SEASON'S
GREETINGS

KAREN,
ALL THE
BEST FOR
2007,

PANTERA

THE POWER OF PRODUCTIVITY

THE POWER OF

PRODUCTIVITY

WEALTH, POVERTY, AND THE

THREAT TO GLOBAL STABILITY

William W. Lewis

William W. Lewis

THE UNIVERSITY OF CHICAGO PRESS   Chicago & London

WILLIAM W. LEWIS was a partner at McKinsey & Company for twenty years and the Founding Director of the McKinsey Global Institute. He held several policymaking positions in the U.S. Departments of Defense and Energy and also served in the World Bank for four years earlier in his career. His work has appeared in the *Wall Street Journal,* the *New York Times,* the *Financial Times,* and the *Economist.*

The University of Chicago Press, Chicago 60637
The University of Chicago Press, Ltd., London
© 2004 by McKinsey & Company, Inc., United States
All rights reserved. Published 2004
Printed in the United States of America

13 12 11 10 09 08 07 06 05 04   1 2 3 4 5

ISBN: 0-226-47676-6 (cloth)

Library of Congress Cataloging-in-Publication Data

Lewis, William W., 1942–
     The power of productivity : wealth, poverty, and the threat to
global stability / William W. Lewis.
          p. cm.
     Includes bibliographical references.
     ISBN 0-226-47676-6 (hardcover : alk. paper)
     1. Industrial productivity. 2. Economic policy. 3. Competition,
International. 4. Consumption (Economics) 5. Investments,
Foreign. 6. Wealth. 7. Poverty. 8. Economic stabilization.
9. Economic development. 10. Microeconomics. I. Title.
HC79.I52 L49 2004
338'.06—dc22

                                                    2003023252

CONTENTS

ACKNOWLEDGMENTS

I am pleased to acknowledge the contributions of several people to the creation of this book.

Jim Levine, my agent, wisely led me to the University of Chicago Press. Alex Schwartz, my editor at Chicago, skillfully managed me through the editing of the book.

Bob Solow, my former McKinsey partners Stuart Flack and Vincent Palmade, and my wife, Jutta, read and commented on the entire manuscript. Bob sent me three letters with detailed comments. Stuart has been a constant and close collaborator over the past twelve years in the communication of the results of my work, including the production of this book.

Others read and commented on selected parts of the book. They were Robert Montgomery, Erik Calonius, Susan Lund, Charles Shaw, Mark Templeton, Tim Broas, Danielle Lewis M.D., Christopher Lewis M.D., and Monica Lewis.

Orley Ashenfelter, Jared Diamond, and Erik Calonius gave me good advice about how to get a book published. Orley and Erik suggested that I go beyond the economic analysis of the first nine chapters into the political economy of why countries have different economic policies.

Omar Ancheta and Frank Scaldaferri from McKinsey computer support set me up with voice recognition software, which I used to dictate the first draft of the manuscript. My assistant, Jennifer Larsen, handled the logistical aspects of the production of the manuscript.

My former McKinsey partners Lenny Mendonca and Diana Farrell encouraged and supported me throughout this endeavor.

Finally, I want to recognize the 251 McKinsey consultants around the world who worked on McKinsey Global Institute projects over the past twelve years. The leverage they provided me is unprecedented. Also, thirty-five academic economists served diligently on the academic advisory committees for these projects. The consultants and advisers are listed in each of the McKinsey Global Institute reports.

For the purpose of helping you decide whether you want to read more than the first page of this book, I am listing here my ten main conclusions.

One, many people look for the causes of poor economic performance primarily in macroeconomics. *An evaluation of economic performance requires an analysis at the level of individual industries, such as automotive, steel, banking, and retailing. This is the "sector" level. You must also look at the sector level for causal factors for economic performance.*

Two, beyond macroeconomic policies, economic analysis usually ends up attributing most of the differences in economic performance to differences in labor and capital markets. *This conclusion is incorrect. Differences in competition in product markets are much more important. Policies governing competition in the product markets are as important as macroeconomic policies.*

Three, the Washington Consensus of the 1990s argued that such elements as flexible exchange rates, low inflation, and government solvency are the critical factors in economic health. *One factor that was profoundly underestimated was the importance of a level playing field for competition in a country.*

Four, many people believe that the educational attainment of a nation's current labor force is responsible for the success or failure of its economy. *The importance of the education of the workforce has been taken way too far. In other words, education is not the way out of the poverty trap. A high education level is no guarantee of high productivity. The truth of the matter is that regardless of institutional educational level, workers around the world can be adequately trained on the job for high productivity.*

Five, many people see access to capital as the determining factor between a productive growing economy and one that is not. Therefore, they feel that if rich countries sent capital pouring into poor countries, the poor countries would become richer. *The solution does not start with more capital. The solution, rather, is in the country's productivity or the way it organizes and deploys both its labor and its capital. If poor countries improved productivity and balanced their budgets, they would have plenty of capital for growth from domestic savers and foreign investors.*

Six, most people consider "social objectives" to be "good." Import tariffs, subsidized loans for small businesses, government disallowance of layoffs, and high minimum wages are all examples of economic policies designed to achieve social objectives. *We can't have it both ways. These measures distort markets severely and limit productivity growth, slow overall economic growth, and cause unemployment. Rather than support these measures, it is better to level the playing field, create a bigger economic pie, and manage the distribution of that pie through the tax code for individuals.*

Seven, most people don't recognize the destructive power of big government on economic development. *Big governments demand big taxation. When part of the economy is informal, and untaxed, the burden falls heavily on legitimate businesses. This is a burden today's rich countries did not have when they were poor.*

Eight, many people think the salvation is in the elites, the educated technocratic, political, business, and intellectual groups, who cooperate to manage economies through government. *The elites are responsible for big government. Particularly in the poorer countries, the elites license business activity, control international financial and material goods flows, promote unaffordable social welfare systems, and favor government-owned businesses. Too often, the elites reward themselves richly.*

Nine, some people think that nations should protect their own industries but also ask outside nations for capital. *This is wrong. Direct investments by the more productive companies from the rich countries would raise the poor countries' productivity and growth rates far more effectively than sending them money. Poor countries have the potential to grow much faster than most people realize.*

Ten, many people think that production is all that is needed to create economic value. This is why government sometimes protects businesses, regardless of their performance. *They fail to make the link between production and consumption. The goods produced have value only because consumers want them. If they don't want them for some reason (such as high price), the business producing them needs to die.*

Only one force can stand up to producer special interests—consumer interests. Most poor countries are a long way from a consumption mindset and consumer rights. As a result, they are poor.

These conclusions come from the studies conducted by the McKinsey Global Institute over the past twelve years. This work is based on how individual businesses—from state-of-the-art auto plants to black-market street vendors and everything in between—actually behave and perform on a daily basis. The understanding of an economy comes from the ground up rather than the top down; a grassroots view versus a bird's-eye view. This book is going to provide the evidence and the arguments for my conclusions listed above.

How Did I Get Here?

In August 1990, I flew from Washington D.C. to Bangor, Maine, and drove a rented car to Bar Harbor. Meeting me there in his boat was Marvin Harris. I had run Marvin down a couple of weeks earlier through the University of Florida, where he was a partially retired research professor. Marvin had formerly been chairman of anthropology at Columbia and was a past president of the American Anthropological Association.

I had wanted to see Marvin because, by chance, one of the first things I did after learning that I would be the founding director of the McKinsey Global Institute was to read Marvin's recently released book, *Our Kind*. I had read the book while holed up in a cabin in the West Virginia mountains over a rainy three-day Memorial weekend. *Our Kind* was a marvelous anthropological history of our species. It convinced me that Marvin's approach might help me some in setting direction for the McKinsey Global Institute.

McKinsey had created the McKinsey Global Institute in June 1990 to develop a better understanding of where the world was going. The specific issue on the minds of many was a phenomenon coming to be called "globalization." Globalization seemed to be so powerful that it could affect the evolution of human society. Thus, it was potentially of anthropological scale.

I had gotten all sorts of advice from many quarters about the factors that were causing and constraining globalization. Culture, religion, ethnicity, climate, and politics were all thought to matter. I needed help in sorting out the relative importance of these factors. I thought Marvin could do it. I was right.

Marvin and I spent several hours sitting in the sun at his summer house on one of the islands in the waters off Bar Harbor talking about my problem. Over a wonderful cold salmon lunch, Marvin and I agreed on the outline of a research project to sort out these factors. What I did not know at the time was that Marvin's lifetime research had already worked out the answer I needed.

During the course of the next six months, Marvin educated me about his theory of Cultural Materialism. Cultural Materialism says that there is a direction in the evolution of our species. That direction is that societies with higher productivity inevitably replace societies with lower productivity. Marvin validates his theory with a large number of case examples. In these case examples, Marvin digs down deeply to the productivity roots of things. The examples range from sacred cows in India to prohibitions against pork in Muslim countries. These case examples explain why many aspects of human behavior considered to be cultural or ethnic or even religious have been adopted because they make societies have higher productivity.

Societies with higher productivity have overcome to a greater degree whatever cultural, religious, ethnic, climatic, and political barriers have constrained productivity. These higher productivity societies have been successful in competition with lower productivity societies. They have been successful either through conquest or through simply surviving the hardships of nature.

In more recent times, this competition has often been commercial. This competition has led to the adoption of higher productivity practices by lower productivity societies. Globalization, through the transfer of higher productivity practices, might be the current method through which lower productivity societies achieve higher productivity. Thus, understanding productivity differences around the world and barriers to the transfer of higher productivity practices might reveal how globalization would proceed.

Initially, I had no appreciation of the huge differences in productivity around the world today. These differences mean that more productive societies have replaced less productive societies to a much greater degree in some parts of the world than in others. I had no idea that understanding the reasons for these differences in productivity would be the central theme of a twelve-year research program. Such a program held the potential for revealing how less productive societies could accelerate the process of becoming more productive. I, of course, did not see this potential then. However, Marvin Harris's research got me started off in that direction.

I could get started because I could connect productivity to the business world in which my colleagues in McKinsey and I had significant experience. If the most important factors in the evolution of societies were cultural or religious, then neither McKinsey nor I would have much basis for understanding where the world was going.

Productivity, on the other hand, is the most important objective that businesses and their management try to improve all around the world. The reason, of course, is that productivity is very closely connected to profitability. Productivity is simply the ratio of the value of goods and services provided consumers to the amount of time worked and capital used to produce the goods and services. If a firm produces more goods and services for the same effort or it produces the same goods and services for less effort, its profitability increases. Such a firm is likely to invest the funds from its increased profits in building a bigger business. The firm then makes even more profits. This process continues until other firms note the success of the more productive firm and copy its more productive ways. The profitability of the innovative firm returns to normal. However, the productivity of all firms is increased. Since the productivity of a society is simply the average (weighted) of the productivity of all the firms operating within it, understanding the productivity of firms around the world must be important. Why are firms in some societies more productive than firms in other societies? The answer has got to help us understand where the world is going.

Buried Statistics

Back in 1990, the most important question about where the world was going was whether the U.S. economy was going down the drain. Conventional wisdom both in the United States and abroad held that Germany and Japan had emerged from World War II with a superior economic model. The United States was either going to have to copy that model or fall behind. In fact many people assumed that Germany and Japan had already passed the United States in economic performance. At that time the most widely used measure of economic performance, GDP per capita, was calculated using market foreign exchange rates to convert GDP from one currency to another. At the market exchange rates prevailing at the time, it was true that the GDPs per capita of Germany and Japan exceeded that of the United States.

Shortly after visiting Marvin Harris, I picked up that week's *Economist* one Saturday just before going to play tennis. After a quick reading, I glanced briefly at the economic statistics buried at the back of the magazine. There I saw the current Organization for Economic Cooperation and Development (OECD) statistics for GDP per capita using purchasing power parity (PPP) exchange rates. By this measure, the GDP per capita of the United States was still some 20 percentage points above that of Germany and Japan. Purchasing power parity exchange rates, although subject to data gathering and statistical analysis difficulties, are conceptually the right way to convert GDPs from one currency to another for comparison purposes. I thought immediately that if this result is right, then conventional wisdom is wrong. Moreover, if the result is right, why is it right? Conventional wisdom included many explanations of why economic policies and practices in Germany and Japan were superior.

In October 1990, I convened a meeting of five people including Marvin Harris and Tom Shelling, formerly chairman of economics at Harvard and then at the University of Maryland. The meeting was to discuss what topics the McKinsey Global Institute should study to contribute to an understanding of where the world was going. At that meeting, I showed the latest OECD statistics based on purchasing power parity exchange rates. I had found that the OECD buries these statistics in an appendix of their international comparisons report.

Tom confirmed that using purchasing power parity exchange rates was the right way to do the comparisons. I allowed that if these numbers were right, then most of the assertions in the debate in the United States about economic performance were wrong. To Tom's credit, he reflected and said, "I don't think my colleagues and I have a good handle on the health of the U.S. economy." I said, "Tom, what do we do about that?" Tom responded that we should get a group of his friends together and talk about it. I asked him who his friends were. He said Bob Solow, Francis Bator, and a couple of others. Bob is a highly regarded Nobel Laureate and Francis is one of the leading macro economists. Tom then helped me organize a meeting that included Bob and Francis to discuss the health of the U.S. economy. That meeting took place in February 1991.

Research Strategy

That February 1991 meeting ended with the idea that shaped the work of the Global Institute over the next twelve years. The idea was to do case studies of a sample of economic sectors to determine differences in productivity across countries and the reasons for those differences. We got to that idea by first confirming the importance of resolving the apparent contradiction with conventional wisdom in the OECD statistics. Clive Crook, economics editor of the *Economist,* and Bob Bartley, editor of the editorial page of the *Wall Street Journal,* were in the meeting and helped us to reach this conclusion.

Second, we felt that the differences in GDP per capita should show up in differences in productivity across countries. The reason for this assumption is that in most countries the fraction of people who work is about the same. GDP per capita is simply the product of the fraction of the population that works and average worker productivity. Thus differences in GDP per capita should reflect primarily differences in productivity. We learned over the twelve years that this is true broadly around the world.

In our meeting, we reviewed the structure of modern economies and saw that service industries now dominate. In developed economies, employment in service industries accounts for 70 to 75 percent of all employment. Manufacturing accounts for 20 to 25 percent, with agriculture at less than 5 percent. The productivity of any economy is simply the average of the productivity of each individual worker. Thus if there were differences in productivity across the advanced economies, there had to be differences in productivity in the service industries because of their sheer size. Thus we concluded that if we were to tackle the conventional wisdom question, we would first study service industries. Since there would be no hope of studying all service industries, the idea was that case studies of productivity differences in a sample of service industries might reveal whether conventional wisdom was wrong, and if so, why.

The February meeting was followed quickly by a Saturday-morning meeting at Francis Bator's house in Cambridge MA. In addition to Francis, Bob Solow and Tom Schelling were there. We organized the first project of the Global Institute. A team of McKinsey consultants would study five key service industries in Japan, Germany, the United Kingdom, France, and the United States. We ended up choosing airlines, telecommunications, retail banking, retailing, and restaurants.

The project took a year to complete and ended up confirming the OECD statistics that the GDP per capita in the United States was significantly higher than in the other advanced economies. In all the case studies, the productivity in the United States was higher. In some cases, it was dramatically higher. For instance, the productivity of retailing in Japan was only 44 percent of retailing productivity in the United States. Productivity of telecommunications in Germany and the United Kingdom was only about 50 percent of the productivity in the United States. Productivity of retail banking in Germany and the United Kingdom was only about 65 percent of productivity in the United States. In countries where capital is freely available, where the workforce is well educated, and where technology and other business innovations are readily available, it was amazing that such large differences in performance existed.

Because the productivity results contradicted conventional wisdom, it was crucial to determine the reasons for the results. We started at the bottom within individual businesses. The productivity of an economic sector is simply the average (weighted) of the productivities of all the firms in the sector. Differences in the services delivered and in the way those services are delivered in each firm have to explain the differences in productivity. For instance, much of Japan's retailing services are delivered by small, unproductive mom-and-pop retailers. In contrast, retailing services in the United States are dominated by large, highly productive supermarkets and discount stores. Moreover, with a similar telecommunications infrastructure, U.S. businesses make far more telephone calls than their counterparts in Germany and the United Kingdom. Thus the capital invested in the telecommunications industry in the U.S. is used more productively. The burning question was, What causes these differences? Why have business managers and owners made decisions that have led to such differences in business operations, with their very different productivities? Fortunately, unlike many efforts in this area, we had the resources and experience to tackle such questions on a large scale.

Manufacturing Wrong Too

Another reason for our working first on service industries was our assumption that the United States had to be behind Japan and Germany in manufacturing. After all, in the early 1990s the newspapers were full of stories of how Japanese manufacturers were flooding the U.S. market with their products and wiping out U.S. companies and jobs of American workers. The automotive and steel industries got the most attention, but other industries including machine tools and consumer electronics had similar results. My assumption was that U.S. superiority in the much larger service industries was overcoming U.S. shortfalls in manufacturing.

Towards the end of our service sector project, Martin Baily, one of the economists on the committee reviewing our work, mentioned that some rough work in the economics literature suggested that the United States still had a significant lead in manufacturing productivity over Japan and Germany. Given our success in conducting case studies in service industries, I decided that we would conduct a similar project in manufacturing. Beginning in October 1992, we conducted nine industry studies in manufacturing over the next twelve months. We studied automotive assembly, automotive parts, machine tools, steel, computers, consumer electronics, food processing, beer, and soap and detergents in Japan, Germany, and the United States.

The most important thing about our results was that they explained Japan. We saw clearly that Japan had a dual economy. Sure enough, in automotive, steel, machine tools, and consumer electronics, Japan had the highest productivity in the world, exceeding the United States by 20 percent in automotive and 50 percent in steel. Japan's high-performing industries corresponded exactly to the industries in which Japan was having extraordinary success in trade. However, there was another Japan that was not involved in trade and was hidden from the global view. In food processing, for instance, the productivity of Japanese workers was only one-third that of workers in the United States.

Food processing is a huge industry in virtually every modern economy. In Japan, there are more workers in food processing than in steel, automotive, consumer electronics, and machine tools combined. Since the productivity of the whole manufacturing sector is the average of the productivities of each individual worker, the very low productivity of the large number of Japanese workers in food processing pulls the Japanese average down below the U.S. average. Thus we found Japan's economy to be composed of a few manufacturing industries with the highest productivity in the world alongside manufacturing and service industries with much lower productivity than in the United States.

Our results for Germany were not as dramatic as for Japan. In all but two cases, productivity in Germany was lower than in the United States. In machine tools and steel it was about equal to the United States. In automotive, productivity in Germany was about 70 percent of the United States figure. U.S. productivity was higher in automotive because of direct competition with the more productive Japanese industry. Japanese car makers not only exported to the open U.S. market but also built automotive plants in the United States that operated at close to Japanese productivity. Japanese cars accounted for about 30 percent of the U.S. market but only about 15 percent in Germany. The more intense competition in the United States with global best practice forced U.S. automotive firms to improve faster than automotive firms in Germany.

Payoff

I was surprised at how clear a picture our service and manufacturing results gave of the world's leading economies. The clarity of the picture clearly came from the industry studies themselves. The industry studies allowed us to relate our economic results to everyday circumstances, such as the large number of Japanese cars in the United States and the very high prices of retail goods in Japan. At the same time, it seemed miraculous that our industry study results and the overall OECD results were consistent. After all, they were developed in totally different ways. The OECD results came from adding up all the sales to final users in each country's currency to get GDP and then converting the totals to a common currency using purchasing power parity exchange rates. These exchange rates are calculated by finding the prices in local currencies of a large sample of the same items in different economies and using these price relationships to convert the GDP numbers to a common currency. Thus the OECD results came from two huge data-gathering and statistical analysis operations. On the other hand, our industry studies were based on counting physical products such as cars and tons of steel and then adjusting the physical counts for relative quality and other characteristics of value to consumers. That the two totally independent approaches gave the same results was deeply reassuring about our conclusions.

Outside Reaction

The outside reaction to our results was also surprising. They immediately became news stories. Sylvia Nasar, who at the time was writing economics columns for the *New York Times,* wrote about our results on the first page of the *Times* business section. She called our results "the most authoritative comparison to date" of country economic performance. News stories also appeared in the *Wall Street Journal,* the *Economist,* and the *Financial Times.* Such attention indicated a deep public interest in the real health of the U.S. economy and the importance of a satisfying explanation of why the conventional wisdom was wrong.

Our first service sector report was issued in the middle of October 1992, some three weeks before the 1992 presidential election. Of course Bill Clinton had campaigned that the U.S. economy was going down the drain and needed fixing. On the day of the release, Nasar's column appeared. By 10:00 that morning, I had received a half-dozen phone calls from Little Rock as the Clinton campaign tried to figure out what was going on. I of course made all our results available to them immediately. At the same time, some of my Republican colleagues immediately recognized the significance of our results for the presidential campaign. They tried very hard to bring these results to the attention of the senior

Bush's White House but were unsuccessful. The only reference to our re-sults on the Republican side came from Barbara Bush on one of the morning talk shows. Needless to say, the Democratic side kept quiet.

Once elected, Clinton appointed Laura Tyson as chairman of his Council of Economic Advisers and Robert Reich as his secretary of labor. Tyson was an advocate of managed trade and believed that much of Ja-pan's success came from emphasis on strategic industries. She thought the United States should copy Japan in this regard. Reich, on the other hand, was an admirer of the German labor market and thought the United States should copy a substantial part of it. Our results showed that the U.S. model actually worked better than the German and Japanese mod-els. Thus, U.S. economic policy should focus on making the U.S. model work better and not on copying the Japanese and German models.

Fortunately for the country, economic policy proceeded along this line. A former Clinton administration official, who later came to work at McKinsey, told me that our work had contributed substantially to their abandoning their initial policy direction on trade and labor. Clin-ton had clearly been wrong about the health of the U.S. economy. Adam Meyerson, a former editor of the "Manager's Journal" column in the *Wall Street Journal,* remarked to me one morning on the Washington subway that our productivity studies had changed the economic debate in the United States.

The reaction in Japan and Germany to our results about the health of the U.S. economy was strong. In Japan there was complete denial. The Japanese were understandably highly proud of their economic recovery after the war. Moreover, Japan has been the only country in the world to go from being a developing country to a developed country within the past hundred years. Even in 1950, 50 percent of the workers in Japan worked in agriculture. By 1990, that fraction had declined to less than 10 percent and was in line with other developed countries.

On the other hand, the Japanese had been misled by their success in international trade, and by the extraordinarily inflated values of their stock market and their real estate. At the beginning of the 1990s, the Japanese stock market index was five times its current value, and the pa-per value of the Imperial Palace grounds in central Tokyo was equal to the value of all real estate in California. The Japanese themselves missed the fact that they had a dual economy. Their overall productivity was only about 65 percent of that of the United States, and much of Japan's impressive economic growth had come from the massive application of labor and capital. However, with the exception of about half its manu-facturing sector, that labor and capital had been applied relatively unproductively. Of course there are limits to how many people can work and to how many hours each worker works. Moreover, there are only so many pieces of equipment that a worker can use. The Japanese stock market and real estate market behaved as if this input-intensive growth could go on forever. In the early 1990s as Japanese workers achieved shorter, not longer, working hours, and as much of the massive investment of the late 1980s remained unused, Japanese growth stalled. It has remained stalled for the past ten years.

Not only were the Japanese proud of their economic success, but many other parties in Asia were also proud of the Japanese success. After five centuries of Western leadership in economic progress, finally an Asian society was perceived to be the leader. In early 1994 at a conference of business leaders in Taiwan, my results were met with disbelief. One gentleman remarked that he knew I came from a reputable firm, but my results were nonsense. He said there was no way I could have adequately taken into account the far superior quality of Japanese products. I responded as calmly as I could that the products of most of the leading Japanese manufacturing companies were sold in the U.S. market. U.S. consumers do pay a price premium over U.S. products when the quality of Japanese products is higher. That premium is the additional economic value to consumers of the higher quality of Japanese products. So when we counted the number of midsized cars produced in Japan, we increased the count by the ratio of the price of a Toyota Camry to the average midsized car produced in the United States. I doubt if I convinced that audience in 1994 that I was right. However, one member of that business community told me within the last year that he still remembers that I was the first person to explain Japan to them.

The reaction in Germany to our results was similar in many respects to the reaction in Japan. Germany also was understandably proud of its economic recovery after the war. Of course, in the early 1990s, even though Germany had already been reunified, when we talked of the German economy, everybody really had the West German economy in mind. Germany viewed itself as the strongest manufacturing economy in the world and had little regard for the importance of service industries. Moreover, West Germans had been misled by their success in competing with the rest of Europe once the European Common Market had been formed.

At a conference of global business leaders in Washington in 1992, I presented the results of our service sector case studies. The CEO of Siemens at the time, Karlheinz Kaske, said he was puzzled about the role of service industries in an economy and wondered why we paid so much attention to them. I showed the group some recent results from our analysis of the interconnectedness of the U.S. economy. We had found that for the economic value reflected in the sale price of a consumer good, two-thirds of that value was created by the consumer good manufacturing firm and one-third of the value was generated by the transportation, wholesaling, and retailing functions that got the good from the manufacturer's loading dock to the hands of the consumer.

Moreover, of the total value produced by the manufacturing firm, one-fourth of that value was created by accounting, banking, legal, consulting, janitorial, and other business services. Thus, services accounted for one-half of the value to a consumer from the purchase of a good such as a CD, a can of beans, or a car. On top of this, one-half of all services are delivered directly to consumers and not to firms. In this light, it's easy to see why services make up about 75 percent of the total value created in an economy. Germans were not taking their performance in service industries into account in forming their perception of the performance of their economy.

Employment and Growth

In the early 1990s, as we were finishing our productivity work on manufacturing and services, the most serious economic issue in Europe was not productivity but high and rising unemployment. Every time Europe had a business downturn, unemployment rose. Every time there was a business upturn, unemployment stayed constant. The net result was that unemployment rates in Europe were two to three times as high as in the United States. At the urging of my colleagues in Europe, we decided to see whether our industry study approach would yield new insight into the reasons for the differences in employment performance.

We quickly found that in the decade of the 1980s the United States had created far more new jobs relative to the growth of the working-age population than in Europe. The question was why. We started with the relationship that employment levels are the result of dividing the overall level of production of an economy by the productivity of the workforce.

This simple relationship has led to one of the most serious public misunderstandings about how economies work. It is tempting to conclude that if productivity increases, then employment must go down. After all, if the workforce works more efficiently, then fewer workers are needed. This line of thought stops too soon. It fails to consider what happens after productivity is improved and workers are available to be redeployed somewhere else in the economy. It assumes incorrectly that the amount of business activity in an economy is fixed. In fact, if workers are available, entrepreneurs can match them with new business ideas and investment capital and thus increase the total amount of business activity in an economy. The production of goods and services thus increases, along with the productivity increase, and employment levels do not have to decrease.

After all, 250 years ago virtually all people who could work worked in agriculture. Since that time, productivity in agriculture has increased tremendously. Now, in the advanced countries, less than 5 percent of the workforce is able to feed their entire population and then some. However the remaining 95 percent of the potential workers are not sitting around simply eating what the 5 percent produces. Obviously, over time these workers had been redeployed to new business activities that produce the huge variety of goods and services that characterize all advanced economies. This change is the natural evolution of all economies.

By this time in our work, it was clear that we were venturing far beyond simple productivity comparisons. We were looking at the fundamental forces that determine how economies grow and the employment consequences of growth. Economic work on these questions long ago pointed out quite logically that growth depended on an increase in the amount people work and the amount of equipment they use and on an increase in the efficiency with which people work and the capability of the equipment they use. Somehow in Europe, the efficiency of the workforce was increasing but the available labor was not being matched with new business ideas and additional equipment to create growth and employment. The natural evolution was proceeding differently in Europe than in the United States.

We looked at the structure of the European and U.S. economies and found that the employment distribution was quite different. The U.S. had far more people working in services than Europe did. In fact, the biggest differences were in residential construction and retailing. We asked why this is so. What we found is that many of the factors that distort the nature of competition and result in lower productivity also limit the production of more goods and services.

I did not realize it exactly at this time, but by enabling an understanding of productivity, growth in goods and services, and employment, our industry study approach provided a new way to understand country economic performance.

Country Economic Performance

In the spring of 1994, I was meeting with Christian Caspar, my McKinsey evaluator. In McKinsey, European partners evaluate the performance of U.S. partners and vice versa. Christian is Swedish and was the partner in charge of our Scandinavian offices. In reviewing my work on manufacturing and service productivity and unemployment, Christian asked if I would add Sweden to the cross-country comparisons. Christian may have thought he had a little extra leverage on me at the time. I reflected for a second and replied that if we added Sweden to all the productivity and employment performance comparisons, we would really have a picture of Sweden's fundamental economic performance as a country. I asked Christian if he was prepared for me to come out with a point of view about Sweden's performance. To his credit, he said yes.

This was the starting point of a series of thirteen country studies covering all the major economies in the world, with the regrettable exception of China. The initial three years addressed OECD countries, where McKinsey's practice had been well established for a long time. As soon as we had confirmed that our industry study approach was going to work in Sweden to yield a point of view about that economy, we immediately started a similar project in Australia. That was followed by a joint study on France and Germany at the same time. Then came Japan and our first real stumbling block.

In 1996 we attempted to do a similar country study for Japan. At that time in Japan, there was some concern about Japan's economic performance. Japan had grown very little since the stock market and real estate bubbles had burst in the early 1990s. However, most of the country was still in denial. The conventional wisdom was that the old input-led growth strategies would lead Japan forward. I found virtually no acceptance of the view that productivity was the fundamental engine of growth. As a result, I was unable to persuade my Japanese McKinsey colleagues to start at the beginning with productivity. As a result, we conducted a project that devoted most of its effort to thinking of new, interesting products that current Japanese companies could add to their production.

My academic advisory committee for that first Japanese project included Masa Aoki, a highly regarded Japanese economist in the Stanford Economics Department. Masa suffered through that first project without complaining, even though we did not get down to the real issues of Japan. By 1999, the no-growth picture of Japan was inescapable to all observers. At that time, the Global Institute had a worldly young Japanese consultant who could lead a second try in Japan to get at the real issues. That person was James Kondo. James was a graduate of Harvard Business School who liked the work of the Global Institute so much that he'd already had two stints with me. James was a true Global Institute veteran, having spent six months working on our projects on capital productivity and on France and Germany, and then a full year on our project in Russia. James knew how productivity was the key to economic performance. Near the end of the second project on Japan, Masa made the remark to James in Japanese that the second project seemed much better than the first.

Within the OECD countries, I had not yet dealt with an apparent paradox. Every time I discussed my results with Continental Europeans, I got one retort I could not handle. That retort was that if the U.S. economy is so great, how come the United Kingdom, the other "Anglo-Saxon" economy, is doing so poorly. This was clearly an apparent paradox. The universal perception was that Margaret Thatcher had deregulated the UK economy to make it similar to that of the United States. Yet the UK GDP per capita was only 70 percent of the U.S. figure and somewhat behind France and Germany. What I knew was that Margaret Thatcher had deregulated the UK capital market and labor market, but I knew nothing about the industry-level restrictions governing the conduct of individual businesses and therefore determining the nature of competition in the United Kingdom. My hypothesis was that the United Kingdom had to have significant industry-level market distortions. However, I had no evidence, and I found little interest among my UK colleagues in resolving the paradox.

My opportunity came when the Labor government took office in 1997. Shortly thereafter, Gordon Brown, the new chancellor of the exchequer, contacted me through Adair Turner, a former partner of mine who was then head of the Confederation of British Industries. The chancellor was anticipating the British assumption of the rotating chairs of both the European Union and the G-7. He was concerned about the economic performance in the rest of Europe and wanted to use this opportunity to improve Europe's performance. He said that during the UK election, our study of France and Germany was the best economic analysis he had read. I replied that he would not be able to lead economic policy improvement in Europe without a diagnosis of the UK economy also. He agreed and offered to pay something for a UK study. I declined the money because the results of a study even partially financed by one political party would be suspect. Thus I got my chance.

Of course what we found was that whereas the United Kingdom

had Anglo-Saxon capital and labor markets, it had a "Continental" product market, the market where goods and services are bought and sold. Moreover, UK firms adhered to the regulations to the letter. Competition was severely distorted in many sectors. In particular, the development of the retailing and hotel sectors was severely constrained by planning regulations. These regulations, for instance, made it tortuous to attempt to improve any property with a structure on it over one hundred years old. The paradox of the UK economy was resolved, and Gordon Brown got a plateful of improvements needed at home.

The Rest of the World

After finishing our country study of France and Germany in early 1997, I was confident that we could do country studies of OECD countries. Of course, we did subsequently conduct country studies of the Netherlands, the United Kingdom, and Japan a second time. However, with the economic reforms around the world of the early 1990s, substantial interest had arisen in "emerging markets" economies. Since McKinsey's practice was growing rapidly in these markets, it seemed possible that the Global Institute could conduct country studies in developing countries.

Korea and Brazil were the obvious first candidates to study. Korea was one of the few middle-income countries, with a GDP per capita at the low end of the range of the OECD countries. In fact, Korea was joining the OECD as we conducted the study. Korea is the largest of the "Asian Tigers," with the most comprehensive economy. Brazil was at the top of the poor countries, with a GDP per capita about 25 percent of that of the United States. Brazil has half the GDP and half the population of all of South America.

Korea

Our work in Korea turned out to be very similar to our work in Japan. This is because we found that Korea was following the Japanese development path almost exactly. Koreans worked extraordinarily long hours and invested enormous sums in plant and equipment. This led to substantial growth in GDP per capita but at relatively low productivity. The one difference from Japan was that Korea had borrowed substantially from other countries to finance its investment. Therein lay the seeds of its financial crisis, which occurred in late 1997 as we were conducting our study. The capital productivity of Korean firms in such sectors as automotive, semiconductors, and steel minimills was so low that they were unable to meet the debt service requirements of their loans, which were at international interest rates. Foreign lenders were unwilling to extend additional loans and the crisis was precipitated.

The IMF of course prescribed its traditional remedies of reforming the banking system and opening the country to trade. Our work showed that these remedies would leave Korea vulnerable to another crisis. This was because the much larger domestic sector also needed drastic reform in order to create jobs to replace those that would be shed in the manufacturing sector because of the IMF remedies. Reform of zoning laws was especially needed to allow for shopping centers and large-scale single-family housing developments.

Brazil

Brazil turned out to be the first truly developing country we tackled. The issue was whether we could gather sufficient data to conduct industry studies. In Brazil many businesses operate and many people work on an unofficial basis. This means they don't pay taxes, government regulations don't apply, and they don't show up in the national economic statistics. In retailing, for instance, about half the people work in this "informal" way. We found that studies in Brazil had analyzed a large enough sample of this informal activity that we could piece together a good enough picture of the microeconomic dynamics of individual industries. We had to supplement this information with extensive interviewing of individual businesses.

For instance, one of our young consultants spent two days recording everything that went on in a small cardboard-constructed retailing business in the middle of one of the huge slums that surround São Paulo. The consultant also provided day care services for the child of the woman who was running the business. This service probably improved her productivity above what it normally was. Even then, it was only 8 percent of the U.S. retailing average. Thus, in Brazil, we first came into contact with perhaps the most fundamental change needed for much higher living standards in poor countries. That change is the evolution of workers from low-productivity jobs in informal firms to much higher productivity jobs in formal firms.

Russia

Having shown that we could obtain results in Brazil, I decided we had to try Russia. The failure of the Russian economy was viewed in the late

1990s as perhaps the most serious economic problem in the world. The replacement of the centrally planned economy in the Soviet Union with a "market economy" in Russia had resulted in a drop in GDP per capita of an amazing 20 to 30 percent. Russia had shown that a market economy could clearly perform much worse than a centrally planned economy. We had to find out why. What we learned is that it is possible to distort the competition in a market economy sufficiently so that the outcome is worse than from central planning. Some firms not paying their taxes and energy bills while others do is just one example of these distortions.

Poland

In the course of our work in Russia, I took notice of how the other countries formerly in the Soviet sphere were performing economically. Poland clearly stood out. Most of the former Soviet sphere countries had dropped in GDP per capita since 1990. Poland was the only country where GDP per capita was higher in 1999 than it was in 1990. Poland was up by about 20 percent. Thus as part of our Russia study, we began to investigate why Russia and Poland had gone in opposite directions from roughly the same starting point in 1990.

Out of the blue one day I got a telephone call from the executive assistant to Leszek Balcerowicz, the deputy prime minister and finance minister of Poland. Balcerowicz was the legendary reformer responsible for Poland's success. The assistant said that Professor Balcerowicz had read about our study of the United Kingdom in the *Economist* and that he wanted us to do a similar study on Poland. Even though the McKinsey practice in Poland was not well enough established to support such a study, I could not turn down a request from Balcerowicz for some help.

In Poland, a quick survey indicated Poland had done many things right. Its macroeconomic policies seemed consistent with current best thinking, including having a flexible exchange rate. As a result, Poland had been affected very little by the "Asian financial crisis" that swept around the world in 1998, plunging many developing countries, including Russia, into economic chaos. Poland did have naggingly high unemployment, ranging from 10 to 15 percent. The source of this problem was at the core of Poland's domestic economy, in residential construction and retailing. These industries are the most difficult for any country to get right. Poland's failure to privatize urban real estate and end subsidized rents was preventing the retailing and housing construction industries from growing and creating jobs. Moreover, zoning laws were preventing suburban development from taking off.

India

Even after studying all these countries, we still had not addressed economic conditions under which most of the people in the world live. Brazil, Russia, and Poland all have GDPs per capita of 20 to 25 percent of that of the United States. Even though they still have 20 to 30 percent of their employment in agriculture, their structure looks roughly similar to the most developed countries. Manufacturing employment accounts for 20 to 30 percent of all employment, and employment in services is already higher than in manufacturing or agriculture. The structure of economies, however, changes dramatically as GDP per capita goes below this level. *The majority of the world's people still live in economies where agriculture accounts for at least 50 percent of all employment.* Thus in order to understand today's global economy, we had to study at least one of the world's poorest countries.

Of course, the two strongest candidates are obvious: China and India. My choice had to be India. McKinsey's practice in India was well established, we could work in English, and India had a number of well-trained and globally respected economists with whom we could work. One of my two serious regrets from the past ten years of work is that we have not done China. However, within the next ten years India is likely to become the world's most populous country, and it has a GDP per capita of only 6 percent of that of the United States. India is clearly a major anchor point for understanding the economies of the world's poorest people. (The second regret is that we did not study South Africa and thus have learned nothing about a whole continent. However, India alone has 200 million more people than the entire African continent.)

Starting in December 1999, I thus undertook a study of India. It turned out to be the largest project we conducted over the last twelve years. It took eighteen months to complete, and we studied fourteen separate economic sectors. The highest number of sectors before had been ten in Russia. In India we had no choice but to study agriculture for the first time. As a result, we conducted sector studies in dairy and wheat. We found that dairy in India had the largest employment of any sector anywhere in the world in absolute numbers of people. Indians get much of their protein from milk and not meat.

We found that India had created a development trap for itself. Farmers have no incentive to further invest in mechanization. The farmers are not dumb. There are so many workers in rural areas with no alternative but to work in agriculture that rural wage levels are incredibly low. They are so low that farmers are better off employing these work-ers than investing further in, for instance, combines for wheat harvest-ing. Thus agriculture in India will not move much further until enough jobs are created in manufacturing and service industries to drain the ex-cess workers out of agriculture. Then, rural wages will increase and farmers will have the needed incentive to invest and thereby improve their productivity. However, India has by far the most restrictions and barriers on the development of the manufacturing and service industries of all the countries we have studied. Restricting the manufacture of 836 products to small-scale industries and prohibiting investment in India by the world's most productive retailers from France, the United Kingdom, and the United States are just two examples.

U.S. New Economy?

As the 1990s drew to a close and we were finishing our work on India, the newspapers were full of stories about how our starting point, the United States, had a "new economy." Thus to close my survey of the global economy, I concluded that I needed to loop back and revisit the perfor-mance of the U.S. economy.

The new economy stories threw in everything: a never-ending rise in the stock market; paper shares in information technology companies that traded for real money without the companies having ever made a profit and sometimes without having any revenues; computers found everywhere all connected by the Internet; computer scientists and MBAs being lavishly recruited and with starting salaries that approached the salary of the president of the United States, etc. However, in economic terms, there were only two dimensions in which the United States might have a new economy. The first was that the United States was having the lowest unemployment rate since the war and at the same time the low-est inflation rate since the war. These two factors are thought to move in opposite directions, not the same direction. Second, after twenty-five years of productivity growth of about 1.5 percent per year, starting in 1995 the productivity growth rate accelerated to an average of about 2.5 percent for the period 1995 to '99.

The unemployment and inflation paradox was not something that the work of the Global Institute was likely to help resolve. On the other hand, we had learned a lot about productivity over the past ten years. Moreover, Alan Greenspan was making the argument that the produc-tivity acceleration explained the unemployment and inflation performance. He believed that because the productivity acceleration caused an acceleration in real wages, workers were less inclined to press for additional wage increases as the labor market got tighter. Thus it seemed clear that we should tackle the causes of the productivity acceleration.

Needless to say, the idea of investigating the productivity acceleration occurred to many economists. At the time we began our work in September 2000, several points of view were already on the table. At one extreme, Bob Gordon at Northwestern concluded that all the productivity acceleration came from the increased performance of the computers we were producing and from "cyclical" factors that were part of the normal fluctuation of an economy and which would not persist. At the other extreme, the *Economic Report of the President* issued in January 2001 concluded that a fundamental change associated with the widespread application of information technology had indeed occurred in the U.S. economy in the 1990s. Alan Greenspan's justification for not tightening monetary policy and for letting the economy roll seems to have been based on agreement with the view expressed in that last Clinton economic report.

All these conclusions were based primarily on extremely complex, data-intensive "regression" analyses standard in economics. Regression analyses always have great difficulty explaining causality in an understandable and satisfying way. Our hope was that our traditional approach of industry studies would allow us to identify exactly where the productivity acceleration had occurred and what businesses had done to cause the acceleration.

In the end the industry study approach worked. We found that the United States did not have a new economy nearly to the extent that Clinton and Greenspan claimed. Sadly, this result has been validated by the disappearance of vigorous economic growth and huge budget surpluses.

The revisiting of the U.S. economy was a good way to end my journey through the global economy. It reconfirmed the role that competition plays in stimulating innovation and productivity improvement. In every sector in which productivity accelerated in the United States in the second half of the 1990s, competition intensified. Sometimes the increased intensity was triggered by regulatory changes, as in mobile telephone services and the reduction of the price per trade in securities. Other times, it came from business innovation like Wal-Mart's. Information technology was just part of the story. The bigger story was competition causing more productive business enterprises to replace less productive ones. This conclusion is of course reassuring to those worried about the health of the U.S. economy. However, it provides even more reason to worry about all the people living in economies where protection and distortion of competition allow unproductive enterprises to persist and cause these people to fall further behind, but even more importantly, to remain in poverty.

CHAPTER ONE

Findings: The Global Economic Landscape

The disparity between rich and poor is the most serious and the most intractable problem facing the world today.

In the global economic landscape, 800 million of the world's 6 billion people live on a high economic peak. They reside in 18 countries mostly in Europe and North America, with a GDP per capita between $25,000 and $35,000 per year. Five billion people live in the "lowlands," 111 countries with per capita income of $8,000 or below. Only 340 million people live in between the lowlands and the peak (Exhibit 1.1).

GDP per capita is the amount of goods and services a country produces per person. It is the best single indicator of material standard of living. It is hard to grasp that 5 billion people live in countries where the GDP per capita is 25 percent or less than it is in the United States; actually, the majority of them live where it is less than 10 percent.

Most business visitors to these countries are severely misled by what they see. They go to São Paulo, Rio, Moscow, St. Petersburg, Mumbai, and Delhi and stay in hotels and eat at restaurants that are indistinguishable from those in the rich countries. The Oberoi hotel chain in India is perhaps the best hotel chain in the world. Its architecture, interior design, and service levels are as good as any place on earth. Moreover, the local people we meet are very much like us. They are well educated, they speak good English, they live comfortably, and they are worldly.

These impressions disguise the reality of life outside international business circles. There, life is hard. It is, of course, better than it was fifty years ago when many more faced starvation and disease took a much greater toll. The Green Revolution and the transfer of public health practices and modern medicines have dramatically increased life expectancy. However, many of these people are illiterate, live in mud or cardboard houses, and are visibly undernourished. They have little prospect of improving their lives and those of their children.

Exhibit 1.1: World Distribution of GDP per Capita by Country

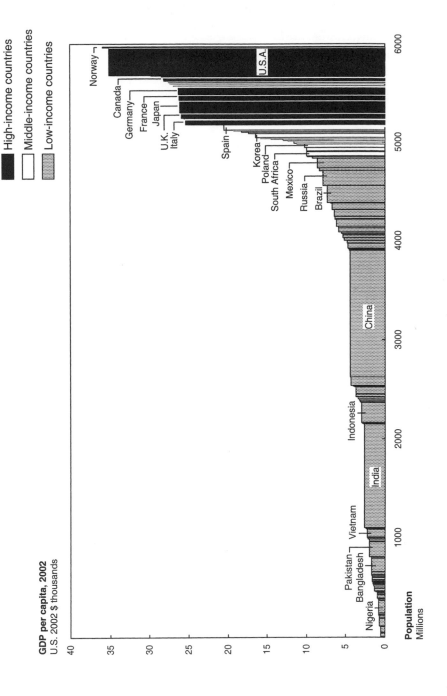

GDP per capita, 2002
U.S. 2002 $ thousands

High-income countries
Middle-income countries
Low-income countries

Population
Millions

The gap between rich and poor nations threatens global stability. Immigration pressures are becoming unsustainable; the poor see moving to the rich countries as the only way to improve their way of life within their lifetime. The frustration, envy, and wounded pride of the poor are causing rogue nations to seek power and influence through the development of weapons of mass destruction and individual extremists to lash out against rich countries through terrorism.

Fifty years ago the population numbers were smaller and the gap somewhat less pronounced, but the distance between the peak and the plain was no less awesome and no less worrisome. A vast array of international institutions was created to remedy this situation. For half a century, the United Nations, the World Bank, the IMF, and countless not-for-profits and foundations have devoted great effort to attacking this problem, but they have failed. Conventional wisdom assumed that improvements in technology, global capital, education, and health care would eliminate stark distinctions between rich and poor nations. But the lot of the world's poor is little improved and their numbers have doubled. Even if the poor countries could grow per capita income at the extraordinary rate of 7 percent per year, it would take fifty years for them to catch up. At the current rates of performance, it would take them a couple of centuries to catch up, if they could at all.

There are very few people living in "foothill" countries on the global economic landscape, countries at the bottom of the peak but with prospects of moving up. Only 340 million people, or 5 percent of the world's population, live in 23 middle-income countries with GDPs per capita between 25 and 70 percent of the U.S. GDP per capita. These countries include Korea (48 million people), South Africa (44 million), Spain (41 million), Poland (39 million), Argentina (38 million people), Taiwan (22 million people), Saudi Arabia (22 million), Greece (11 million), the Czech Republic (10 million), and Hungary (10 million).

Each country has its own story, but the small number of people on the foothills is worrisome; it means that all of the poor nations on Exhibit 1.1 today will be poor nations ten or twenty years from now. Economic development is a slow process, but the lack of more foothill countries also shows how ineffectual development economics has been since the Second World War.

Our solutions to this problem have failed because they don't address the real causes of persistent poverty.

The difference in economic success, I will argue, is not a matter of nature, intellect, or genetics. The problem—and the solution—lies in public policies. But effective policies can be created and implemented only if one truly understands what makes the economies of poor (or rich) nations grow. But even during the 1990s, when development economics seemed most promising, it lacked that understanding.

The Failure of Development Economics

At the beginning of the 1990s, the fall of the Soviet Union precipitated a wave of market reform that swept around the world. Brazil, Russia, Argentina, Poland, Mexico, India, Chile, and New Zealand were the leading examples. A consensus emerged about good economic policies for development. Dubbed the "Washington Consensus," it included such elements as price decontrol, privatization, flexible exchange rates, low inflation, government solvency, good corporate governance, and good market regulation. With the exception of Russia, the countries on this list were thought to be doing virtually everything needed. Even Russia made many of the prescribed reforms, although not in corporate governance.

However, the results have been disappointing. By the end of the 1990s the growth rates of most of these countries had returned to levels so low that the profile of the global economic landscape was not changing at all. Disenchantment among the poor has spread quickly. Their impatience has been reinforced by the elites, who in many cases have not really given up the idea that socialism is better than capitalism or that we need something in between. However, the so-called third way has proved illusive.

The political reaction was quick in some cases. A populist labor leader, Inácio Lula da Silva ("Lula"), has been elected president of Brazil, and the electorate in Poland has returned the party formed by former Communists to power. Argentina is struggling to emerge from chaos, India is not growing nearly as fast as China, and Mexico and New Zealand are performing far below potential.

Development economics is in disarray about where to go from here.

All Rich Countries Are Not Equal

Conventional economics has also failed to explain the persistence of disparities in wealth among those nations at the peak of the global economic landscape.

Twenty-five years ago, the general expectation in economics was that the economies of the United States, Europe, and Japan would converge. We had entered an era in which technology and business practice

Exhibit 1.2: Economic Development Paths

Percent U.S. 1995 level

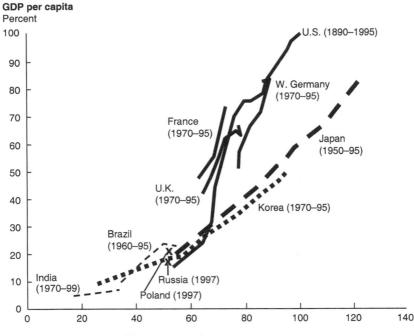

GDP per capita
Percent

Total labor and capital inputs per capita

flowed freely among these countries, capital was readily available, and the workforces were healthy and well educated. Moreover, the products and services desired by these workforces seemed highly similar based on what they spent their money on. Thus any successful new product or service or any better way of providing a product or service would transfer quickly among all these rich countries.

But large disparities of wealth even among rich countries remain because Japan has been following a low-productivity path and because Europe has been making unnecessary distortions in its markets to achieve its social objectives. The development path exhibit (Exhibit 1.2) shows that Japan's growth has been caused more by a massive increase in the hours worked and plant and equipment applied in economic activity than in the Western democracies. The hours worked increase came from an increase in the fraction of people of working age and an increase in the fraction of those people who worked. Alwyn Young, followed by Paul Krugman, pointed out that the increase in hours worked could only go on for so long and that massive inputs of capital not earning an economic return would eventually lead to diminished growth. In fact, this is exactly what was vividly exhibited in the Japanese economy in the 1990s.

Both Europe and the United States have followed a high-productivity path. Europeans as individuals work fewer hours and fewer individuals of working age actually work. The net result is of course a lower GDP per capita. However, Europeans appear to be making a trade-off that reflects individual preferences for how people want to live. Many people would say, "I would rather be European." But the trade-off is not fully what it first appears to be. Unemployment rates in Europe have persistently been at least twice as high as in the United States, much more of the unemployed are individuals who remain out of work for a long time, and many people have given up trying to find work.

Some might argue that Europe has been following a lower poverty path than the United States. Thus Europe is making a different kind of trade-off to create a society that many would prefer: trading a higher GDP per capita for a lower poverty rate.

But this understanding of the lower poverty rate of the European countries is just as flawed as the conventional understanding of the higher poverty rate among nations on the plains of the global economic landscape. Both interpretations fail because they are grounded in analysis of economies at the macroeconomic level. It's like trying to understand our physical universe using only the telescopes of astronomy. Any real understanding comes from studying how the tiniest particles in the universe interact in the depths of massive stars.

Most economists utilize this macro approach; a more fine-grained microeconomic approach is beyond their means. They simply can't afford the time and resources that it would take to look, in detail, at how the economy of an entire country works.

At McKinsey, over the last twelve years, we have had that luxury, and the results yield an entirely new understanding of the disparities between rich and poor nations—and even of the disparities among the richer nations.

Research Approach

In 1990, McKinsey & Co. decided to try to understand globalization. What was it? Where was it going? Why was it occurring? Since most economic analysis is about countries, we started with questions about what was happening to the economies of countries in the context of globalization.

As founding director of the McKinsey Global Institute, it was my responsibility to oversee an unprecedented study: a combination of macro- and microeconomic analysis conducted over twelve years in thirteen countries. We conducted systematic individual reviews of the economic performance of the United States, Japan, Germany, France, the United Kingdom, Sweden, the Netherlands, Korea, Australia, Brazil, Russia, Poland, and India. Each study compared the performance of one country with the performance of a sample of comparison countries. Each year-long study involved a team of six to eight McKinsey consultants and economic specialists working full-time.

I did not realize until near the end of this twelve years of work that we had accumulated a new understanding of why the global economic landscape looks the way it does and what could be done to change it. But indeed our work, and the method of research we were able to use, gives a new understanding of why workers and managers produce goods and services around the world at such different efficiencies. Our work is based on the detailed studies of individual businesses—from state-of-the-art auto plants to black-market street vendors. It builds an understanding of the economy from the ground up, rather than the top down; a grassroots view versus a bird's-eye view.

In contrast, most economic analysis is done at the level of entire economies, the macro or macroeconomics level. According to Princeton University economist Orley Ashenfelter, a frequent adviser on our projects, "macroeconomics consists of identities and opinions." The opinions are often based on massive data analyses, which attempt to find out what economic events occur at about the same time as other economic events. However, this co-relationship does not prove that one event causes the other in any sense that an ordinary person would use causality. Moreover, these analyses are usually unable to determine the direction the causality flows from one event to the other.

This is not true for microeconomics. Microeconomics is about the behavior of firms in the same market. These firms are in the same market because they're trying to sell the same goods and services to the same customers. Thus these firms interact intensely with the same customers and among themselves. The nature of these interactions is rooted in human behavior, which we understand something about intuitively and scientifically. Thus we can understand why firms and customers behave the way they do. That means we can understand causality within markets.

Since economies are the sum of all their micromarkets, or "sectors," as they are called in economics, if we could simply add up the behavior of all individual markets, we would have the total economy, or macroeconomics. The problem is more complicated because there are constraints on the total economy such as the size of the potential labor force, customer preferences across all goods and services, etc. Thus, what happens in one micromarket influences what happens in other micromarkets. However, combining the micro behavior in individual markets with the identities and constraints at the macro level yields total economy outcomes.

This situation is intuitively familiar to me because of my initial training as a theoretical physicist. In physics, great progress has been made in explaining the physical world around us by understanding precisely the nature of the interaction among the tiniest particles in the universe and then summing up how all these particles behave subject to macro constraints such as the walls of a box or curved space. Because physics knows precisely the interactions among the most fundamental particles and because the mathematical techniques developed for adding them up are incredibly powerful, physics can give an explanation of why the universe looks the way it does.

In economics, it is not possible to accomplish the same thing that physics has. The reason is that the nature of the interaction among firms is much more complicated than the interaction among fundamental particles. Moreover, there are many more different kinds of firms than there are different kinds of fundamental particles. Until recently, the idea of adding up all these interactions for enough firms in enough sectors to understand total economies was hopeless. However, in the last few years, we have had massive improvements in economic data collection and data analysis coming from modern information technology. As a result, we found we could do enough industry studies to understand country economic performance and enough countries around the world to understand the global economic landscape. Even doing this work on such a sample basis requires enormous resources. At the moment, McKinsey is the only organization in the world with the global scope and resource depth to conduct such a research program.

It's Productivity

Over the course of our research a single theme emerged: the importance of productivity. Our initial goal was to explain the reasons for the differences in GDP per capita around the world, as depicted in Exhibit 1.1.

Exhibit 1.3: Productivity and GDP per Capita across Countries

Index U.S. = 100 in 1996

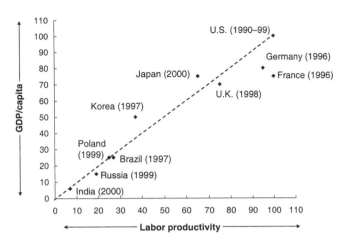

GDP per capita is widely regarded as the best single measure of economic well-being. GDP per capita is simply the product of labor productivity—how many goods and services you can produce with a given amount of workers—multiplied by the fraction of people who work. The fraction of people who work varies somewhat around the world. Interestingly, however, it doesn't vary much.

Productivity, however, varies enormously around the world. The differences in productivity explain virtually all of the differences in GDP per capita (Exhibit 1.3). Thus, most of our work sought to explain the reasons for the differences in productivity around the world.

As I explained earlier in this chapter, we can truly understand causality only at the industry level. The productivity of a country is the average productivity of all industries (weighted appropriately by size). If we understand the causes of productivity performance in enough industries, we then understand what causes a country's productivity to be what it is. Thus, an evaluation of economic performance requires an analysis at the level of individual industries, such as automotive, steel, banking, and retailing. Many people look for the causes of poor economic performance primarily in macroeconomics, but *we found that you must also look at the industry level for causal factors for economic performance*. Industry-level work reveals what could be done differently in an economy to increase productivity. Making these changes does not automatically increase GDP per capita. You have to make sure that workers stay employed as they change what they do and move from firm to firm. And so our approach also included assessments of the degree to which employment would be maintained as productivity increased.

Because productivity determines GDP per capita, the productivity of every worker matters. The average productivity of an entire economy is simply the average of the productivities of all workers. In today's rich countries, most workers work in service industries. Only about 20 to 25 percent work in manufacturing and about 5 percent in agriculture. That means the standard of living in the rich countries is determined primarily by the productivity of service industry workers. Thus, it's not high-tech workers in computers and biotechnology and it's not Wall Street. It's more the productivity of the massive number of workers in retailing, wholesaling, and construction that give the United States the highest GDP per capita in the world.

From our studies of Brazil, Russia, and India, it is clear that without macroeconomic stability, countries will be unable to increase productivity and lift off from the poverty plain. In these circumstances, firms concentrate on making money from the macroeconomic instability rather than by improving their productivity. Countries have to control inflation and have flexible exchange rates. Flexible exchange rates are necessary in order to absorb the inherent volatility in the global economy. However, macroeconomic stability is not sufficient to reach the peak, as both Japan and Korea show. Japan and Korea have both had the macro policies needed for stability. However, neither have had the micro policies most countries need to reach and stay on the peak. Japan has reached the peak and Korea has approached the peak because their hard work and high savings and investment have made up for bad micro policies distorting competition.

Russia, or more correctly the former Soviet Union, shows that it's possible to have macro stability but to distort competition so much through micro policy that productivity increases do not lift the economy off the plain. Thus, the profile of the global economic landscape seems to be explained by a simple pattern. Without macro stability, it is not possible to increase productivity. Even with macro stability, micro policy may distort competition so much that productivity does not rise. With macro stability, lesser degrees of micro distortions should allow economies to reach the foothills. Since we don't have many foothill countries, the micro distortions must be pretty bad. They certainly are in Brazil and India.

Our finding of the importance of productivity is not a stunningly original insight, even though productivity does not get the attention it deserves. The key is what follows from investigating why productivity levels are so different around the world. There we did find several important unconventional ideas:

- As mentioned above, you have to look at the industry level for causal factors of economic performance.
- Education is not as immediately important as most people think.
- If poor countries take care of their productivity problems, they will get the needed capital.
- Foreign direct investment has the potential to cause poor countries to grow faster than anybody thinks.
- Distortions in competition in product markets are much more important than labor or capital market problems.
- The Washington Consensus about good economic policy for developing countries profoundly underestimated the importance of a level playing field for market competition.
- Distorting markets to achieve social equity objectives is usually a bad idea.
- Today's big governments in poor countries are a handicap today's rich countries did not have when they were poor.
- The elites in poor countries have not accepted the hard lessons from the economic experiments of the past fifty years.
- Consumers are the only political force that can stand up to producer interests, big government, and the technocratic, political, business, and intellectual elites.

The next sections in this chapter show how these ideas emerged from our study of productivity differences.

It's Not Education and Capital

Many people believe that the educational attainment of a nation's current labor force is responsible for the success or failure of its economy. *The importance of the education of the workforce has been taken way too far. In other words, education is not the way out of the poverty trap. A high education level is no guarantee of high productivity. The truth of the matter is that regardless of institutional education level, workers around the world can be adequately trained on the job for high productivity.*

In the early 1990s, the conventional wisdom was that Germany and Japan were passing the United States in economic performance. One of the principal reasons cited was the poor education of the U.S. workforce. A substantial part of this book is about how wrong that perception of German and Japanese economic performance is. However, it was true that in a handful of industries, Japanese productivity was the highest in the world. Japanese firms in those industries, and particularly in automotive, built transplant factories in the United States and achieved 95 percent of home country productivity. They achieved this productivity with the U.S. workforce. They did it by training U.S. workers on the job. This training cost them only a 5 percent productivity penalty. More broadly, as this book shows, U.S. workers achieve the highest productivity in the world in most economic sectors. Whatever weakness exists in the U.S. education system, it is being made up for by on-the-job training.

Our work shows that what has been true in the United States can also be true in the poor countries of the world. They do not have to wait until they build much bigger and better educational systems and until they put a whole generation of workers through such systems. If their local businesses follow the proven approaches for organizing labor, all poor countries are capable of very rapid productivity improvement from their workforces. If illiterate Mexican immigrants can reach world-class productivity building apartment houses in Houston, there is no reason why illiterate Brazilian agricultural workers cannot achieve the same in São Paulo.

Moreover, many people see capital as the determining factor separating a productive growing economy from one that is not. They feel that if rich countries sent capital pouring into poor countries, the poor countries would become richer. *The solution does not start with more capital. The solution, rather, is in the country's productivity or the way it organizes and deploys both its labor and its capital. If poor countries improved productivity and balanced their budgets, they would have plenty of capital for growth from domestic savers and foreign investors.*

As chapter 8 on India describes in detail, only about 20 percent of employment in India is in firms that look like firms you find in the rich countries. However, the average labor productivity in these firms in India is only 15 percent of the U.S. level. Without any additional capital, these firms could increase their productivity to about 40 percent of the U.S. average. They can do this by simply reorganizing the way work is conducted. Indian workers have the ability to be trained to work in these new ways. Suzuki, one of the six high-performance Japanese auto companies, invested in India in a joint venture in 1983. Suzuki had operational control. It built plants like the ones in Japan, it organized the work as in Japan, and it trained workers to work as in Japan. It achieved a productivity that was 55 percent of the U.S. auto industry average. Sadly, a morass of misguided economic policies have not allowed other Suzukis to do their thing in India. Recently, a couple of private Indian retail banks have achieved productivity near global best practice.

Some people think that nations should protect their own industries but ask outside nations for capital. *This is wrong. Direct investments by the more productive companies from the rich countries would raise the poor countries' productivity and growth rates far more effectively than sending them money. Poor countries have the potential to grow much faster than most people realize.*

What conditions need to change in poor countries for this to happen?

Undistorted Competition in Product Markets Is Essential

Most economic analysis ends up attributing most of the differences in economic performance to differences in labor and capital markets. *This conclusion is incorrect. Differences in competition in product markets are much more important.*

As chapter 7 on Russia and chapter 8 on India show, intense, balanced, local competition is critical for productivity improvement and economic growth. The only other factor of equal importance is macroeconomic stability. However, macroeconomic stability gets all the attention. Most economists and politicians seem to have no idea how severely distorted competition in most markets around the world really is. *The Washington Consensus of the 1990s profoundly underestimated the importance of a level playing field for competition in a country.*

That's a problem. It's a problem because competition is the way more productive firms win out. Productivity increases as more productive firms expand and take market share away from less productive firms. Sometimes the less productive firms go out of business. Other times they react to the competitive pressure and increase their own productivity. Either way, overall productivity increases.

Firms become more productive through innovations. The innovations may be new products and services. They may also be new ways of manufacturing products and delivering services. We really don't understand why innovations occur when and where they do. Why did the innovations of Toyota, Wal-Mart, and Intel occur as they did? We just don't know. What we do know is that innovations occur. Valuable innovations allow the innovator to charge higher prices, make more profits, invest in more capacity, take market share away from competitors, make even more profits, etc. The process goes on until competitors react by copying the innovation or inventing something equivalent of their own. Profits for all competitors return to normal levels and the industry may very well be stable for a while. However, it is stable at a higher level of productivity. Consumers and workers have achieved a permanent gain. Investors in the original innovator enjoy temporarily high returns. However, through competition those returns soon become normal. They remain normal until the next innovation.

Competition is what makes this process work. The more intense and evenly balanced competition is, the faster the process works. The faster the process works, the faster productivity increases. If conditions in the market exclude some potential competitors, then competition is less intense and productivity growth is slower. If conditions in the market favor less productive competitors, then innovators cannot expand and productivity growth is slower. Over and over again, we found markets where more productive innovators were excluded and where less productive firms were favored.

Even in the rich countries this is a problem. In the United Kingdom, France, Germany, and Japan, zoning laws and planning regulations prevent global best practice retailers from expanding as fast as they could. Sometimes these restrictions are for valid environmental reasons. Most times, they're not. Tesco, the global best practice food retailer in the United Kingdom, has been unsuccessful in obtaining planning authority permission to build a modern supermarket on the site of a derelict hospital, broken windows and all, near central London. The hospital is of no architectural value. Yet it cannot be touched because it is over one hundred years old. The result is lower productivity for the UK economy and higher food prices for the UK consumers. In Japan, such restrictions, along with subsidized loans and distortions in the tax code, are used to protect mom-and-pop retailers from going out of business. The result is that an unsalable hat has sat on the shelf of a mom-and-pop shop in central Tokyo for the past fifteen years. The proprietors don't have to sell the hat. They get subsidized loans, and their bequest will easily cover the loans. Their shop sits on some of the most valuable real estate in the world.

Most people consider the "social objectives" motivating zoning laws and small-business subsidies to be "good." *However, we can't have it both ways. These measures distort markets severely and limit productivity growth, slow overall economic growth, and cause unemployment. Rather than support these measures, it is better to level the play-*

ing field, create a bigger economic pie, and manage the distribution of that pie through the tax code for individuals.

Such market distortions explain most of the difference between the GDP per capita of the United States and the other rich countries. However, the United States is not immune to these distortions. The recently enacted tariffs on steel imports and subsidies for farmers diminish competitive intensity for U.S. steel and agricultural industries. The result is lower productivity and higher steel and food prices in the United States.

The Big Distortions Are in Poor Countries

The really big market distortions show up in the poor countries. Russia is unfortunately a very good example. After the fall of the Soviet Union, a flurry of new business activity took place. It was easy to assume that this business activity was more productive firms replacing the old, unproductive Soviet firms. Surely Russia was rapidly on its way to becoming rich.

Not so. The new firms were no more productive than the old Soviet firms they were replacing. More productive firms either tried to enter and failed or didn't bother to try. Carrefour, perhaps the best international retailer in the world, concluded it could deal with the red tape, bribery, and even threats to physical security in Russia. However, it could not deal with not making money. And it could not make money in Russia. The reason was that Carrefour, like virtually all multinationals, pays its taxes. Its competitors in Russia, the open-air markets, do not. These markets are even favored by tax law. Moreover, before the ruble crashed, these markets sold smuggled or counterfeit goods at prices Carrefour could not match. Carrefour decided not to enter Russia.

Finally, we come to India. India has even more market distortions than Russia. The distortions are everywhere. India reserves several hundred consumer goods products for manufacture in small-scale plants. China doesn't. China builds world-scale plants. The result is that China gets the export markets available to cheap labor economies, not India. China even exports into India. India has passed an absolute prohibition against foreign direct investment in retailing. Global best practice food retailers, led by Carrefour, have stimulated supermarkets and hypermarkets to gain a 40 percent market share in Thailand, 35 percent in Brazil, 18 percent in Poland, and 10 percent in China. In India, these stores have a 2 percent market share and are much less productive than in these other countries. In housing construction, competition among developers and construction firms has nothing to do with productivity. It's all over gaining control of the scarce parcels of land with clear ownership titles. Over 90 percent of land titles in India are subject to dispute. Nobody is going to build housing on land they might find someone else owns. There is so little price competition among construction firms that they have not even felt the need to adopt the innovation of the wheelbarrow.

Why are these distortions to competition in the product markets so pervasive? First of all, they are hard to find. Distortions in each individual market have to be painstakingly dug out. It's a big effort and it requires special skills. Second, significant political forces gain from their existence. These forces are business special interests, big governments, and technocratic, political, business, and intellectual elites.

The Enemies of Economic Growth

We understand that in the commercial world, special interests exist. We see them every day. We expect such behavior. Owners, investors, managers, and workers are looking out for themselves. David Hume first said this is true for all of us. In the Western democracies, special interests are generally not allowed to have their way to the extent that it undermines the common good. We do not understand how widespread the influence of special interests is in the rest of the world.

In the poor countries, protection of special interests is pervasive. Certainly in Russia and India. The Moscow government allocates housing contracts to the old Soviet construction companies. Local governments in Russia don't allow the energy companies to cut off small factories that can't pay their bills. India doesn't allow large factories to make any of some eight hundred consumer goods products. Domestic retailers in India are protected entirely from foreign direct investment by global best practice retailers. In poor countries today every domestic firm is a potential special interest. That's because global best practice firms have shown that they can go virtually anywhere in the world and operate at productivity well above local firms. The result of course is that local workers earn higher wages and local consumers enjoy lower prices. However, owners and managers of unproductive local firms stand to lose.

Workers at these unproductive firms also think they stand to lose. Most people fear changing jobs. This fear is especially strong in poor countries. There the risk is not just a job at a somewhat lower wage, but falling back to near subsistence living. Owners and managers often hide behind a social concern for the jobs of their workers. However, if poor countries want to become rich, unsuccessful owners and managers have to be allowed to fail and workers have to find new jobs. In a healthy economy, workers come out all right in the end. Undistorted competition in the product market makes economies healthy. That's why product market distortions are much more important than labor market distortions. However, part of a healthy economy is that unsuccessful owners and managers do not come out all right in the end. That's why they fight so hard for protection. That's part of the reason globalization is under such attack.

Brazil has made remarkable progress over the past decade in reforming its economy to eliminate favoritism for business special interests. However, Brazil has another big problem. Most people don't recognize the destructive power of big government. *Big governments demand big taxation. When part of the economy is informal, and untaxed, the burden falls heavily on legitimate businesses. This is a burden today's rich countries did not have when they were poor.*

Brazil's government spends 39 percent of Brazil's GDP. The U.S. government spends about 37 percent. Brazil already looks a little out of line. However, Brazil is in a dramatically different position for raising the money to pay for that much government spending. Government spending has to be financed primarily by taxes. The U.S. government is able to tax most business entities and most individuals. The U.S. government can do this because virtually all businesses and all people are registered with the government. The government knows who they are and where they are. If some don't pay their taxes, the government comes after them.

Not so in Brazil. About 50 percent of the workers in Brazil are not registered with the government. Many small businesses are also not registered. Often, these people are desperately poor and living near subsistence. No country has the heart to go after these people for tax money. Even if they did, they would collect very little from each person. However, because we're talking about roughly 50 percent of the workers in Brazil, the total tax revenue forgone is substantial. But collecting this money is not a possibility even if the government wanted to. The workers and small businesses would be virtually impossible to find. The costs of collecting taxes from them would probably be more than the revenue raised. This means that most of the tax revenue has to come from larger businesses and some individuals.

Unlike the United States, Brazil has chosen to collect most of its taxes through corporations. Thus today, taxes paid by corporations in Brazil are almost twice as high as in the United States. However, that's not the right comparison. We should be making a comparison with the United States in 1913. That's when the United States had the same GDP per capita as Brazil today. In 1913 the U.S. government spent only 8 percent of GDP. Thus, as a percentage of GDP, the corporate tax burden in Brazil today is seven times that of U.S. corporations when the United States was at Brazil's current GDP per capita.

Big Government Distorts Competition

This difference in tax burden has a pernicious consequence. The more productive firms in Brazil pay taxes and the less productive ones don't. Moreover, the tax rates on the firms that do pay taxes are extraordinarily high. The consequence is that the costs of doing business for the more productive firms are about as high as the costs for the less productive, informal firms. Thus, the productive firms have to charge prices about as high as the unproductive firms. The prices in modern convenience food retailing chains are about the same as in cardboard nooks with a few shelves. This means that modern productive enterprises cannot easily take market share away from unproductive enterprises. The natural evolution of Brazil's economy is thus stymied.

Brazil (and India) got such a big government because in the second half of the twentieth century, technocratic, political, business, and intellectual elites around the world thought that government management of economies of poor countries was the way to make them rich. *These elites are responsible for big government. Particularly in the poorer countries, the elites license business activity, control international financial and material goods flows, promote unaffordable social welfare systems, and favor government-owned businesses. Too often, the elites reward themselves richly.*

Governments, staffed by the technocratic and intellectual elite, were thought to be smart enough to figure out which industries to invest in and which industries to nurture and protect. The common perception was that Japan was successfully doing this. So everybody else should too. Japan managed its economy to a much lesser extent than commonly perceived. Moreover, Japan got away with what management it did apply because entrepreneurs in automotive, steel, machine tools, and consumer electronics were operating outside the government system and were fabulously successful in global competition. Finally, in the 1990s we saw stagnation resulting from Japan's approach.

With the fall of the Soviet Union, substantial rethinking about the planning approach has occurred around the world. Intellectual elites have been the most reluctant to give in. They seem inherently uncomfortable with capitalism, even in its modern social welfare form. They seem to wish that socialism would just work because they wish the world were such that it would.

In any case, once government functions are established, history shows they are very difficult to abolish. The poor countries today do not have to reinvent the wheel. Innovations already exist around the world, which if applied in the poor countries through globalization, would make them rich. However, the rich countries of today have given the poor countries a curse. That curse is not globalization. It is big government.

Policy Directions

Chapter 11 of this book is about how poor countries might get out of this poverty trap. It necessarily takes me into political economy and political philosophy. Those thoughts did not come out of the twelve years of economic analysis of the Global Institute. They are personal.

It seems to me that many people think that production is all that is needed to create economic value. This is why government sometimes protects businesses, regardless of their performance. *They fail to make the link between production and consumption. The goods produced have value only because consumers want them. If they do not want them for some reason (such as high price), the business producing them needs to die. Only one force can stand up to producer special interests— consumer interests. Most poor countries are a long way from a consumption mindset and consumer rights. As a result, they are poor.*

I believe consumer rights rise fundamentally from political philosophies based on individual rights. Included in the notion of individual rights is the right to be a consumer, the option to buy what you want with the money left over after providing for food and shelter. This consumer right includes the freedom to buy these goods and services from anybody who wants to sell them to you, including "start-ups." Consumers want to buy from firms with better products and services or with lower prices. Those are the firms that survive if competition is equal. Thus, consumer interests are served if competition is not distorted. Poor countries will remain poor until their societies serve consumer interests through respect for individual rights.

Education is important for this evolution (even though, as I said earlier in this chapter, it's not important for immediate productivity increases). Through education we are exposed to different ideas about how to organize societies. We learn that the natural experiments of the past show that societies based on individual rights are the only societies to become rich and we can understand why this is so. We still are not compelled to live in such a society. However, if we want to be part of a rich society, we had better do so.

We will begin to change the shape of the global economic landscape for the better when we begin to act with the understanding that economic progress depends on increasing productivity. Increasing productivity depends on undistorted competition. Undistorted competition depends on consumers claiming their rights through the political process. Such consumer action depends on societies having democracies based on individual rights.

PART ONE

RICH AND MIDDLE-INCOME COUNTRIES

Japan: A Dual Economy

Over the past thirteen years, I have bought five automobiles manufactured by Honda. One was manufactured in the United States. They have been perfect, no trouble, a pleasure to drive, and stylish. I have stood on the train platform in Atami just southwest of Tokyo and felt the compression waves as the long-distance bullet trains sped by every five to six minutes. On a night ride on the Super Bullet between Tokyo and Kyoto, we rocked gently right and left as the high-speed train tilted on the banked curves necessary to keep the train on the track at those speeds. The Japanese name for bullet trains, "shinkansen," even sounds like power and precision.

Yet for all this industrial muscle, one can stand in Kyoto, amidst a couple of million people, in temples with gardens designed and maintained to provide islands of peace and tranquility, if there are any on earth. The meticulous service of a sequestered Japanese inn carries over to a Japanese restaurant owned by a Japanese family in the mountains of southwestern Virginia. The Japanese can even train Americans to make cars and serve food the way it's done in Japan. In short, the Japanese have made us believe they can do anything they want to, and do it better than almost anyone else. Indeed, Japan is the only country that went from poor to rich over the last one hundred years.

Japan is still an economic powerhouse. Yet its condition is precarious. For the past decade, the Japanese economy has stagnated. Today, Japan's GDP per capita is about 30 percent below the United States'. Real per capita economic growth since 1990 has measured just 0.6 percent annually. Unemployment has increased from about 2 percent to between 5 and 6 percent. Since 1996, the Japanese standard of living has not improved at all, and the gap between U.S. and Japanese per capita income has grown by 13 percentage points since 1991.

Despite So Much Success, Japan Is Failing

What went wrong? Japan had virtually all the conventional characteristics listed in chapter 1 as those considered by economists as necessary for good economic performance. Japan had a highly educated workforce. It had a well-developed capital market. It saved a lot and thus invested a lot without having to borrow much from abroad. Its labor market worked well enough to keep unemployment low. It had low inflation, low interest rates, and low public debt.

Yet in Japan, all the factors that economists traditionally think contribute to economic prosperity are not enough. Despite the unrivaled success of such big names as Honda, Sony, and others, the Japanese severely distort competition in most of their markets where goods and services are sold. There, productivity ranks among the middle-income countries, not the richer ones. These product market distortions simply overpower labor and capital market factors, and limit the potential influence of macroeconomic policy.

The Japan We Do Not See

This is the Japan that we do not see. It's the Japan of the small farmer, the small shopkeeper, the small milk plant, the lone carpenter, and the long lines at the university medical centers. Here, small is not beautiful; it's inefficient and unproductive. The result is products and services at such high prices that consumers don't want them. The story of the success of Japan's big global industries is well known. Unfortunately, they contribute at most 10 percent of Japan's GDP. The vast majority of the economy is made up of the production and delivery of more mundane products and services that are consumed within Japan—food, clothing, housing, health care. To understand why Japan's economy is stagnating, you must look at what is happening in these unglamorous but large parts of the economy. As I said in chapter 1, the devil is in the industry-level detail.

The problem in these domestic parts of the economy is lack of competition. A string of land restrictions, tax policies, loan subsidies, and other market regulations prop up small, inefficient firms while stifling more enterprising and efficient firms. The result is a dual economy (Exhibit 2.1). The few shining export sectors—autos, consumer electronics, steel—are the face of Japanese industry to the world. But the much larger domestic industries remain inefficient, subscale, fragmented, and, as a result, have very low productivity. And this is the majority of the

Exhibit 2.1: Dual Economy in Japan

11 industries

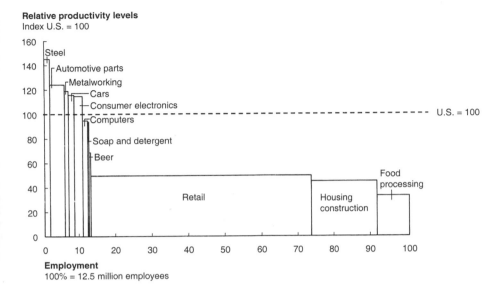

Relative productivity levels
Index U.S. = 100

Employment
100% = 12.5 million employees

economy. To understand an economy's productivity, one needs to understand the productivity of every single worker in it, and most workers are not like Toyota employees. In this chapter, I will spend most of my time on the unseen side of Japan's economy, from mom-and-pop retail stores to tiny dairy plants to individual carpenters, to explain how this part of the economy operates and what is holding it back.

The Japanese are resourceful people. *They have been devoting their extraordinary talents to propping up an economic structure with limited future development potential.* They have done this very successfully and for too long a time. They are capable of doing much better. However, the changes needed for better economic performance will require leveling the playing field for competition in such a way that the more productive modern enterprises will cause the small operations to fail. This will be hard to swallow. Notions of social equality and maintenance of self-respect make it almost impossible for the Japanese to accept such dynamics. Even more difficult is the political reality that the many small shopkeepers, carpenters, farmers, and doctors form the backbone of the Liberal Democratic Party (LDP), the political party that has ruled Japan almost continuously since the war. These special interests benefit from

the current system and thus perpetuate it. Finding the way to end decades of protection and subsidies has so far been impossible.

Such change may come with another generation, but that's a long
wait. However, without accepting substantial change within a generation, Japan's economy will lag further and further behind those societies
that do accept such change. Thus the Japanese face a genuine trade-off:
current notions of domestic tranquility versus economic growth.

Conducting our work in Japan was very difficult. As I mentioned in
the Prologue, my first attempt at a country study of Japan in 1996 was
thwarted by the unwillingness of my Japanese colleagues to engage in
this kind of work. Even they, who had trained at some of the most reputable universities and business schools in the West, found it extremely
difficult to dissect their own economy. The Japanese have an obsession
about correctness. To dissect or to analyze requires identifying causality. For less than perfect outcomes causality implies that things could've
been done better. That means there is a risk that someone has not performed as well as he should. Should that shortcoming be identified, the
individual would lose face. Everyone around would be uncomfortable.
The Japanese go to great lengths to avoid this discomfort. Thus they
avoid causality. They avoid causality by denying the problem. Japan de-
nied its current economic problems for almost ten years.

However, by 1999 the problems were undeniable. The last defense
was to claim that everything was already known about causality and
that the remedy was clear. It is very difficult to admit in Japan that one
does not know something. Again, it would entail a loss of face. However, by 1999 it was clear that the remedy applied by Japan, massive
fiscal stimulus, was unsuccessful. Only at that time were we able to do a
detailed diagnosis. This chapter is the story of what we found.

Autos: The Best in the World

Autos are the most visible evidence of how good the Japanese are in the
good part of their dual economy. The Japanese automotive industry has
probably had more beneficial effects for the economies on the peak of
the global economic landscape than any other single industry in any
country. It has shown that perfection, usually referred to as "quality," is
a much better way of making things than the previous way of "make and
then fix." It has shown that workers around the world from the United
States to India can be trained in factories to achieve close to this perfection, regardless of their previous education and skill level. Finally, the
development of the Japanese auto industry shows the powerful and

beneficial effects of intense competition with firms who are better than you are.

In the 1960s in the United States, no one would have predicted that thirty years later the Japanese auto industry would have had such an effect on the world. Some of us can remember Toyotas broken down on the side of the road, often with smoke billowing out from under the hood. They did not look like much competition for the big three U.S. automakers, led by General Motors, by far the largest manufacturing company in the world. However, what we also didn't pay attention to was that General Motors had a 40 percent market share in the United States, was unlikely to be allowed by the antitrust authorities to gain more share, and had become complacent. All Ford and Chrysler had to do was to make cars that ran to stay in business. The United States had a sleepy oligopoly. Perhaps the biggest mistake ever made in U.S. antitrust law was not to break up General Motors and create more intense domestic competition. Fortunately, the Japanese took care of that problem for us.

The Japanese did have intense domestic competition. Six domestic producers fought intensely over market share. Out of this competition emerged Toyota, first as the leading automotive producer in Japan and, later, in the world, and probably the best overall manufacturing company anywhere. Toyota's leadership came simply from its being by far the most productive auto manufacturer in the world. This means that it can make more cars per worker than anyone else. Toyota's productivity lead means that it can produce an equivalent car with only 70 percent of the labor hours used in the United States. It is even further ahead of the German industry.

Toyota itself is some 30 percent more productive than the rest of the Japanese industry. Since Toyota has a 40 percent market share in Japan, much of the lead of the Japanese industry comes from Toyota alone.

Toyota has achieved this large productivity edge by recognizing that doing things right the first time is by far more efficient than making things with defects, which are fixed later. Over the years, Toyota has worked out inch by inch how to delegate responsibility and organize work on the production line so that cars are made right the first time. This way of manufacturing takes fewer labor hours. The car produced has fewer defects when sold to the customer and is more reliable over time. That means the car is more valuable to the customer. Thus Toyota produces a more valuable product with less work.

Toyota has also helped the hundreds of its suppliers to deliver quality parts, thereby improving their own productivity. The other Japanese producers have had to improve rapidly to stay in business, but none of them have come close to catching up with Toyota, with the possible exception of Honda.

Toyota's Innovation Felt around the World

The superiority of "quality" manufacturing, and, for that matter, "quality" services, has been recognized around the world for a couple of decades now. Hundreds of firms now work towards this standard. Consumers benefit worldwide. It all really started with Toyota. Thus Toyota has probably had more impact on the global economy today than any other single firm. Someday, it might be Intel, Microsoft, or Wal-Mart, but today it's Toyota. Why Toyota? Nobody really knows why the quality innovation first occurred there. It just did. It turns out innovations occur all the time. What we can learn from the Toyota case is how economic policies affect the rate at which innovations spread around the world and become available to everybody.

Innovations spread through competition. From the beginning, Toyota attempted to penetrate the U.S. market. This may have stemmed from a strategy of becoming one of the world's best. Since in the 1960s, the best was in the United States, Toyota may have come here initially to learn. After Toyota got so good, it came here to take market share and make profits. The effect was dramatic for the world's auto industry. Japanese car exports to the United States exceeded 20 percent of the entire U.S. market in the early 1980s.

The Japanese had a little luck because the small, fuel-efficient cars developed for the Japanese market were exactly what many Americans wanted after the steep rise in the price of oil around 1980. However, the main reason for Japanese car success was that Americans loved the "good buy." The Japanese cars were much better than American-made cars at the same price, and much cheaper than similar quality cars from Europe. The Japanese drove many of the European producers, with the exception of the luxury car makers, out of the U.S. market in the 1980s. In the early '90s, the Japanese finally entered the luxury car segment and took significant market share from Daimler-Benz in the U.S. market, where Daimler made much of its profit. Daimler conducted a massive revision of its products and work ways as a result.

The biggest impact, however, was on the U.S. auto industry. Chrysler nearly went bankrupt, Ford struggled for survival, and very slowly General Motors began to change. The ultimate indicator of General Motors' problems was that it agreed to form a joint venture (NUMMI) with Toyota to make Toyota-designed cars in California, under Toyota operational management. Slowly but surely, American-made cars got better as the U.S. industry adopted Japanese ways. The most important factor causing this change was the success of the Japanese "transplant" auto manufacturing plants in the United States.

The Japanese manufacturing plants in the United States have about a 15 percent share of the U.S. market. They have achieved home country quality standards at productivity levels about 95 percent of those in Japan. Transplants are important for many reasons: the workers are local and thus contribute to the productivity of the U.S. workforce; transplants put direct competitive pressure on domestic producers because the plants are targeted solely on the U.S. market; best practice techniques are transferred as managers move from transplants to domestic producers; and transplants show that Japanese levels of quality and productivity can be achieved under local U.S. conditions and, in particular, with U.S. labor. Thus, they take away all excuses of domestic management that they can't compete with the Japanese because of the shortcomings of U.S. labor. It turned out the problem wasn't with U.S. labor; it was with U.S. management. That's an easier problem to fix.

It Wasn't MITI

Another myth dispelled by the Japanese automotive case is that Japan's trade success was due to actions by the Japanese government and, in particular, the Ministry of International Trade and Industry (MITI). In the 1980s and early '90s, several academics, including Laura Tyson, President Clinton's first chair of the U.S. Council of Economic Advisers, were calling for the United States to create a similar "strategic trade industrial policy." This vague notion was based on the belief that the Japanese government protected its domestic automotive market from foreign competition, while supporting national champions attacking the open U.S. market.

On the contrary, if anything, MITI acted in potentially counterproductive ways. They tried, for example, to reduce competition in the domestic Japanese market by attempting to persuade one or two Japanese producers to withdraw from the market. Fortunately for the Japanese economy, these producers refused. The Japanese may have made it difficult for foreign producers to penetrate the domestic Japanese auto market. However, the high priority the Clinton administration placed on opening up this market for U.S. auto parts was ludicrous. Everyone in the industry knew that the Japanese parts industry was so much more productive than the U.S. industry that opening up the Japanese domestic market would make no difference.

The Japanese developed perhaps the most successful industry in the world the old-fashioned way, "they earned it." Of course, the old-fashioned way is simply being 40 percent more productive than anybody else in the world. So far, the Japanese and the Americans have gotten most of the benefit of the Toyota innovation. The United States got the benefit because of its open market to trade and investment. The same is not true for Europe. All the major countries in Europe have domestic auto producers. They have protected their domestic markets and limited the Japanese market share to less than 15 percent. In the smaller European markets without domestic producers, the Japanese market share has been around 25 percent, or about the same as in the United Sates. Thus, most Europeans lose the old-fashioned way, by protecting their domestic producers.

Retailing: Small Is Not Beautiful

If the Japanese automotive industry represents what's best about Japan, then retailing represents what's worst. A combination of misguided zoning laws, taxes, and subsidies have distorted competition and allowed the smallest, most inefficient retailers still to account for slightly over half of all retailing employment in Japan. Around the corner from the McKinsey office in Tokyo is a mom-and-pop shop where the same unsalable hat has sat on the shelf for the past fifteen years. For reasons I will get to in this case, the shopkeeper does not have to sell this hat to stay in business.

Labor productivity in the retail sector in Japan is only 50 percent of that in the United States. Unfortunately for Japan, much more of its economy is like retailing than like autos. About 220,000 workers in Japan assemble autos. About 7.5 million work in retailing. Another 2.3 million work in housing construction, and 1.3 million, in food processing.

To understand why Japan's performance in retailing is so low, we have to understand what retailing really is. When we undertook our first retailing industry study as part of the Service Sector Productivity project in 1991, I thought retailing was simply moving goods from the back door of a retail store to the shelf, where I picked up the good and paid for it at the checkout counter. Thus to me, the value provided by the retail industry was simply moving goods through this last stage of the distribution chain from the manufacturer to me as the final customer.

It did not take long for Herman de Bode, at that time the McKinsey retail expert in Europe, to straighten me out. He pointed out that retailers compete not only on price but also on a number of service dimensions. We as customers, of course, want it all. We want low prices, we want convenience, and we want a gratifying social experience when we shop. The price dimension is pretty clear. However, convenience has many aspects which most of us don't consciously register. We want to shop when we have time to shop. Thus, the opening hours of retailers are very important to us. Also, when we do shop, we want to walk away with something we're happy to have bought. If we're looking for a specific item, we want to find it, in the size and color we want. If we have a need to buy something, say for a gift, we want to find something that will do. We're willing to pay more for opening hours convenient to us, for stores that stock what we're looking for, and for stores that know us well enough to have something we will like even if we don't know specifically what we're looking for. We're also willing to pay for the "atmosphere" that makes us feel good.

Dramatic innovations have occurred globally in retailing over the past fifty years. In 1950, retailing was primarily made up of small-scale stores selling food or a general assortment of nonfood items. Since then, distinctive retailing formats have developed that are designed to provide different aspects of what we want from retailing. Convenience stores, such as 7-Eleven, open all the time and within walking distance of many neighborhoods, have proliferated. Chains of stores specializing in electronics or clothing have developed to give us a very good chance of finding exactly what we want in their area of specialty. Radio Shack and The Gap are good examples. Finally, huge "big box" formats such as Wal-Mart allow us to get many of life's needs in one place at "every day low prices." Wal-Mart now has the highest total sales of any company anywhere in the world. In the United States, all of these modern retailing formats have about twice the productivity of the traditional general stores in the United States.

Japan Still Has Mom-and-Pops

Japan's productivity in retailing is only half that of the United States because the mix of store formats in Japan has evolved much less towards the modern, specialized (and high-productivity) type of store. Moreover, the traditional mom-and-pop stores in Japan are especially small-scale, with productivity only one-third of that of the traditional stores left in the United States. Fifty-five percent of all workers in retailing in

Japan are in these mom-and-pop stores. Only 19 percent of the retail workers in the United States are left in traditional stores. Twenty-three percent of Japanese retail workers are in specialty chains, compared with 35 percent in the United States; 8 percent are in supermarkets, compared with 21 percent in the United States; and 4 percent are in big box stores, compared with 14 percent in the United States.

The Japanese format mix is so different from the one in the United States because it is virtually impossible for a Japanese or, for that matter, foreign business to open a large supermarket or big box general merchandise store in Japan, and tax laws and government subsidies favor traditional stores. The two problems are connected since the traditional shopkeepers in Japan have been an important political support base for the LDP, the ruling party in Japan. Sure, in the United States we're nostalgic about Wal-Mart's wiping out most of our traditional "Main Street" general stores. However, when it comes down to our pocketbook, we choose to spend at Wal-Mart because the prices are so much better. The behavior of Japanese living in the United States or here as tourists indicates that Japanese consumers would behave in the same way if they had a chance. But they don't.

They don't because of the Large-scale Retail Store Law in Japan. For many years, this law simply prohibited the building of stores larger than 1,000 square meters. Virtually all the modern supermarkets and big box general merchandise stores in the United States are larger than this. Under pressure from the United States, Japan replaced the previous law in 2000 with the Large-scale Retail Location Law. This law does not outright prohibit large stores. It indirectly limits their entry through "social" screening criteria related to the environment. Such factors as traffic, noise, and trash are considered. Decisions are made at the local level, where the political influence of the incumbent shopkeepers is high. Moreover, the local authorities get most of their tax revenues as transfers from the central government. Thus, they have little incentive to approve the development of higher tax base enterprises.

Japanese tax law also strongly favors the maintenance of mom-and-pop shops. Many of these shops are sitting on some of the most valuable real estate in the world, in the center of Tokyo. This is true even after deflation of the real estate bubble in Japan of the late 1980s. Many of these mom-and-pop shopkeepers have a net worth of more than half a million dollars. Not bad for a tiny store maybe 15 feet by 20 feet, with a bed and a stove just behind the back wall. They have strong incentives to sit on their property because property taxes are low, capital gains taxes are high, and inheritance taxes are low. They have little incentive to improve productivity because the government guarantees loans for them to meet any cash flow needs.

The government and most Japanese people think these policies are a good thing because they achieve the social objective of keeping the mom-and-pop stores in operation. That's one way of keeping these elderly people warm, dry, and fed, albeit in cramped quarters. As I will get to later in this chapter, the Japanese are underserved by alternatives such as retirement communities, assisted living facilities, and nursing homes. However, as I pointed out in chapter 1, the social support for mom-and-pops distorts competition and causes lower productivity and lower economic growth. It would be better in Japan to let the retailing industry evolve to more productive formats and thus create a bigger economic pie. Some of the extra income should be used to finance unemployment benefits for mom-and-pops who cannot find other work and retirement services for those ready to stop working. As I mention above, the United States went through this process and survived. It's sometimes painful, but only in the sense that all change involves some pain. That's life if we want to develop.

The stagnation of the Japanese retailing industry is important. First of all, the hard-working Japanese consumers deserve better. When they do have better services, they respond. When the Japanese clothing manufacturer Uniqlo reduced the price of its fleece jackets by half and focused its marketing efforts to sell them, it sold 8 million jackets in one season—or one for every fifteen people in Japan. In the past five years, the number of Uniqlo stores has increased threefold to make it the largest casual wear retailer in Japan. Uniqlo stores are not large enough to be affected by the Large-scale Retail Store Law. However, the world-class stores of Wal-Mart and the French hypermarket Carrefour are. Carrefour, undoubtedly the most successful international retailer in the world, with stores from Brazil to China, seems to be giving up on the Japanese market. The only place it found where mom-and-pops could not block its opening a store was on newly reclaimed land where there were no mom-and-pops nearby. There's not enough reclaimed land to allow Carrefour to open enough stores to reach efficient scale.

Good Retailing Improves Manufacturing and Wholesaling

The failure of Japanese retailing to evolve has another important consequence: the performance of most consumer goods manufacturers remains terrible. Retailers, not manufacturers, are in the best position to know what customers want. They see them every day and they know exactly what they buy and why. Since a significant part of the manufacturing in any economy is the production of consumer goods, having a sophisticated retailing sector is essential for producing the goods consumers value most. Moreover, as I will discuss in the Japanese dairy case later in this chapter, in many countries the manufacturing of consumer goods is still done in small, low-productivity plants. Just like Toyota improved the productivity of its parts suppliers, large-scale retailers improve their efficiency in part by buying in bulk from efficient, large-scale manufacturers. Thus, world-class British supermarkets, Carrefour, and Wal-Mart have worked with suppliers in many countries to increase their scale of operations through consolidations. These consolidations have improved productivity significantly in the manufacturing sector itself. The same potential for productivity improvement exists in Japan. For instance, as I will get to in the next section of this chapter, Japanese productivity in food processing is only 39 percent of that of the United States.

Moreover, the world-class retailers have reached a scale that allows them to bypass the wholesale sector and buy directly from manufacturers. This arrangement has put enormous pressure on wholesaling to improve its performance. Wholesaling up until now has been another sleepy oligopoly or outright monopoly in virtually all countries. A regional market can typically support only one wholesaler to supply the small numbers of each individual item that different retailers need. In these circumstances, wholesalers have typically made large profits without having to improve performance much. However, with the consolidation of retailing into large stores and large chains, retailers now buy large quantities on a regional basis. They can improve their productivity by going directly to manufacturers or by setting up their own more productive wholesaling operation.

In the United States, wholesalers have finally taken notice of this change and in the 1990s, as I will describe in the chapter on the U.S. economy, began to consolidate their warehouses and improve the productivity of the operations in those warehouses. This change was the largest single contribution to the productivity acceleration in the U.S. economy in the late 1990s—not the efforts of Microsoft or Silicon Valley. Thus, evolving to a more productive retailing format mix has large spillover effects in improving the productivity of consumer goods manufacturing and wholesaling. The Japanese are not getting these benefits either, as I will describe next in food processing.

Food Processing: Small-time Retailers Beget Small-time Food Processors

The problems of Japan's retail sector spill over into much of its consumer goods manufacturing. We studied food processing to illustrate this because it is a surprisingly large part of manufacturing. In virtually every country, food processing is the largest employer of manufacturing workers. Eleven percent of all manufacturing employees in Japan work in food processing. It has more employees than the combined total of cars, steel, machine tools, and computers. Since the productivity of the entire economy is the average of the productivity of every single worker, food processing has more of an impact on the standard of living in Japan than cars, steel, machine tools, and computers combined.

And in contrast to the manufacturing excellence of cars, steel, machine tools, and consumer electronics, the performance of Japanese food processing is poor (Exhibit 2.2). Its productivity is 39 percent of the United States'. Thus even in manufacturing, Japan has a "dual economy." How can such inefficiency exist in the country of Toyota? The answer is Toyota has created its own supply world in Japan and competes intensely both in Japan and around the globe to sell cars. On the other

Exhibit 2.2: Productivity and Employment in Japan

9 manufacturing industries

Relative productivity levels
Index U.S. = 100

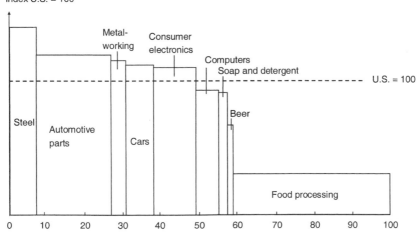

Employment
100% = 2.7 million employees

hand, food processors serve a galaxy of small, fragmented retailers. And as it turns out, only small, inefficient food processors can supply these retail stores.

Milk is a good example. The average milk processing plant in Japan produces 16 tons of milk a day. The corresponding average for the United States is 150 tons. The Japanese milk plants are scattered all over the country and close to the retail food stores they supply. They are close enough to supply the retail stores directly without intermediate distribution centers. On the other hand, large-scale milk plants in the United States supply a large regional market, composed mainly of large supermarkets, and use intermediate distribution centers. The volumes are large enough to justify the cost of these distribution centers. But in Japan, large milk plants would be unable to supply directly the fragmented retailers. The costs of long-distance supply of small quantities to the fragmented retailers would be higher than the cost of small milk plants located close to the retailers. Establishing intermediate distribution centers would reduce the cost somewhat, but small milk plants would still have lower costs because they don't have to have distribution centers at all.

Another problem is that Japanese milk plants also do not use extended shelf life technology (super pasteurization). In order for the milk not to be spoiled, it has to be delivered three times a day. Switching the production lines among milk products three times a day makes the productivity of the small milk plants even smaller. However, large milk plants located long distances away from retailers cannot compete on freshness because of the time it takes to deliver. They alone cannot afford to undertake the marketing costs of persuading Japanese consumers that extended shelf life technology is perfectly fine. Thus, the Japanese consumers do not get the benefit of milk produced at lower costs in large-scale plants. The situation is stable with high-priced milk produced at low-productivity, small-scale plants.

Bring on the Retailers

How do countries break out of such a situation? After all, at some stage of the development of the dairy and retailing industries, all economies must look like Japan. We know that in the United States there's another configuration that is two to three times more productive. That configuration consists of widespread chains of large supermarkets, such as Safeway, Albertsons, and Giant, and large-scale regional dairy processing plants, most of which we have never heard of. Sometimes the volume of milk sold by a supermarket chain in a region is so large that the super-market operates a regional distribution center to take the huge quantities of milk from the milk processors and deliver it to individual stores. Some large supermarket chains, such as Safeway, actually own the large milk processing plants.

The evidence from many countries is that the movement from the low-productivity configuration to the high-productivity configuration is caused by retailing modernization. First, retailers are in a better position to judge consumers' reaction to change. Second, food stores can be expanded in relatively small increments, both in terms of individual store size and number of stores in chains. On the other hand, food processing plant development occurs in discrete jumps. For dairy, the two main steps are automation, of packaging for instance, and extended shelf life technology. Both of the steps require significant capital investment and large-scale operations.

Thus the development of dairy products production and distribution starts with food stores growing larger and larger and combining into chains. At some point, their volume of dairy products becomes sufficiently high that the retail firms begin to negotiate large-volume contracts with milk plants that can consolidate into a large-scale, high-productivity operation using extended shelf life technology. The secret then is to unleash retailing so that individual firms can reach a scale at which it is in the retailers' interests to negotiate volume contracts with dairy processors. In Japan, this process cannot get started because of the constraints on retail store size and the many tax policies and subsidies that allow the mom-and-pop stores to survive.

One of the common responses in Japan to our analysis has been that Japanese consumers like their milk delivered three times a day to the store and like the amazing product variety. However, Japanese consumers do not have a choice between low-price, high-volume products of limited range and the high-priced product variety existing today. Given a choice, the Japanese consumers would likely do what consumers in both the United States and France have done. In both these countries, the majority of consumers have chosen low price over variety, especially when consumer market research gets good enough to identify the products consumers really want. However, in both countries, specialty food stores providing a wide variety of delicacies exist for consumers who want to spend their money that way. In Japan, just because consumers buy what is offered today does not mean that consumers would not buy something else, especially if that something else were priced much lower.

Housing Construction: Long-forgotten U.S. Standardization Missing in Japan

Housing construction in Japan is a good example of just how complex industry analysis can be. However, it shows how such analysis can explain why clearly visible things such as housing develop as they do.

The lack of competition and low performance of Japanese retailing and its suppliers, like food processing, stem largely from zoning regulations, tax policies, and loan subsidies that keep mom-and-pop stores in business while blocking out larger competitors. But competition can also break down even in the absence of such explicit government policies.

Japanese housing construction is a good example. Markets perform poorly when firms do not have to compete strongly on price and when customers cannot assess well the value of products. Both of these conditions exist in housing construction in Japan. They exist because housing construction methods in Japan have not been "standardized."

Over the years, much has been made of the small, cramped houses in which the Japanese live. The average Japanese housing unit is only 60 percent of the size of housing units in the United States. However, a casual overview of a Japanese residential neighborhood from a raised motorway, or even from a neighborhood street, suggests a more fundamental difference. Japanese neighborhoods are a jumble of small, angular houses, all looking different and often fitting together in a jarring pattern or no pattern at all. The Japanese houses may be jewels of taste and tranquility inside, but not on the outside. In contrast, most U.S. neighborhoods are made up of houses revealing some basic architectural similarity that creates a pattern to the eye. Underlying this difference in pattern are huge differences in housing development, construction methods, and productivity.

Housing construction labor productivity in Japan is only 45 percent of that of the United States. For such a large industry, which accounts for 3 to 4 percent of all employment, this is a huge difference. Many people assume that customized goods—including houses—are of better quality. After all, don't rich people in the United States build custom houses? Most Japanese single-family housing is customized but of poor quality. The average life of a Japanese house is twenty-six years, compared with forty-four years in the United States. The problem with Japanese houses is that they are built one at a time by craftsmen who may no longer be masters, and consumers have none of the choices and protections of the United States.

Some of the difference in productivity is due to different construction methods. The predominant housing construction method in Japan for single-family houses is "post-and-beam." In this method, vertical posts at the corners carry the structural weight of the house. Horizontal beams lie across the tops of the posts. The connection joint is complicated. Thus, the operation takes time. Moreover, 150 different post-and-beam systems are used across Japan. With this proliferation, none of the approaches have been optimized.

In contrast, the universal single-family housing construction method in the United States is "two-by-four." In this method, small standardized pieces of lumber are positioned vertically all along a wall so that each of these "posts" bears relatively little weigh but in total can hold up the house. Because of the lower stresses, the connection "joints" with the horizontal boards to stabilize the walls and support the floors can be simple. The boards are nailed to each other.

For these reasons, the Japanese post-and-beam system has a potential productivity of about 80 percent of the simpler two-by-four system. However, the Japanese realize with the post-and-beam system only 30 percent of the productivity of the U.S. two-by-four system. Thus the Japanese are realizing less than half of the productivity potential of the post-and-beam system. The reason is that each post-and-beam house is built inefficiently and not in large-scale developments as in the United States. The problem is lack of standardization.

Standardization Often Helps

Standardization has been an important step in the productivity improvement of many industries. It is beneficial when the cost reduction results in lower prices, which are more important to the consumer than the variety of products forgone. Sometimes, one large firm has enough market share to standardize an industry by itself. In the 1960s, IBM standardized the mainframe computer industry. In the 1990s, Microsoft standardized the operating system for the PC and server computer architecture. Sometimes, governments need to intervene when an industry is not self-standardizing. One of the best examples of good government intervention is MITI's standardization of the Japanese machine tool industry starting in the 1950s. At that time machine tools were highly customized and produced on a small scale around the world. MITI standardized the tolerances of machine tools in Japan. The standardization allowed the Japanese to industrialize the production of machine tools by introducing large-scale assembly lines. The Japanese then applied their electronics technology to automate the assembly lines. The Japanese producers thus achieved a double technological advantage over the rest of the world. They drove U.S. and German machine tool producers into niches. In all our studies of Japan, this is the only action by MITI that we found to have had a significant beneficial impact on the Japanese economy.

What the Japanese did in machine tools, the United States did in housing construction. And the United States did it in the 1920s. At that time different geographic regions had slightly different sizes and grades of lumber, as well as different construction methods. In 1922 the U.S. Department of Commerce met with large purchasers of lumber to standardize sizes and grades. Other standardizations followed. Brick went from forty-four sizes to one. Industry associations and the Federal Housing Administration began to set guidelines for home design. The standardization allowed widespread appraisal services to develop since appraisers could rely on the tested and approved standardized construction methods in judging the quality of housing construction. The appraisal system gave banks the confidence to finance housing and gave consumers confidence in the quality of the products they were purchasing. The result was that consumers knew the price and quality of the houses offered.

In Japan If You Want a House You Build It

Moreover, house builders in the United States had to compete on price and quality with a large volume of existing houses being sold on the secondary market. The percentage of existing houses sold each year in the United States is seventeen times higher than in Japan (Exhibit 2.3). The secondary market in the United States is highly developed primarily because customers and banks have confidence about the quality of the housing. It is more developed also because everybody knows the price of new and existing home sales. Not so in Japan. Individuals will not risk equity and banks will not risk loans for existing housing because they do not know housing quality or the prices of previous house sales. (The government does not make public the price of new and existing home sales.) The lack of price and quality competition in the overall Japanese market means construction firms have not been forced to look for more productive ways to provide housing as in the United States.

The lack of a market for existing houses forces Japanese seeking single-family housing to build a new house. Because construction methods are not standardized, the only assurance of quality is to work with

Exhibit 2.3: Secondary Housing Market

Number of existing houses sold per thousand dwellings

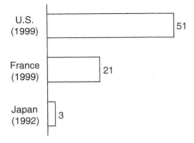

a builder who is known to the purchaser and can be trusted. This condition severely limits competition since purchasers spend most of their time trying to find builders they can trust as opposed to comparing prices across a wide range of existing housing. Thus builders feel little pressure to innovate, increase productivity, and lower prices.

Ironically, the lack of standardization in the Japanese housing construction market has a double impact on productivity. Not only does this lack curtail price-based competition, it also directly lowers productivity. Simply changing the 150 different post-and-beam construction methods to best practice would increase single-family housing productivity by two-thirds. Post-and-beam would then be 50 percent as productive as U.S. two-by-four construction.

No Large-Scale Housing Developments in Japan

Another reason why single-family housing construction in Japan has such low productivity is that houses are built there one at a time and not in large housing developments with economies of scale. Without the quality assurance that comes with standardization, no one would buy a mass-produced house. However, even if standardization were established, large-scale developments would not occur. The reason is the same as the reason large-scale retailing stores don't develop. Land is simply not available at prices which allow large-scale housing developments to compete substantially with the traditional one-at-a-time single-family housing construction. Low property taxes and inheritance taxes and high capital gains taxes give Japanese families strong incentives to hold on to their land forever. Land accounts for 67 percent of total bequests in Japan compared with 25 percent in the United States. These tax effects along with zoning laws and tenant protection laws have restricted the development of multifamily housing as well, thus further limiting competition in the housing market.

It would have been much better if the Japanese had standardized their housing industry right after the war. Because so much housing has already been built, the effects of standardizing now would take several decades to show up in a fully functioning secondary market. Moreover, special interests, who would lose from the increased competition, are much stronger now than they were earlier. The construction industry is one of the main supporters of the LDP. That's why Japan faces gridlock in housing construction today. It's not the only industry where special interests are holding Japan back. Health care is another.

Health Care: Regulations Favor Providers Not Patients

In looking at Japan, we thought for a long time about which case studies to conduct. At the time of our study, 1999–2000, the story of the Japanese auto industry was well known. We knew that the problems of the Japanese economy were deeply buried in the domestic part. Thus it was easy to choose retailing, housing construction, and food processing. We also knew that the potential for productivity improvement in these industries was so large that Japan would create a lot of unemployment if it moved rapidly to best practice performance in these industries and did nothing to create jobs elsewhere. We needed an industry study where people in Japan wanted significantly increased service levels, which, if provided, would generate many new jobs. Health care turned out to be ideal. Not only does it have substantial potential to create new jobs in Japan, but it is also an industry in which it is possible to increase productivity substantially at the same time.

Health care is a very difficult sector for countries to get right. No country is currently close. Markets simply don't work well in health care. Consumers have very little ability to judge the quality of the service they receive and whether the price is reasonable. Furthermore, some people need lots of health care, whereas most people need relatively little. Thus we need insurance schemes to protect us against the chance that we are one of those needing lots of health care. Designing good health insurance schemes has proved difficult everywhere, including in the United States. Finally, for many diseases, it is virtually impossible to measure the difference in outcomes from different types of treatment and from different medical service providers using the same treatment.

Thus, it is difficult to generate strong competition among providers of health care services.

When markets don't work well, we have to supplement them with regulations. Health care is so complex that the difference between good and bad regulation yields enormous differences in performance. Of the four countries whose health care systems we have studied, Japan's regulations are much worse than those of Germany, the United Kingdom, and the United States.

In attempting to assess productivity in Japan, we were unable to compare outputs of the health care systems. However, we could identify differences in inputs that had no known relationship to differences in health outcomes. These differences in inputs indicated that on this dimension, Japan's productivity was about 75 percent of the United States'. Moreover, in Japan, only 4 percent of employment is in health care, compared with 8 percent in the United States. Comparable consumer satisfaction surveys indicate that only 67 percent of the Japanese are satisfied with their health care system, compared with about 90 percent of people in Canada, Germany, the United Kingdom, and the United States.

Good Regulations and Bad Regulations

The most dramatic difference in treatment is that the average length of stay in a hospital in Japan is twenty-four days, compared with eleven in Germany and six in the United States. Nobody can make a scientific argument that the extra hospital days result in better health care outcomes. When these results were discussed with the CEO of a U.S. hospital, he was appalled by the risk that Japanese patients run of contracting infections from other hospital patients by staying in the hospital so long. The reason hospital stays are so long in Japan and so short in the United States is a difference in the regulation of how hospitals are paid for their services. In Japan, hospitals are simply paid a fixed amount for each day a patient stays in the hospital, a "per diem." One Japanese hospital administrator told us "the only reason to release the patient is if you have a new one to admit." Hospitals have a powerful incentive to keep all their beds full all the time.

In the United States, the regulation is much more complicated. The U.S. government agency administering the government program paying for health care for the elderly (Health Care Financing Administration) established fixed payments to hospitals for the complete treatment of specific diseases (Diagnosis Related Groups). U.S. hospitals are free to organize the treatment of diseases however they choose consistent with accepted medical practice. Nobody knows how innovation will progress in improving outcomes and reducing the costs of disease treatment. Thus, the government uses a trial-and-error method of reducing the fixed payments to put pressure on hospitals for cost reductions and then relaxing the fixed payments if the cost reductions go too far. The net result has been that the average length of stay in U.S. hospitals has come down dramatically over the past two decades. In addition, U.S. hospitals have moved rapidly to introduce improved procedures for disease treatment. Microscopic surgery for gallbladder removal accounted for 90 percent of all such procedures in the United States in 1993. Japan did not reach the same percentage until 1999. In 2000, five of the ten top-selling drugs worldwide were not available in Japan (Prozac, introduced in the United States in 1987; Paxil, in 1992; Zoloft, in 1991; Lipitor, in 1996; and Claritin, in 1993).

Japanese Doctors Have Big Conflicts of Interest

The second major area of dissatisfaction in Japan is seeing a doctor when the patient doesn't need to stay in a hospital. U.S. doctors spend an average of twenty-five minutes with the patient on such visits. Japanese patients, on the other hand, often endure long waiting times and see doctors only five minutes on average. On top of this, the patient often has to go through this all over again a short time later just to renew a prescription. Japanese doctors, of course, are paid on a per visit basis. Thus they have an incentive for as short a visit as possible and for as many visits as possible. The Japanese visit the doctor an average of fourteen times per year compared with four times per year in the United States. Americans still manage to spend more time with their doctor in a year than the Japanese.

Japanese doctors prescribe about twice as many drugs per capita as American physicians, despite Japan's having lower disease and injury levels. Japanese doctors behave this way to generate more office visits. They also behave this way because they are allowed to own pharmacies and to take as profits the large gap between the regulated cost of wholesale pharmaceuticals and the retail price. Providers of health care are not allowed to own pharmacies in the United States because of the potential conflict of interest.

A final example of how good regulation can help make up for

poorly performing markets is accreditation and licensing. When consumers cannot judge the quality of the service they receive, someone who can has to provide that assurance. The U.S. Joint Commission on Accreditation of Health Care Organizations (JCAHO) has existed for seventy years as an independent, nonprofit organization for monitoring and accrediting all types of health care providers. To acquire and maintain accreditation, hospitals must undergo extensive on-site reviews conducted by multidisciplinary committees composed of physicians, nurses, hospital administrators, and health care policymakers. JCAHO accreditation assures patients a quality of care consistent with generally accepted medical practices. U.S. health care providers cannot survive without this accreditation.

Without such an assurance, Japanese seek out other sources of confidence. The only source of assurance they have found is university hospitals and other prestigious hospitals. The Japanese believe they get superior service they can trust at these hospitals. The result is they all try to go to these hospitals and the lines are even longer and the visits shorter.

Japanese Are Shortchanged on Health Care

We found that Japan could make all these productivity improvements and at the same time increase services to such a degree that employment in health care would go up by one million. After adjusting for differences in disease levels, we found that labor inputs in health care in Japan were 80 percent of U.S. labor inputs. Japanese patients get lower service across all care settings, including elderly nursing care, acute care, and ambulatory care. Japanese hospitals often have four patients per room and lack rehabilitation and physical therapy services. Adjusted for population, there are eight times as many trained physical, occupational, psychological, respiratory, and speech therapists in the United States as in Japan. On the same basis, there are twice as many nursing home staff in the United States. About 700,000 work in home health care services in the United States. These services are virtually nonexistent in Japan.

The irony is that the Japanese could pay for all this by getting rid of their excess consumption of drugs and excess hospitals. Thus the Japanese people pay an enormous price in quality of life for favoring producers and not consumers through health care regulation. Life expectancy in Japan is the highest in the world. But that's because the Japanese have a healthier life style, not because their health care system serves patients well.

An Immature Democracy

So, what about Japan? We can all agree now that the Japanese economic model is not working. Japan is a country of "small timers," as my partner Yoshi Yokoyama says. Japan is dominated by small shopkeepers, small milk plants, small groups of carpenters, small houses, and short visits to the doctor. Within this economy, a few enclaves of big companies operate with the highest productivity in the world—Toyota and Honda, Nippon and Kawasaki Steel, Sony and Matshushita, and Fanuc Machine Tools. This structure worked to make Japan the only country to move from being a low-income country to being a high-income country in the twentieth century. This model does not, however, have the capability of making Japan an advanced economy of the twenty-first century.

Japan's way forward towards becoming an advanced economy is clear in concept. What Japan needs to do to resume growth is very simple. It is the old-fashioned way all countries have grown. Japan needs simply to increase the productivity of the domestic part of its economy (retailing, housing construction, food processing, etc.) and reallocate the freed-up resources to provide the increased services Japanese consumers want (more and better health care, etc.). The simple result would be that the same number of people would end up working, and, as a whole, they would produce more. That's growth.

In practice, the change will be wrenching. Elderly mom-and-pop shopkeepers cannot be converted to physical therapists. However, some of the younger ones can. Or at least to hospital transporters. Moreover, for sure their children need to be headed in this direction. Safety nets have to be put in place. For now, the Japanese provide a safety net by business as usual. However, this has to change if Japan wants to remain among the advanced economies.

Why Not Just Fix Japan?

Growth does not occur now in Japan, because a tangle of regulations prevents modern businesses from entering the market and competing with the small timers. We have seen how productivity improvement in retailing is stymied. The production and distribution of food and other consumer goods thus does not feel the pressure to improve from modern retailers. Regulation of health care, the largest sector in all advanced economies, causes waste of resources and poor services. Instead of spending money on roads that go nowhere and bridges that cross nothing, the Japanese government could restructure the health care sector and generate growth without spending any extra money.

Why doesn't this happen? Japan has elected prime ministers, from Hosokawa to Koizumi, promising reform. It hasn't happened. The more things change, the more they are the same. Karel van Wolferen was right in his book *The Enigma of Japanese Power;* the balance of power in Japan prevents the needed leadership from emerging. A large number of Japanese benefit, but only in the short term, from the current structure of the economy. They are the small timers: farmers, shopkeepers, carpenters, and doctors. These groups form the core of the support for the LDP. To stay in power, the LDP protects these groups and many others in the low-productivity 80 percent of Japan's economy.

This situation has been stable for a long time—ever since the Second World War. It's been stable because the LDP has been so powerful. It's been like the Democratic or the Republican party has been in control of Congress for the past fifty years. Only it's been much more than that. Japan has a parliamentary system. So the ruling party in the Japanese parliament, the Diet, also has charge of virtually all the functions performed by the president of the United States and the executive branch of government. So it's more like the same party has had control of both the White House and the Congress for fifty years. On top of all this, the only real opposition party has been the Socialists, who never have been a threat to the LDP.

But still Japan is a democracy. Why doesn't the majority insist on real reform and overpower the LDP and its special-interest support base? The reason is that these special interests have a working majority in Japan. Thus democracy is working. We wouldn't want it any other way. How do democracies get out of this trap? Well, that's not very well understood. As Nobel laureate economist Bob Solow says, "All discussions of productivity and growth end up in amateur sociology." My contribution will be no exception. I make no apologies, however, because the state-of-the-art in understanding how societies evolve is so primitive.

The big reforms in economic policy in the United States occurred as a result of abuse of power or economic calamity. The abusive behavior of the rail and other monopolies in the late nineteenth century and early twentieth century led to much of U.S. antitrust and competition law. The financial market excesses of the 1920s and the Depression of the 1930s led to financial market reform and social safety nets. This story suggests Japan will not change until the majority of Japanese believe things are so bad that the LDP must be replaced in power by a party whose full membership is dedicated to reform.

It May Take a Long Time

The Japanese people seem a long way from concluding that things are really bad, and no genuine reform party is in sight. The truth is things are not so bad in Japan. Most people in the world would believe they had died and gone to heaven if they lived in a country with as high a standard of living as Japan's. Moreover, Japan does not depend on the rest of the world for money. Thus, international investors cannot discipline Japan if its returns on investment are low because of low productivity. The only way the capital market can affect Japan is for Japanese investors to get tired of their low rates of return in Japan and to take their money out of the country. This may happen someday, but again, we don't seem to be close. So far the Japanese have been content to let the LDP use their savings to placate the LDP's strongest special interest supporters and run up big government debt in doing so. It will probably take another generation of Japanese to decide they don't want their standard of living to stagnate and they want their savings to earn as much as possible. That's a long time to wait.

If this situation is so difficult to get out of, it's only natural to wonder how Japan got into it in the first place. Like many societies, Japan evolved over the centuries alternating between autocratic rule of elites and anarchy. Paul Johnson's description of Japan in the first half of the twentieth century is one of anarchy. The navy was a power unto itself. The Japanese people never had a chance to develop the confidence that they could control their destiny with their own hands. The United States then imposed democracy on Japan only fifty years ago. However, the Japanese people have behaved more like sheep governed by the wolves of their society than like a free people confident of their rights and demanding that their government serve their interests. As we have seen in the retailing, housing construction, and health care cases, the Japanese government has favored producer interests and not consumer interests. Change will only occur when consumers rise up and elect a government with their interests at heart.

Any consumer movement in Japan is likely to start with the increasingly numerous elderly and the increasingly independent housewives. These groups are the least directly tied to producer interests. However, any doubts about the potency of the producers have been removed by their effectiveness in opposing the attempts at reform by Koizumi and his cabinet over the past couple of years. While it is still possible that some progress may be made in health care and construction, the small retailers have run to the Diet to stop attempted retailing reforms in their tracks.

Individual Japanese, and especially the elderly and the housewives, need to think more for themselves. Japan's education system doesn't help much in this regard. It needs reform, but that's another subject. Japan's democracy is well entrenched; it's just immature. The upcoming generation in Japan is substantially different from their parents. With this generation will likely come substantial progress towards more mature democratic processes and the advanced economy that this development allows.

Ironically, the United States bears significant responsibility for the way Japan looks today. As John Dower carefully documents in his book *Embracing Defeat,* the U.S. occupation government at the end of the war initially planned for a thorough reform of all aspects of Japanese society, including abolishing the emperor, breaking up the giant corporations, reforming education, and liberating women. The rapid turn of U.S. geopolitical concerns to the spread of Communism, including worries about Communist movements in Japan, caused the United States to shelve most of these plans.

Who knows what Japan would be like today if thorough reform had proceeded at the end of the war? What we do know is that it is very important for Japan to succeed now. Japan is clearly the most advanced Asian society. It is a democracy. Democracies may not always do the right thing, but they have a good track record of not doing terrible things. Since Japan is a democracy, it will eventually work out its problems. That's OK; it will just take longer than anybody has believed could be possible.

CHAPTER THREE

Europe: Falling Behind

Europe is a very important piece of the global economic landscape. Taken together, the countries of the European Union have an economy roughly equal in size to that of the United States. Europe and the United States together account for about half of the total GDP of the world.

Europeans are integrating their economies more every day. Most of the countries of the European Union now have a common currency. Entry into the monetary union carries conditions on fiscal policy about deficit financing and total debt levels. Thus, much of macroeconomic policy in Europe is harmonized. The ability of the European Union to discipline members not conforming to fiscal policy and whether that policy is flexible enough is currently being tested. Also being tested is whether one monetary policy can accommodate the different rates of growth among the members of the monetary union.

The laws and regulations governing how business is conducted, how competition is managed, how capital is allocated, and how labor markets work are still determined almost exclusively at the national level. There are some important differences across countries in these laws and regulations. I will describe these differences later in this chapter. However, in thinking about how to describe the European part of the global economic landscape, I have decided to start with generalizations about Europe and then show some of the variations among countries.

The alternative is to treat one country, such as Germany, in great detail. However, the common patterns across Europe even in the laws and regulations governing microeconomic behavior are very strong and more important than the individual country differences. Moreover, we have conducted country studies of Germany, France, the United Kingdom, Sweden, and the Netherlands. These countries account for two-thirds of the total GDP of the European Union. Thus, we have a very good sample from which to generalize. The one missing piece of Europe is the Southern Tier, most importantly Italy and Spain. However, we included Italy and Spain in our Employment Performance study in the early days of the McKinsey Global Institute. Thus we seem to have sufficient information for me to talk about Europe.

Things Didn't Work Out as Expected

Moreover, we need a clear picture about Europe because things are not working out the way many people thought they were going to ten years ago. Europe is falling behind the United States economically. Since 1991, GDP per capita in France has fallen 5 percentage points further behind the United States, and in Germany, 8 percentage points further behind. GDP per capita in the European Union is now about 70 percent of that in the United States. Ten years ago, many people in Europe and in the United States thought that Germany had passed the United States, that the German economic model was superior, and that the United States was going to have to change its model to keep up. Loose talk by Lester Thurow and Paul Kennedy contended that the twenty-first century would be the century of Europe. That may still turn out to be so. However, long-term trends suggest otherwise, at least for the next couple of decades.

The war-damaged European economies, especially France and Germany, grew rapidly in the 1950s and '60s. However, convergence with the U.S. economy slowed significantly in the 1970s and '80s and became divergence in the 1990s (Exhibit 3.1). Such smooth behavior suggests fundamental structural causal factors at work. In 1992, when we published our Service Sector report, we reported the OECD GDPs per capita at purchasing power parity exchange rates. As I mentioned in the Prologue, those results showed GDP per capita in Germany to be about 20 percent lower than in the United States. The strongest criticism of these results came from the senior partner in McKinsey's German office. He simply could not believe the results and said they had to be wrong. To him and many others, the strong deutsche mark meant a strong German economy, and using the market foreign exchange rate showed that German GDP per capita was higher than U.S. GDP per capita (although not higher than in Japan, which had an even stronger currency). Today, the use of purchasing power parity exchange rates to make these comparisons is widely accepted. However, in 1992 it was new. By the way, not all my European partners questioned my results. In Scandinavia and Switzerland, both more neutral about the U.S. and European rivalry, my partners found little of surprise in my results.

Exhibit 3.1: GDP Per Capita

Index U.S. = 100; 1995 PPPs

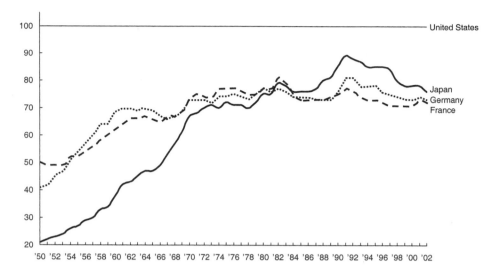

Why did my German colleague have such a wrong impression? His belief came heavily from the extraordinary success of German manufacturing. And German manufacturing was extraordinarily successful. With the formation of the European Common Market in the 1980s, European manufacturers were able to compete on even terms across Europe, while at the same time still being protected from the full force of global competition. The productivity of German manufacturers in most industries was higher than in the rest of Europe, and Germany was thus able to export strongly throughout Europe. This success caused many European manufacturers, especially in Germany, to take their eye off the global ball. They missed seeing that improvement in Japanese manufacturing was resulting in the highest manufacturing productivity in the world in several industries. The open U.S. market quickly got a wake-up call from the Japanese, but Europeans didn't. Moreover, in Germany especially, manufacturing was considered to be the important part of an economy; services were simply supporting at best and somewhat frivolous at worst. There was simply no good understanding of the essential role services play in modern, complex economies. As I explained in the Prologue, by the time a manufactured good reaches the consumer, half the value represented by the price the consumer is willing to pay for the good is contributed by the service sector. The service sector in all advanced economies is much bigger than the manufacturing, construction, utilities, and mining sectors combined (Exhibit 3.2). Thus, the productivity of the service sector is much more important in determining the economic standard of living than these other sectors.

Overlaying this success of German manufacturing was a widespread belief in Europe, but especially in Germany, that substantial economic gains would come from the formation of the Common Market. The idea was that European firms could now grow to the size of U.S. firms because they had a market of similar size. The benefits of economies of scale and market power would be substantial. The calculations of the economic benefits of economies of scale and internal European competition always showed modest gains of about 5 percent of GDP. Little attention was paid to the potential gains resulting from more global competition. If more attention had been paid to that, then perhaps the innovations in Japan in manufacturing and in the United States in services would have been noticed. But they were not, and in the decade of the 1990s, when the benefits of the Common Market should have been felt ever more strongly, Europe began to fall behind.

Articles in such respected journals as the *Economist* and the *New Republic* have claimed that Europe is not really falling behind. They cite the widely published OECD figures on GDP and hours worked to conclude that, actually, productivity in France and Germany and a few other Northern European countries is higher than in the United States by 5 to 10 percent. They go on to infer from these numbers that the U.S. lead in GDP per capita comes from Americans working harder and not from higher productivity. Thus, Europeans are choosing to have a lower GDP per capita because of a higher preference for leisure over material standard of living.

It is correct that the GDP per capita gap between the rich countries in Europe and the United States is explained primarily because of more work per person in the United States. However, the situation is not as simple as it may seem. Unemployment rates in Europe are consistently twice as high as in the United States. That means that the European economies are not providing as much work as Europeans would like. A significant number of Europeans are not working because they can't find a job and not because of a preference for leisure.

The productivity picture is even more complicated. No national or international statistical agency can measure the value of goods and services produced by the government, by education, and by health care. If you are thinking that means we really don't know what GDP is, you are right. However, we can measure the value of goods and services in the

Exhibit 3.2: Sector Employment Shares

Percent of total employment

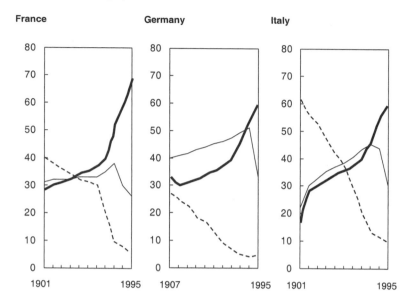

market sector (the other 70 percent of the economy, made up of manufacturing, agriculture, and services except for government, education,
and health care). We can measure the value of goods and services in the
market sector because there market prices reflect the value to consumers
of goods and services. In the market part of the economy, productivity
in rich European countries is about the same as in the United States.

Moreover, these measured numbers overstate the true efficiency of
operations in Europe. In food retailing in the United States and the
United Kingdom, a large number of workers paid at the minimum wage
provide services such as bag packing, checkouts, floor cleaning, and
stock rotation not found nearly to the same extent in France. These
workers have low productivity. They pull the average food retailing productivity down in the United States and the United Kingdom. If food
retailing in France provided the same services, its productivity would decline by about 17 percent. France does not provide these services because the high minimum wage in France makes these services uneco-
nomic to provide. Thus, the equivalent low-productivity workers in
France are unemployed rather than working as in the United States and
the United Kingdom. The same thing is true in all services that employ

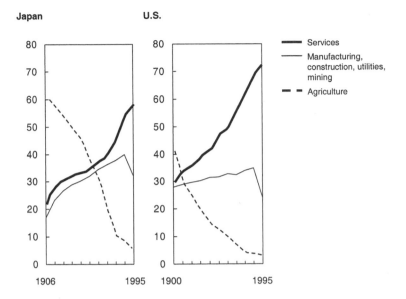

Japan   U.S.

large numbers of workers near the minimum wage in the United States and the United Kingdom.

Finally, all other things being equal, Europe should have higher labor productivity than the United States. That's because Europeans have invested about 10 percent more for plant and equipment per hour worked in the market sector than the United States. That should make labor productivity higher in Europe than in the United States, but it doesn't. The reason is that the capital in Europe is used much less productively than in the United States. Capital productivity in Germany is about 65 percent of that of the United States. That means overall productivity (considering both labor and capital) in Germany is 85 to 90 percent of the overall productivity in the United States, as measured in the market part of the economy. Moreover, the measurements overstate productivity for Germany as in France.

Social and Economic Policies Don't Mix

What is the basic reason for why things are working out in Europe as they are? The reason is quite simple. Europeans commingle social policy and economic policy to a much greater extent than the United States. They do this by attempting to achieve social objectives through distortions in the way markets would naturally work. All modern economies distort markets for these reasons, including the United States. However, distortions in Europe are so great that Europe suffers a substantial economic penalty relative to the United States. Examples include a high minimum wage, which is intended to achieve income distribution objectives but which results in high unemployment of low-skilled workers. Another example is planning regulations in the United Kingdom that effectively prohibit the development of land with any buildings over one hundred years old on it. The result is that modern supermarkets cannot replace abandoned, derelict buildings of no redeeming architectural value.

The creation of the European Union may have made this problem more severe. The Maastricht treaty includes a social charter. Read literally, the Social Charter requires that all members of the European Union "harmonize" their social policies, and, in achieving this harmonization, no member will be required to reduce its social benefits. Thus, unless the highest social benefit country voluntarily reduces its benefits, all members have to increase their social benefits to the highest level. No member of the European Union is in conformity with the Social Charter. Such conformity would incur unacceptable economic costs. The United Kingdom finally signed the Social Charter when the Blair government took power, but then promptly set its minimum wage at the U.S. level and not that of the Continent. The Social Charter is a good example of the muddle Europeans get into when they set social policies without understanding the economic trade-offs and trying to minimize the magnitude of the trade-offs.

There is nothing wrong with the European social objectives. In fact, many people in the United States believe that U.S. social objectives should be more like Europe's. In some cases, there is a legitimate trade-off between environmental and social safety net objectives, on the one hand, and GDP per capita, on the other. However, we found many cases where the trade-off made in Europe is not necessary. Income distribution objectives can be met by using the Earned Income Tax Credit to redistribute income through the tax code to achieve whatever after-tax income distribution is desired. The United States adopted such a tax credit in 1975, more than twenty-five years ago. With this tax credit, the minimum wage need not cause unemployment, the total economic pie is larger, and thus there is more economic purchasing power to be distributed however a society chooses to do so. At the same time the United

Kingdom set the minimum wage at the U.S. level, it also adopted the Working Families Tax Credit, which works the same as the Earned Income Tax Credit.

The Politics of Poverty

Still, many in Europe and the United States would say that Europe has been on a low poverty path and that they would rather have that path than the path of the United States. Poverty is a highly charged political issue. Even its measurement is fraught with controversy. In Europe, income levels defined as poverty are taken to be a certain percentage of the median income of the entire society. Thus poverty levels in Europe are really an income distribution question. In the United States, poverty is defined differently. Poverty corresponds to a certain level of purchasing power that allows individuals to buy a certain set of "necessary" goods and services. Thus in the United States, poverty is defined without reference to the income levels of those in the society who are not in poverty. This difference in the definitions of poverty makes any comparison of reported national poverty levels invalid.

Work by the Luxembourg Income Studies group allows a consistent comparison of poverty levels. That work takes the income level in different European countries and the United States corresponding to the national poverty level and calculates the income in all the other countries that would yield the same purchasing power. Their analysis goes on to show the fraction of people living in each country below that common level of purchasing power. Using simply gross salaries and wages, their analysis shows that the United States has a smaller fraction of people living below these absolute poverty levels than European countries. Thus, the U.S. economy produces less poverty in an absolute sense than European countries.

A different picture emerges, however, after taking into account income redistribution by the government. After redistribution, most of the European countries have less poverty than the United States. However, this redistribution is a matter of social policy and political outcomes and not a result of the performance of the economies. The income tax code can be used to affect the poverty levels, regardless of whether poverty is measured in absolute terms or in income distribution terms. After all, it is after-tax income that should be used to measure the real purchasing power of individuals.

European countries have commonly resorted to distortions in the markets of their economies in attempting to reduce poverty, in addition to a redistribution of income. Europe would get a better outcome by removing the distortions on their markets, generating a bigger economic pie, and then using the income tax code to redistribute that bigger pie to achieve whatever after-tax income distribution society can agree on.

The poverty picture for Europe as a whole looks worse than for the individual countries studied by the Luxembourg group. That's because the Luxembourg group studied only the richer Northern European countries. If the poorer southern countries were included in an assessment of poverty in Europe as a whole, then poverty for all Europe taken together would be higher than for the northern countries. Portugal and Greece have per capita GDPs that are only two-thirds of that of the northern countries. Thus including them would increase European poverty whether it's measured on a distributional or an absolute basis.

Moreover, the poverty levels for Europe taken as a whole will get much worse as ten Eastern European countries join the European Union. Six of these countries have GDPs per capita similar to Portugal and Greece. Moreover, the largest of the ten, Poland, and the three Baltic states, Estonia, Lithuania, and Latvia, have GDPs per capita that are on average only one-third of the average GDP per capita in the Northern European states. It is clear that by an absolute definition, poverty will increase substantially. It will also increase substantially on a distributional basis because the median income will not change much and most of the population of these new states lives below that level. How Europe will handle the pressures for redistribution of income from the rich northern states to the poorer eastern and southern states remains to be seen. This will be increasingly difficult as the EU attempts to integrate more of its foreign and economic policies to compete with the United States.

Of course the United States had a similar problem of income disparity between North and South following the Civil War. However, the flexible and mobile U.S. markets for labor, capital, and products took care of this problem by themselves in the 1960s and '70s. Now the per capita income of the South equals that of all other regions in the United States. Europe's markets today are not close to being this flexible.

Doubts about Competition

Even more fundamentally, however, there is more reluctance in Europe to let competition work. Competition is increasing in Europe, and, in this case, the European Union authorities in Brussels are leading the way and struggling to overcome national support of incumbents. However, competitive intensity is increasing even faster in the United States. Europeans are still uncomfortable with competition because many believe that with competition comes the necessity of reducing labor to increase productivity and this process causes increased unemployment. If there are constraints on the creation of new business, as is the case in Europe, then Europeans are correct to some degree. These constraints on the creation of new business are just another limitation on the nature of competition to prevent the productivity improvement mechanism from working and to preserve existing employment.

This process is simply too complicated to be managed in the way Europeans would like to. Global competition forces some productivity improvement. High minimum wages and constraints on new businesses do mean high unemployment. The unemployment rate in Europe is roughly twice that of the United States. The youth unemployment rate in France is 20 percent, and much of it is long-term unemployment. Thus now in Europe many young people are having difficulty entering the workforce at all. Europe's GDP per capita is 30 percent below that of the United States because productivity is lower and fewer hours are worked. Some of the fewer hours worked is voluntary, in that Europeans choose more leisure than Americans. However, the high unemployment rates in Europe mean that European economic policy is not generating as much work as the members of those societies want.

Europe's falling behind the United States is likely to get worse before it gets better. The age profile of the people in most European countries means that over the next decade a substantially higher fraction of the workforce will retire in Europe than in the United States. That means that a smaller fraction of the population will be working in Europe. Mechanically, this factor will increase the GDP per capita gap between Europe and the United States by 2 to 3 percentage points over the next decade. Thus, Europe will avoid losing more ground to the United States only by improving productivity faster than the United States. The only way to do this is to remove the market distortions affecting the nature of competition as fast as possible.

Autos: Competition at Work

The global auto industry is the best example we have studied of the importance of competition in causing productivity improvement. The European auto industries are the most intricate part of this story. In the 1980s, because of the formation of the Common Market, Europe had one competitive dynamic going on in its auto industry. At the same time, a global competitive dynamic was developing, caused by the dramatic productivity innovations of the Japanese auto industry in the 1970s and '80s. This global dynamic first showed up in the U.S. market in the 1980s. From the Common Market dynamic of the 1980s, the German auto industry wreaked havoc among most of the rest of the European auto industries. (Ironically, Ford Europe and Opel, owned by General Motors, were part of the Common Market dynamic and highly independent of their parents, who were caught up in the global dynamics triggered by the Japanese.) In the late 1980s and early 1990s, the competitive reaction of the rest of the European auto industry and belated competition with the Japanese wreaked havoc with the German industry. Attempts by the European governments to keep the Japanese out of the European market were probably counterproductive. Because of the delayed competition with the Japanese in Europe, the Japanese probably ended up with a larger market share than if this competition had occurred earlier.

In 1980 the German auto industry produced cars at a 10 percent lower cost than for equivalent cars made in France, and 30 percent lower than in Italy and Spain. German wages were higher, but higher productivity more than made up for the wage disadvantage. The net result was that exports grew in the 1980s by 18 percent of total 1980 production. The corresponding numbers for France and Italy were 8 percent and 4 percent. The major Italian and French auto producers, FIAT, Peugeot, and Renault, lost money in the early 1980s, whereas the German producers, VW, Daimler-Benz, and BMW, either broke even or made money.

Not surprisingly, the French, Italian, and Spanish producers reacted. Their productivity growth in the 1980s was between 4 and 5 percent per year. Employment in the auto industries in France and Italy declined at slightly over 3 percent per year for the twelve-year period from 1980 to 1992. However, the competitive success and profitability of the German industry led to complacency. During this same period, productivity growth in Germany was only half the rate of the rest of Europe. Moreover, real wage growth in Germany over this same period was three times the rate in France and Italy. The net result was that by 1992 France had almost equaled German productivity and had a 38 percent lower cost position. Italy and Spain now matched the German cost position. This competitive reaction contributed significantly to the steady fall of the German auto trade surplus during the 1980s.

The second factor that contributed to the competitive pressure on all European auto industries was the appearance of the Japanese. Even in 1980, the Japanese auto industry had the highest productivity in the world, 10 percent higher than the United States, 40 percent higher than Germany, and more than twice as high as France and Italy. On top of this, Japanese wages were half the rate in the United States, 30 percent lower than in Germany, and about the same as France, Italy, and Spain. The net result was that Japan had a massive cost advantage over the rest of the world's auto industries. Japan was able to exploit this position first in the United States because the U.S. market was initially fully open and easy to enter. The governments of Europe, on the other hand, seeing the Japanese success in the United States, worked out formal and informal understandings with the Japanese to protect the national markets in Europe with substantial domestic auto industries.

No Avoiding the Japanese

The European industries, however, could not avoid competition with the Japanese. First of all, in the 1980s European exports to the United States almost disappeared, with the exception of the luxury car segment, important primarily for the German industry. Second, by the early 1990s, the Japanese auto makers had achieved market shares of 20 to 30 percent in all the smaller European markets without significant domestic auto industries. The Japanese even acquired about 25 percent of the Swedish market, even though Volvo and Saab were major global auto companies. The reason was that Volvo and Saab produced near-luxury cars, a segment the Japanese had not yet entered, and which did not yet need to be protected. Thus the Japanese took export markets away from German, Italian, French, and Spanish producers both in the United States and in the smaller markets in Europe. This pressure helped cause the restructuring of the Italian, French, and Spanish industries in the 1980s and then finally the restructuring of the German industry in the late 1980s and early 1990s. Employment in the German auto industry peaked in 1991 and fell precipitously for the next five years.

The final blow to the European auto industry came with the Japanese entry into the luxury car segment. Up until the 1990s, much of Daimler-Benz's profitability had come from the United States. When Toyota and Honda began to sell luxury cars in the U.S. market, with close to German quality, but at a price 30 to 40 percent lower, U.S. consumers switched amazingly quickly to the Japanese cars. Lexus became the highest selling luxury car brand in the United States. This finally caused a restructuring at Daimler-Benz in the first half of the 1990s. Sweden was also affected. In 1980, Sweden had the highest auto productivity in Europe and was close to the United States and Japan. However, almost total lack of competition caused Sweden to fall 25 percent behind the United States and Japan by 1992. The entry of the Japanese into the luxury car segment solved this problem too.

The UK auto industry is a special case. Following the war, a long history of labor difficulty and government subsidy made the industry uncompetitive with almost everybody, and as a result it was decimated. Today, the UK auto industry is almost entirely owned by companies headquartered outside the United Kingdom. Car production in the United Kingdom is only 40 percent of the level in Germany. Productivity is half that in Japan and 70 percent of the levels in the United States and Germany. However, the United Kingdom was the production site chosen by Nissan, Toyota, and Honda for their first manufacturing facilities in Europe. Amazingly, these Japanese manufacturers have shown that they can use local labor even from the United Kingdom and achieve close to home country productivity. This is yet another example of how the labor forces of all the advanced countries are capable of producing global best practice labor productivity. Labor inputs are not the constraint; lack of competition with global best practice is.

Europe has not fallen further behind the United States in the 1990s because of the auto industry. The United States and European auto industries have about the same relative position now that they had two decades ago. The United States got the Japan shock in the 1980s, at the same time the European industries got the German shock. Then all the European industries felt the Japan shock in the late 1980s and first half of the 1990s. The United States felt the shock directly in its home market. The German industry felt the shock indirectly through its export markets. The force of the shock turned out to be about equal. This is a great example of how unless a country runs a closed economy, its tradable goods sector is going to run into global best practice. The world's auto industry and consumers are better off for it.

It's not so easy in service industries, where goods are not usually traded internationally and firms have no choice but to set up shop under local conditions to serve local customers. National governments have been much more successful at preventing the setting up of more productive service industries than they have been at keeping out exports from more productive manufacturing firms. The next industry study, retailing, will show how European governments have done this and thus contributed to Europe's falling further behind the United States in the 1990s.

Retailing: Having the Best Is Not Enough

Retailing is revealing about why Europe has recently begun to fall further behind the United States. However, the reasons are not obvious to us as we buy imported goods from Europe or as we move quickly between the United States and Europe on business or short vacations. We have some intuitive sense of the differences between the United States and Europe from our stays in hotels, our eating in restaurants, our use of national transportation systems, and our purchase of traded manufactured goods such as cars. However, unless we live for an extended time in a country, we know very little about the most important economic elements of everyday life, shopping (retailing) and housing. These are perhaps the two most important sectors determining economic standards of living. They are big. U.S. employment in retailing is 11 percent of total employment, and housing construction is 2 percent.

I had learned some things about retailing in Europe before we studied it. Consultants from Germany working on Global Institute projects talk about how shopping is almost impossible for them in Germany. They work such long hours at McKinsey that the opening hour restrictions mean the stores are almost never open when the consultants can shop. I experienced another difference in France, doing a week's grocery shopping for our extended family staying in a rented house near Aix-en-Provence one summer. I had been extremely pleased to find a wonderful hypermarket where I could not only get everything I wanted for a week but also found food of at least as high quality as I was used to in Washington. I did think the prices a little high, but I was on vacation. The shock came when I took my two fully loaded shopping carts to check out. The checkout person rang up my goods and slid them to the space behind her on the counter. They just stood there, as the counter got more and more crowded. I glanced over at the next checkout counter and saw a woman packing her own bag. I looked for bags; there were none. I knew I was in trouble; I had not brought my own bags. Realizing my plight, the checkout person was quite helpful. But I still had to pack the bags she produced. I painfully learned that there are some skills in packing grocery bags so that the eggs are not on the bottom and the ice cream doesn't melt. I have appreciated the baggers in U.S. supermarkets ever since.

Minimum Wage Equals Job Killer

These two stories explain why we found that employment levels in re-tailing in France and Germany are only about two-thirds of the U.S. level. The principal reason is that France and Germany have minimum wages of about twice the U.S. level. The sophisticated French and German retailers have found that they make more profits by not hiring the bag packers and paying them the high minimum wage. European consumers react to the even higher prices that would be necessary to pay these wages by reducing their shopping lists and shopping elsewhere. The value to the customer of the services of these low-skilled workers is less than their high wage. The skills of bag packing may be beyond me, but they are simple to acquire. Opening hour restrictions in Germany further reduce employment in retailing.

These factors cause lower employment across the board in retailing in high minimum wage countries. In France, Toys "R" Us employs 30 percent fewer workers than in the identical store in the United States. The wages of 35 percent of the U.S. retail workers are below the minimum wages in France and the Netherlands. Most of the equivalent of these people in France and the Netherlands end up unemployed. UK food retailers, on the other hand, employ a higher fraction of the workforce than U.S. food retailers. Sure enough, the United Kingdom had no minimum wage until 1998, and then it set the minimum wage at about the U.S. level.

The large European hypermarket and supermarket chains equal or exceed the productivity of their U.S. equivalents. Carrefour in France and Tesco, Sainsbury, Safeway, and Asda in the United Kingdom are clearly global best practice. They have been successful not only in Europe but have led the transfer of global best practice in retailing around the world. Carrefour is to retailing what Toyota is to autos.

In the mid-1990s when we measured retailing productivity, we found that productivity in France and Germany was at least as high and maybe higher than in the United States. There is a problem, however, with the measurement of retailing productivity when the service levels are not the same. The OECD purchasing power parity exchange rates cannot capture the differences in services when stores with the same service level do not exist in both economies. The services provided by low-skilled workers in the United States are therefore likely to be missed by the OECD. We corrected for this factor by calculating the productivity of the French and German retailing industries if they employed similar numbers of low-skilled workers to provide the "bag-packing" services found in the United States. The result was a reduction of productivity in French and German retailing by about 15 percent, to a level somewhat below the United States. In the Netherlands, we constructed our own purchasing power parity exchange rate for retailing by comparing the prices of identical items in IKEA stores in similar locations. The result was to reduce retailing productivity in the Netherlands by about 15 percent. Measured productivity in food retailing in the United Kingdom was about 10 percent below that of the United States also in the mid-1990s.

As I will describe in the next chapter on the United States, productivity growth in U.S. retailing accelerated to about 5 percent a year in the second half of the 1990s. In Europe, productivity growth was only between 1 and 2 percent per year. Thus now without question, U.S. retailing as an industry has higher productivity. The principal reason is that the best practice retailers in the United States, and especially Wal-Mart, are relatively free to expand across the country as fast as possible. We in the United States complain about the resulting closing down of the local mom-and-pop stores. However, we don't shop in those stores when we can find what we want all in one shopping trip to Wal-Mart and all at considerably lower prices. The competitive dynamic in the United States is now to the point that Wal-Mart is putting intense competitive pressure on the other large retailing chains. They are responding by increasing productivity now at a rate as fast as Wal-Mart.

In Europe, this evolution in retail development has not gone as far. France has tried to outlaw hypermarkets and the shopping centers that often surround them. The hypermarkets have gotten around the restrictions somewhat, but the shopping centers have not. The result is fewer high-productivity specialty stores, which naturally surround the anchor store in a shopping center. In Germany and the United Kingdom, environmental concerns have resulted in laws giving local planning authorities the ability to restrict expansion of high-productivity retailers. Incumbent retailers have substantial influence with the local authorities and have been successful at thwarting competition. High-productivity retailers have been more successful establishing large hypermarkets and shopping centers in East Germany, where incumbents often don't exist and consumers are hungry for goods at the price levels of hypermarkets. The expansion of UK food supermarkets is limited by formal planning regulations and processes. Many times, these restrictions are obviously valid in preserving beautiful open space and architectural treasures.

However, the restrictions are now applied in a mechanical way, for instance to all buildings over one hundred years old.

As we were conducting our work in the United Kingdom, local consumers and the UK government were complaining about the high prices and profitability of the UK supermarkets. The problem is not with the supermarkets themselves. The problem is that the planning restrictions keep the supermarkets from expanding and having to compete with each other by lowering prices. The planning restrictions make it too easy for the supermarkets now. They can easily compete with the traditional stores at the high prices traditional stores charge. Because the supermarkets are so much more productive, at those prices the supermarkets make a lot of money. (Planning restrictions in the United Kingdom also constrain hotel development. On June 26, 2003, the *Economist* reported that relative to average-price levels, hotel prices in London are 70 percent higher than in New York.)

Unintended Adverse Consequences

The European Continentals have a high minimum wage for good reason. The United Kingdom has planning restrictions also for good reasons. However, the influence incumbent retailers have on retailing evolution in France and Germany does not come from a good reason but from special interests. Japan is even more extreme in this regard, but Continental Europe is pretty bad at times.

The problem with a high minimum wage and planning restrictions is that they have unintended adverse economic consequences. The minimum wage leads to more unemployment; the planning restrictions lead to low productivity and high prices. Europeans don't have to make these trade-offs. The United States has a low minimum wage and uses the Earned Income Tax Credit to make the after-tax income distribution somewhat more equal. Europeans could do the same thing and make their after-tax income distribution even more equal than in the United States. There is no right answer to income distribution. Every society has to settle this question through its political process. However, Europeans can achieve whatever after-tax income distribution they want by using the Earned Income Tax Credit and not distorting the labor market so much with a high minimum wage. Similarly, the UK planning authorities need to discriminate between architectural treasures and the abandoned, derelict hundred-year-old hospital that Tesco cannot replace with a supermarket. Without change here, Europe will fall progressively further behind the United States in retailing.

Housing Construction: Higher Prices Don't Always Mean Higher Quality

When traveling between Europe and the United States, most people get the impression that housing is significantly different. In Europe, multifamily dwellings (apartment houses) are much more common. In the United States, the middle-class suburbs of single-family housing on relatively spacious lots seem to go on forever in Atlanta and Denver. Such impressions are valid. The average American has about twice as much housing space as the average European.

The principal reasons for this difference are twofold. Productivity in all the European countries we studied, with the exception of the Netherlands, is significantly lower than in the United States. Housing construction productivity in Germany is 70 percent of that of the United States; in France, 80 percent. The second reason is that relative to the prices of other things in each economy, housing is much more expensive in Europe. Relative to all other prices in the economy, land for housing construction in Germany costs four times as much as in the United States. On top of this, construction costs are about twice as high. Germany is extreme, but there is no question that housing in Europe is much more expensive than in the United States. Of course, the higher construction costs are caused in part because of the relatively low productivity in this industry.

Our productivity results for housing construction in Germany raised perhaps the strongest feelings in Germany that we were wrong. The conventional wisdom in Germany is that U.S. houses are made out of sticks and are on the verge of falling down any day. If U.S. houses are so cheap, they have to be of inferior quality. No German would want to live in them. If we made appropriate quality adjustments, we would find that productivity in Germany was not below the United States.

We were reasonably confident of our results because we had faced the same issue in our earlier study of Sweden. There we found Swedish academic work showing that under similar climatic conditions, American housing is some 30 percent cheaper than in Sweden for the same quality. Moreover, Skanska, the big Swedish construction firm, had explored building Swedish-quality houses in the upper Midwest United States and found they could build the houses at about the costs of U.S. housing. Our results showed that housing construction productivity in Sweden was 80 percent of the level in the United States.

The Swedish example was not good enough to be convincing in Germany. However, we got lucky. We found that the Netherlands had the same housing construction productivity as the United States, and the cost of new housing was about the same in both countries. Moreover, the Netherlands productivity advantage over Germany derived from the same factor we had found to give the U.S. industry an advantage. This factor was large-scale developments in which many single-family homes were built at the same time. Some of this housing was built close to the German border, for instance, near Aachen. The clinching factor was that Germans seemed perfectly satisfied to live in this much cheaper Dutch housing and commute to work in Germany.

The one big innovation in housing construction in the last fifty years has been large-scale construction of many single-family homes at the same time on the same site. The savings from lower overhead, better utilization of labor and equipment, and similar architectural designs are significant. Moreover, price competition from a large supply of housing causes big developers to apply "design to cost" techniques to reduce labor and materials. Why don't developers in France and Germany build several houses at the same time on the same site to improve efficiency?

The reason is they can't get the land. The usual assumption is that they cannot get the land because there is not enough of it. Europe is just a very crowded place already. Thank goodness for the Netherlands case. The Netherlands is the most crowded European country, and it makes enough land available for large-scale single-family housing. It turns out it takes only a tiny fraction of the total land for such developments. In the Netherlands, only 8 percent of the total land area is used for housing. Forest and other designated natural areas take 13 percent. About 70 percent of the land in the Netherlands is still devoted to agriculture. The Dutch could double the land devoted to housing, not disturb "green space," and reduce agricultural land by only 10 percent.

Misaligning Authority and Responsibility

The reason the Dutch (and the Americans) can make large tracks of land available for single-family housing development is that both countries align the responsibility for infrastructure with the authority to finance it. Both countries give the same level of government the responsibility for providing roads, water, sewers, and schools and the authority to tax the value of housing to pay for the financing costs of this infrastructure. In the Netherlands, this level of government is the federal government. In the United States, it's the lowest level of cities and counties. In Germany and France, local governments have to pay for infrastructure but they do not have the authority to tax to finance it. Thus the local authorities make very little land available for housing development in

France and Germany because they cannot afford to do otherwise. In this way, France and Germany are unable to apply the innovation of large-scale development of single-family housing to improve productivity.

The second consequence of so little land being available in France and Germany for development is that land prices are very high. When these high land prices are combined with the high construction costs coming from lower productivity, the costs of housing in Europe are much more relative to other things than in the United States. Thus, Europeans over the years have built less housing. Between 1985 and 1994, the United States built 164 square meters of new housing per 1,000 people, compared with 82 in France and 94 in Germany.

Land prices are clearly artificially high. Europeans are behaving as if land is more scarce than it really is. They then choose to spend their money on more of other things. They buy so much of these other things that the value to them of more goods and services is less than the price they have to pay, given that the price has a floor set by a (high) minimum wage for the labor involved. This mechanism is one of the principal causes of unemployment. Clearly, if land prices in Europe were lower and closer to their true scarcity, Europeans would buy more housing. Construction jobs are high-paying. They equal manufacturing wages in most countries. They are thus well above the minimum wage. Therefore, this increased purchase of housing would result in an increase in the total number of jobs. (Skills are not a constraint as I will discuss in the next chapter, which includes a section on housing construction in the United States.) Thus, unemployment in Europe would go down and output would grow faster than it otherwise would. Sounds like a good deal.

Software: First in Takes All

Software has been a great example for us around the world. It has revealed so many things about how economies are developing at the frontier today. First of all, software is the only "high-tech" industry with enough employment to make a difference in the national employment statistics. In the United States, software accounts for about 0.5 percent of total employment. It employs about seven times as many people as the semiconductor industry and about three times as many people as the computer hardware manufacturing industry. Software employs almost as many people as all high-tech manufacturing sectors combined. These manufacturing sectors, including computers, instruments, drugs, chemicals and plastics, consumer electronics, machine tools, etc., provide only about 0.7 percent of total U.S. employment. Thus, European dreams about solving employment problems with government support of high-tech manufacturing industries are only dreams.

Second, software is a good example of how service industries provide good jobs. The conventional wisdom in Europe throughout most of the '90s was that most service jobs were not worth having. They were mostly "hamburger-flipping" jobs. In our Employment Performance study, we had found that median weekly wages in service sectors in the United States had reached 95 percent of the level of manufacturing industries. Moreover, the OECD Jobs Study had shown that the United States was creating twice as many jobs in the professional, technical, administrative, and managerial categories as in the clerical, sales, and service category. Since all the net jobs created in the United States were in the service industry, the OECD results meant that the United States was creating two high-paying service jobs for every hamburger flipper. Software is a wonderful illustration of the creation of good service industry jobs.

Software shows the most dramatic difference between Europe and the United States of any case we have studied. The amount of software produced in France, Germany, and the United Kingdom is only 20 to 30 percent of the amount produced in the United States on a per capita basis. Software industries in Europe are simply much smaller than in the United States. Employment levels in software in France, Germany, and the United Kingdom are about 30 percent of the U.S. level, again adjusted for population differences. The productivity levels in these European countries are higher, but still only about 75 percent of the U.S. level.

The biggest difference is in "packaged" software, which accounts for about half of all software. This is the software sold around the world in standardized, identical forms. IBM has been the leader in packaged software for mainframe computers, and Microsoft, for PCs. The United States produces ten times as much packaged software per capita as France, Germany, and the United Kingdom. Packaged software illustrates the powerful effect of being the "first mover" in an industry in which there are great benefits from standardization, and thus in which there are natural monopolistic tendencies.

How come the United States was the first mover in packaged software and not Europe? Well, it has to be that firms providing such software and customers wanting such software came together at the same time first in the United States. Much has been written about the differences in the supply side of this equation. The entrepreneurial, risk-taking culture of the United States clearly shows up in start-up software firms and venture capital firms financing them. This difference from Europe is well known. European governments have tried to make up for this difference by intervening in the market, without success. The evidence that government agencies are not good at picking good entrepreneurs is substantial and, by now, widely accepted. What is still not understood is the crucial role played by other industries (software users) in the initial development of the software industry around the world.

Software Needs Customers Under Pressure

Over the past twenty years, computers and software applications have given businesses a new way a giving customers better services at lower costs. However, these changes have been painful for business management to make. They have involved changing the way businesses operate. That meant moving people around and giving them different things to do. Computer applications have also often directly reduced costs by replacing people. Although in the early computer days, these changes were "no-brainers" in business logic, they took substantial management will to implement because they were hard. Most people don't like change, and they especially don't like to be laid off.

In the United States, managers in many industries faced a draconian choice: either change or go out of business. Managers in the United States faced this choice to a much greater degree than their European counterparts in the early computer days. The reason was that competitive intensity in the United States, especially in service industries, was much higher than in Europe. Retail banking and airlines are good examples. In the early 1980s, when mainframe computers were becoming widely available at low prices, the United States deregulated both retail banking and airlines. This deregulation set off intense competitive pressure in these industries. Retail banks now had to compete on price because interest rates on deposit accounts were no longer fixed by regulation and mutual fund companies were offering checking services on money market accounts. Thus banks had to compete for customers by increasing the interest they paid on deposits. They could only continue to meet their payrolls by reducing their costs.

Mainframe computers were the ideal way for retail banks to reduce costs. Much of the business of retail banking is the recording and processing of standardized information, most of which is in numerical form. This is an application for computers made in heaven. In the 1980s in the United States, retail banks invested massively in mainframe computers and packaged software to run applications that had previously been

Exhibit 3.3: Impact of U.S. Banking Deregulation

Index 1980 = 100

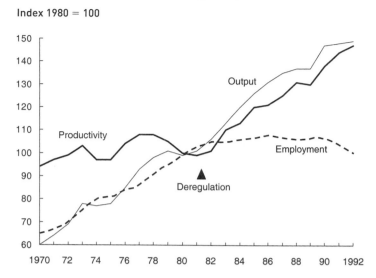

done by people using pencil and paper. Retail banks drastically cut back the number of people in their processing ("back-room") operations. After stagnating for many years, productivity began to grow rapidly in this industry (Exhibit 3.3). No similar increase in competitive intensity occurred in Europe at this time. The application of computers to retail banking was much less extensive, and often not accompanied by the reduction in people. Thus retail banks in Europe ended up with simply higher costs and no productivity improvement. The U.S. deregulation of retail banking was initially triggered by competition from money market mutual funds, which began in the late 1970s to offer checking services with money market interest rates on the deposits. Such checking services were not allowed in Germany until the late 1990s, or about twenty years later.

A similar story occurred in the airline industry in the United States. The deregulation of the industry in the late 1970s triggered price competition and a huge increase in demand. The application of computers allowed the industry to expand at a high rate and provide customers with some better services. For instance, computer applications made it possible for central reservation systems to give immediate information on the telephone about flight availability and for reservations to be immediately confirmed. Much more complicated applications for the optimization of flight schedules allowed airlines to introduce "hub and spoke" systems. These systems provided connections among many more cities for greater customer convenience. Again, at this time in Europe air travel between any two European countries was a regulated duopoly, under which flights were limited to the two national carriers of the two countries involved. Moreover, if one national airline happened to increase market share, it had to share its increased revenues with the other national airline. Europe has moved considerably to deregulate air travel since then. However, the United States went first. Thus the benefits of the spillover effects to the mainframe computer and software industries went primarily to IBM.

A similar story could be told about packaged software for PCs. The competitive intensity in the United States, and especially in services, caused U.S. industries to invest much earlier and much more intensely in PCs. In the early 1990s, the United States had twice as many PCs per capita as any other major economy. As I will report in the next chapter on the United States, in the late 1990s the United States undoubtedly overinvested in PCs. However that may be, the demand for applications for PCs in the United States was high, and that led directly to Microsoft's ability to sell standardized applications, as well as standardized operating systems. The difference from Europe was that U.S. service firms had to be at the leading edge of providing customer service and convenience and cutting costs in order to stay in business.

There's not much Europe can do about the United States' first-mover advantage in packaged software. However, other technological and business innovations that affect the provision of computer applications will occur over time. Whichever economy has the most incentive for managers to perform better will lead in the application of these innovations. If the innovations lend themselves to being standardized, then that economy will gain a first-mover advantage. The current trends would indicate that the United States would again be the best bet over the next decade or so. However, that is a story for the next chapter.

Europe Needs to Raise Its Economics Game

Our findings reveal why Europe did not catch up with the United States economically and why it has begun to fall further behind over the past ten years. Europe has come out OK in the automotive sector because that industry was sufficiently engaged in the global marketplace. Competitive pressure from Japan eventually forced restructuring of the European automotive industry, in the same way that pressure had forced restructuring in the United States almost ten years earlier. However, retailing has not been the employment engine in Europe that it has been in the United States. And Europeans have not had nearly as much housing to enjoy as Americans. Finally, Europe missed entirely the first-mover advantage in packaged software.

The reasons Europe did not have as strong a performance in our service sector industry studies as the United States are clear-cut. Europe's high minimum wage and zoning laws and other retail regulations constrained expansion of modern retail stores. The mismatch of responsibility and authority concerning land development, along with restrictive zoning laws, caused less housing to be built. Finally, low competitive intensity across the board, primarily in service industries, prevented the demand for packaged software from developing as early in Europe as in the United States.

On the other hand, Europe does not have the extremely low-productivity industries of Japan. Food processing productivity is twice as high in Germany as in Japan, though it's about 75 percent of U.S. productivity. The principal reason for the difference between Germany and Japan is that retailing is so much more consolidated in Germany. The protection of mom-and-pop stores is not nearly so strong. That means that industrial-scale food processors can serve retailers directly and thus put craft shop food processors out of business.

As I discussed in each of my industry examples, the restrictions in Europe are in place for good social reasons. At least, the restrictions can be justified that way even if, as is likely the case, they also serve to protect incumbents and other special interests. Nevertheless, as long as they can be justified socially, they will not be changed. However, our work showed that the same good social objectives could be achieved in ways that distort the economic markets less. The result would be achieving virtually all of the current social objectives and better economic performance at the same time.

The Earned Income Tax Credit is a better way of achieving after-tax income distribution objectives than a high minimum wage. Giving the same government body responsibility for land development and taxing authority to finance such development would result in cheaper land and larger tracts of land for more productive and thus cheaper housing construction. More discriminating planning rules and processes would reach a better balance between preserving truly valuable green space and architectural treasures and making old but rundown areas available for modern retail and housing developments. Finally, the competitive pressure that would result from these changes and others would make it more likely that Europe would not miss the next "first-mover" opportunity that comes along.

Why hasn't Europe made these changes, and does it matter anyway? After all, international polls often show that France is the country most people would like to live in. Moreover, the United Nations' Human Development Index usually has a few European countries at the top. However, as outsiders, our impressions of Europe are usually formed from visits to the affluent city centers and the beautified countryside. The economic and social problems of Europe are in the suburbs. Moreover, with economic power comes potential political power. It is ironic that Europe begins to move towards a military force independent of the United States just as the total European economic pie stops catching up in size with the United States and begins to fall further behind. Moreover, the aging of the European workforce means that European social programs are becoming harder and harder to finance. Europe will simply not meet its social and political objectives nearly as well if it does not improve its economic performance.

As an American, I have an emotional reaction of "just as well." Europe caused the world an awful lot of trouble in the first half of the last century. It seemed at times to be thwarting American efforts towards preventing this from happening again in the second half of the last century and the beginning of this one. But that reaction is not right. It is very important for Europe to succeed as a society. This is not the place to recount European contributions to civilization as we know it today. Europe is the founder of democracy, "our last, best hope." Because Europe is a democracy, I have to believe it will succeed. However, democracies work better the more knowledge the people have. Europe needs to upgrade its economic knowledge.

Economics at the Breakfast Table

As we conducted our country studies of Germany, France, and the Netherlands, we were surprised by the misunderstandings in the public economic debate. Sweden and the United Kingdom were considerably better, but France and Germany were surprisingly weak. For instance, on the Continent virtually no one knew about the Earned Income Tax Credit. Moreover, most public economic discussions assumed that productivity was the enemy of employment. Changes in regulation that would lead to more competition and faster productivity growth would just generate more unemployment.

In the United States, on the other hand, Alan Greenspan has made productivity a household word. The quarterly productivity statistics often appear on the front page of the business section of the *New York Times*. The economic debate in the United States takes as a point of departure that productivity is the engine of economic growth. Moreover, a consensus seems to be forming that the United States was able to achieve record levels of low unemployment in the late 1990s because of faster productivity growth. Faster productivity growth meant faster real wage growth. Thus workers were less inclined to ask for higher wages, which would have been inflationary and caused the Federal Reserve to increase interest rates and slow down growth. This unusually low unemployment though is likely to be temporary as workers catch on that even though their real wages are increasing, they're not increasing as fast as productivity.

It is not easy for a society to have good economic knowledge and a good economic debate. Economics is not easy. An economy is a huge system of millions of actors interacting among themselves and doing things that add up to the GDP. The system is either stable (in "equilibrium") or unstable (in "disequilibrium"). Unstable economies are bad news. Accelerating hyperinflation leads to currencies of no value, the destruction of all savings, and often political chaos, as the Weimar Republic illustrated. We know how to prevent unstable economies and they now rarely appear. Fortunately, for Europe, we really have to think only in terms of stable economies. Even that's not so easy.

The economic question we need to consider is this: What will happen if we change some of the conditions influencing the economy? For instance, what would happen if we let the Japanese car companies build transplant factories in our country? As a physicist, I was used to taking a formula describing a system and then expressing the effects of change in a string of ever-decreasing factors. When the effects got small enough to be negligible I stopped. I had the answer. Not so in economics. The difference is that in physics we can often write a formula describing the whole system because we know exactly what the interactions are between all the elements of the system. In economics, the elements of the system are people, and not even the most gifted psychoanalyst could start to write a formula describing the interaction among people. Nevertheless, in economics we try anyway. And if we are very careful, we can gain some useful information.

So if we consider the question of the effects of the Japanese transplants, we know that the workers in those plants will be more productive than our current workers. Moreover, the Japanese transplants will take market share from our current auto plants. In an effort to preserve profitability, our own plants will also increase their productivity. Thus we will end up with fewer workers producing the same number of cars. Unemployment will go up, and letting the Japanese transplants in is a bad idea. It is possible that the process does stop here and that we have a stable economy with the same number of cars produced but more unemployment.

I believe it is only through the experience of such events in specific economies that we know that the important effects of the introduction of the Japanese transplants do not stop simply with more unemployment. We know that if capital is available, and laws and regulations do not prevent the formation of new businesses producing new goods and services, then entrepreneurs will form new businesses to produce the new goods and services that the now richer auto workers want. The entrepreneurs will employ the displaced auto workers (or other members of their families). We are back to another stable economy. This one is better, however, because not only do we get the same number of cars, we also get the new goods and services from the new businesses. And unemployment stays the same. Needless to say, this example is oversimplified. Nevertheless, it shows the main difference between the European and U.S. points of view about productivity growth. The outcome envisioned by the United States is clearly better. We also know it happens unless our laws and regulations prevent it. This conclusion is not well understood in Europe and, for that matter, in most of the rest of the world.

You Can See a Lot by Looking

So why don't Europeans look around and see how the world works? Of course many do, but also many don't. Where would Europeans look? Europe's economic performance is higher than virtually all the world. Japan is about the same. The obvious place to look is the United States because it is the only comprehensive economy with economic performance significantly above Europe's. However, Europeans are very reluctant to look at the United States, and knowledge about the United States is surprisingly weak in Europe. Why is this? Here I will indulge again in amateur sociology. In the Japan chapter I expressed the view that obsession with correctness and denial of problems was the reason Japan was not dealing with its economic problems. For Europe, I think it does not learn the economic lessons from the experience of the United States because of "wounded pride."

This wounded pride is understandable. After contributing so much to civilization for the past five hundred years, the performance of many European societies in the first half the twentieth century was so bad that it is taking a long time to recover psychologically. This wounded pride behavior is expressed particularly towards the United States. Of course, this in large part is because the United States played such a major role in bringing stability to Europe again. However, the lack of understanding of the United States goes deeper. Europeans just cannot understand how the United States performs as it does. After all, in the nineteenth and early twentieth centuries, the United States was settled by immigrants from Europe who came to the United States to escape poverty or persecution, or who thought opportunities were better in the United States. Thus, for much of its history, the United States was settled by people who were rejecting Europe, and who were considered in Europe to have been unsuccessful. This combination has led to Europeans being genuinely puzzled about how such a country could perform as it has done, and to an understandable denial of its performance.

Europe's reluctance to look at the United States has been longstanding. In 1997, when Chancellor Kohl spoke in Washington at the fiftieth anniversary of the Marshall Plan, he remarked about how surprised German industrialists had been at the advanced state of U.S. manufacturing when they visited U.S. plants under the Marshall Plan. Kohl said that the belief in Germany before and during the war was that the economic strength of the United States came primarily from agriculture and natural resources. I even heard this view expressed in Germany in the early 1990s. It's surprising how many of the economic policies and business innovations that have shaped the U.S. economy to this day were put in place in the first part of the last century. These changes seem to have escaped the attention of Europeans. Perhaps that was because of all the turmoil at the time in Europe. However, as I mentioned above, I think it was deeper.

France doesn't make many of the needed economic reforms because of the threat of civil disobedience on the part of those workers who would have to change what they're doing. Consistent with that view, at a lunch at Princeton in 1970, Helmut Schmidt, who at the time was Germany's defense minister, said that many on the Continent thought U.S. society was falling apart over the Vietnam War protests. I was astounded to realize that such protests in Europe would be thought to be the precursors of anarchy because society would not set limits on the degree to which they infringed on the rights of others. When democracies do not set such limits, that means the majority of people sympathize with the protesters. Margaret Thatcher recognized this limit had to be tested when she forcibly stopped the civil disobedience in the coal miners' strike in 1984. Thatcher succeeded because the majority of the people in the United Kingdom were well enough informed about the issue to feel that their liberties and their pocketbooks were being unduly diminished by a minority unwilling to change.

Thus, the fear of civil disobedience over economic reform in France must mean that the political leadership believes that the majority of French people would sympathize with those protesting reform. This situation calls for real leadership. One of the crucial traits of real leaders in a democracy is the ability to help people become better informed so that society can make better choices. This brings us back to the need in Europe for a better understanding of the natural economic experiment that has been taking place in the United States.

Help may be on the way for Europe from the dramatic expansion of the EU to include many Eastern European countries in 2004. The EU will suddenly not be dominated by France and Germany anymore. These new additions don't suffer from wounded pride. They are still recovering from real wounds inflicted first by fellow Europeans and then by the Soviet Union. They are more favorably inclined towards the results of the natural experiment of the United States. This is especially true for Poland, by far the largest of the new additions.

Knowledge about how things are done in the United States, or anywhere else for that matter, does not oblige us to copy those things. We can learn the lessons we choose. However, we first have to have the knowledge of what happened, in this case in the U.S. economy. That's what the next chapter is about.

CHAPTER FOUR

The United States: Consumer Is King

As I have discussed in the previous chapters, in 1990 the conventional wisdom around the world was that the U.S. economy had seen its day. That point of view was wrong. In the second half of the 1990s, productivity growth rates accelerated in the United States to almost twice the level seen for the previous twenty-five years. The conventional wisdom became that the United States had a "new economy," unlike anything seen before. This point of view was made official in President Clinton's last Economic Report of the President, of January 2001. This point of view was also wrong.

The most remarkable thing about the performance of the U.S. economy has been how steady it was. For each of the past three decades, the average annual growth rate in GDP per capita has been exactly 1.7 percent per year. In contrast, for Japan the corresponding growth rates were 4.3 percent in the '70s, 3.4 percent in the '80s, and 0.6 percent in the '90s. The corresponding numbers for France were 2.6 percent, 1.7 percent, and 0.7 percent. We don't have a similar time series for Germany because of reunification, but the growth rate in GDP per capita for unified Germany in the 1990s was 0.7 percent. The United States had some acceleration in performance in the second half of the 1990s. However, about half of the factors causing the acceleration are not sustainable for the next five years. Moreover, the factors that will carry over are not permanent and will mostly dissipate by the end of the next five years. This doesn't mean that other factors won't take their place. However, those factors have not shown up yet and we have no way of knowing whether they will.

The Grass Looks Greener Elsewhere

In 1990, the problems most commonly assumed about the U.S. economy were these: no industrial policy orchestrated as MITI was doing in Japan; too low a savings rate to provide enough investment, especially long-term investment; and too much poverty. Across a broad range of manufacturing and service industries in Japan, there are only two instances where MITI's intervention was a significant cause of good economic performance. The first was MITIs standardization of the Japanese machine tool industry starting in 1956. The second was MITIs requirement that to enter the Japanese market in the 1960s, IBM had to share its computer patents with Japanese companies.

Both actions were good economic policy. It's appropriate for government to set standards when large economic gains would result and industry is not self-standardizing. IBM's forced sharing of computer patents prevented IBM from having a mainframe computer monopoly in Japan. However, these steps were a long way from the conventional view that MITI was identifying and supporting a broad array of "strategic" industries, and that this action was giving Japan a strategic economic advantage over the United States.

With regard to poverty, the view, especially in Europe, was that the U.S. economic system created unacceptably high levels of poverty for that system to serve as a model for anybody else. Moreover, doubts were raised about the stability of U.S. society under such conditions. As I discussed in chapter 3, the work of the Luxembourg Income Studies Group showed that the U.S. economy, before income redistribution, produced more purchasing power per capita for the lowest income group than any other comprehensive economy. That same work showed that most European countries redistribute considerably more income than the United States, for instance in unemployment benefits. The result is that on an after-tax and after-welfare basis, the lowest income groups in some European countries have higher purchasing power than in the United States. However, income redistribution is primarily a social and political issue, not an economic policy issue. The United States could make political choices to redistribute more income than it does and achieve a considerably higher after-distribution purchasing power for the lowest income group.

How about savings and investment? Where productivity is higher in Germany and Japan, is it higher because of more investment or more long-term capital? As I reported earlier, productivity is higher than for the United States in only a few manufacturing industries in Japan. In none of these industries was more capital investment the reason for higher labor productivity in Japan. In auto assembly, the amount of capital applied per hour worked is higher in the United States. General Motors uses more robots per worker than Toyota.

Still the amount of capital applied per person overall is 13 percent higher in Germany than in the United States, and 22 percent higher in Japan. Yet, the United States has a GDP per capita 25 to 30 percent higher than both these countries and a household net financial wealth about 50 percent higher than both these countries. What is the resolution of the paradox I first heard stated by Francis Bator in 1994, "If the United States saves so little, how can it be so rich?"

The answer is much higher capital productivity in the United States. Capital productivity in Germany and Japan is 35 to 40 percent lower than in the United States. The lower capital inputs in the United States are more than made up for by this. The higher capital productivity in the United States also caused the financial return on investment to be much higher than in Germany and Japan. Over the period from 1974 to 1993, the financial return in the U.S. corporate sector was 9.1 percent, compared with 7.4 percent in Germany and 7.1 percent in Japan. I was relieved that the higher financial return came from economic fundamentals in the real economy and not from financial gimmicks. The higher financial return in the United States over twenty years more than made up for the lower investment levels and resulted in 20 percent more new financial wealth accumulation per capita in the United States.

The reasons for the differences in capital productivity were similar to those for labor productivity. Twenty to thirty percent of the gap was caused by laws and regulations that directly constrained capital productivity potential. Examples include short store opening hours and underground telecom cable requirements in Germany. However, managers could choose to change other factors to make up for the rest of the gap in capital productivity. They don't do it because they don't have to. Less intense competition allows them to earn sufficient returns to satisfy their owners, which in some cases, such as telecom in Germany, is the government.

From One Extreme to the Other

In the late 1990s, pessimistic comments about the U.S. economy gave way to euphoria. Beginning in 1995, the annual productivity growth rates began to exceed the average rate of the past twenty-five years. They did this for enough years so that by 2000 it was clear that something fundamental had happened and that these results were not coming from business cycle effects or statistical fluctuations. The economic performance in the second half of the '90s was clearly different from that of the first half of the '90s. This time the difference was not across coun-

Exhibit 4.1: The Solow Paradox

CAGR, percent

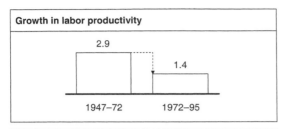

Growth in labor productivity

2.9
1.4

1947–72   1972–95

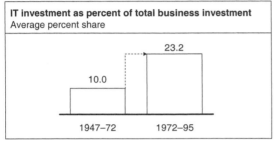

IT investment as percent of total business investment
Average percent share

23.2

10.0

1947–72   1972–95

tries but over time in the same country. What change in factors caused this change in the labor productivity growth rates? Since the total labor productivity growth rate for the whole economy is a slightly complicated weighted average of the labor productivity growth rates for each industry, the answer had to lie within individual industries.

The conventional wisdom about the answer was clear. In 1987, Bob Solow had quipped, "You can see the computer age everywhere but in the productivity statistics" (Exhibit 4.1). Now that we saw the productivity statistics dramatically improve, most people automatically assumed that the computer age was finally showing up in the statistics. This was easy to assume since the growth rate in investment in information technology increased from 11 percent to 20 percent, starting in 1995. Everybody began to say the United States had a new economy caused by computers and the Internet, and everybody believed it because everybody else was saying it.

This issue attracted the attention of several of the most respected economists in academia, as well as at the Federal Reserve. They, of course, took their traditional approach of running regressions between productivity growth rates and many other variables, including investment in information technology. They also tried to account for the increased labor productivity growth in terms of capital stock increases and business cycle effects. All these approaches have problems. Because of the massive investments in computers and other information technology equipment in the second half of the '90s, the amount of capital stock increased faster than average. However, just because the growth in capital stock accelerated at the same time that productivity growth accelerated does not mean that the capital acceleration caused the productivity acceleration. It depends on how the capital was used. It turns out that much of that information technology capital, especially in telecommunications, is still not being used. The consequences of all that capital investment can really be understood only by investigating how it was used in each industry.

The results of the traditional economic analysis were contradictory and unconvincing. The most optimistic analysis came from the Council of Economic Advisers in January 2001. That report claimed there were no business cycle effects in the statistics and that the productivity acceleration had come from the production and widespread application of information technology. At the other extreme, Robert Gordon at Northwestern claimed the productivity acceleration came only from the production of information technology equipment and from business cycle effects.

The difference in points of view was critically important. The growth of the U.S. economy depends primarily on the labor productivity growth rate. Whether the high growth rates of the late 1990s will continue depends heavily on what caused them in the first place. Unfortunately, many people assumed that just because two factors move together in the regression analysis that the change in one factor was causing the change in the other factor. The most obvious potential error was to assume that because the big increase in information technology investment occurred at the same time as the acceleration in the labor productivity growth rate, the investment increase caused the productivity acceleration. Many people made this error.

This error caused the Council of Economic Advisers and the Congressional Budget Office to project that the labor productivity growth rates of the late 1990s would extend over most of the next decade. These projections mechanically resulted in projections of huge U.S. government budget surpluses. The surpluses were so large that all government debt would be wiped out over the next decade or two. For a very short time in 2001, we actually were worried about how we were going to conduct monetary policy without a U.S. Treasury bond market. We didn't worry about this very long. The projections of huge budget surpluses opened the window for a debate over whether the government should collect all the tax revenue from current law just to generate surpluses or whether we should have a tax cut. In the end, we got a big tax cut building up over the next ten years. At the same time, it became clear that the projections of surpluses based on the productivity growth rates of the late 1990s were unrealistic. The conclusions I give in this chapter contributed to this reassessment. Thus, after the tax cut and after reassessment, we're facing deficits rather than surpluses. It's doubtful that the tax cut would have made it if the tax cut had been seen as creating deficits as opposed to simply reducing surpluses. The new economy hype of the late 1990s will haunt us for some time to come.

The Economic Frontier

The United States is the productivity leader in virtually every industry. The only significant exceptions are automotive, steel, machine tools, and consumer electronics in Japan and retail banking in the Netherlands. Moreover, the United States has achieved these high productivity levels and created enough jobs to have an unemployment rate half of Europe's and about the same as Japan's.

Most of our work has been in the "market" part of the economy. This is the part where consumers can determine the value, including quality considerations, of the goods and services offered. Consumers can compare the value of the product and the price and decide whether to make the purchase. In these circumstances, price is a good indicator of the relative value of goods and services if there is competition among firms. If there is little or no competition, then relative prices are distorted because firms can charge what they want to and prices are not set at the balance of value to customer and cost to produce.

The market part of the economy accounts for about 70 percent of GDP. The remaining 30 percent is made up of health care, education, and government services. Of these, health care is the most market-like in the United States. Moreover, practically speaking, there is some hope of defining a meaningful measure of the product of health care. No convincing concept has been found for measuring the products of education and government services. Thus, we really can't measure economic performance in those parts of the GDP. Thus, in this chapter I will summarize our findings on the performance of the market part of the U.S. economy in the late 1990s and also give the results of our separate study on the productivity of the health care systems of Germany, the United Kingdom, and the United States.

New Economy?

In the second half of the 1990s, only six of the sixty sectors making up the U.S. economy accounted for about 75 percent of the total gross productivity growth acceleration of all sectors with some productivity acceleration. These six sectors were wholesale trade, retail trade, security brokers, microprocessors, computer assembly, and mobile telephone services. Many sectors had small productivity growth decelerations such that the total net productivity growth acceleration for the whole economy was almost exactly equal to the productivity acceleration in the six sectors. Thus an explanation of the productivity acceleration in the six sectors gives a very good explanation of the overall productivity growth acceleration.

Of course, it's a little unnerving that the whole new economy question boiled down to what happened in just six of sixty industries. Just how unusual was this? How had productivity growth occurred before the 1990s? Did most sectors just uniformly improve productivity, or did sectors increase productivity in fits and starts? The answer is both surprising and revealing about the nature of productivity growth. First of all, the number of sectors with significant productivity accelerations in the period from 1995 to 2000 was not unusual. It was about average. Thus the focus on six sectors should not be surprising.

What was unusual about the six sectors was that they either had an extraordinarily high productivity acceleration (microprocessors, computer assembly, mobile telephone services, and security brokers) or they had unusually large amounts of employment (wholesale trade, retail trade). In either case, each separate sector made a significant contribution to the productivity growth acceleration. Taken together then, the six sectors explain most of the unusually strong U.S. economic performance in the second half of the 1990s. Thus it should not have been all that surprising that if productivity acceleration occurred, it occurred in a few "jumping" sectors. Thus, in retrospect it is not surprising that the overall acceleration occurred because the sectors that jumped either had unusually big jumps or the size of the sectors was unusually large.

Of course, productivity jumps are necessarily associated with an abrupt acceleration in the rate of improvement in a sector. These abrupt changes are likely to be associated with the effects of innovations. After all, innovations are about better products and services and better ways of producing them. Again, it was tempting to imagine that all the jumps were caused by the computer and Internet innovations taking place all around us. This conjecture is true to only a limited extent.

The only productivity jumps in the six sectors that were "new economy" in nature were online securities trading and mobile telephone services. Online securities trading was not possible without the Internet. Mobile telephone services only became widely used in the United States after the application of digital electronics technology made possible by computer controlled switches and other communication technology innovations. Perhaps the most surprising finding of the whole study was that the productivity acceleration in microprocessors was not caused by technological innovation; it was the result of traditional microeconomic competitive dynamics. In the middle 1990s, Intel, challenged by a competitor for the first time, changed its product line strategy to bring its more powerful chips to the market faster. This action alone abruptly increased the value of the microprocessor chips sold to the market. Since these microprocessors determine the power of PCs, the products of the computer assembly industry also abruptly increased in value. The productivity growth in both sectors accelerated.

In the general merchandise part of retail trade, Wal-Mart's innovative way of retailing had captured a sufficiently large market share by 1995 that Wal-Mart's competitors faced a choice of either getting as good as Wal-Mart or going out of business. Many began to accelerate their rate of productivity improvement in an attempt to match Wal-Mart. That caused a productivity growth acceleration. Finally, the biggest contribution to productivity growth acceleration of a sector came from wholesale trade. In the early 1980s in the United States, wholesale trade was still a fragmented, nonindustrialized business. For a variety of reasons, including the threat that big retailers were bypassing them, the wholesale industry began to industrialize by investing in such early twentieth-century technologies as conveyor belts, and to convert from paper systems to computer-based electronic systems, as had been done by many sectors of the economy in the 1970s and '80s. This is not exactly new economy stuff.

Now What?

All these innovations have some life left. Their continued application will keep productivity growth above average certainly for the next five years. However, all innovations have a finite life; once virtually everybody is using them, they have no place else to be applied and the rate of improvement associated with their application goes away. Some of the other causes of productivity acceleration in the six sectors have already gone away. The value of asset manager services included in security brokers is proportional to the value of the assets managed. An increase in the stock market value automatically translates into productivity improvement. Since 1999, the stock market has gone down, not up, and nobody expects it to grow over the next five years the way it did in the second half of the 1990s. Thus this source of productivity growth acceleration has already disappeared.

Moreover, the United States had made a massive one-time investment in information technology infrastructure. Some of this one-time investment was caused by the standardization of client-server computer architecture around Microsoft operating system software. This standardization required a huge one-time increase in computer system power. Now the infrastructure is in place and the standardization has occurred. Thus the rate at which companies and individuals will have to upgrade their computer systems has decreased. Fewer microprocessors and PCs will be sold. The reduction in the production growth rates will reduce the rate of productivity growth.

When all these factors are taken together, we estimated that productivity growth in the United States over the next five years would still be somewhat above the twenty-five-year average, but almost certainly below the high rate of growth of the second half of the 1990s. Moreover, it's impossible to tell what will happen after that. It all depends on things that are not visible to us yet. What is clear is that the United States got carried away with the new economy hype. We thought we were going to be a lot richer than we will likely be. Under the circumstances, it's easy to see how those big budget surpluses became big deficits, especially after a tax cut agreed upon because many believed we really did have a new economy.

Microprocessor Chips and Computers: More Competition, Not Moore's Law

The manufacturing of microprocessor computer chips and the manufacturing of computers based on these chips contributed 20 percent of the total productivity growth acceleration in the second half of the 1990s. In the context of the entire economy, these are tiny industries. The semiconductor industry, including all memory chips as well as microprocessors, has only 0.16 percent of total U.S. employment. Computer manufacturing has only 0.07 percent. Thus, in these industries, 0.23 percent of all employment contributed 20 percent of the total productivity growth acceleration.

The only way this can be possible is for the productivity growth jumps in these industries to be huge. And they were. In semiconductors, the productivity growth rate jumped by 22 percentage points starting in 1995, and in computer manufacturing, it jumped by 33 percentage points. These jumps were even more astounding because they came on top of an extraordinarily high base productivity growth rate. In the period from 1987 to 1995, productivity growth in semiconductors was 43 percent per year, and in computer manufacturing, 27 percent. During this entire period, the number of employees stayed about the same, increasing slightly in semiconductors and decreasing slightly in computer manufacturing. Thus, virtually all the productivity growth and the productivity growth jump has to be explained by increases in the total value of the products produced by these industries.

So what happened? Well, the number of computers manufactured grew at a high rate of about 15 percent per year throughout the 1987–95 period. However, the growth rate had only a tiny jump of about 2 percentage points in 1995. The huge change came in the value of each computer produced. The growth rate of that value jumped 24 percentage points (from 7 percent per year to 31 percent per year) starting in 1995. This increase in the value of computers came almost entirely from the increased capability of the microprocessors in the computers.

The story of how we know how much the value of each computer increased is a success story for U.S. government statistics and economic analysis. After all, the most obvious data that might tell us something about how the value of computers was changing, namely the computer prices, were decreasing not increasing. The rate of decrease actually accelerated in 1995 from minus 5 percent per year to minus 10 percent per year. At the same time, it was obvious that the computers we were buying were rapidly becoming more powerful. I am right now dictating the manuscript of this book using voice recognition software. To achieve an acceptable error rate and computer reaction time with my diction requires a 700 MHz computer. Thus, I could be producing this manuscript this way only since about late 1999. My computer is certainly not less valuable to me even though McKinsey paid less for it than for the computer it bought me four years ago.

Taxpayer Money Well Spent

The Bureau of Economic Analysis (BEA) in the U.S. Department of Commerce has worked out the appropriate adjustment factor for the actual computer price data to calculate the real value of the computer. The calculation of the adjustment factor starts with the collection of an enormous amount of data about the different prices consumers are prepared to pay at one point in time for computers with widely varying capabilities. From this data the BEA calculates how much the increments in capability are worth to us. The government statisticians also gather data about how much the performance characteristics of computers change from year to year. They apply the information about how much the increased capability is worth to calculate how much the value of the computer has really gone up. This same technique applied to semiconductors shows that virtually all the productivity growth jump comes from a jump in the capabilities of microprocessors shipped starting in 1995. This work is a good example of a valuable government service. Without this work by the U.S. Department of Commerce, we would have no idea of what was really happening in the overall computer and semiconductor industries.

Since the jump in computer capability came primarily from the jump in microprocessor capability, we need to know what happened in microprocessors. In the past couple of years, many people have just assumed that the jump in microprocessor capability starting in 1995 had to come from "Moore's Law." Gordon Moore, a founder of Intel, predicted in the early 1960s that the number of transistors that semiconductor manufacturers could fit onto a single chip would roughly double every eighteen months. The industry developed so consistently at this rate that Moore's prediction became known as Moore's Law. The problem with the assumption that Moore's Law caused the productivity growth acceleration in microprocessors is that Moore's Law predicts a constant rate of growth of capability, not an accelerating rate of growth. There is some question about whether Moore's Law accelerated towards the end of the 1990s; the evidence is inconclusive. What is conclusive is that competitive dynamics in the microprocessor industry caused Intel in the late 1990s to shorten the time between its introduction of state-of-the-art microprocessors.

Prior to 1996, the chip manufacturer Advanced Micro Devices (AMD) operated under a disputed licensing agreement through which it produced some of Intel's chip designs and paid royalties to Intel. Moreover, AMD had to wait for Intel to set the microprocessor standard before releasing chips of its own design. However, in January 1996, the disputed licensing agreement was settled, and AMD acquired the right to manufacture many of Intel's chip architectures. The lag time between Intel's and AMD's introductions of equally capable chips was reduced from about twenty months around 1995 to ten months by 1998 and essentially disappeared by 2000. Intel's competitive response was to develop designs which AMD had no legal right to produce and to bring state-of-the-art microprocessors to the market more frequently.

If state-of-the-art microprocessors are brought to the market more frequently, then the average chip sold moves closer to the technological limit set by Moore's Law. An acceleration in the capability of the total basket of chips sold would occur. This acceleration caused the productivity growth rate acceleration in microprocessors in the late 1990s. Of course, this accelerated rate of productivity growth cannot continue indefinitely. As the overall basket of chips gets closer to the technological frontier, the growth rate has to slow and go back to the growth rate allowed by Moore's Law. Most of this accelerated productivity growth rate will be sustainable through 2005. After that, the growth rate will inevitably slow down.

It is ironic that in perhaps the most "new economy" of all sectors the accelerated productivity growth rate of the late 1990s came not from anything new but from a straightforward increase in competitive intensity. It's nice to see that the most fundamental force causing economic development applies at the very cutting edge of the economic frontier.

Retailing and Wholesaling: The Wal-Mart Effect

Retailing and wholesaling contributed 50 percent of the entire U.S. productivity growth rate jump in the second half of the 1990s. Productivity growth in retailing jumped by 4.3 percentage points, from 2.0 percent to 6.3 percent. Productivity growth in wholesaling jumped by 5.3 percentage points, from 2.9 percent to 8.2 percent. These jumps came in huge economic sectors. Retailing has 11 percent of all U.S. employment, and wholesaling, 6 percent. When almost 20 percent of U.S. employment has a productivity growth jump of 4 to 5 percentage points, the national productivity statistics take notice.

Of course, retailing and wholesaling have several subsectors. The findings here are for a sample. In retailing, the sample is general merchandise, which has about 15 percent of total retail sales. Even so, its total sales in 1999 were $379 billion.

The productivity growth jump in general merchandise retailing was caused by the "Wal-Mart Effect." The innovation of Wal-Mart, started by Sam Walton in Bentonville, Arkansas, in the early 1960s, showed up in the national productivity statistics in the second half the 1990s. General merchandise retailing contributed 16 percent of retail trade's contribution to the national productivity growth jump. That amounts to about 4 percent of the total national jump. Virtually all that 4 percent was caused by Wal-Mart.

Just as I am writing this part of the manuscript, the Fortune 500 has been released showing that Wal-Mart now has the largest sales of any company worldwide. This is the first time a service firm of any kind has been No. 1. For years, the company with the largest sales has been an auto company, General Motors, or an oil company, either Exxon Mobil or Royal Dutch Shell. If nothing else, this transition marks the age of the service economy. On top of this, Forbes has just issued its list of the ten richest people on earth. Of course, the list included Bill Gates and Paul Allen, the founders of Microsoft. The most notable characteristic of the list, however, was that four people had the same last name. That name was Walton. Thus, the second half of the 1990s was more the day of Sam Walton than it was of Bill Gates.

Many of us who live in city centers and consider shopping a waste of time know much more about the products of Microsoft than about the services of Wal-Mart. As I drove through the suburbs of Washington or down Interstate 81 by the rural Virginia towns in the Shenandoah Valley, I of course noticed the appearance of the huge Wal-Mart stores. I went into one of these when I was moving my mother into an assisted-living apartment in Blacksburg, Virginia, and I needed picture hangers.

First of all, the floors were gleaming, they were so clean. Second, the cross aisles were so long that I could not see from one end to the other. How could I ever find anything here amidst the acres of clothes, sporting goods, food, gardening products, and hardware? One question to a smiling, readily apparent salesperson solved that problem. I found picture hangers in all the sizes I wanted and noticed that the racks for the sizes I didn't need were also full. Checkout was no sweat. On top of all this, I left knowing I had gotten the lowest prices possible. I began to understand why Wal-Mart has been so successful.

One Company Moves the Economy

Wal-Mart caused the national productivity statistics to move in the second half of the 1990s because it had gotten so good that its competitors faced the choice of either becoming about as good as Wal-Mart or going out of business. In 1987, Wal-Mart had 9 percent of the general merchandise market. However, it had a 44 percent productivity advantage over the rest of this subsector (Exhibit 4.2). By 1995, Wal-Mart had a 27 percent market share and had increased its productivity advantage slightly. Starting in 1995, Wal-Mart accelerated its productivity growth

Exhibit 4.2: Wal-Mart Sales and Productivity

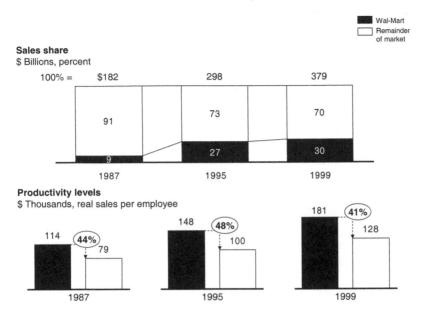

rate from 3.3 percent per year to 5.1 percent per year. The competition, however, increased its productivity at an even higher rate of 6.4 percent per year. When Wal-Mart captured 27 percent of the market in 1995, it could no longer be ignored. The race for survival was on. By 1999, Wal-Mart had increased its market share only slightly, to 30 percent. One-third of the productivity growth jump in general merchandise retailing came from Wal-Mart's accelerated rate of improvement. Two-thirds came from the competitive reaction of Sears, Costco, Target, Meijer, Kohl's, MacFrugals, etc. By 1999, the rest of the subsector had become about as productive as Wal-Mart had been in 1990.

How important was information technology in the general merchandise productivity growth acceleration of the second half of the 1990s? Well, the most important causal factor of this jump was that Wal-Mart forced the rest of the general merchandise subsector to adopt the "big box" store. Wal-Mart invented the big box store back in the 1960s, when information technology was too primitive to be a major factor in the innovation. The idea of big stores with regional distribution centers providing the wholesaling function was a simple business innovation not dependent on new applications of technology beyond the telephone and the fax machine. That innovation alone had the potential to wipe out all the mom-and-pop stores in the United States. Over the next thirty years, this is what happened. By the 1990s, all that was left was random general merchandise chains with stores of varying size and efficiency. There were exceptions. Sears had tried its own innovation for longer than even Wal-Mart. Kmart made a weak attempt to imitate Wal-Mart. By the 1990s, it was clear that the Wal-Mart innovation was the winner.

Of course, Wal-Mart got better and better over the years. Wal-Mart was the leader in the use of information technology in retailing and pioneered a number of IT applications. These applications include use of computers to track inventory in distribution centers (1969), scanning using standard barcodes (1980), radio frequency (RF) guns to track merchandise (late 1980s), and complicated electronic data and satellite communications systems to manage logistics and keep the right items in the stores and in stock (late 1980s, early 1990s). These applications involve old IT and provided the basis for Wal-Mart's accelerated improvement in the 1990s. Thus one thing is for sure. The Wal-Mart success was not because of information technologies typically associated with the "new economy." These technologies are the Internet and the PC and computer server architecture standardized on the Microsoft operating system. Since the competitive reaction of the rest of the subsector in the late 1990s to Wal-Mart brought everybody else up to about where Wal-Mart was in 1990, that reaction was also based on old IT.

Because Wal-Mart has shown that much higher productivity is possible in general merchandise retailing, the rest of the subsector will go on improving for several years. Moreover, Wal-Mart's current improvement rate is so high that the frontier will also keep moving. However, the rate of improvement will inevitably decline, once virtually the entire sector has converted to the big box store. It has taken more than thirty years for the full effects of this innovation to be felt in the economy. It should not be surprising for these strong effects to last for ten years. However, after that, another innovation will have to take over or the rate of improvement will decline. Perhaps it will be Internet sales. One thing is for sure, however. Internet sales were not the story in the late 1990s. Internet sales contributed roughly 2 percent of the overall retail productivity growth jump. In the late 1990s, the story was Wal-Mart.

1920s Industrialization, Not New Economy

The Wal-Mart effect goes beyond retailing into wholesaling. I described earlier in the chapter on Japan how modern retailers have caused improvement in wholesaling and consumer goods manufacturers. These modern retailers saw an opportunity to bypass the inefficient, monopolistic wholesaling sector and acquire goods much more cheaply. Wal-Mart set up its own distribution centers, which bought directly from manufacturers. Modern food supermarkets did the same thing. A few wholesalers noticed and realized they were going to have to compete. We studied this reaction in detail for pharmaceuticals. This subsector has led the way for the rest of the industry.

McKesson was the only national pharmaceuticals wholesaler in 1992. Dramatic consolidation in the industry over the past twenty years has resulted in four companies having 95 percent of the market by the end of the 1990s. Pharmaceuticals wholesalers found that consolidating warehouses and improving their operations led to a much lower cost configuration than the previously fragmented system. The scale allowed the mechanization of the movement of goods in the warehouses, and with mechanization came automation. The story reminds me of the dramatic change in the Japanese machine tool industry that resulted from standardization. There it was government action of standardization that caused industrialization and then automation. In U.S. wholesaling, it was competitive pressure from retailers going into wholesaling.

Wholesaling is a remarkably simple business. Goods that come in one side are resorted and shipped out the other side. The industry was naturally monopolistic because one wholesaler could provide all the needs of a local market for one line of products. These wholesalers grew up with paper-based systems for managing the business and legwork and carts for moving the goods around. Without fundamentally new business innovation, scale advantages of trying to serve a larger market would be more than offset by increased transportation costs. And there were virtually no scale advantages from adding additional product lines. All the current wholesalers were happy with this highly profitable situation. They had no incentive to spoil the party. It would take an outsider. Finally, that outsider came as retailers got big enough to say enough is enough. They brought wholesaling into the industrial age.

It's amazing that this process only gained momentum in the 1990s. Only about 25 percent of the wholesaling industry had been converted by 2000. Thus, the very rapid rate of productivity growth in wholesaling is going to continue for the next five to ten years. After that, innovation will have penetrated most of the wholesaling sector. Then productivity growth will slow, unless another equally powerful innovation comes along in the sector.

Many people in the United States have been surprised that in the midst of all the new economy hype, the biggest contributions to the improved U.S. economic performance in the second half of the 1990s came from a 1920s-like industrialization of wholesaling and from a business innovation originating in Bentonville, Arkansas. It has been even more surprising to people outside the United States. There, economies are virtually synonymous with the production of goods. How consumer wishes are taken into account and how goods get into consumer hands are considered matters of little importance. By and large they have a producer mentality. It's different in the United States. Consumers are king. It should not be surprising then that the biggest story in the U.S. economy over the past twenty-five years and the biggest contributor to the improved U.S. economic performance in the second half of the '90s has been the sector closest to the customer. That sector of course is retailing. Not only did retailing improve its own performance, but its innovations spilled over to revolutionize wholesaling too.

Health Care: The Elephant at the Table

Health care was never part of the "new economy" story in the United States. Health care is widely considered to be the most problematic sector in the U.S. economy. It is huge. The United States spends 14 percent of its GDP on health care. The most any other country spends is 10 percent. Since the GDP per capita in all other advanced countries is 25 to 30 percent below that of the United States, the United States devotes twice as many resources to health care as any other country on a per capita basis. Yet, our newspapers are full of stories about the inadequacies of our health care system.

Many of these stories are about the plight of the 30-some million Americans without health insurance. Hospital emergency rooms are required to treat these people when they are sick or injured. And they do so at substantial cost. However, a serious issue is that the uninsured clearly do not get health checkups and health maintenance services. If they did, the United States would be even more out of line with the rest of the world on health care spending. Whether the United States will provide universal coverage is a political question, not an economic one.

The crudest measure of health care performance suggests the United States is not getting its money's worth. Average life expectancy in the United States is below that of many advanced countries, most notably Japan. However, life expectancy depends not only on the interventions of the health care system but also on the shape of the population it has to work on. Lifestyles in Japan are healthier than in the United States.

The proper way to measure the performance of health care is to measure the difference it makes in the quality of life of people who come for help. We simply do not know how to do this. No government agency, university, or hospital systematically measures the results of health care. Thus we have no nationwide accounting for the products and services delivered by health care. We can't tell by how much those products and services grow each year nor can we tell how the total compares with other countries. All we know is how much we spend. What we need to know is whether the higher level of spending means the United States is much less productive in health care than other countries.

In an attempt to test the limits of knowledge here, we studied the treatment of four diseases—diabetes, cholelithiasis (gallstones), breast cancer, and lung cancer—in three countries: Germany, the United Kingdom, and the United States. These three countries were the only countries for which comparable data existed for these diseases, either nationwide or for large regions. Even then we could not get data for diabetes in Germany. For the cancer cases we used an output measure of life expectancy after treatment. For diabetes and cholelithiasis, which have low mortality rates, we used a complex index developed by others to measure the quality of life after treatment. None of these measures of the products and services of health care are very good. However, they are a lot better than nothing, and good enough to tell us whether the United States is much less productive in these diseases than other countries. For the resources used in health care, we counted the "real" operational resources devoted to disease treatment. We counted such things as doctor and nurse hours, pharmaceutical consumption, hospital capital costs, etc.

Surprisingly Good Productivity

The results were counterintuitive. The United States is more productive in all these diseases except for diabetes in the United Kingdom. The reasons for this result can be traced directly to the huge differences in the way the health care sector is organized and governed across these three countries. The UK health care system is almost entirely government owned and run. The government has maintained very tight budget control of the system, and doctors are mostly government employees on salaries. The result has been that the United Kingdom has not invested as quickly in technologies that have dramatically improved the diagnostic capabilities of medicine and significantly reduced recovery time. For instance, the United Kingdom was slower than the United States in adopting laparoscopic surgery. (Laparoscopic surgery is done with tiny surgical instruments and a tiny flexible scope with a light, all inserted through a small incision to minimize tissue damage.) As a result, the United Kingdom had to keep cholelithiasis patients in the hospital considerably longer than the United States. The United Kingdom did not invest as much in CT scanning of lung cancer patients. Their cancers were not staged as well. The result was that lung cancer surgery was performed on a less optimal set of patients. On the other hand, the centrally managed UK system took a life cycle approach to the treatment of diabetes, a long-term disease. Most of the resources used in the treatment of diabetes come from the treatment of complications, which usually show up after many years of the disease. The United Kingdom invests more in early treatment of diabetes and thus has a lower complication rate.

Germany, on the other hand, has a system more like the United States had twenty years ago. In Germany, medical expenses are paid for on a task-by-task basis for services of doctors and hospitals. As a result, hospitals in Germany have no financial incentive to reduce length of stay. As I noted in the chapter on Japan, average length of stay in hospitals in Germany is eleven days, compared with six in the United States.

High Prices and Administrative Nightmare

So if the United States is more productive in health care than Germany and the United Kingdom, why does it spend so much more? The spending total in the United States is the result of having an extremely complicated system based on the principles that have been so successful in the market part of the U.S. economy. These principles are to have as much private ownership, profit incentive, and competition as possible and to use price cap regulation to correct for market failures. (The market fails in health care because patients cannot judge the quality of their care and thus cannot stimulate competition among care providers by bargaining over price. Moreover, because the incidence of the need of health care is highly variable, insurance systems are needed. Thus, there is no natural limit on the demand for health care services because patients are paying insurance premiums and not directly for the services they ask for.) The result has been doctors operating as thousands of small businesses, a large health care insurance industry, and micromanagement of health care by the government and insurance companies. In the midst all this, patients (and sometimes doctors) feel a great loss of control. They are overwhelmed by the monstrosity we have built.

The large health care insurance industry and the government health care insurance schemes for the elderly and the poor generate tons of paperwork in the reimbursement process. This paperwork is especially burdensome for the tiny administrative operations in doctors' offices. The net result is that the administrative expenses of running the U.S. health care system are at least one-third higher than in any other country. On top of this, the salaries of health care workers and the prices of pharmaceuticals and other supplies are much higher in the United States. The United States pays its doctors twice as much as Germany and the United Kingdom. Most of this income difference is readily understandable. Average professional wages in the United States are 25 percent higher than in Germany and 40 percent higher than in the United Kingdom. Moreover, it shouldn't be surprising that doctors' incomes in the United States exceed those in Germany and the United Kingdom by more than the U.S. professional average exceeds the averages in those countries. Doctors in Germany and the United Kingdom are mostly salaried government employees, who are paid well below private sector levels. Thus the expenses of administering the insurance schemes and the thousands of small doctors' practices seem to be the problem.

The other side of this coin is that the United States gets far more competition in its health care industry. Doctors and hospitals do compete for patients. Patient satisfaction is a big deal for hospitals these days. Moreover, the "price cap" regulation introduced by the government insurance sets a limit on the total reimbursement for a case of a specific disease. This type of regulation has been very successful in the United States in creating incentives in the telecommunications and electricity generation sectors to reduce costs through improving productivity. It is working the same way in health care. Hence the reduction of length of stay in U.S. hospitals to about half the time of Germany and the United Kingdom and 25 percent of the time in Japan.

This price cap regulation seems to have achieved much of the effects that we might expect from the profit incentive under competition. In the end, not-for-profit hospitals have about the same incentive because they have to struggle to avoid running out of cash under the price caps. Moreover, for-profit health care providers seem to be especially vulnerable to the charge that they are cutting corners on health care to earn a dollar. We don't care if cookie manufacturers might be doing this to us. We can simply stop buying from them. We can't stop buying health care. Thus price caps are working pretty well. However, the system has to be much more complex than for telecommunications and electricity. In those industries, the price caps apply to telephone calls and kilowatt hours.

These products are much simpler than the huge variety of complicated diseases and procedures in health care. Thus the big question is whether the extra costs of administering such a system in health care are worth it.

This is a big experiment the United States is conducting, and we will have to wait and see how it comes out. We will see it through to the end, however. There is no taste in the United States for a government run system like the one in the United Kingdom. Doctors and patients want more freedom than such a system allows. The German system is no option because under it, health care costs would explode in the United States. The only direction for reducing administrative costs in the United States is to simplify insurance schemes and consolidate doctors' practices. The simplification of insurance schemes seems feasible, although it would require legislative intervention to cause it to occur. It would amount to the government's creating standards for an industry when the industry didn't do it for itself. The benefits would be substantial and this should probably be done.

The conversion of doctors' small practices into large professional corporations with central administrative services and performance evaluation systems for the distribution of income seems a long way off. Doctors could do this at any time. So far, they haven't wanted to and nobody is going to make them. I don't think patients want it either. We keep wanting a lot of freedom about which doctor to see. That's understandable. Nothing is more important to us than health care. Nor is information technology going to solve important aspects of the administrative cost problem. IT will help move all the information around faster and without error. However, much of the administrative cost is caused by disputes arising in the micromanagement of health care. These disputes are a necessary consequence of an insurance system trying to cover a large and complex array of services under the price controls of a price cap system. Thus, trying to use the fundamentals of the market economy in the United States for the health care system seems terrible, until you look at all the alternatives.

Competition Is Good for Consumers

The OECD GDP per capita data show that the gap between the United States and the other advanced economies is large and has been growing over the past ten years. Moreover, our analysis of productivity growth and the demographic facts of life indicate it is likely that the gap will continue to grow over the next ten years. After that, nobody knows. We do know that the sources of the productivity growth acceleration in the United States in the second half of the 1990s will dissipate over the next five to ten years. Other sources of acceleration might take their place. We just don't know. However, at the beginning of the twenty-first century, the U.S. economy seems to be in a class by itself. Why is that?

Not much can be said about fundamental causality for demographic changes. Moreover, the United States may very well be following the European path with a ten- to twenty-year lag. We can, however, say something about causality for the accelerated productivity growth in the United States. Our case studies showed that the fundamental cause was increased competitive intensity. AMD began to compete head-to-head with Intel. Wal-Mart forced other general merchandise retailers to accelerate their rate of improvement or go out of business. In telecommunications services, a case I have not discussed in detail, increases in competitive intensity forced the price of digital telephone services down to the point that use of mobile telephones exploded in the United States. Sure, the application of lower-cost digital technology made the price reduction possible. However, it was not happening while U.S. regulation allowed only two mobile service providers in each region. With the auctioning of more spectrum and the resulting competition among seven to eight potential providers, prices declined dramatically.

Of course, some of these productivity accelerations are possible because of innovations. Some are technical innovations, such as digital mobile telephone service. Others are ordinary-looking business innovations. Wal-Mart and industrialized wholesaling are like this. No work has satisfactorily explained why innovations occur when and where they do. However, under increased competitive intensity, superior innovations win out more quickly. Productivity increases faster and so does GDP per capita.

So why does the United States have higher competitive intensity? I think the reasons go a long way back. *The United States adopted the view that the purpose of an economy was to serve consumers much earlier than any other society.* The United States continues to hold this view more strongly than almost any other place. Other countries take more of the view that economies are about firms that produce and workers in those firms. In these countries, economic policy choices are considered more heavily in terms of the effects changes will have on firms and workers. In the United States, the effect on consumers is considered the most important. In the United States, it is easier to get agreement on constructive economic policy changes that will benefit consumers. After all, everybody is a consumer. In other countries, economic policy changes that benefit firms often hurt workers, at least in the short term, and vice versa. Thus, it is more difficult to reach agreement.

Why Competition Matters

Of course, Adam Smith explained in the late eighteenth century the mechanism of how economies work to benefit consumers more. One firm figures out how to make a more valuable product at little extra cost. The firm can charge customers a price reflecting the increased value of the product. The firm then makes a larger profit because its profit now becomes the difference between the new higher price and its costs, which increased little. However, other firms notice these higher profits and begin to produce the more valuable product themselves. To take sales away from the first firm, the new firms have to price the product lower. This is price competition.

This process has no stopping point until the prices get so low that profits are just barely acceptable. Of course, with the lower prices, consumers buy more and more of the more valuable product, which takes about the same amount of hours worked to produce as the old product. If we keep track of the higher value of the product, then we will measure a productivity improvement.

If this economy had had a producer-and-worker orientation, it might have protected the innovative firm from competition which would threaten its position. The economy might have prevented new firms from entering the market to make the new product because firms making the old product would go out of business and their workers would have to change jobs or be unemployed. The net result would be that fewer workers would end up making the new product and productivity would not increase as much. Of course, in this case a few people end up being better off than in the high-competition economy. However, in the high-competition economy, far more people are somewhat better off and the total gain is greater.

This analysis has always made me feel better about the extraordinarily high compensation of chief executive officers in the United States compared with the rest of the world. If done right, compensation is used as an incentive for executives to innovate or to follow quickly the innovations of others. Intense competition ensures that most of the value of innovations will go to the consumer. Even the highest compensation is a tiny fraction of the value created by many business and technical innovations. The problem with executive compensation in the United States is not with this idea. The problem is that in many cases the high compensation levels persist even when innovations do not occur and reactions to the innovations of others are slow.

Deep Historical Roots

So where did this consumer orientation in the United States come from? I have admired Gordon Wood's analysis in his book *The Radicalism of the American Revolution,* which came out in 1991. This analysis describes the difference between eighteenth-century societies in Europe and the United States, just as economies were evolving beyond agriculture to the production of goods and services. This transition began because productivity in agriculture had improved to the point that agricultural workers produced more than they needed to feed their families. Thus farmers traded their surplus of food to townspeople for goods and services. The difference was that in Europe, the farmers were big landowners, in a social class to themselves. Since agricultural workers worked for them, they owned the agricultural surplus. Thus initially in Europe, consumption of goods and services was a privilege of the aristocracy. The purpose of agricultural workers was to produce food and the purpose of craftsmen in towns was to produce goods and services for this aristocracy.

In contrast, in eighteenth-century America, the agricultural surplus belonged to a few million independent farmers. They became the first consumers in America. Moreover, if they could be consumers, then independent craftsmen in towns could be too. Thus in America, consumption was a privilege of the middle class. Gordon Wood describes how these conditions led to an explosion of entrepreneurial, adversarial, and competitive economic behavior following the American Revolution. That's more than two hundred years ago. Things have changed hugely in Europe too. However, vestiges of the producer-and-worker orientation linger.

In the past couple of decades, a new contention has arisen in Europe about why Europe has little to learn from the United States. That contention is that the entrepreneurial, adversarial, and competitive American economy is "soulless." I'm not sure what "soulless" means. I think it means that if you are spending your time suing somebody or competing with them intensely, you cannot have a genuine personal connection with them. That's probably true. However, competition is a natural way aggression is expressed. Americans are aggressive people. But so are Europeans. I think the outlets for their aggression are more constrained, including in economic activity.

Perhaps these constraints come from a romantic view about human nature. I mean "romantic" in the philosophical sense. That we should be guided more by our emotions and our will rather than by our reason and our common sense. Romanticism has always been stronger on the Continent than in the United Kingdom and the United States. Isaiah Berlin, the highly respected Oxford don of political philosophy, spent much of his career educating us about this difference and its consequences. Romanticism seems to have led to both more utopian and more totalitarian views. It may have also led to somewhat deeper interpersonal relationships. However that may be, the price has been high at times. The practical, "unromantic" view is that consumer wishes never seem to be satisfied anywhere around the world, continuous attempts to satisfy those wishes cause productivity increases, competition stimulates more rapid productivity increases, and more productive societies replace less productive societies.

CHAPTER FIVE

Korea: Following Japan's Path

As I noted in chapter 1, Korea is one of the 23 middle-income countries in the world (Exhibit 5.1). I arbitrarily define middle-income countries as those with GDPs per capita between 25 and 70 percent of the GDP per capita in the United States. I pick this range because it is very wide yet only 340 million people live in countries within it. There are 5 billion people in the 111 countries below 25 percent and 800 million in the 18 countries in the relatively narrow range above 70 percent. I addressed in chapter 1 how the findings of this book explain why there are so few middle-income countries.

Korea's GDP per capita is now 47 percent of the GDP per capita in the United States. Korea helps us understand how a country can emerge from the group of poor countries. Korea also tells us something about where the Korean way of development leads.

The answer to both these questions is that Korea is following the Japanese development path (Exhibit 5.2). Koreans work very hard, save a lot of what they earn, and invest heavily in industries that have been favored by the government. These actions have caused record-breaking economic growth. In 1970, Korea's GDP per capita was $2,500 in to-day's dollars. In 1995, it was $12,600, or five times higher. It took the United States almost a hundred years (1857–1954) to cover this same ground. Japan did it slightly faster than Korea, taking twenty-one years (1952–1973).

However, in both Korea and Japan, protection of domestic manu-facturing industries and regulations constraining the development of services have resulted in low labor productivity and low return on cap-ital invested. Moreover, if anything, Korea has not developed as efficiently as Japan. Korea has not developed any world-class industries, as Japan did in automobiles and electronics. Thus, without further re-

Exhibit 5.1: World Distribution of GDP per Capita by Country

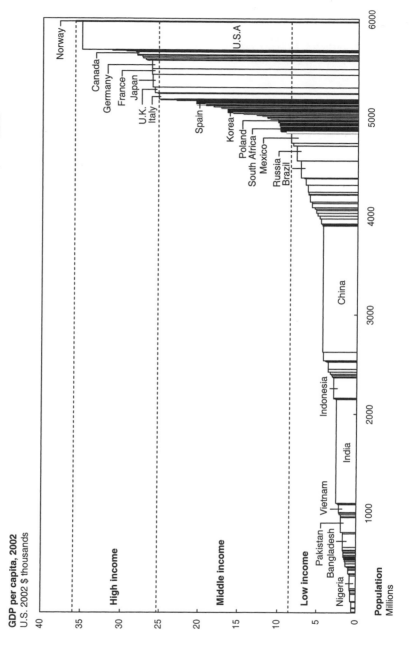

GDP per capita, 2002
U.S. 2002 $ thousands

■ Middle-income countries

High income

Middle income

Low income

Population
Millions

Exhibit 5.2: Economic Development Paths

Percent U.S. 1995 level

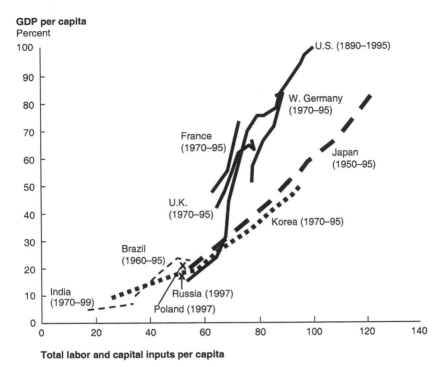

GDP per capita
Percent

Total labor and capital inputs per capita

form, Korea, like Japan, will inevitably began to stagnate as it approaches the economic frontier.

On a per capita basis, Koreans work 40 percent more hours than Americans do and even 20 percent more than the Japanese. However, its labor productivity is only 36 percent of that of the United States. Its capital inputs on a per capita basis are high for a middle-income country, although still only 47 percent of those in the United States. If Korea's hours worked and investments in buildings and equipment are added together, the total inputs to its economy are almost the same as for the United States on a per capita basis. Thus Korea is making the same economic effort as the United States. Yet Korea gets only half the economic benefit out of this effort that the United States does. Korea's overall productivity (total factor productivity) is 51 percent of that of the United

Exhibit 5.3: Components of GDP per Capita (PPP)

Index U.S. (1993–95 average) = 100

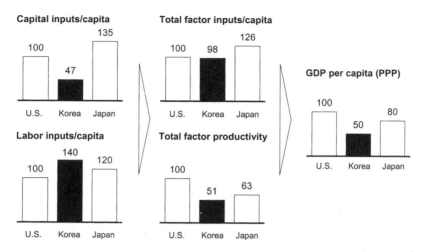

States (Exhibit 5.3). Thus Korea looks a lot like Japan, whose total factor productivity is only 63 percent of that of the United States.

Unlike Japan, Korea has already felt the adverse effects of following the Japanese development path. This happened with the financial crisis of 1998. Prior to that time, the government had directed that massive amounts of capital be applied in favored industries. The result was that the amount of capital available to each Korean worker in manufacturing as a whole was 80 percent of the U.S. number. In semiconductors, automotive, and confectionery, the amount of capital per worker was equal to that of the United States. However, in these industries the products produced were only about half the value of the products produced in the same industries in the United States. These circumstances caused the financial returns on private capital investments in Korea to be much lower than the corresponding returns in the United States, and slightly below the cost of debt, unlike in the United States and Japan (Exhibit 5.4).

Korea, Not Japan, Got the Financial Crisis

In an effort to accelerate development, Korea had borrowed significant amounts of capital for favored industries from Japanese, European, and U.S. banks. The financial crisis in Thailand in 1997 caused these banks

Exhibit 5.4: Return on Investment and Cost of Debt in the United States, Japan, and Korea

Average, 1981–95

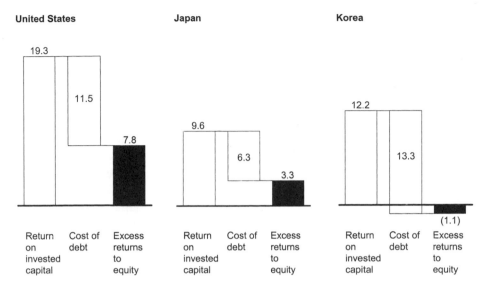

to look closely at the return on their investments in developing countries around the world. They did not like what they saw in Korea. As some Korean manufacturing firms went bankrupt because of their low capital productivity, the banks began to call in their loans. The Korean government ran out of reserves trying to protect the value of the currency, thus precipitating a foreign exchange crisis as the currency plummeted. The real economy was deeply affected because all businesses using imports suddenly found their costs to be dramatically higher. They could simply no longer conduct business in the usual way, because the prices at which they would have to sell their products and services would be higher than Koreans were willing to pay. This condition precipitated a substantial dislocation in the economy as businesses searched for domestic sources to replace high-cost imports and consumers stopped buying because the prices were too high. A disturbance of this magnitude takes many months or even a few years to work itself out to a new balance. The loss in standard of living is substantial.

The IMF of course came to the rescue with a loan to the government to rebuild reserves and a reform package requiring the banks to become independent of the government and trade barriers to be lowered to generate foreign competition with domestic manufacturing industries. If the IMF program had been followed, however, Korea would have traded a financial crisis for an employment crisis. Imported goods, especially from Japan, would have forced labor productivity to increase in Korean manufacturing and many jobs would have been shed. Moreover, efficient banks would have required failing firms to fail rather than being bailed out by throwing good money after bad. The large number of displaced workers would not have been absorbed quickly in the service industries because of regulations constraining their growth. The result would have been massive unemployment. The reality turned out to be that Korea did not follow the IMF program, the banks have still not been straightened out, and Korean manufacturers are feeling only a little more foreign competition. Thus Korea remains vulnerable to another crisis down the road.

An obvious question at this point is, Why didn't Japan have financial crises as it moved along the same development path? As I discussed in chapter 2, Japan now doesn't owe the world any money. Thus outside investors can't precipitate a crisis. However, this has not always been true. I remember a Harvard Business School case on Japan taught in a World Bank course on corporate finance in 1973. That case explained how in the 1960s Japan had gone to the U.S. financial markets to raise money to finance the redevelopment of Japan following the war. The money was raised on the argument that these were investments in the future of Japan. That argument turned out to be right for long enough for the investments to be fully repaid. The Japanese used that money and their own savings to create world-class industries in steel, automotive, and electronics. These industries were so good that their exports to the world's markets earned enough foreign exchange to repay all the early investments. Korea never achieved such foreign exchange earning power. Their industries did not become world class like the Japanese ones, and, by coming along later, they had to compete in world markets with the Japanese. Bad luck.

The Exception That Proves the Rule

Of course, there is always the exception. In Korea, the exception is POSCO, Pohang Iron & Steel Company. POSCO produces 60 percent of Korea's steel and may have the highest productivity of any integrated steel producer in the world. (The poor performance of Korean minimills keeps the Korean steel industry from being world class as a whole.) Moreover, POSCO has been government owned for most of its life (it was privatized in 2000). In virtually every industry we studied around the world in which some firms were government owned, the government-owned firms had substantially lower productivity than the private firms.

So how did POSCO happen in Korea? Well, POSCO happened because the president of Korea asked General Park to build a world-class integrated steel company. General Park did this by having engineering and construction firms from Japan design and build the plant to best Japanese standards and by benchmarking the operating performance of the plant against world best practice. He insisted that these standards be met and they were. General Park was quite a manager.

There is nothing that prevents good managers from running government-owned industries. It just turns out that most such managers are not in General Park's class. However, there are other examples of government managers achieving extraordinary standards. After all, Adm. Rickover was the mastermind of the design, development, construction, and operation of the U.S. nuclear submarine fleet. He also oversaw the development of the naval officers commanding the boats. This program is perhaps the most complex program ever undertaken by anybody anywhere in the world. The success of the U.S. strategy to have an assured retaliatory strike capability if the Soviet Union ever started a nuclear war with the United States relied most heavily on Adm. Rickover's accomplishments. General Park was Korea's Adm. Rickover.

However, General Park's steel company is a tiny sliver in Korea's economy. Steel accounts for 0.34 percent of the working population in Korea. It's just not big enough to have the beneficial effects on the Korean economy that the automotive, electronics, and steel industries did in Japan. The effects of POSCO on the Korean economy are swamped by, for instance, retailing. Retailing productivity in Korea is 32 percent of the U.S. figure, and retailing accounts for about 8 percent of total employment in Korea. Seventy percent of all employment in retailing in Korea is still in mom-and-pop stores, in contrast to 19 percent in the United States. Korea's biggest challenge is to modernize its service industries.

Automotive: Couldn't Follow the Japanese

The Korean automobile industry is a great case for understanding how government development plans for building a "strategic" manufacturing industry can work out. These plans are based on the notion that governments can accelerate development by nurturing large organizations in which skilled personnel and capital can be concentrated and applied to build favored industries with large numbers of high-wage jobs (high-productivity industries). The idea is that economic development would proceed faster than it would otherwise.

Korea was simply following the Japanese model in this respect. In the late nineteenth century, the Japanese government orchestrated the creation of the *zaibatsu*. These were large industrial conglomerates organized to leverage the limited managerial skills and capital available in Japan at the time. Japan chose this path for its "crash" modernization program. This modernization program was based on the conclusion that to maintain its independence from the United States and Europe, Japan needed a modern economy. An important aspect of this policy is the protection of fledgling industries from foreign competition ("infant industry policy"). This policy is needed initially because infant industries are not able to compete against imports from more developed countries. The new industries have to learn how to operate their factories before they can compete.

This policy served Japan well for most of the last century. Japan is the only country to go from poor to rich in the last one hundred years. However, as I discussed in chapter 2, Japan ran into problems in the last decade of that one hundred years. Japan did not realize that to have a fully modernized economy at the end of the twentieth century, a modernized traded goods sector was not enough. *It also needed a modernized service industry and local manufacturing industry.* Moreover, as I indicated above, Japan would have run into trouble earlier if it had not been for the extraordinary export performance of its automobile, electronics, and steel industries. The really interesting fact is that the leading Japanese automobile companies, Toyota, Honda, and Nissan, and the leading electronics company, Sony, were not part of this *zaibatsu* (now called *keiretsu*) system. Independent entrepreneurs founded these companies. Sure, they benefited initially from protection from imports. However, they used this time the way they should have. They got good enough so that they didn't need the protection anymore, even if it was left on. These companies, through exports, earned the foreign exchange that has allowed Japan to stay independent of the IMF.

The Korean automotive industry is no Toyota or Honda. The big three Korean automobile companies, Hyundai, Daewoo, and Kia, have all been part of industrial conglomerates, called *chaebols* in Korea.

Exhibit 5.5: Automotive Labor Productivity Growth

Vehicles produced per employee

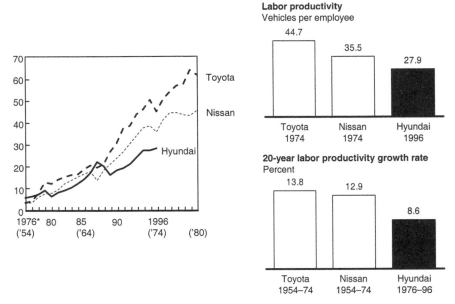

Labor productivity
Vehicles per employee

Toyota 1974	Nissan 1974	Hyundai 1996
44.7	35.5	27.9

20-year labor productivity growth rate
Percent

Toyota 1954–74	Nissan 1954–74	Hyundai 1976–96
13.8	12.9	8.6

*Time shift based on production output—1976 for Hyundai (19,200) and 1954 for Toyota (22,000) and Nissan (22,800)

These companies have achieved the growth objectives of government policy. That growth has been remarkable. As recently as 1985, Korea produced virtually no cars. Korea is now the fifth-largest automobile producer in the world. Korea produces more cars than the country in which the industrial revolution started in the late eighteenth century, viz. the United Kingdom. Korea also produces more cars than Italy. However, Korea uses massive amounts of capital and labor to produce these cars. Korea's capital productivity and labor productivity are both about half of the levels in the United States. Labor productivity in Korea is about one-third of that in Japan. The Korean automobile industry has been improving its productivity, but not nearly as rapidly as the Japanese at the same stage of development (Exhibit 5.5). In the twenty-year period from 1976 to 1996, Hyundai's labor productivity grew at 8.6 percent per year. However, when the Japanese automobile industry was at the same stage of development, from roughly 1954 to 1974, Toyota's labor productivity grew at 13.8 percent per year, and Nissan's, at 12.9 percent per year.

The reason Korea's automotive productivity is so low is that it has not made much progress in adopting the lean, high-quality manufacturing process of the Japanese. Hyundai has 125 problems per 100 vehicles produced; Kia has 275. In contrast, Toyota has 64, and Nissan, 78. Korea uses almost twice as many labor hours per vehicle as the Japanese in the welding, painting, and assembly steps in the manufacturing process. Korea has only half the percentage of common parts across different models that Japan and the United States have. Moreover, the Korean car companies have tried to do too much too soon. They expanded into virtually all car segments in the 1990s. The result has been a proliferation of different car structures (platforms), with relatively low production for each platform. Daewoo produces 121,000 cars per platform, and Hyundai, 157,000. Ford, GM, Honda, and Toyota all produce 300,000 to 400,000 cars per platform. Thus the capital applied in designing a platform and building the manufacturing line for a platform does not yield as many cars in Korea as in Japan and the United States. Capital productivity and return on capital are thus much lower in Korea. The Korean automobile companies have never earned a return on capital as high as the interest rates they have to pay on their debt.

Whereas the Japanese automobile industry contributed significantly to Japan's international financial stability, Korea's automobile industry contributed significantly to its 1998 financial crisis. No one can go on forever paying higher interest rates than the rates they earn on the investment of the money borrowed. Kia was simply not viable and had to be merged into Hyundai. It's not clear how this will solve the real problem in the longer term. Kia did have only one-third the production per platform of Hyundai. However, Hyundai itself has too many platforms. This action was probably just a face-saving way of shutting down most of Kia. Daewoo went bankrupt and has now been bought by General Motors. Why have the Japanese and Korean automobile industries made such different contributions to their economies?

Korea Copied the Rest of Japan, Not Toyota

The explanation starts with Toyota. As I discussed in chapter 2, no one knows why the high-quality, lean manufacturing innovation occurred at Toyota. It just did. The difference is in the reaction of the Japanese industry and the Korean industry to this innovation. In Japan, the other automobile companies were not protected at all from Toyota. Because they were independent, they could not rely on cross-subsidies from profitable businesses in other parts of an industrial conglomerate. Thus, they either had to follow Toyota or die. In Korea, the car companies were protected completely against Toyota in the domestic market. They did have to compete with Toyota and the other Japanese car companies in export markets. They lost money doing this. However, the chaebols' objectives were not to make money, but to grow. They could get away with this because some of their other businesses made a little money, and because the government pressured the Korean banks to lend to the chaebols no matter what.

This process can go on for a long time. Most investments made by companies are financed by cash generated by the companies themselves and not from capital intermediated by the capital markets. Thus, most companies have relatively little debt relative to their assets. In these circumstances, their cash flow can run down to very low levels before they are unable to meet their interest payments. Even then, they can pay their interest if the banks loan them additional money to do so. This is what happened in the Korean automobile industry. The first signal of trouble was Kia running out of cash. The chaebols were largely privately held, and information on the profitability of individual businesses within the chaebols was not available, even to the chaebols themselves because they didn't care. The immature Korean equity market did not have institutional analysts capable of assessing the market value of these conglomerates as a whole. Thus there were no early signals of trouble. The only signals were the astounding growth, which in the world to which the Japanese, European, and U.S. banks were accustomed, usually meant good financial performance.

So how could Korea have done better? First and foremost, the automobile industry should have been exposed to Toyota in the domestic market. Exposure in the export market was not enough given the behavior of the chaebols and the banks. Exposure through opening up the domestic market to exports from Japan would undoubtedly have resulted in a better outcome. However, Korea probably would have ended up with a smaller automobile industry than it had the potential to have. The best outcome would have been to open up the domestic market to foreign direct investment so that Toyota could build manufacturing plants in Korea. The idea would be to trade access to the Korean market for the transfer of best practice to Korea in transplant factories.

Everybody would gain from this situation, except the inept chaebol owners and managers. Having this possibility is one of the advantages of coming along the economic development path later than others. Developing economies don't have to invent everything themselves.

The Korean automobile industry also illustrates how tricky it is to apply an infant industry policy beneficially. Yes, some protection is needed initially, but most of the time that protection allows the creation of a low-productivity industry. Japan was lucky. It had Toyota. That forced the Japanese automobile industry to compete with the best. But there's only one Toyota. Other countries simply have to remove their protection or invite Toyota in to force their automobile industries to achieve high productivity. That's hard to do after creating strong domestic special interests through the nurturing of domestic industrial conglomerates and allowing them to get used to having an easy time through protection. That leads me to conclude it's just better to invite Toyota in to build a plant in your country from the beginning.

Steel: The Biggest Exception to the Global Pattern

In all our 118 industry studies around the world over the past twelve years, steel in Korea is the only case in which we found government-owned operations to achieve productivity equal to the best in the world. Needless to say, it's important to understand why this occurred in steel in Korea.

Labor productivity in the Korean steel industry is about 10 percent higher than in the United States, although it's about 10 percent lower than in Japan. However, capital productivity in the Korean steel industry is about 15 percent higher than in both the United States and Japan. Thus, total factor productivity in Korea is 10 percent higher than in the United States and about equal to that of Japan, the highest in the world before Korea entered. The labor productivity difference from Japan comes entirely from minimills, where Japanese productivity is 40 percent higher than in Korea. For integrated mills, the two labor productivities are equal. Integrated mills produce 60 percent of Korea's output and are all in one company, POSCO.

The reasons for the lower labor productivity in minimills in Korea are not surprising. U.S. and Japanese minimills were invented to compete against the integrated suppliers. They chose initially a simple product mix, minimized management, and maximized flexibility. They used multifunctional teams, multitasked jobs, and continuous improvement and cost reduction programs. It sounds similar to what Toyota did in automobile manufacturing. Whereas U.S. integrated mills have been unable to compete with low-cost production in developing countries, minimills have flourished in the United States. With their success, minimills have begun to produce more and more complex products. More steel is now produced by minimills in the United States than by integrated mills.

The minimills in Korea have adopted these techniques to a much lesser degree. The reason is that they have not had to do so in order to survive. Steel has been a strategic industry favored by the Korean government. The government found minimills to be an attractive way to develop its steel industry because of low initial investment and easy technology to import. The government protected minimills against imports from abroad. It also protected minimills against POSCO by drawing a clear line between the products minimills and POSCO produce. Even so, the early 1997 bankruptcy of Hanbo Steel, a Korean minimill, was perhaps the most visible of the events alerting foreign investors to the weak financial condition of many Korean firms in which they had invested.

POSCO Is Amazing

In contrast to the minimill story, the really surprising finding about steel in Korea is the performance of POSCO. POSCO succeeded because the government simulated the conditions of market competition. General Taejoon Park, chairman of POSCO from 1968 to 1994, made sure that POSCO remained profitable under those conditions. In establishing POSCO, the government agreed to three conditions of General Park for his taking the job. They were as follows: no government influence in the procurement of equipment, goods, and services by POSCO; no government influence in the hiring and management of POSCO personnel; and no political donations allowed from POSCO. General Park was strong enough to make these conditions stick. POSCO bought its equipment from around the globe and was free to hire the best people available. However, POSCO had a domestic monopoly for the production of most flat steel products and it was protected by tariffs from imports. It could still have made money at low productivity by charging high prices.

The government took care of this potential problem by using the best practice technique found for regulating industries with natural monopolies, such as local telephone service and local electricity distribution. The technique is called "price cap" regulation. Independent regulators with consumers' interests at heart progressively squeeze down the price allowed for services. This technique forces progressive productivity improvement. Of course, it is a matter of judgment about the rate of price decline, and sometimes regulators go too far. The rapid price increases in health care in the United States now suggest that the government held down prices too long as cost pressure built up.

For steel, the government regulators in Korea have had an easier time. The reason is that there is an international price for steel delivered to Korea. The government made sure that POSCO's prices were below these international prices. We checked and found that sure enough, prices for hot- and cold-rolled coil and for hot-rolled plate were 10 to 15 percent lower than in the EU, the United States, and Japan. Under these conditions, General Park made sure POSCO made a profit. He used the best of modern techniques to do so, such as continuous benchmarking of operations against the Japanese and net present value financial analyses of new investments. POSCO is the only instance in Korea where we found these techniques to be seriously applied.

We don't know what would have happened if POSCO had begun to lose money. Would the government have allowed POSCO to raise prices above the international level? Would the government have directed the banks to loan POSCO more money? The pressure on the government to relax the conditions would have been enormous. There's no question that most governments would give in on the grounds of supporting a strategic industry and preventing unemployment. The difference in Korea is that General Park made sure this dilemma did not develop. Thus he seems to have been the factor that differentiates this government-owned operation from every other one we studied. It's too bad government-owned industries around the world don't have more General Parkses.

Semiconductors: Capital Productivity Matters

The Korean semiconductor industry has not been a success. Its lack of success has not come from the problems associated with "infant industries" protection policies, as was the case for Korean automobiles. Rather, its problems have come from not having performed the financial analysis necessary to see that the economic value of the products produced would not be great enough to provide a return on the enormous amount of capital necessary to build a semiconductor industry.

In the 1970s, the Korean government chose semiconductors as a "strategic" industry to be developed with government support. Semiconductors has been perhaps the "prestige" industry in Korea. At the government's direction, huge amounts of capital were channeled through Korean banks to this industry. Semiconductors, telecommunications, and electric power require the most capital per worker of any of the twenty-nine industries we have studied over the past twelve years. *For semiconductors, capital costs account for about 70 percent of the total costs of production. In comparison, the average for the total economy is about 30 percent for capital and 70 percent for labor.*

The capital productivity of Korean semiconductors is about 50 percent of that in the United States, although it's about the same as in Japan. (Japan has the same problems in semiconductors that I will describe below for Korea.) Labor productivity is also about 50 percent of that of the United States. However, labor productivity is not so important in this industry.

The reason capital productivity is so much lower in Korea than in the United States is that almost 80 percent of Korea's production is for standard memory chips. In the United States, one-third of all production of semiconductors is for microprocessors. The rest is mostly other types of simpler logic chips. Standard memory chips have only 10 percent of U.S. semiconductor production. The economic value of microprocessors is huge compared with memory chips. The other logic chips also have higher value. We saw in chapter 4 how the increase in the value of microprocessors produced in the late 1990s in the United States was so great that it increased the national productivity growth rate. Microprocessors are very hard to design and produce. Only one company in the world, Intel, has really been successful at designing and producing microprocessors. However, microprocessors make computers work. Thus we value them highly and are willing to pay high prices for them.

We also need standard memory chips to make computers work and for many other purposes. However, memory chips are built to the same standard set of specifications worldwide and are relatively easy to design and manufacture. They are "commodities." They do require enormous amounts of capital to produce, but the world has lots of capital. Capital availability is almost never an important constraint if an investment will earn a reasonable rate of return. The problem is often that capital is available even when investments don't earn an adequate rate of return.

The Commodity Cycle

The reason capital invested in standard memory chips does not produce high enough economic value to justify the investment is that much of the time, the world produces too many memory chips. Memory chips go through a form of the "commodity cycle." The rapid technological improvement in the number of transistors that can be placed on a silicon chip ("Moore's Law") has meant that every few years we can make standard memory chips with dramatically increased memory capability. At these points, semiconductor manufacturers in the United States, Japan, Korea, and a couple of smaller producing countries race to build manufacturing plants to produce these more capable chips. Initially, producers can charge much higher prices for the chips produced because the chips are much more valuable to computer manufacturers and other users than the previous generation of chips. However, because the new generation of standard memory chips can be produced by several companies, more and more plants are built based on the assumption that their chips will also get the high prices. That assumption turns out to be wrong.

The reason it is wrong is that we need only so much memory capacity. As the production of the new generation of memory chips exceeds that demand, prices fall. The reason prices fall is that producers still are better off producing at lower prices than not producing at all. And the reason for this is that most of the costs of production have already been paid in the building and equipping of the production plants. Those costs are already gone ("sunk" in the initial investment). The additional costs of producing more chips from the plants already built are primarily labor costs. Thus, chip prices can fall almost to these incremental labor costs before producers would be better off shutting down their plants.

Computer manufacturers and other users of these chips know this. Thus, the users go to the chip producers and say we will buy chips from you but only at a lower price. Some producers are afraid to say no because they fear other producers will say yes and they will be left with no customers. This process goes on until prices have spiraled downwards to near the incremental costs to produce chips once the plants are built. In these circumstances, it is easy to see how the costs to build a plant are never recovered through the sale of chips. In the United States, semiconductor companies have almost never earned a return on their capital equal to the cost of that capital.

Intel Moved Out of Commodities Early

The big exception, of course, has been Intel. Intel's returns to shareholders from 1985 to 1998 were four to five times the returns of the next best semiconductor companies in the United States. But Intel was not producing standard memory chips. It was producing chips that almost nobody else could make. As a result, it could manage the balance of supply and demand for its microprocessors better so that it didn't build too much capacity. Perhaps more importantly, customers couldn't threaten Intel with buying from somebody else (although as I noted in chapter 4, this is now changing). Of course, Intel and its customers could play a big game of "chicken." Customers could threaten not to buy at all and Intel could refuse to lower its price. However, Intel had the stronger hand because customers feared that other customers would pay Intel's price and produce the most advanced computers, leaving them behind. Thus, everybody ended up paying Intel's price.

The market doesn't get either of these two situations perfect. For that matter, the market probably doesn't get any situation perfect. However, inefficiencies arising from too much supply relative to demand are costly when the capital costs to build capacity are especially high. Just to be clear, wasted capital is not just a loss of wealth for shareholders. In the end, we have made our material world by the sweat of our labor and the natural resources we found around us. Part of our material world is the capital stock of structures and equipment. We have built this stock to produce the goods and services we consume. If we waste this capital, we are wasting the labor and natural resources ultimately used up in producing that stock.

Capital costs are high for both microprocessors and memory chips. Fortunately, most of the rest of the economy is not this way. There, labor costs dominate capital costs. Most labor costs can be varied up and down to adjust to imbalances in supply and demand. Fewer resources end up being wasted.

Intel's pricing power has been strong enough to allow it to cover up any capacity mistakes it might have made. We'll never know whether this was the case. We do know that a lot of capital has been wasted in memory chips. The Intel problem seems less serious. Intel's position is based on unique technological achievement. It seems reasonable to reward that achievement, but only for so long. The hope would be (for everybody except Intel's shareholders) that extraordinary profits would stimulate alternative technological developments that matched Intel's. More than two hundred years ago, Adam Smith thought this was how things would work. As I described in chapter 4, competition did develop for Intel in the second half of the 1990s. There is no guarantee that competition will develop in every case. So far, it seems to have done so.

For commodities like memory chips, we do not have a good solution. Time and time again, temporarily high prices cause current producers to build more capacity than needed or new companies to enter the market. Often those new entrants are from developing countries. Petrochemicals has been perhaps the largest commodity subject to these cycles. In the early 1980s, Formosa Plastics from Taiwan made a huge entrance into this industry and helped create overcapacity that lasted for a long time. In semiconductors it was Korea. The only hope in commodity businesses for productive use of capital is for producers to be reasonable about new capacity additions. However, this is difficult because how do you decide who gets to add the new capacity needed to meet real increases in demand? Any producer would reasonably fear that competitors would get the capacity expansion and they wouldn't, if they didn't expand themselves. Hence, everybody expands. Sometimes even new entrants appear.

Collusion in taking turns over who gets the next capacity expansion seems reasonable. However, it faces two problems. That collusion would also create the temptation to limit supply to less than demand to make high prices possible. Moreover, how do new entrants ever get a chance to participate in such markets? We just don't have a solution, and we may never. However, it does seem clear that it is unwise for developing country governments to direct the people's savings into investments such as memory chips, where the chances of wasting capital are very high.

Of course, the inevitable has happened in Korea. The financial crisis of 1998 revealed that two of the three Korean semiconductor firms were nonviable. They were Hyundai and LG. The government directed that the semiconductor businesses of these two chaebols merge into a new company (Hynix). Since most of the costs of the semiconductor industry are in production plants, it's not clear what this merger will achieve. Perhaps the benefit is that one firm will waste less capital than two. Micron from the United States reached an agreement with the Korean government and Hynix's management to buy the new company. Micron's productivity in memory chips has been almost twice that of the two companies merged in Korea. Micron seems to have been an exception in this commodity business in making better timing decisions about capacity additions. Korea would have saved a lot of capital if it had invited Micron in from the beginning. This story sounds a lot like the automobile case, where Korea would have been better off if it had invited Toyota in at the start. However, Korea is not getting its Toyota in semiconductors even now. After the union threatened to strike and the Hynix shareholders complained about the purchase price, Hynix's board rejected Micron's offer. Looks like more capital will be wasted here.

Retailing: Much Like Japan

Late one night in the spring of 1997, I was on my way to my hotel from the airport in Seoul. Once the taxi left the freeway from the airport and the main city streets, it entered a series of narrow winding roads up to my hotel on a hill. All the building fronts were dark and the streetlights were widely spaced apart. In contrast, the taxi's headlights were so bright that it was difficult to make out anything not in their beam. Eventually, by looking out the side window, my eyes adjusted. I began to notice a few scattered open storefronts, each about ten feet wide and lighted by a single dim electric light bulb. Nobody was on the street, and certainly no customers were in the stores. But the tiny stores were open. I wondered if I was really in the country that produced the third-largest number of semiconductors in the world.

Retailing Is Backward in Korea

Retailing is backward in Korea because for a long time the government directed capital and other development support to "strategic" manufacturing industries. It is also backward because up until the late 1990s, the government protected small stores from competition with modern retailing. The result is that productivity in Korean retailing is about 30 percent of that of the United States and only 60 percent of that of Japan. Korea has one retail establishment for every one hundred people. The United States has half as many per person. Seventy percent of Korean retail workers are in mom-and-pop stores, compared with 20 percent in the United States and 50 percent in Japan. The average number of workers per store is two in Korea, five in Japan, and eight in the United States. Moreover, 70 percent of Korean retail workers earn no wages. They are working proprietors and unpaid family members.

No one views retailing as a strategic industry. Yet in Korea, retailing employs about 30 percent as many people as all manufacturing combined. Moreover, it is the sector receiving constant and immediate feedback from consumers about what they want. The government chose to support the chaebols in developing manufacturing industries such as automobiles and semiconductors. It actually placed some restrictions on chaebols entering retailing. As a result, capital did not flow towards retailing. Korean workers in automobiles and semiconductors have the same amount of plant and equipment per worker as workers in the United States. Retail workers in Korea, on the other hand, have only 25 percent as much capital per worker as in the United States.

Moreover, the Korean government protected these small shops from competition with modern retailing stores until the late 1990s. Before then, only relatively low-productivity Korean department stores were allowed. Large-scale foreign discount stores, such Carrefour and Wal-Mart, and shopping centers were not allowed. The foreign stores were restricted to store sizes far below minimum efficient scale. As a result, they did not enter Korea until 1996.

Zoning regulations have prevented the development of large shopping centers in Korea. The land around urban areas is the logical place for shopping center development. This land is the only place that is both close to urban shoppers and has undeveloped tracts large enough for shopping centers. Until 1993, retailing was not allowed in these areas. In 1993, retail developments of up to 30,000 square meters were allowed here. However, this is still not enough land for modern shopping centers.

The More Things Change, the More They Are the Same

The government removed virtually all restrictions on foreign direct investment in retailing in 1996. Moreover, some of the size restrictions in the zoning laws were removed following the crisis of 1998. Thus, retailing has the potential for rapid modernization and productivity improvements. However, Japan did the same thing and not much changed in retailing. The reason is that Japan had another layer of indirect restrictions on retail development. Korea has that same layer of indirect restrictions. All stores larger than 1,000 square meters have to be approved by a local government advisory board. Members of these boards often have strong connections to existing retailers. These boards block many new openings or restrict business hours and operating days so much that stores decide not to open. Moreover, the bureaucratic process of registering to build a large store can take two years. Many foreign retailers choose not to go through this process. Thus it remains to be seen whether retailing will rapidly modernize in Korea or not.

One thing is sure. Koreans are rich enough to afford the service and convenience of more modern forms of retailing. However, the government has been and may still be making it difficult for Koreans to have this. If it's hard to consume, the only thing left to do is to save. That's what the government has wanted Koreans to do for the past several decades. By denying good retailing services, the government has forced savings. However, as the automobile and semiconductor cases show, the savings have not been used very well. The playing field between consumption and savings should be more level so that Koreans can decide more for themselves how they want to use their money.

Housing Construction: Another Good Government Action

The computer programs generating the flight schedules for the international airlines seem to have all flights from the United States to Seoul arriving at night (of the following day!). After several trips to Seoul for our project on Korea, I finally arrived during daylight hours after a flight from Tokyo. Only then did I notice, in the distance off to the left of the freeway into Seoul, a large group of medium-height buildings, gleaming white in the sun. Even though I had traveled the same road in the opposite direction in daylight several times when leaving Seoul, I had not noticed these buildings. I guess the fourteen-hour time difference from Washington plus working Korean-length days had taken their toll. These buildings seem to go on forever. When one group finally ended, soon another group started. Each group looked like a whole city. I did not learn what these buildings were until we started the residential construction case in Korea.

Housing construction has been a success in Korea, at least up until now. The government has seen to it that virtually everybody has a decent place to live. In 1989, the government set out to resolve the housing shortage, and approximately 3 million housing units were constructed from 1991 to 1995. For a country with a population of only 50 million, these units accommodated about 25 percent of the total population. Virtually all this housing was apartment buildings like the ones I saw on the outskirts of Seoul.

Government actions were almost entirely responsible for this phenomenon in Korea. Government made sure that banks channeled the required capital to the construction industry. Zoning laws made land very expensive. Since apartment houses of the size in Korea provide four times as many square meters of housing per acre of land as single-family housing, 80 percent of this housing was apartment buildings. The U.S. housing mix during the same period was almost the reverse, with 70 percent being single-family houses. Finally, the government imposed a price cap on new housing to make this housing affordable by all. The result was these absolutely huge clusters of identical apartment buildings. I didn't go inside one of the apartments in these buildings, but my Korean colleagues described them as "apartment shells," with four walls and little content.

It should not be surprising that Korean construction companies were able to build these apartment houses with relatively high productivity. Overall housing construction productivity in Korea is 70 percent of that of the United States. That's probably the limit for housing of this type. The only way to get higher productivity in apartment construction is to build apartments with more attractive designs and more built-in content, such as cabinets, refrigerators, ovens, fireplaces, carpets, etc.

Government Can't Take It from Here

The other way to achieve higher productivity is to build more single-family housing. Single-family housing is inherently more productive than multifamily housing because of the value of privacy and of customized design and content. In Korea, single-family housing is built at 50 percent higher productivity than apartment buildings. Relatively little of this single-family housing is in large-scale developments, which are more productive than single houses. Land is just too expensive to be used this way. However, to take advantage of single-family housing construction, land has to be relatively available, and land prices must be determined by overall income per capita, not by artificial scarcity caused by zoning laws.

Many Koreans want better housing than they can get. Just like in Sweden, they now want something different from what government intervention caused to be built. Either they will be stuck in the current housing, or the government will make enough land available for more single-family housing to be built and they will move out. So it looks like either many Koreans will not get the housing they want, or some of the newly constructed apartment houses will not be lived in for the life of the buildings. In either case, Korea falls short of its economic potential.

However, I don't want to sound too negative about Korean housing construction. Korea done so much better than so many countries. In some respects, it has even done better than Japan. Japan now builds a mix of apartment houses and single-family houses about midway between that of Korea and the United States, or about half-and-half. However, as I discussed in chapter 2, zoning laws and lack of housing construction standards have caused single-family housing in Japan to be built at very low productivity (about 30 percent of the U.S. figure). The result in Japan is that overall housing construction productivity is about 50 percent of the level in the United States and about 70 percent of the level in Korea.

Retailing in Korea has not fared as well as housing construction. In principle, the same land availability problems that I discussed for retailing should apply to housing construction. And they do in most respects. However, the government has made sure that housing construction proceeds despite the high land prices. Specific laws allow large apartment complexes to be built in specific areas. Shopping centers have no such privileges. Moreover, the government itself purchased land and passed it on to the construction companies. They then made the housing affordable with price caps. The construction companies in turn built bare-bones apartments. At least people got modern housing. Retailing still includes a lot of tiny shops with dim light bulbs. There is nothing modern about them.

Thus, for housing construction strong government intervention has been successful up until now in providing a minimum standard of housing for most people. Korea has reached the middle income level of the global landscape in this way, not only in housing construction but in many other industries. The question is: How does Korea proceed from here? Many young middle-class Koreans with professional incomes want single-family housing. However, government housing policy is not geared towards satisfying their preferences. Only by meeting their demand will the housing construction industry improve its productivity. The risk is that the construction industry will be stuck in the current configuration. Radical change in land use policy and careful attention to standardization of single-family housing construction will be necessary for Korea to move forward from here. Otherwise, like Japan, Korea will begin to stagnate in housing construction. This may happen to much of the rest of the economy as well.

What Korea Needs to Do Now

Korea has shown one way for a country to go from low income to middle income. Korea concentrated its managerial and business talent in large industrial conglomerates (chaebols). These conglomerates had the organizational skills to mobilize large amounts of capital. The government directed the Korean banks to provide some of this capital. Other capital came from banks abroad. Internal cash flow generated additional capital. The conglomerates also had the skills to use this capital to build large modern factories, often with the best equipment money could buy.

The Korean people also have worked very hard to become middle income. They work 40 percent more hours per person than in the United States. Korea has shown that simply using the best equipment the world has to offer and working very hard are enough to rise from low income to middle income. However, as our industry studies have shown, Korea has used this equipment and hard work only about half as productively as the United States uses its equipment and hours worked. As a result, Korea is middle income and not high income.

As I pointed out earlier, Korea has been following the Japanese development path. This fact alone gives reason for concern about Korea because of the stagnation of the Japanese economy when it reached 75 to 80 percent of the GDP per capita of today's economic frontier. Japan has so far not been able to convert its economy from high capital investments and hard work to high productivity. Moreover, as Korea has moved up the Japan development path, Korea has run into economic difficulties earlier than Japan did. Japan has had no financial crisis yet like the Korea crisis of 1998.

The reason is, as I mentioned in the first section of this chapter, that Japan has had a few economic sectors, most notably automobiles and electronics, that have not followed the "Japan path." These sectors have done almost everything right and achieved the highest productivity in the world, as I explained in chapter 2. Through export success, the sectors have earned the foreign exchange that has made Japan independent of the international financial system. Unfortunately, automobiles and electronics in Korea have been following the Japan path, and Korea has no equivalent to Toyota and Sony. Thus Korea remained dependent on financing from abroad. When those investors became concerned about the low financial return on their investments in Korea, they began to withdraw their money, precipitating the 1998 financial crisis. Of course the low financial return came mechanically from Korea's low productivity. Korea will remain vulnerable to repetitive financial crises as long as it depends on capital from abroad and its productivity remains low. Japan has shown that a country can go further up the Japan path, but only if it has Toyotas and Sonys. Korea does not have them. Thus, the only way out for Korea appears to be to switch to the high-productivity path.

How Does Korea Do This?

- Korea's no-longer-infant manufacturing industries need to be exposed, in the Korean market, to direct competition from the world's best companies.
- Koreans need to recognize that all high-income countries are primarily service economies.
- Korea needs to change laws and regulations to allow the most modern forms of the service industries to develop in Korea.
- Korea needs to make land available around its cities for modern shopping centers and single-family housing developments.
- Korea needs to understand and accept the consequences of this relaxing of control over how its economy develops.

Hard to Change Mindset

This will not be easy in Korea. Korea is an ancient and proud civilization. It grew out of the great Chinese civilization. As Jared Diamond points out, the modern Japanese people are descended from Korea, although the Japanese try to ignore it. Korea has been an unfortunate location, in between the Chinese and the Japanese. In this respect, Korea is like Poland, which has been unfortunately located between Germany and Russia. In recent times, Korea has been swept over, occupied, and dominated by the Japanese. Virtually nothing very old is left in Korea. The Koreans built out of wood, and the Japanese burned virtually all of it down. Finally the Korean War of the early 1950s left the country destitute.

Koreans have been deeply influenced by the Japanese. Despite the horrid relationship, the government and business leadership in Korea has modeled itself after the Japanese. Prior to the Korean War, most of them went to Japan to be educated. What an irony. The difficulty for Korea now is that Japan is not a good model from this point on. There is a huge amount of experience in the rest of the world about different paths. Some of these paths have led to the high income to which Korea aspires. However, the understanding of these alternative paths is not very deep in Korea.

In January 1993, in the depth of the bitterly cold Korean winter, I was in Seoul for the official opening of the McKinsey office there. I was having lunch with a group of top managers in one of the chaebols, and the conversation turned to one of the first bankruptcies of a sizable firm in Korea. It was clear from the tone of my Korean company that this event was viewed highly unfavorably. I interjected that in the United States, a moderate number of bankruptcies was viewed as indicating that the economy was performing in a healthy way. The polite silence following my remark indicated to me that these Koreans thought I was from the moon. To them, large companies that operated were the means of going from low income to middle income. The important thing was for the company to operate at all. If it failed and did not operate, that was a loss on the road to middle income. I'm sure that the "loss of face" associated with business failure also influenced their view. But this exchange indicated to me that these top Korean managers did not understand how the "creative destruction" process leads to higher productivity companies replacing lower productivity companies.

All business involves some unknowns and therefore some risk. The way managers decide to organize and operate their company may not work very well. After all, some of the most sophisticated managers in the United States in the early 1970s decided that conglomerates would be a good idea. The idea was that exceptional managers could apply their skills to a variety of businesses and improve the performance of them all. It turned out that didn't work. Individual businesses were sufficiently complex that concentrated general management attention gave better results. We didn't know this in advance. We had to learn from experience.

In addition, even the best market research may be wrong about customer acceptance of new products and services. Finally, there may be technological risks as well. The important point for economic policy is to accept these risks and find out what works and what doesn't as fast as possible. Then we need decisive actions to continue what works and to stop what doesn't. Bankruptcy is the stopping of what doesn't work. It is simply a natural part of the process of increasing productivity. If bankruptcy is not accepted, then the labor and capital resources devoted to the continuation of the low-productivity enterprises are wasted to some degree. These resources could be better used elsewhere. Of course, sometimes bankruptcy results from simply bad management. In this case, it is obvious that the firm should not continue operating as it has. Perhaps simply changing management would be enough.

It's Efficiency, Not Raw Growth

An even more fundamental point is the lack of understanding in Korea that there are other paths. Near the end of our study of the Korean economy in 1998, the senior Korean member of the team said he had learned one very important thing on this project. He said, "I have learned that you have to put something in the denominator." By that, he meant that simply increasing absolute sales, absolute profits, and absolute GDP was not enough. These increases had to be viewed relative to the effort made to generate them. That meant for instance calculating the ratio of profits to capital invested, sales to total assets, and GDP to hours worked and capital employed. In Korea, just growing sales, profits, and GDP were enough to go from low income to middle income. And to be clear, most of the people in the world live in countries that have been unable to do even this. However, my Korean colleague meant that to go from middle income to high income required using capital and labor much more efficiently than Korea has done.

The most telling point of the story is that my colleague did not understand this point before our study of Korea. Neither his educational background nor his business experience in Korea had made him aware of this point. He was recruited into and trained by a global professional management consulting firm. After our project, he went on to become a partner in McKinsey's Seoul office. If he didn't understand this point, then almost nobody in Korea does. That is a big problem.

As I discussed in chapter 3, even Europe has only recently accepted the merits of these factors, and then reluctantly. However, they are necessary for high income. Koreans have shown that they can learn the Japanese path very quickly. Perhaps they can also learn about the high-productivity path equally quickly. The difficulty Korea is experiencing in rationalizing its lower productivity assets following the 1998 crisis suggests this learning will be neither automatic nor easy. Moreover, it has to permeate all aspects of Korean society, including government policy-making institutions, businesses, and the public. That sounds like a couple of decades at best.

President Kim Dae Jung was elected as a reformer to put Korea on a new path. He faced enormous difficulties for some of the reasons above. However, he made some progress in moving Korea towards a more productive path. Unfortunately, he got sidetracked by naive aspirations for reunification with North Korea. (North Korea's GDP per capita is only 5 percent of that of the South, yet its population is about half. The corresponding ratios for East Germany were 50 percent of West Germany's GDP per capita and only 25 percent of the population. The difficulties of German reunification look like a piece of cake next to the difficulties of Korean reunification.)

Kim Dae Jung was also unable to avoid scandals involving both his family members and close colleagues. As a result, he finished his term seriously discredited. That is a setback for reform in Korea towards a more productive path.

The new president, Roh Moo Hyun, seems even more naive about reunification with North Korea and disinterested in economic reform. Just because Korea's economy is temporarily doing OK does not mean it will do well in the long run.

PART TWO

POOR COUNTRIES

CHAPTER SIX

Brazil: Big Government Is Big Problem

With Brazil, we started our examination of low-income countries. These are countries with GDPs per capita below 25 percent of the figure in the United States (Exhibit 6.1). *Eighty percent of the world's people live in low-income countries.* Nobody can see how we can go on indefinitely with this huge difference between how the richest 20 percent and the poorest 80 percent of the world's people live. Sure, it's important to understand how Europe, Japan, Korea, and even the United States can get richer. However, those issues are minor compared with improving the economic standard of living in low-income countries.

That so many people live in low-income countries and so few in middle- and high-income countries indicates that economic development is hard. Why is it so hard? That's what this chapter on Brazil and the following chapters on Russia and India are about.

Brazil's per capita income is 23 percent of the United States'. Brazil is one of the richest of the low-income countries. Yet Brazil is half as rich as Korea. Since Brazil is so much poorer than the advanced countries, and even Korea, you ought to notice a significant difference by just looking around. You can, and I don't mean the Copacabana beach scene.

The big difference you see is the vast settlements of cardboard, paper, cloth, and canvas shelters on the outskirts of the big Brazilian cities, and especially São Paulo and Rio. When you fly into São Paulo, these settlements (*favelas*) seem to go on for miles. These settlements do not exist in the advanced countries, nor in Korea. In Korea, the corresponding housing is the vast tracts of gleaming white, identical apartment houses on the outskirts of Seoul. The favelas suggest that the people living in them have a different kind of economic life. They of course do. They are living outside the legal framework of their country. They are unregistered as workers, they pay no taxes, the enterprises in which they work don't look like anything seen anymore in the rich countries, and

Exhibit 6.1: World Distribution of GDP per Capita by Country

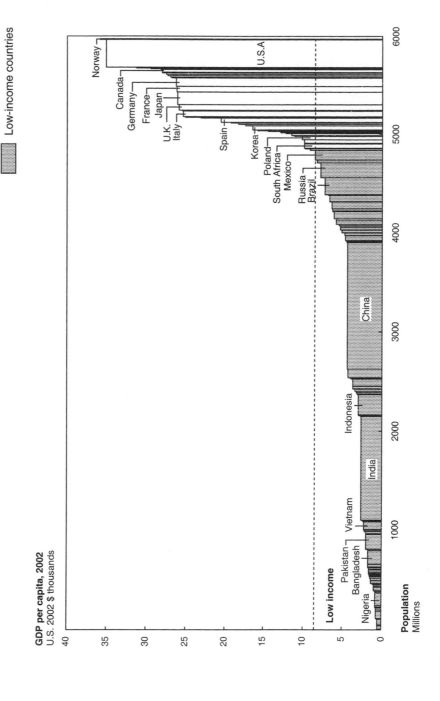

Low-income countries

GDP per capita, 2002
U.S. 2002 $ thousands

Exhibit 6.2: Informality in Brazil

Percent urban employment

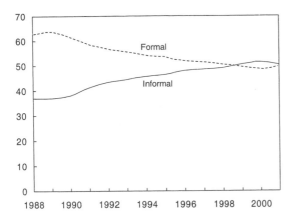

their productivity is on average about 15 percent of the average productivity in the United States. *Fifty percent of all workers in Brazil fall into this category, called the "informal" economy.* It includes at least one-third of the workers outside agriculture. The percentage of informal workers has been increasing over the past decade (Exhibit 6.2).

At the same time, you see much that is familiar in Brazil. The city centers are remarkable for their modern office building skyscrapers, good restaurants, and interesting housing. Thus there is also a fully modernized segment in Brazil. After all, Brazil produces the airplanes flown by many U.S. commuter airlines, Brazilian steel and chickens are exported around the world, and the largest investment bank outside New York and London was in São Paulo until it failed and was taken over in the financial crises of 1997–98. You also see in Brazil vast tracts of empty landscape. In part, that's because Brazil simply has so much land. Brazil has half the land (and half the population) of all of South America. However, the land is also empty because few people live in rural areas anymore. Only 25 percent of employment in Brazil is in agriculture. Korea has 13 percent in agriculture. This small difference cannot explain Brazil's being half as rich as Korea. Brazil has already evolved out of agriculture to a significant degree. The difference has to come elsewhere. The difference is the favelas and how their occupants earn a living.

When It's Good, It's Really Good

The formal sector in Brazil (non-agriculture, non-informal) is almost as far along as Korea. Its average labor productivity is 37 percent of the United States', compared with 36 percent for Korea, which is virtually all formal. Korea is twice as rich as Brazil, not only because of informality in Brazil, but also because Koreans work 35 percent more hours per capita than Brazilians. In terms of hours worked then, Brazil looks like the United States does now, not like Korea or like the United States when it was at Brazil's stage of development. At that point, U.S. workers had longer hours than even Koreans do now. There is nothing necessarily wrong with Brazil's working hours; still, the harder you work, the richer you usually are.

The formal part of the Brazilian economy has some industries and, within industries, some firms with very high productivity. *The top-performing private retail banks, Itau and Bradesco, are 95 percent as productive as retail banks in the United States.* The poultry segment of food processing is 68 percent as productive as U.S. poultry. Hypermarkets in Brazil achieve productivity within 15 points of the U.S. average for all food retailing. Thus, high labor productivity close to the economic frontier can be achieved in Brazil. So why doesn't all Brazil's economy look like these examples? Why has informality actually been increasing recently in Brazil?

Well, there is much left for Brazil to do. There are still too many restrictions on international competition in the Brazilian market, and there is still too much government ownership in some sectors. However, the highest priorities of the government and of the World Bank in its support of Brazil are not the binding constraints right now on rapid economic growth in Brazil.

It's Not Capital and Education

The conventional wisdom in economic development is that labor productivity in poor countries is so low because labor is cheap and capital is expensive. Therefore, labor is used in place of capital, causing low labor productivity. Additional capital investments are not economic, and countries have to wait for wages to rise before these capital investments should be made. The constraints are really education and infrastructure. With more education, workers will be able to perform more high-skill jobs, wages will rise, and capital will then be invested. Finally, the road, rail, and port systems are so bad that poor countries cannot develop the scale of operations necessary to achieve high productivity. In Brazil, (and in Russia and India), none of this conventional wisdom is true.

In Brazil, we studied steel, telecom, airlines, food processing, automotive, retail banking, food retailing, and housing construction. Averaging (on a weighted basis) across all these industries, almost one-third of the productivity gap with the United States was caused by lack of investment. However, of that missing investment, 75 percent is economically viable even at today's wage rates. Only about 8 percent of the total gap can be attributable to nonviable investments in Brazil today. *Thus, Brazil's labor productivity potential today is slightly more than 90 percent of the U.S. level.* The two-thirds of the labor productivity gap not attributable to missing capital comes most importantly from inefficient organization of the activities of labor and inefficient arrangement of equipment in the production process. Scale, product design, mix of products produced, and capacity utilization explain the rest.

This result means two things:

· Investments could be made now to increase Brazilian labor productivity across the board.
· Not nearly as much capital as currently assumed will be needed to add capacity as Brazil grows.

Brazilians are very aware that Korea invested 33 percent of its GDP to achieve about an 8 percent growth rate. That looks hopelessly high compared to Brazil's current investment rate of 19 percent. However, by achieving its current capital productivity potential, Brazil would need an investment rate of only 26 percent, or halfway in between Brazil's current level and the Korean level. That level is attainable by Brazil if they do the following:

· Reduce the costs of investment goods by opening up those markets.
· Remove the drain on national savings from the high cost of inefficient (unproductive) financial intermediation.
· Reduce the loss of national savings to finance the government budget deficits.

Lack of education of the Brazilian workforce is just an excuse today for poor economic performance. There are just too many examples from banking to food processing and automotive where firms have been able to match productivity levels at the economic frontier with the Brazilian workforce. These findings just reinforce what we found in every other country we studied. The primary means through which workers attain the skills to perform at the economic frontier is through on-the-job training. Brazilian workers are equally trainable in this regard to workforces all around the world. There are many important reasons to increase the educational level of the Brazilian people, including making Brazil's popular democracy work better. However, removing a constraint on current economic performance is not one of them.

Finally, only in steel is there a physical infrastructure constraint on current productivity growth. There, high port costs protected the domestic market from steel imports and made domestic iron ore prices low because Brazil's surplus of iron ore had to be exported at the international price. Thus the Brazilian steel industry did not face as much competition in the domestic market and the low price of ore made it easy to make a profit. Even in steel, it is not clear how much of the high port cost came from physical infrastructure constraints and how much from inefficient port operations.

Informality Is a Bigger Problem Because of Big Government

Our industry studies also revealed the problem with informality. Sure, informality is a problem because of the low productivity of the businesses in which it appears. However, that's a problem that should take care of itself as more productive, formal businesses, with lower prices and better services, overtake the informal enterprises. However, this process is not happening very quickly in Brazil, and informality is increasing. What's going on here?

The problem is that the more productive formal enterprises cannot take advantage of their higher productivity by charging lower prices and thereby increasing market share. *The reason their prices are not lower is that they pay taxes on employment, value added, sales, and profits, and the informal enterprises do not.* In both food retailing and housing construction, taxes significantly distorted competition. The counter stores, street vendors, and open-air markets in retailing and the special trade companies using informal labor in housing construction were competitive with the larger, much more productive formal companies. Presumably, all economies have informality at early stages of development. The United States must have had it to a significant degree in the early part of the twentieth century when it was at Brazil's economic level. The difference is the tax levels on the formal companies are much higher now in Brazil than they were in the United States almost a hundred years ago. And the reason they are so much higher now in Brazil is that Brazil now has a big government, whereas the United States had a small government one hundred years ago.

Today total tax revenues as a percentage of GDP are 33 percent in the United States and 29 percent in Brazil—not all that different. The difference is that the United States raises its tax revenue from virtually all the workers and all the firms in its economy. In Brazil, however, tax revenues can only be raised from the 50 percent of the workers in formal firms and from these formal firms themselves. That means that the tax burdens on these workers and their firms have to be higher, relative to income, than in the United States. Moreover, in Brazil the tax burden is skewed more heavily towards corporate taxes than in the United States. The result is that formal Brazilian corporations pay 85 percent of all taxes collected, compared with 41 percent for U.S. corporations. Brazilian corporations end up paying taxes equivalent to 25 percent of GDP, compared with 14 percent for the United States. Thus, formal corporations in Brazil bear a much higher tax burden than U.S. corporations do today.

The relevant comparison, however, is with the United States in 1913. Then, total tax revenues in the United States were only 6 percent of GDP (compared with 29 percent in Brazil today). The biggest tax item was property taxes, at 3.4 percent. Corporations paid some of that. However, other corporate tax items of income tax, sales tax, trade tariffs, etc. amounted to only 2 percent of GDP. So total taxes paid by corporations probably amounted to 3 to 4 percent of GDP. In other words, the corporate tax burden in the United States when it was at Brazil's state of economic development was so low that informality did not hold back the growth of the formal sector. Unfortunately, that's not true for Brazil.

A Lot of History

The other thing Brazil has against it is its history. Brazil doesn't need to look at the economic experiences of the rest of the world to draw lessons about good economic policy. With the exception of a Soviet-style centrally planned economy, Brazil seems to have tried everything. Brazilians often point with some pride to the 4.5 percent per year growth rate they achieved in the 1970s. This growth was achieved under authoritarian rule like in Korea and with some of the same tactics. Substantial capital was borrowed from abroad and invested, often in unproductive state-owned enterprises. Brazil had a crisis in the early 1980s much like Korea had in 1998. Brazil could not pay its international debt. To be fair, international interest rates spiked to unprecedented levels, but Brazil was headed for trouble in any case. Its productivity improvement from all this investment was no better than Japan's or Korea's during their high-growth periods. That led to stagnation in Japan and financial crisis in Korea.

From there, Brazil indulged in hyperinflation, claiming with firm conviction that it did not matter because everything was indexed. For the entire decade of the 1980s, Brazilian managers focused on making money out of inflation rather than making money out of becoming more productive. Even in 1997, Brazil resisted lowering import tariffs because the government believed the high exchange rate made protection of many domestic manufactures from imports necessary. The government was unwilling to implement a flexible exchange rate because they were sure that, with so much indexing still in place, the surge in import prices would immediately rekindle inflation. In 1998, the international financial market forced Brazil to go to a flexible exchange rate, and inflation was no problem.

From all this, Brazil has emerged with much better economic policies. However, as I will get to at the end of the chapter, it must do something about its big government.

Automobiles: Brazil Let Multinationals Go to Sleep

Brazil's automobile industry shows the terrible effects of a historical legacy of bad economic policy. The expectations were so different in the 1970s. Then Brazil had the apparent good fortune of four of the world's most capable industrial concerns building automobile plants there. General Motors, Ford, Volkswagen, and Fiat all came. These firms are not Toyota, but they have shown that they can achieve 60 to 70 percent of Toyota's productivity in their home countries. In Brazil, they achieve 20 percent of Toyota's productivity, 30 percent of Japan's as a whole, 35 percent of the United States' as a whole, and only 85 percent of Korea's. What's going on here?

About everything went wrong that could. In 1956, the Brazilian government banned all imports of cars. Even as late as the end of the 1980s, imports were still banned. So the multinationals came. They faced no international competition. Moreover, unlike the domestic Japanese automobile companies, the multinationals in Brazil did not compete intensely with each other. The U.S. and European automobile companies in the 1970s were very experienced with oligopolies. They knew the benefits to themselves of such an arrangement if they could get away with it. They could in Brazil. Up until the end of the 1980s, only two of the multinationals competed in each car segment in Brazil.

Under these conditions, the multinationals had little incentive to improve productivity. However, things got worse. In the 1980s, Brazil entered its decade of hyperinflation. It also controlled the prices of cars. Under these conditions, no firm in its right mind would invest good money and top management in trying to improve productivity. These firms were no fools; they didn't.

The result was that in the early 1990s, the automobile industry in Brazil was in a 1970s, "pre- Japan" world instead of a 1990s, "post Japan" world. Its products were not designed for easy manufacturing; it had adopted none of the Japanese "lean manufacturing" techniques; and it had not made investments in automation, economic even at Brazilian wage rates.

Finally Competition

Brazil's stabilization and market opening policies established in the early 1990s brought dramatic changes to the automobile industry. Brazil allowed imports and began a progressive program of reducing tariffs from 85 percent to 20 percent by 1995. The Brazilian auto industry increased productivity at about 17 percent per year from 1991 to 1995. However, the industry was so far behind that this improvement was not enough. Imports rose rapidly, reaching 23 percent of the market in 1995, with no end to their growth in sight. The government had no choice but to raise tariffs. They overreacted, however, and raised them all the way up to 70 percent, thereby pricing imports out of the market. They may have felt they needed to do this because, unfortunately, Brazil was trying to maintain a policy of very slow foreign exchange devaluation. The flood of car imports put foreign exchange reserves at risk.

This is what happens without a flexible exchange rate. With a flexible exchange rate, the buying of other currencies to purchase imported cars would lower the international value of the Brazilian currency. This would make imports more expensive, lower the demand for them, and reduce the reserve drain. For the Brazilian auto industry, it would've been far better for the exchange rate to adjust to maintain some international competitive pressure on the domestic industry. Instead, the Brazilian government went back to yet another multiyear plan of reducing tariffs on imported automobiles.

By coincidence, I was in Rio speaking at a World Bank conference in 1995 when Brazil abruptly reinstated the high tariffs on automobiles.

The Brazilian finance minister, Pedro Milan, had been scheduled to speak also at the conference. However, the World Bank's vice president for Latin America publicly criticized the Brazilian government for raising the tariffs, and Milan canceled his speech. The underlying point, however, was that both the Brazilian government and the World Bank were flying blind about the rate at which the Brazilian automobile industry could be expected to improve. Neither one knew Brazil's productivity and unit cost position relative to international competition. Also, neither one knew the rate at which other automobile industries had been able to increase productivity under competitive pressure.

The 17 percent per year increase in productivity in Brazil from 1991 to 1995 looks awfully good to me. It's better than the Japanese, the United States, and the Koreans ever achieved. Of course, it should be because these European and U.S. multinationals knew exactly how to achieve productivity levels two to three times their current performance in Brazil. Thus, in retrospect, it looks like the Brazilian market opening for automobiles in the early 1990s was somewhat overaggressive. Moreover, they learned from experience and adjusted, although probably too much. In 1997, the new tariff reduction schedule matched the productivity improvements that could reasonably be expected of the Brazilian industry. This time the government had it about right, although not because the government knew the rate at which productivity could increase. On the other hand, the World Bank's position of no tariff increase seemed doctrinaire and uninformed.

The irony, of course, is that all this back and forth on tariffs was overtaken by the 50 percent devaluation forced on Brazil by the international financial market in the 1998 emerging market financial crises. At these exchange rates, automobile producers in Brazil should not have to worry about imports. Thus, international competitive pressure is off. The Brazilian government has a new problem. How does it force intense competition among the domestic producers? Antitrust policy and enforcement is very difficult. By far the quicker and more effective route is additional competition from new producers. A couple of big Japanese automobile factories in Brazil would take care of this situation. Brazil's huge domestic market and low-cost position should make it especially attractive. The risk, of course, is Brazil's long-term economic and political stability. Brazil's record for the 1990s is on balance good. Brazil now needs to show it can have a change of government with the continuation of good economic policies. Brazil has to prove it will not go the way of Argentina.

Retail Banking: Private versus Government Ownership

Retail banking is an important sector for all economies, and especially for developing economies. Without a money system and the retail banks that enable us to manage that money, we would be stuck with a barter economy. Every time we wanted some bread or cheese, we would have to go to a central marketplace with some goods of our own and trade them physically with somebody who had bread or cheese. The exchange of goods takes place at the same time. With a money system (and appropriate markets for goods and services), we can sell the results of our labor at one place and at one point in time for money and buy the results of the labor of others at a different place and time with that money.

What Banks Do

It's easy to see why a barter economy cannot function once a society moves beyond the simple production of food and shelter for subsistence living. There would just be no way to physically make all the trades in goods and services. Money and markets allow us to make the trades multiparty, with different pieces of the trades transacted at different times. Since money has face value purchasing power, we need to handle it carefully. Most of us are uncomfortable storing significant amounts of money under our mattresses and carrying significant amounts of money around to buy things. We need a safe place to keep it. We need a place with a big safe. That's where retail banks first came in. We could store our money there and instruct the bank to pay anyone to whom we owed amounts of money we were not comfortable carrying around. Since virtually all the people we owed also have their money in a bank somewhere, the banks could just make a paper note that we had less money with them and the people we owed had more. One can see already that this is a business made in heaven for computers. And that's where this story will end up. For the small transactions for which we pay cash, we could go to the bank (or computer-operated ATM now) and get the cash we needed.

What I have just described in the last paragraph is the payments system, which retail banks run for individuals. We can also see from this paragraph that sometimes we will have a surplus of money if we are paid for our efforts before we complete our trades for goods and services produced by others. At other times, we will want to acquire the goods and services of others before our efforts have yielded enough purchasing power to complete the trade. Buying a house is perhaps the best example of this situation. Most of us prefer to buy a house before we have saved enough money to purchase it with cash. Because the money is more valuable to us early when we don't have enough money to buy the house than it would be if we waited until we had saved the full price, we are willing to pay extra for that money early. That's "interest." We can see now how retail banks would naturally begin to loan the surplus money of some to others who want to make purchases in advance. Those are the deposit taking and lending functions of retail banks. Because those of us who have surplus cash have something valuable to those who don't but need it, we can charge the bank interest on the money we store there.

This phenomenon is actually at the heart of the capitalist economic system. Instead of immediately consuming all the money we earn, we can choose to save some of it so that we can consume even more later. (Some of this saving goes to buying equipment and building plants that allow us to leverage our work more through increasing our productivity. Retail banks don't handle this part of saving; that's wholesale banks and the financial institutions in the equity and bond markets.)

Retail banks thus play a special role in an economy. They are necessary in a monetized economy. And a monetized economy is necessary to get anywhere at all. I think that's why governments historically have paid so much attention to retail banks. Governments have heavily regulated them and in many cases outright owned them. However, in another respect, retail banks are just like any other sector in an economy. Retail banks perform certain functions, and labor and capital are used to conduct those functions. The efficiency (productivity) with which these resources are used matters in retail banking just like any other sector. It turns out that all this special attention from government through regulation and ownership has often damaged retail banking productivity. This has certainly been the case in Brazil.

How Banks Perform

Retail banks have three functions: making payments, taking deposits, and lending to individuals. Retail banking productivity in each of these functions is just the ratio of the number of payments or number of deposits or number of loans to the hours worked to handle each of these actions. Labor productivity in retail banking in Brazil is 40 percent of that in the United States. The percentages for payments, deposits, and loans are 35 percent, 69 percent, and 31 percent, respectively. The overall productivity of 40 percent is a composite of these three numbers.

Combining them is a technical issue without a perfect method. However, we can see from the components that 40 percent cannot be a bad number.

It is surprising that this number is not higher. As you can tell from the above description of retail banking, retail banks do the same thing everywhere. It should be a simple matter of just copying best practice. Moreover, in Brazil a couple of private banks do just that. Their productivity is 95 percent of the U.S. level. Why isn't this the case for all banks in Brazil?

The biggest reason is that the government owns half the retail banks in Brazil, both in terms of share of deposits and share of employment. These banks and some of the private banks have not taken either of the two steps taken by best practice banks around the world in the last thirty years. The first step is to centralize the processing of all the information related to payments, deposits, and loans in one big centralized "back office," and the second step is to replace the paper-based systems and many of the people in this back office with computers. Instead, most of the Brazilian banks still conduct these functions in the subscale back offices of branches. Back offices of Brazilian branches have 25 percent of the total employees of the bank, compared with about 8 percent in the United States. Overall, private banks in Brazil are twice as productive as government-owned banks. All Brazilian banks suffer about a 20 percent penalty relative to the United States because the government requires retail banks to accept all bill payments, and tellers have to handle the majority of these transactions. Nevertheless, even with this penalty, the best private banks in Brazil achieve 95 percent of U.S. productivity. Without this penalty, these private banks would be well above the U.S. average. The government banks and the rest of the private banks don't get this good because they don't have to.

Competitive intensity among Brazilian banks is very low. It is low because the public banks have such a large share and they don't have to perform because the government will not let them fail. The government requires that all public employee salaries and government financial assets be deposited in these banks. Thus these banks are guaranteed a certain market share. Moreover, the government fixes real interest rates on the most popular savings account product in Brazil. Thus, there is little price competition for deposits. For this reason, the large private banks have not been able to use higher interest rates to gain share. However, because their productivity is so much higher, they have made large profits. As I explained earlier about food retailing in the United Kingdom, more productive companies are happy when government regulations make it such that they do not have to compete intensely against each other through lowering prices. Then, they can make large profits.

Another reason most Brazilian banks have low productivity is that during the hyperinflation of the 1980s and early '90s, they made enormous profits from their "float." All retail banks make some money from their float. The float is the money retail banks hold for the time between their drawing the money down from your account and their paying the person you owe the money to. In hyperinflation times, the banks can earn very high interest rates on this money and yet pay out only the nominal amount of the payment. In 1993, 50 percent of all bank income in Brazil came from float income. By 1995, this percentage had dropped to 4 percent. Banks had to get back to earning money the old-fashioned way. However, during hyperinflation, they didn't have to worry about increasing productivity through reducing costs. The retail banking case in Brazil is perhaps the best example of the fallacy that hyperinflation didn't matter because everything is just indexed.

Big Government Needs Its Own Banks to Finance Itself

So why hasn't Brazil made more progress towards rationalizing and privatizing the government-owned banks? The reason is the government has needed control of those banks. It needed control because it needed those banks to lend money to itself. No private bank would do this to the extent needed. The reason the government needed loans is that Brazil has a continuous struggle to discipline its public finance. Both federal and state governments have been notorious for running deficits, although recently more at the state level. In the late 1980s, almost 50 percent of all bank loans from government-owned banks was to government entities themselves. The government was using government-owned banks to collect deposits from Brazilians and to loan this money to the government. It was the only way the government could finance its deficits. Eventually, the state-level government-owned banks ran out of money and had to be bailed out by the federal government. The federal government eventually got tired of this in the late 1990s and cut a deal for the privatization of the state-level banks in return for the last round of subsidies. Let's hope this deal holds.

The government also needs some state-owned banks to execute its policy of providing credit to agriculture and low-income housing. There's nothing wrong with these social objectives; it's just that the subsidies are hidden in the big government-owned banks. It would be better to privatize the regular retail banking functions of the government-owned banks and to set up separate agricultural and low-income housing banks. In this way, Brazil could get both high-productivity retail banking and the amount of agricultural and housing subsidies society as a whole wants. There is certainly lots left to do to improve retail banking in Brazil.

Food Retailing: Reveals the Real Problem of Poor Countries

The food retailing case in Brazil was the test of whether industry studies could be extended to poor countries. Everyday impressions even from moving in business circles in São Paulo suggested there would be problems in food retailing. On my taxi ride from the Transamerica Hotel to the McKinsey office, I always passed a huge Carrefour hypermarket with an American-sized parking lot in front. Carrefour is the most successful international hypermarket in the world. That part of food retailing is no problem. However, even outside modern office buildings in the business district of São Paulo, the sidewalks were crowded with long strings of street vendors. The street vendors seemed to sell virtually everything. Some were selling food. They were obviously a cash business, and they had no cash registers. They weren't even keeping any paper records. It was obvious that these food retailing operations would be beyond government statistics.

Informality

About 85 percent of employment and about 50 percent of sales in food retailing are beyond government statistics. This caused a triple problem for our study. Our working team had to estimate the employment and sales in these "informal" food retailing businesses, group the different stores by type, and convert the financial data expressed in the Brazilian currency, *reais,* into units that were comparable in real terms with financial data in other currencies, and in particular with U.S. food retail financial data in dollars. The standard method is to use purchasing power parity exchange rates, and these did not exist for food retailing in Brazil.

This situation demonstrated the advantage of doing this kind of microeconomic analysis in McKinsey. In analyzing markets, McKinsey consultants are highly trained in finding and gathering data that go beyond government statistics. They are also highly trained in combining disparate sources of data, some public and some not, to develop information not created before. They are also trained to be relentless in this pursuit. Finally, they are talented, aggressive, and high-energy. They don't like to fail. They didn't for our food retailing case in Brazil.

Government census and industry association data gave us good information about the formal sector. However, for the informal sector, the only source was the 1995 household survey. Household surveys have turned out to be a wonderful source of information in countries with large informal sectors. Establishment censuses do not include informal businesses. Household surveys, on the other hand, include everybody. Usually, information about what everybody in a country is doing is collected in a detailed enough way for us to separate out employment not only for the informal sector but also by appropriate microeconomic category, in this case, by type of store. Then a representative sample of data for sales per employee for each type of store allowed us to estimate the total sales for each store type. The actual process was more complicated than I have described, but this gives the general idea.

That left purchasing power parity exchange rates. Since none existed, our team had to create them. The methodology is well established; it's just so much work that only public institutions such as the OECD and World Bank have done it in the past. Nonetheless, beginning with Brazil, we constructed these exchange rates by sector when they did not exist. For food retailing in Brazil, we used a basket of 400 comparable food products and collected their prices in the United States and Brazil.

The result of all this data gathering and analysis was that labor productivity in food retailing in Brazil was 14 percent of that in the United States. Supermarkets were about 50 percent as productive as the same types of stores in the United States. However, the traditional stores (minimarkets, counter stores, street vendors, and street markets) were about 10 percent as productive as the corresponding convenience stores in the United States. The principal reason hypermarkets and supermarkets are less productive in Brazil is that they have not converted fully to automated checkout and inventory control systems through investments in information technology. In 1996, only 32 percent of Brazilian hypermarkets and supermarkets had such systems, compared with 97 percent in the United States. However, Brazil is rapidly investing in such systems and this problem is taking care of itself.

The reason the convenience segment, which is made up of the traditional stores in Brazil, has such low productivity is that no modern convenience stores exist yet. 7-Eleven, Lawsons, gasoline station minimarkets, and their Brazilian equivalents simply aren't there. By choosing store sites with sufficient local traffic, by combining into chains for scale advantages in logistics, and by investing in information technology for automated sales and inventory management, convenience stores in the United States are able to achieve 90 percent of hypermarket and supermarket productivity. The added service of convenience allows them to compete successfully.

How Can Informal Compete with Modern?

In Brazil, the traditional stores charge prices 30 percent higher than hypermarkets and supermarkets and still stay in business. They do so because of convenience. Modern convenience stores in Brazil could charge prices about 15 percent below the current prices of traditional stores. However, even then the traditional stores could stay in business because they pay no taxes. Their take-home revenue would be cut by 30 to 40 percent, but they would still survive. If they had to pay taxes, their take-home pay would be virtually wiped out and the proprietors would have to do something else. Modern convenience stores would proliferate. Brazilian consumers, many of whom are very poor, would be better off because their food prices would be lower. This doesn't happen now because modern convenience stores would have to struggle too hard to take market share away from the non-taxpaying traditional stores.

The reason we were able to understand this competitive dynamic is that a young Brazilian McKinsey consultant spent a couple of days with the woman operating a typical counter store in a favela in São Paulo. He kept a record of everything that happened in the store. He gained access by agreeing to provide day care services for the woman's child while he was there. He got information on prices, on total sales, and on how the woman spent her time. He found that the woman was idle half her time. Needless to say, there had been no market research about the location of her store. She was just trying to survive. She would certainly have been able to perform one of the low-skill jobs in high-productivity supermarkets or convenience stores. If the child was a problem, she could work part-time. Everybody would seem to be better off.

Taxes to Finance Big Government Are the Culprit

However, this will not happen as things stand today in Brazil. The problem is taxes. It is infeasible, even if it were socially acceptable, to tax the informal retailers. They have no records on which tax returns or tax audits could be based. Moreover, there are obviously too many of them for the Brazilian tax authorities to do in all of them what our consultant did in one of them. The only answer is to reduce the taxes on the productive food retailers. As I explained earlier, that requires a smaller government. I will return to this issue at the end of this chapter.

Even if the tax problem were solved, everybody might not be better off if the woman in our counter store could not get a job in a modern convenience store close to her current location. As I will get to in more detail later, in some sectors, and food retailing is one of them, employment will actually decrease initially as Brazil gets richer. For food retailing, the reason is that Brazil has such a large number of workers in low-productivity food retailing stores. That has been the way Brazil's economy has evolved. As people left rural areas in droves for the prospect of a better life in the city, informal retailing was a way to get started.

I guess it's better than what people left behind. However, food retailing has such high potential for productivity growth, that if this potential were realized, then the employment level in food retailing would go down. So our woman in the counter store in the São Paulo favela might not get a job in a modern convenience store after all. I will return to this subject in a later section in this chapter when I discuss how Brazil's economy might evolve from here. The bottom line, however, is that Brazil's labor market is so flexible that if Brazil increased labor productivity across the board at its potential of 6 percent per year, unemployment would not rise and the amount of informal employment would go down by 20 percent in ten years. Thus, our woman would get a job and possibly a much better job, in a modern general merchandise retailing store or a telephone company, for instance. But Brazil will have to reduce the size of its government first.

Residential Construction: Another Informality Story

Among the 118 industry studies our teams conducted in thirteen countries, a few stand out by providing clinching evidence of a point. Residential construction in Brazil was one of those cases. Time and time again in the advanced economies, the education level of the workforce did not explain the differences in labor productivity. The reason was that companies demonstrated they could achieve best practice productivity through on-the-job training. This conclusion was also true in Korea, one of the very few middle-income countries.

However, in all these countries, including Korea, the great majority of the workforce had substantial basic education. In Brazil, the low education levels might finally limit the trainability of the workforce. Eighty percent of Brazilian workers have less than eight years of education, compared with only 20 percent of Korean workers. The average years of education of Brazilian workers is 5.3 years, compared with 12.3 in Korea. In construction in Brazil, the average years of education is about 4, or at least 20 percent below the average for the country. Many workers in the Brazilian construction industry were illiterate and straight from remote rural areas.

However, It's Not Education

Since there was virtually no best practice residential construction productivity in Brazil, there was no evidence about whether the average residential construction worker could be trained on the job to achieve high productivity. One construction company had compared itself with U.S. multifamily housing construction. It had achieved about 60 percent of U.S. productivity without running into a labor skill constraint. They had trained their workers to perform the tasks of construction at close to best practice levels. However, this contractor still had two productivity penalties. The first was that his scale of operations was too small to keep his trained workers in different crafts fully utilized. He would have needed to be able to subcontract to special trade companies to get the special craft labor when he needed it. However, such special trade companies are not available in Brazil. A second penalty was that he did not use heavy equipment, such as cranes and elevators, because they were not economic at Brazilian wage rates. Clearly, this contractor did not think that trainability of the workforce would be a constraint in achieving best practice productivity. However, this evidence was too thin to be sure.

Ironically, the conclusive evidence came from the United States. Our construction team from Brazil went to Houston, Texas, to do some comparisons. We compared two similar subsidized housing projects in São Paulo and Houston (Exhibit 6.3). In both cases, many of the workers were illiterate and from agricultural backgrounds. However, in Houston the workers were from Mexico and most did not even speak English. Yet, the Mexican workers in Houston were achieving close to best practice productivity. They had been trained sufficiently to work in the more productive operational and organizational systems used in Houston. With this evidence, I never again doubted that workers around the world have a distribution of capabilities similar enough to allow companies to train them in best practice methods.

I must have told this story at least a hundred times over the past five years. We in advanced economies with high education levels usually assume that workers with low education levels will be a constraint on eco-

Exhibit 6.3: Blue-Collar Trainability in the Housing Sector in the United States and Brazil

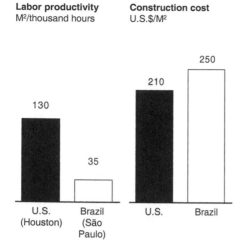

Labor productivity
M²/thousand hours

Construction cost
U.S.$/M²

Construction description	
U.S.	**Brazil**
• 75 M²/unit	• 40 M²/unit
• 209 units	• 20 units
• 1 floor	• 5 floors
• Content	• Content
– 1 bedroom	– 1–2 bedroom
– 1 bathroom	– 1 bathroom
– AC	– No internal doors

Labor productivity: U.S. (Houston) 130, Brazil (São Paulo) 35

Construction cost: U.S. 210, Brazil 250

nomic development. We do this because in our societies, educational level is usually associated with higher capabilities. Thus we slip into the fallacy of thinking that without much education, the workforce in poor countries must not have much capability. However, if you think about it for second, it's obvious this is wrong. Just because people do not have high educational levels does not mean they do not have high capabilities. The Mexican workers in Houston demonstrate this.

If the educational level of the workforce in poor countries were a binding constraint on economic development, then we would have to wait a generation or two before these countries could make much progress. It takes at least a decade or two to build an educational system like those in the advanced economies of today. Even after the system is built, it would require another generation to have had most of the workforce go through it. Korea built such an education system and educated most of its workforce in forty years. The Koreans do everything about twice as fast as everybody else, except for the Japanese. Fortunately, poor countries do not have to wait that long.

As valuable as residential construction in Brazil was in clinching the conclusion about labor trainability, it also had other gems. It vividly demonstrated the penalty Brazil was paying for a history of macroeconomic instability. It also showed how informality was trapping residential construction in a low-productivity position.

A Legacy of Hyperinflation: No Mortgages

Residential construction is a very difficult sector to get right. First of all, the product, housing, is big. Housing is by far the largest purchase of individuals. Housing costs at least ten times the cost of a car. Whereas cars can be produced in one big factory where everything can be seen at once and tightly managed, houses are built all over the place. They may not have the ten thousand different parts of automobiles, but they have a lot. The tasks may not be as technologically complex as assembling a car, but there are specialized tasks such as carpentry, electrical, plumbing, bricklaying, etc. The complexity comes from having to gather all materials and all the specialized labor together at the construction site in the proper sequence and without big time gaps in between steps. Brazil cannot do this well because mortgages are not available and real special trade companies do not exist.

In Brazil, houses are built on a pay-as-you-go system. When the owner saves enough money to pay for the next step, the contractor builds some more on his house. The owner cannot contract for the full house in the beginning because he cannot get a mortgage. *Mortgages do not exist in Brazil.* In fact, there is no twenty- to thirty-year money available for anything. A history of hyperinflation has made loans of that length too risky for anybody to make available. The result is that houses are built piecemeal. This method makes the planning and coordination of material acquisition and workforce deployment impossible for the contractor.

And No Special Trades

Moreover, real special trade companies do not exist in Brazil. In the United States, contractors use these companies to provide the specialized labor at the times in the construction process they are needed. No one contractor would have enough business to have all the special crafts in his company and keep them busy all the time. Special trade companies can move from contractor to contractor and are able to achieve high utilization. Obviously, special trades are more useful for contractors building custom single-family homes than they are for contractors building multifamily housing or large single-family housing developments.

In Brazil, the special trade companies are really simply a source of low-cost labor rather than of skilled craftsmen. The reason their labor is low-cost is that the special trades companies pay no social security,

Medicare, and other benefits for their workers, pay for no holidays for them, and spend no effort training them. Workers can't object to these conditions because the special trade companies don't care if they leave. There are plenty of other potential construction workers who have left rural areas for the city. It makes no sense for the special trade companies to train these workers in craft skills because the companies then would not want to lose them and the workers could demand the benefits. The result of these conditions (plus the lack of prefabricated materials and material standards) is that labor productivity in housing construction in Brazil is 35 percent of the U.S. level.

In principle, a formal construction company using special trades with best practice productivity could underprice a company using untrained informal labor. However, it would take too long for the formal company and the special trades to reach best practice for this leap to be financially viable. Moreover, for single-family housing the project financing problem would also have to be solved for the formal company to reach best practice. Thus lack of mortgages and informality has locked Brazilian residential construction into low productivity. Building a track record of macroeconomic stability will solve the mortgage problem. However, informality is more complex. I will come back to it for both retailing and construction at the end of this chapter.

Economic Growth: How Does It Happen and What Does It Take

The first and only question on the minds of the people in both Korea and Brazil was this: How fast can we grow and how do we do that? These people were behind and they knew it. It was obvious that it was possible to have a much greater GDP per capita. They wanted to know how to get there and how long it would take. There was no choice but to take on the growth question.

I was very reluctant to get involved in growth. Growth modeling had a bad reputation. It had a bad reputation for good reason. Reality turned out almost always to be different from the model results. In addition, the models were "black boxes." By this I mean a set of input data went into a large computer program and another set of numbers came out. However, the manipulation of the input data was so complex that you lost all feel for what was really important and for the amount of uncertainty surrounding the results. I was determined that if we did any work on growth, it would be simple and transparent. I did not, however, hold out any hope that our work would be any better than the rest.

Different Approach

Our team tackled the growth question with an approach different from traditional growth modeling. We started from what we could establish well and what had not been available before our work. We started with the current productivities of a good sample of industries. We also knew what best practice productivity was. We knew why the productivity levels were lower. Thus we knew that if, say, Brazil and Korea removed the barriers keeping their productivity low, their productivity would grow. The question was how fast. There we simply looked again at best practice. How fast had any economy at the same stage of development increased productivity in each of our industry studies? Our team took that empirical evidence as the benchmark for the potential growth rate of labor productivity. That analysis showed that Brazil could potentially increase labor productivity at 6 percent per year (about 13 percent per year in the formal part of the economy and almost no productivity growth in the informal part).

Most growth modeling starts the other way around. These models make assumptions about how fast capital can be invested in a country. They then take the current ratio of output to capital and generate an output growth rate. Sometimes they add in a little extra output growth from improvement in the efficiency (productivity) with which the capital is used. We started with labor productivity because improving labor productivity is what most businesses around the world really work on to improve their performance. Sometimes performance is improved through producing the same thing with fewer workers. Sometimes it's improved through the same workers producing a more valuable product or service. Sometimes it's both. In each case, labor productivity improves.

Performance improvement through labor productivity improvement seemed to us to be the starting point for economic progress. After all, that's how we got started moving out of agriculture more than two hundred years ago. In the United Kingdom, agricultural productivity increased enough that it didn't take everybody working on the land to produce enough food for everybody. Surplus workers were the result. These workers started making products and providing services that the landowners wanted but couldn't get if everybody was working on the land. Thus, the same number of workers produced enough food for everybody plus some goods and services for the landowners. Total economic output increased. That's growth. It started with labor productivity improvements in agriculture. Sure, more was needed, but labor productivity improvement was the starting point.

We thus had a way of estimating how fast labor productivity could potentially improve. In the simplest form of our "model," if you want to call it that, if a country just kept everybody working, then we had that country's potential economic growth rate. GDP per capita equals labor productivity times employment per capita. For Brazil, that meant a growth rate in GDP per capita of 6 percent. Since the working-age population is increasing at about 2.5 percent per year, Brazil has a GDP growth potential of 8.5 percent per year.

Role of Capital

We didn't avoid considering capital. We just put it in its place. Capital is needed for some of the labor productivity improvements in existing businesses. Moreover, if productivity improvements release labor, then capital is needed to build the productive capacity where that labor can work. If labor is not released, but more valuable goods and services are produced, then workers and owners use the additional income from the sale of these more valuable products to buy more of the goods and services produced by others. Capital is needed again for the additional productive capacity to produce these additional goods and services. Labor productivity in these other enterprises also has to go up since for the moment we are assuming that everybody is working.

We could estimate how much capital is needed. In each of our eight industry studies in Brazil, our team calculated how much additional investment was economic at today's wage rates in Brazil. About one-third of the labor productivity gap between Brazil and the United States in these eight industries was caused by lack of capital for automation and other technology improvement. Surprisingly, it was economic for Brazil to invest to close three-fourths of the part of the gap due to capital, even at today's low wage rates in Brazil. From this information, we calculated the amount of capital needed to increase labor productivity at 6 percent per year. To this capital, we then added the capital needed to increase capacity so that everybody stayed employed. It turned out that most of the additional capital needed was to increase capacity and not to increase productivity in existing businesses.

To calculate how much additional capital was needed, our team had to know two things. Where would the additional capacity be built and at what capital productivity? To determine where in the economy the capital would be added, we looked at where other economies further down the development path than Brazil had built the capacity and increased production of goods and services. It turns out that all economies have followed a similar evolutionary path. They all evolve out of agriculture into manufacturing and services. Service employment always increases faster than manufacturing employment. Manufacturing employment increases for a while and then actually begins to decrease as a fraction of total employment. Service employment just keeps increasing as a fraction of total employment right up to today's economic frontier in the United States. Using this evolutionary pattern, we could estimate how much capital is needed, taking into account that manufacturing and electric and telecommunication utilities require much more plant and equipment to produce products than do service industries and construction.

Our team still had to estimate the efficiency (productivity) at which capital could be applied to build additional capacity. We assumed that new investments would apply capital at global best practice efficiency up to the maximum level that was economic at today's Brazilian wage rates. The net result was that Brazil needed to invest each year total capital (including public infrastructure, education, etc.) equal to 26 percent of its GDP to achieve its maximum potential. At first, this result looked too low compared with Korea's total investment rate of 33 percent. However, the difference between the two countries comes entirely from the difference in the business investment rate component of total investment (14 percent for Brazil and 22 percent for Korea).

I pointed out in the last chapter that Korea used capital inefficiently. Its capital productivity in telecom, automotive, and food processing is less than half of the level Brazil could achieve. Thus it's not surprising that Brazil's business investment rate would be much less than Korea's. Since Brazil's current total investment level is only 19 percent, it's not obvious it can reach 26. However, at least half this gap could be closed by balancing the governments' budgets. In the 1990s, Brazil ran government deficits of about 4 percent of GDP. Here again is a problem arising from Brazil's big government. In order to use the savings of the people of Brazil to grow faster, those savings need to go to finance business investment and not to finance government deficits. The remainder of the investment gap can be made up from lower costs for investment goods through market opening and higher productivity in retail banks to reduce the drain on national savings from the high costs of collecting savings deposits and making loans.

There are other more complex aspects of growth that must be considered before reaching a final judgment about Brazil's maximum growth potential. We considered whether Brazil's exports would grow fast enough to earn enough to pay for the increased imports Brazil would need for this fast growth, without Brazil's having to borrow too much from abroad. Neither we nor anybody else can model the complex interactions here fully satisfactorily. It did look likely that with the productivity potential in Brazil and its low labor costs, it should have an enormous international cost advantage in many sectors. Therefore Brazil should have no trouble exporting. Moreover, with the movement to a flexible exchange rate forced on Brazil by the 1998 crisis, exports and imports should remain in adequate balance to keep Brazil from being unduly vulnerable to an international financial crisis.

How about the availability of labor skills for an 8.5 percent growth rate? I have already discussed why productivity can improve substantially without increasing the educational levels of the workforce on the factory floor and its equivalent in other parts of the economy. However, comparing with Chile, it seems that Brazil might have to increase its supply of highly educated workers to fill the needs for management and technical skills.

Will Rapid Productivity Increase Cause Unemployment?

Finally, is the assumption that everybody would stay working correct or not? Would all this productivity improvement just lead to substantial unemployment? In fact, unemployment in Brazil doesn't really happen. People just fall back into subsistence living in rural areas or to street vending in the cities. Would this happen in Brazil?

In order for Brazil to grow fast, it has to remove the barriers to productivity growth. As some workers and owners get richer from this productivity growth, their preferences for goods and services shift. They shift from the goods and services produced by informal workers, primarily in agriculture, construction, and retailing, to the goods and services produced by formal workers, primarily in utilities, housing construction, and service industries such as banking and airlines.

This is what happened in all other countries as they developed from Brazil's current state. In fact, demand grows so fast for these "formal industry" products and services that if the capital is available to build the new capacity, then the output of the formal industries actually grows faster than productivity there. That means employment increases in these industries. The only place to get additional employment is from the informal sector. So informal employment would go down. That means poverty goes down. That's exactly how economic development should work. That's how all economies have evolved out of agriculture and other forms of informal employment to high productivity, formal work.

However, Brazil is in a tough spot. Because it is coming along behind other countries, it has the potential to increase productivity very fast. Thus, if Brazil removes the barriers to productivity growth, rapid productivity increase is very likely to occur in the formal sectors. This productivity growth will occur regardless of whether Brazil builds the additional capacity to satisfy the preferences of workers with higher wages. If Brazil did not generate the capital to provide the additional capacity that the country had the potential to use, it would not pull workers out of the informal sector to formal jobs. A 5 percent per year growth rate is necessary just to hold informal employment even. The fraction of Brazil's people working in informal or subsistence conditions would remain at about 50 percent. That's why it's critical to get the investment rate up. If Brazil mustered the business investment to grow at 8 to 9 percent per year, informal employment would go down from 50 to 40 percent of all employment in ten years. Otherwise, the principal result of productivity improvement will be a further widening of the income distribution and not economic growth for all. That's an additional reason why getting the size of Brazil's government down is important.

Brazil's Potential Is Huge

So what should we make of all these numbers? The important thing is not the actual magnitude of the numbers, but whether they are big or little and why. The growth numbers are big, especially compared with Brazil's GDP per capita growth rate for the past decade of 1 to 2 percent per year. We can have confidence that they are big because we understand why they are big. They are big because Brazil has the potential to increase productivity very fast. The reason Brazil has this potential is that it is coming along behind other countries that have made the numerous innovations yielding high productivity. Brazil simply has to apply these innovations. However, countries coming along behind now have a new risk. Because Brazil can increase productivity so fast, it also needs to mobilize the savings to invest at a considerably faster rate than now. In this way, Brazil could add enough capacity to pull workers out of informality and poverty and into formal jobs. Otherwise, the formal sector workers will get richer and the informal workers will be left behind.

So Brazil has the potential to grow very fast. Will it? That of course depends on many things. It is ultimately a political question. However, even before politics, there is a question of operational feasibility. Is it feasible for businesses in Brazil and for foreign investors to improve current operations and build new plants at the rate required by 8 to 9 percent growth per year? Well, Korea did it for ten years, from 1985 to 1995. So it can be done. However, it was done in Korea through government-directed investments using the banks and through suppressing consumption by de-emphasizing the service sector.

Neither of these conditions apply in Brazil. The Brazilian government is not directing the allocation of capital in the private sector, and Brazilians have plenty of goods and services to consume. This is as it should be because the low productivity associated with the Korean (and Japanese) path leads to trouble down the road.

On the other hand, is the profit incentive, which is the motivator for the high-productivity path, strong enough to cause businesses to improve and new businesses to be built at a rate generating 8 to 9 percent growth per year? There is simply no such example anywhere in the world yet. When the United States was at Brazil's state of economic development (1913), it was growing at 4 percent per year. However, it was having to make the innovations that pushed out the economic frontier at the time. Brazil doesn't have to do that. Perhaps the closest case is the rebuilding of war-torn Germany's economy in the 1950s. Of course Germany's performance was motivated by perhaps the most cataclysmic crisis one can imagine. Maybe it does take a crisis to shake an economy from one development path to another. Korea's experience suggests it takes more than the 1998 crisis to do so. I don't think we wish for a deeper crisis than 1998 in hopes that Brazil will shift to a faster development path. Crises are risky. You never know in which direction they will turn, and there are many possible bad directions. The world will learn a lot about growth from Brazil's experience over the next decade or so.

Big Government Stands in the Way

Brazil ought to be doing better economically than it is. Yes, Brazil suffers a huge legacy from bad economic policy. Brazil has protected its domestic industries, protected foreign direct investment, merrily indulged in hyperinflation, let the government own and run a large part of its economy, and kept a fixed exchange rate too long. As I said earlier in this chapter, Brazil seems to have tried almost everything except a Soviet-style centrally planned economy. Brazil has had lots of hard lessons on what does not work. Nevertheless, economic policy under President Fernando Enrique Cardoso has been improving for the past eight years. Yet Brazil has barely been growing. Why?

Brazil is a hard country to get your arms around. It's not just because it has a huge land mass and 150 million people. Brazil now is a pluralistic democracy. Many points of view are strongly held and there is little conformity. Brazil is strongly egalitarian in philosophy, considerably more so than the United States. It may be that Brazil is too philosophical about everything.

The two big characteristics of Brazil's economy that stand out now are the large amount of informality and the large size of its government. As we have seen, 50 percent of all employment in Brazil is informal. Moreover, the Brazilian government spends an amount equal to 39 percent of GDP, compared with 37 percent for the United States today and about 8 percent when the United States was at Brazil's level of development in 1913. The two are linked. Formal businesses with high productivity cannot take advantage of that high productivity and take market share away from informal businesses. The reason is that formal businesses pay such high taxes that they cannot price below the informal businesses (Exhibit 6.4). This is especially true in the food retailing case.

Exhibit 6.4: Government Revenues

Percent GDP

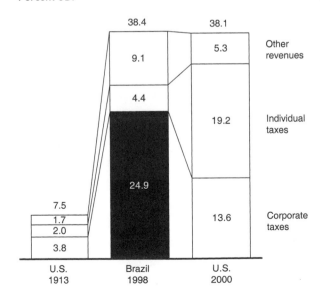

It's also the reason formal special trades companies with skilled crafts-men cannot replace the informal special trades companies providing only cheap labor for residential housing construction.

The reason the formal businesses pay such high taxes is that gov-ernment is so big and that government cannot tax the informal busi-nesses. The formal businesses are where Brazil raises most of its tax rev-enue. Brazil has a very low personal income tax compared with the United States. Even at these high tax rates, the Brazilian government spends even more and runs budget deficits. These deficits soak up na-tional savings and leave less money for business investment.

Why does Brazil have such a large government? My thoughts about this are speculative. The Constitution of 1988, established when Brazil moved from military rule to democracy, guaranteed economic and so-cial welfare rights in the spirit of the modern social welfare states of Western Europe. The government technocratic elite favored these guar-antees ideologically. The political elite saw a chance to reward their con-stituents (and themselves). The business community went along with it as long as the taxes to pay for it didn't come out of their profits.

But the money to pay for all this has to come from somewhere. It ends up coming from the consumers who pay the high prices that result from adding all the sales, value-added, and employment taxes on to the cost of goods and services. Customers avoid these taxes when they can by purchasing from informal enterprises. That directly slows down the growth of the more productive formal enterprises and results in slower economic growth.

There are other reasons to worry about 39 percent of a country's GDP passing through the hands of government. First of all, governments are viewed everywhere as being unproductive. We just have to compare the productivity of government-owned retail banks in Brazil with pri-vate retail banks to realize the potential inefficiency. As we saw earlier, the private banks are twice as productive as the government-owned banks. Moreover, with all that money flowing through government, the potential for corruption is enormous. It's especially risky for Brazil, with the weak judicial and law enforcement institutions typical of a develop-ing country.

How Much Government Is Enough?

I'm not advocating that Brazil today return to a government that spends only 8 percent of GDP. Today's developing countries can have public health standards and educational opportunities that simply were not available in the United States in 1913. It is clear that modern public health and educational programs should be provided by governments in developing countries, even if such expenditures slowed economic growth down a bit. The 11 percent of GDP that Brazil spends on health and education looks roughly in line with Germany's 13 percent and Japan's 9 percent, but definitely higher than Korea's 6 percent. The question really is what about the other 28 percent of GDP spent by government in Brazil.

Brazil's government spends about 11 percent of GDP on the government-run pension system compared with 5 percent in the United States today and close to zero in 1913. The government contribution to the pensions of Brazil's government employees is 4.7 percent of GDP compared with 1.8 in the United States today. Sounds like Brazil's government employees are getting away with murder. Brazil clearly has government employment it can't afford.

I would argue that Japan got along satisfactorily in terms of government services in the 1950s, when it was at Brazil's current level of development. Then, Japan's government spent only 20 percent of GDP. That should be enough for Brazil today. That suggests Brazil's major task is downsizing its government substantially. Brazil's government workers are trying to implement policies and enjoy standards of living as if they were in rich countries. They are not. They are in a poor country that is not growing very much in per capita terms.

I know of only four countries that have substantially downsized their governments as a percent of GDP in recent times. They are Chile, New Zealand, Ireland, and Canada. The struggle in the United States and Europe has been to keep government from growing even larger. It seems that holding even is the best most countries have done so far. Politically, it's easy to see why it's so much easier to increase government spending than to cut it. It may be that the secret to a small government is to never get big to start with. If that's true, then Brazil will never grow nearly as fast as its potential. Generally, I have been saying that coming along the development path later than others is not all bad because these countries don't have to invent everything all over again. However, copying the size of governments of countries further down the path turns out to be a bad idea for developing countries. In this regard, Brazil has tried to leap too fast into the world of rich countries. As a result, it now runs the risk of leaving half its population near subsistence levels of living. That doesn't sound like a sustainable situation to me.

CHAPTER SEVEN

Russia: Distorted Market Economy

Russia has proved that it is possible for a market economy to have a worse economic performance than a centrally planned economy. And Russia does have a market economy. Russia has privatized virtually all businesses and set free virtually all prices. However, powerful forces against reform prevented anything more. The economic costs to the Russian people of woefully incomplete reform have been enormous. Russia's GDP per capita dropped by 40 percent between 1989 and the mid-1990s.

This is not an indictment of market economies, or capitalism, for that matter. It is strong evidence of just how hard it is to realize the potential of market economies for high economic performance.

Sometimes we have to see conditions in the extreme to appreciate their significance fully. Brazil gives a strong hint of how distortions in competition among firms can constrain productivity improvement and thus limit the performance of a market economy. Russia leaves no doubt about the pernicious effects of such distortions. Russia distorts the ground rules for competition to such an extreme that businesses do well not because they do better but for other reasons.

These distortions take many forms. They include government subsidies for some firms but not others, preferential taxes for some but not others, forgiving taxes or electricity and gas bills for some but not others, giving government contracts consistently to some but not others, hassling some with red tape but not others, or allowing some to steal intellectual property from others. Sometimes more productive firms cannot expand because government simply orders unproductive firms not to shut down.

Russia Is Special

Russia holds a special fascination for Americans of my generation. For the first fifty years of my life, the Soviet Union was the one country that could dramatically change my way of life. We will always remember Khrushchev banging his shoe at the UN and saying "we will bury you."

The economic analysis of the CIA was so bad that we thought he might be right. In March 1989, the CIA publication "The Soviet Union in Global Perspective" estimated that in 1985 the Soviet Union's GDP was 60 percent of the United States' GDP and that things changed little through 1989. Given the population differences, that would make the Soviet Union's GDP per capita about 50 percent of the United States'. Thus, the CIA was estimating that the Soviet Union was one of the very few countries in the world to break out of the ranks of the poor and achieve middle income levels. The Soviet Union would have had the same relation to the U.S. economy that Korea has today, except that the Soviet Union had 20 percent more people than the United States, whereas Korea has only 20 percent as many. For all we knew at the time, the Soviet path could have continued its upward trajectory, and it was bigger than the United States (in both population and land mass).

The Soviet Union was a military success and an economic failure. I got a glimpse of the economic failure part while traveling in Russia as a student in 1965. Our group visited a photographic film processing plant on the outskirts of Moscow. There was no automation in the plant and very little mechanization. Strips of film were pushed along the stages of the development process primarily by hand. An engineer from East Germany kept the right solutions in each vat. Halfway through our tour, a British engineering student whispered to me, "You guys don't have anything to worry about." Of course, Russia did have very good engineering. It was all devoted to military production and heavy manufacturing. Consumers didn't count and got next to nothing. A society can go on only so long that way, especially if consumers are well educated and aware that their competitors have both guns and butter. The Soviet Union fell because it could not provide both. In 1989 GDP per capita in Russia was only 27 percent of that of the United States, or half the CIA estimate.

Russian Reform

Since the disappearance of the Soviet Union, Russia has tried to go from a centrally planned economy to a market economy overnight. It quickly took the two most obvious steps to establish a market economy. It placed most of its productive assets in private hands and it stopped controlling prices for most items. It also opened its borders to the imports of consumer goods. By the mid-1990s, however, an apparent contradiction had appeared. Official statistics showed that Russia's GDP per capita had dropped to 15 percent of the U.S. level. Yet my partners in McKinsey's Moscow office were telling me that new businesses were starting up all around and that things had to be getting better. After all, new businesses can get established and expand only if they have better performance than the old businesses they're trying to replace. They make more profits because they produce better products or they use fewer resources or both. They are more productive than the old businesses. Or at least that's what new businesses replacing old businesses usually means.

This is not the case in Russia. In Russia, the most productive firms were not the ones making profits and expanding. It was the firms benefiting from the distortions in competition.

Whether the early Russian "reformers" simply did not understand the importance of a level playing field for business competition we will never know. Many "romantics" about the wisdom of the capital market believe that all you have to do to create a successful market economy is to generate the profit incentive through privatization and allow price competition. The capital market would take care of the rest. It will make sure the best companies survive and expand. Maybe the reformers put their faith in the capital market. However, the "best" companies in the eyes of the capital market are the most profitable ones. And in Russia, the most profitable companies were not the most productive companies.

Another possibility is that the reformers were desperately trying to make a return to the state-owned and centrally planned economy impossible. They could do this by privatizing everything and decontrolling prices. What actually happened was that Russian banks, at the government's direction, simply made gobs of loans to failing companies. They didn't reward productive companies, or even profitable ones. They just created hyperinflation by handing out all that money.

Poland Went a Different Way

It is tempting to conclude that Russia just had to bear this cost. It is the price of almost a century of misguided ideology. The problem with this argument is Poland. In 1989, Poland had about the same economic structure and about the same economic management system as Russia.

Poland's GDP per capita was 21 percent of the United States', or about 25 percent below Russia's. By 2002, Poland's GDP per capita was 29 percent of the United States', and about 40 percent above Poland's GDP per capita in 1989 (Exhibit 7.1). The really important point is that between 1989 and 2002, Poland's GDP per capita on the way up crossed over Russia's GDP per capita on the way down, and ended up 30 percent higher than Russia's.

I'm not going to write a separate chapter about Poland. I will simply point out at times in this chapter how Poland did things differently from Russia. Perhaps the most important thing Poland did differently was that it made sure that competition in much of its economy was sufficiently fair that high-productivity foreign companies wanted to invest in Poland because they could make money there. In 1997, business investment in Russia was 13 percent of GDP. However, foreign direct investment was only 0.8 percent of GDP. In Poland business investment was a little higher, at 16.5 percent of GDP. However, of this, foreign direct investment was 7 percent of GDP, or almost half of all business investment. With this foreign direct investment came, in many cases, global best practice productivity. In particular, the world's best retailers—Tesco, Carrefour, and Wal-Mart—are all there. None of them go to Russia because they can't make any money there.

The Russian experience since 1989 has valuable economic lessons. Sometimes to understand the subtleties of a phenomenon we need to see the phenomenon in extreme conditions so that the effects stand out. In Russia, we have seen extreme distortion of competition in a market economy and its devastating effects. If someone had asked me before we

Exhibit 7.1: GDP per Capita (PPP), Russia and Poland

Index U.S. 1995 = 100

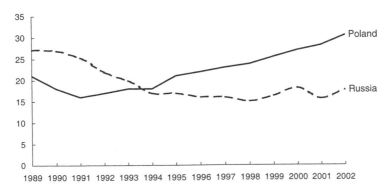

studied Russia whether it was possible to distort a market economy enough to get a worse outcome than from a centrally planned economy, I would not have been sure about the answer. I am sure now. We now know for sure how important a level playing field for competition is.

Lesson from Russia

In Russia, we heard these distortions were put in place for one of two reasons: social concerns or corruption. The social concerns in most cases are an excuse and not a good reason. There are a few company towns where workers would be absolutely devastated if the only factory in town shut down. I will address this issue in detail in the steel case, which follows. However, these cases are rare. The more general concern about factory shutdowns comes from a lack of understanding of how economies evolve, how jobs are always being created and destroyed, and how workers in a modern economy in today's world will have to change jobs several times. Of course, Russia itself has little experience with this, although there is lots of such experience in the rest of the world. In any case, it is certain that these social concerns arguments would have had less influence if the full costs of the market distortions had been understood in advance.

As for corruption, it exists to some degree everywhere. Usually developing countries, and Russia is a developing country, lack the institutions (judicial and enforcement) to successfully combat corruption. The action they can take, however, is to reduce the opportunity for corruption. That means simpler taxes, less red tape, less government procurement, and privatization of virtually everything. Again, if the full costs of market distortions were understood, it seems likely that reformers would do more to reduce the potential for corruption.

Thus, I end up thinking that ignorance about the existence and impact of market distortions on competition is the most important factor. First of all, these distortions are hard to see. They occur not in one big national economic market. They occur in the hundreds of separate micromarkets that make up an economy. Moreover, you can see the impact of these distortions only by determining the productivity of the firms that are surviving and expanding. That's hard to do and takes substantial effort to accomplish. One of my worries is, How will national governments and international institutions ever build the capability to identify these micro distortions and evaluate their impact? They certainly have not done it so far. For now, only the private sector has the scope and the knowledge of how markets work to do this work on a comparative basis around the world. This is a big problem.

Steel: The Good and the Ugly

In 1990 the Soviet Union was the largest steel producer in the world. It produced 160 million tons of steel per year. That was 60 percent more than the next largest producer, Japan. At the time the Soviet Union broke up, Russia alone produced 90 million tons, slightly below Japan but about equal to the United States. That 90 million tons was four and a half times the production of Brazil, a country of roughly the same population and GDP per capita as Russia. The Soviets believed that through heavy manufacturing they would "bury" the West. Steel was the backbone of heavy manufacturing.

I can still remember seeing replays of old news clips depicting the Soviet developments in the 1930s. Those clips highlighted the building and operation of the huge Magnitogorsk steel complex, built on the eastern side of the Urals to protect it from invasions from the West. Even the sound of the name suggests force and energy. In 1990, Magnitogorsk produced about 15 million tons of steel. That was about 60 percent of Brazil's total production. Russia has two other large steel plants: Severstal, almost as big as Magnitogorsk, and Novolipetsk, about half that size.

Russia has very good metallurgy and metallurgical engineering. The Red Army had good steel in its tanks. Russia manufactured the operating equipment and designed and built its steel plants. The plants were good. In 1990, the productivity of these three large plants was 95 percent of that of the U.S. steel industry. Russia also has six other steel plants of somewhat smaller size with total productivity about 70 percent of the U.S. industry in 1990. If the large and medium-sized steel plants were all Russia had today, its steel industry would be in pretty good shape. The problem is that Russia also has thirty-three small steel plants scattered among many towns across the country. These plants use the hopelessly obsolete open-hearth furnace and ingot casting technologies. In 1990 their productivity was only 30 percent of that of the U.S. industry. One-third of Russia's 400,000 steelworkers are in these obsolete plants. These plants would have been closed down long ago in Japan, Korea, the United States, and even Brazil for economic reasons. Beyond that, these plants would not come close to meeting environmental standards in any of these countries.

The Legacy of Central Planning

So the Soviets left Russia with too big a steel industry. Then when the Soviet Union disappeared, the bottom fell out of demand for steel in Russia. Consumption of steel in Russia dropped 75 percent between 1990 and 1998. Imports containing steel poured in, private companies in Russia cut production and invested very little, and the government stopped building infrastructure. Now, a steel plant either operates or it doesn't. You can imagine the problem of trying to shut down a plant with molten metal running all through it and then starting it up again. So unless you are going to shut the plant down permanently, you just run less metal through it. However, since you have to keep everything running, you have to keep all the people. The reduction in steel output per hour worked is straightforward. Between 1990 and 1997, labor productivity fell 32 percent in the big plants, 48 percent in the medium-sized plants, and 54 percent in the small plants. The industry ended up with a labor productivity of 28 percent of the U.S. level and 40 percent of Brazil's.

Because the big plants were so good, they began exporting heavily. That's why their labor productivity fell less than in the other plants. In 1997, Russia exported 60 percent of its total steel production. Even though the world has substantial overcapacity in steel, Russia was able to export because of its low natural gas and labor costs. Good economics tells us that the rest of the world should welcome these low-cost steel imports. Steel workers elsewhere should move on to do something else where they have more of an international advantage than in steel. Russia will not be able to disrupt the steel industries in other countries enough to export its way out of its low-productivity position.

One would think that now the thirty-three small, hopeless steel plants will close. They will simply run out of cash. They won't be able to pay their energy bills; so the electricity and gas will be shut off. They won't be able to pay their taxes; so the government will foreclose on their land. They won't be able to pay their workers; so the workers will go do something else. The destruction half of the creative destruction process through which economies evolve will happen in steel. Not so.

Why Not?

The local governments don't want to lose these plants. These governments control the local distribution companies for electricity and gas.

They order the distribution companies to supply the small steel plants. The small steel plants pretend to pay the local distribution companies with barter goods of steel products, whose value is grossly overstated. The local distribution companies pass these overvalued barter goods on up the chain until they reach the national gas company, Gazprom, and the national electricity company, UES. At this point, the federal budget is left holding the bag with overvalued barter goods. This process finally collapsed with the inability of the federal government to meet its debt service obligations in 1998, thus precipitating a financial crisis. I understand that because of this lesson, it is much more difficult to use the barter subterfuge today. I guess the small steel plants are just piling up their energy bills. The national energy companies can't do anything about this. To cut off the small steel plants, they would have to cut off the whole town in which they operate. That's tough to do, especially in the middle of a Russian winter.

The same thing happened with taxes. One way or another, the small steel plants underpaid or didn't pay at all. If the small steel plants went into bankruptcy, the local government appointed a manager no longer responsible to shareholders. The plants effectively became publicly owned. The public was not going to shut them down. Our team looked at how serious a problem shutting down the small steel plants would be for the towns in which they operated. It turns out that half the plants are in towns where the steel plant workforce accounts for less than 10 percent of town employment. It's hard to see how the loss of this small percentage of employment would be a catastrophe for the town. This result suggests substantial collusion between the plant managers and the local government officials, using social concerns about town employment as the excuse for not shutting the plant down.

And it seems the small steel plants can get away without paying the workers. The reason is the registration system ties social benefits to the worker's current residence. Thus workers have a disincentive to move anywhere. Second, they are very unlikely to find a job anywhere else. For reasons that I will get to in the food retailing and housing construction cases, the creation part of the creative destruction process isn't working in Russia either. Moreover, in Russia, workers can't just move to the outskirts of cities, live in flimsy housing, and hope they can work their way up. The Russian winter, again, will not allow what is possible in Brazil. So the workers in the small steel plants are stuck trying to live by growing potatoes rather than making steel. Actually, it's probably a good thing they are stuck because we couldn't see anything else for them to do right away. It's better for them to live this way until Russia starts creating jobs in the areas the Soviets hugely underemphasized, consumer goods and services.

Oil: Opportunity Squandered

Russia is probably making its biggest mistake in oil. Oil could solve a lot of problems for Russia. It could provide the export earnings that would allow Russia to import all the capital equipment it needed to achieve its high economic growth potential. It also could provide the government sufficient revenue so that Russia could have a social welfare system well above what other developing countries without oil can afford. Brazil has to worry about both these problems. Russia does not. However, Russia's current path in the oil sector will fail to yield these benefits.

Russia has the largest oil reserves outside the Middle East after Venezuela. It is currently the world's second-largest oil producer. However, its oil industry is in rapid decline. In 1988 Russia produced 12 million barrels of oil a day. By 1998 that rate had declined to 6 million barrels per day. Russia stopped drilling more wells and stopped investing in increasing the yield from existing wells. Under these conditions, the decline in this industry is inevitable. The recent spurt in oil production and oil exports in response to the sharp rise in world oil prices is not sustainable. It's a shame because this decline is so unnecessary.

Oil is one of the most mature sectors in today's global economy. Moreover, oil is one of the most global sectors. The sector has several large firms that compete intensely at the retail level all over the world. At the crude oil production stage, the world has a production cartel, OPEC, to which many of the major oil producing countries belong. OPEC agrees to limit supply. This causes the world price of oil to rise to the point that high-cost producers are brought into the market to satisfy demand. The low-cost members of OPEC then make huge profits. Russia is not a member of OPEC, but it is a low-cost producer. Russia's lack of oil exporting infrastructure and its drop in overall production mean that Russia is leaving an enormous amount of money on the table. If Russia does not start investing heavily in its oil industry, it will end up being a net importer of oil in ten years.

This is simply not necessary. The world's oil industry could provide the capital needed to develop new oil fields with the best of modern technology. It also has the technology to significantly improve the performance of existing fields. Under favorable investment conditions and application of best practice technology, Russia could return to produc-

Exhibit 7.2: Future Russian Oil Scenarios

Millions of barrels per day

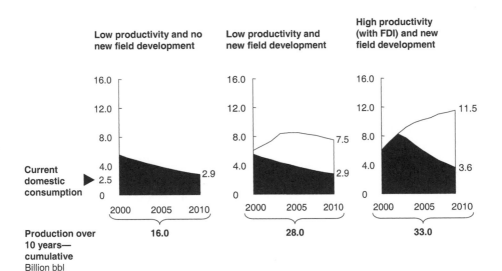

tion of about 12 million barrels a day in ten years (Exhibit 7.2). Only 4 million would come from existing fields; 8 million would be from new fields. Even more importantly, 7 to 8 million barrels a day could be exported, compared with 3 to 4 million barrels a day in 1999. This increase in oil exports could be done without increasing Russia's share in the world oil market. However, Russia would need to triple the capacity of its export infrastructure.

What's Wrong at the Well Head?

To determine just how bad Russia's performance in oil was, we benchmarked it against the performance of the onshore oil industry in Texas. The Texas industry is close to global best practice. Overall productivity (total factor productivity) is the right measure for comparing the two industries. Overall productivity is the ratio of the oil output to the capital and labor resources used to produce the oil. To make the results comparable, we had to adjust for differences in geology, age of fields, crude oil quality, well depth, and climate. After these adjustments, Russia's overall productivity in oil was 30 percent of Texas's productivity.

Lower output per well explained about half of the productivity gap. The biggest reason for lower output per well was lack of application of modern recovery technologies, primarily hydrofracturing. This technology uses water under pressure to break up underground structures preventing access to pockets of oil in the field. The water pressure also forces more oil to the surface.

About 25 percent of the gap came from extra capital per well in Russia. The oil industry creates most of its own capital. That capital is a well drilled and ready for production. In Russia it takes twice as long to drill a comparable well. It's not because the Russian drills have a slower mechanical drilling speed. Russia switched almost entirely to faster "turbo" drilling in the 1960s. Western oil companies made this switch only in the 1990s. Russia bet that its drill bit industry could meet the higher quality requirements of turbo drilling. It could not. The more rapid wearing out of the drill bits more than offsets the higher drilling speed (Exhibit 7.3). This is because drill bit replacement involves lifting a string of drill pipes up from a well that may be two miles deep. Today the drill bit market worldwide is dominated by four large manufacturers who have vast experience and substantial R&D efforts. Only in the 1990s did drill bits become good enough to justify economically turbo drilling. Modern drill bits produced with polycrystalline diamond cutters have five times longer life than the standard Russian drill bit used today.

Extra labor in the oil fields explains the remaining 25 percent of the productivity gap. The Russian oil industry still uses large numbers of functional specialists to manage its reservoirs, whereas Western oil companies have converted to smaller multidisciplinary teams. In addition, Russian oil companies, especially the small ones, have a large overhang of administrative personnel left over from Soviet days.

Why No Deal?

So it would seem that there is a deal made in heaven in Russian oil. Western technology and Western capital applied against huge untapped reserves yielding good business for the oil companies and government revenue in the form of dollars for Russia. At least that's how it must have looked in the early 1990s. Too bad it hasn't worked out. It hasn't worked out because the two sides don't trust each other. Russians don't trust Western oil companies because they're afraid Russia will be raped.

Exhibit 7.3: Drill Bit Durability

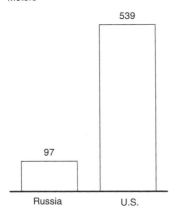

Drill bit distance before replacement
Meters

539

97

Russia   U.S.

Moreover, the private Russian owners, who "stole" the Russian oil assets in the infamous "loans for shares" deal cut with President Yeltsin and his reformers, don't want the Westerners in. They have become fabulously wealthy without the Westerners, and they see no reason to risk losing any control.

The Western oil companies, on the other hand, have been burned as minority shareholders. Holding companies have used transfer pricing and share dilution to "milk" their subsidiaries, which included oil companies. Moreover, the Western oil companies have not been able to get comfortable about the chances of Russia's living up to agreements specifying how profits will be shared between investors and the government. Since the return from the investment in the development of a new oil field may be spread out over thirty years or so, this confidence factor is important. In addition, the Russian government controls all oilfield equipment and service imports through a convoluted and nontransparent licensing process.

Finally, the Russian government has kept the domestic oil price low for strategic uses (agriculture, defense, etc.) by controlling exports. It controls exports through the state-owned pipeline monopoly Transneft. Oil export infrastructure is operating at full capacity and has not been enlarged since 1991. The Russian government appears to be afraid that if it built more export infrastructure, the Russian oil companies would simply increase exports without investing to increase production. Of course, even that outcome would be better than the current situation. Russia would have more exports. The higher revenues could be used to explicitly subsidize the "strategic" users of oil, who would then have to pay the world price.

It will be interesting to see whether Russia can get oil right or not. The industry could use about $200 billion in investment over the next ten years. To maximize production, about 40 percent of this investment should come from foreign sources, who would bring technology with the money. With that, Russia could be producing 12 million barrels of oil a day in ten years instead of the projected 3 million. The increased production over only the investment period would be worth slightly over $300 billion at $20 per barrel. The increased production would of course carry over well beyond the investment period. The potential benefits for all sides, but especially Russia, are huge, and the "deal" involves only big sophisticated negotiators. The BP investment of $6.75 billion announced in early 2002 is a start, but only a small start. Major progress on oil is probably a leading indicator of whether reform in Russia is progressing constructively or not. It will be fascinating to watch.

Housing Construction: Lots of Change but Little Progress

The housing construction sector in Russia has undergone dramatic change since the dissolution of the Soviet Union. All construction companies have been privatized; half of all housing construction is being done outside the Soviet-era companies that existed in 1990; and half of all housing built is now high-end multifamily housing and single-family housing. These two types of housing accounted for only 10 percent of new construction in 1990. Then, 90 percent was Soviet-style multifamily housing, either from prefabricated panels or bricks. Despite all these changes, labor productivity declined slightly between 1990 and 1997. It is now about 10 percent of the U.S. level and one-third of the level in Brazil. Clearly, in this case, change has not been an indicator of performance improvement.

The obvious implication of these facts is that the productivity at which these new types of housing are being built is about the same as the productivity of the old Soviet companies building Soviet-type housing. Here, we have a chance to reconcile the impression of substantial change in Russia's economy with declining performance. First of all, in 1997, 30 percent of all housing constructed was single-family housing, compared with about 5 percent in 1990. However, it turns out that

90 percent of this single-family housing is being built by the homeowner himself on a brick-by-brick basis. Whenever he saves a little money, he builds a little more on his house. The reason single-family housing is being built this way is that no mortgage financing is available. That's the same as in Brazil.

What is different in Russia is that no small construction companies using informal labor are available to construct single-family housing. The productivity of these small companies is pretty bad, but it's better than that of the average Russian building a house for the first time. Yet Russians, like everybody else, want single-family housing when they have a choice. In 1995 only 15 percent of the housing stock in Russia was single-family houses. In contrast, single-family housing accounted for 90 percent of the housing stock in Brazil, 60 percent in Korea, and 70 percent in the United States. The productivity of an individual building his house brick-by-brick in Russia is roughly 5 percent of U.S. housing productivity.

Most single-family housing in Russia is being built without any of the advantages of scale. Individuals and not companies are doing the building, and houses are being built one at a time. Probably the principal reason large-scale single-family housing developments do not exist in Russia is the absence of a land code. The ownership of land has not been sorted out since Soviet times, when the state owned everything. As a result, agricultural land on the outskirts of cities and towns is not being converted into large-scale single-family housing developments. In addition, Russia has not sorted out the responsibility for providing infrastructure for such new developments nor the authority to tax to finance infrastructure. Finally, the general hassle associated with obtaining the hundred or so permits needed to start construction deters any business-minded entrepreneur from getting into small-scale single-family housing development. That leaves only the average Russian, who is already living somewhere and already has some land, as the only party willing to proceed with single-family housing construction.

State Companies in Private Clothing

The other reason housing construction productivity is so low in Russia is that the formerly state-owned construction companies are still around. They are operating as if nothing has changed. They build the same Soviet-style panel or brick multifamily houses, still financed by federal and local governments. The governments give them contracts often under the condition that they not lay off workers. Sometimes these companies simply built flats for themselves to use as barter at overvalued prices for payment of taxes. They have little incentive to improve since they have assured business from the governments in return for their not changing.

Their days are numbered, however, because governments are much less able to finance housing than they were before 1990. The result has been that the output of these Soviet-style companies has dropped by about 50 percent between 1990 and 1997. Productivity in these companies has dropped 30 percent, which is somewhat less than the output drop because employment has declined from natural attrition. Their productivity is now about 10 percent of U.S. productivity and 20 percent of multifamily housing productivity in Brazil. The reason the productivity of these Russian companies is so low is that it was bad in Soviet times and has just gotten worse since then.

The Soviet housing construction companies lagged behind their Western counterparts in almost every respect. They did not use the modern resource utilization planning techniques needed to have materials, equipment, and labor all arrive at the right place at the right time. The companies tried to provide all the craft specialties in-house because no special trades companies were included in the Soviet plans. Moreover, the companies had no incentive to try to reduce costs through lower-cost designs and getting rid of excess labor. Thus, a bad situation has just gotten worse. It will remain so until the governments start a fair and open bidding process for public housing. The governments still finance 25 percent of all housing. It would be even better if the governments got out of so much public housing and worked on making land available, providing infrastructure and reducing red tape for private developments. As Brazil has shown, performance in housing construction can be much higher than in Russia even without a mortgage system.

The performance of the remaining 25 percent of construction is a surprise. This is the construction by the new private companies, which primarily build high-end multifamily housing. One would think that they would have good productivity. Unfortunately not. It's only about 20 percent of U.S. multifamily housing productivity and 40 percent of that of Brazil. Even the best of these companies achieve only 40 percent of U.S. productivity. They have all the same operational performance gaps as the old Soviet companies, only somewhat less so.

The resolution of this puzzle is that these companies are responding to sudden demand from a modest number of cash-rich Russians for high-end housing. The construction companies build what these people want as fast as they can without having to worry about costs. This situation, of course, will change over time as the burst of demand is satisfied. At this point, the situation will just get worse as these new companies have less business.

The only remedy is for governments to make the changes in land policy, infrastructure provision, and permitting listed above. In this way, these new companies could begin to provide lower-cost housing for average Russians. Moreover, if the governments cut the old Soviet companies loose, then the old Soviet companies and the new companies would have to compete for this market. Under these conditions, productivity would surely improve up to at least Brazil's level. That would be a huge improvement.

The Toughest Industry to Examine

The construction industry was perhaps the most difficult industry to examine in Russia. It was difficult because the state statistical office, Goskomstat, did not keep employment data for housing separate from the rest of construction. What Goskomstat did have was the number of square meters built for each type of housing. However, a complete picture still required knowing the productivity of the different types of housing construction. The only way to do this was through numerous interviews of construction companies, including the old Soviet companies, who were not anxious to talk to anyone about their performance. Our team also talked to the government officials in charge of housing about how they allocated land and construction contracts.

In one of these interviews, a former Soviet construction company boss said it was dangerous to be asking these questions in Russia. Construction has been a dirty industry in many countries. Post-Soviet Russia was undoubtedly one of the worst. I had just been at an interview with the principal owner of one of the "stolen" Russian oil companies while guards with submachine guns stood outside the door. I wondered if we should really proceed with the project. Soon afterwards, the Moscow police arbitrarily picked up the Japanese consultant on our team while he was simply walking down the sidewalk. They held him for an uncomfortably long time in the back seat of their car. They were presumably looking for a bribe.

At this point the senior consultant on our team in Moscow became unnerved and called me back in Washington with some distress. I worried that I was putting our team at undue risk of harm. I had all of them register with the United States Embassy in Moscow and carry the Embassy phone number with them at all times. In addition, I told them that if they ever became so uncomfortable that they felt they should leave, they should go immediately to the airport and catch the first plane out. No questions would ever be asked. Just the knowledge that they had some control through a license to leave at any time seemed to relieve anxiety somewhat. In any case, we had personal contact with many parts of the Russian economy not explored before by outsiders. We managed to finish our job and left without any serious mishap. Russia was the only country of the thirteen studied by the Global Institute where I felt there was some physical risk to the team. However, the risk seemed manageable and the work was important.

Physical security risks are often cited as an important reason why foreign firms don't go to Russia and set up operations. However, other factors related to the distortion of competition to the extent that foreign firms can't make money are much more important. Our team's own experience in construction is consistent with this. Data is hard to get in construction and the industry is difficult to work with. It would prefer that many of its practices not see the light of day. But that did not stop us.

Food Retailing: No Supermarkets

Sitting around the conference table in McKinsey's Moscow office, I heard several times about how the *gastronoms* worked. Gastronoms were the Soviet food retailing stores. You had to see one to believe it. Walking back from lunch one day, I got our team to take me into one. Sure enough, they were for real.

The first impression was misleading. The shop was relatively spacious, seemed reasonably clean, and was staffed by several women in crisp, white coveralls behind each counter. Moreover, each counter had an interesting variety of high-quality food products. I remember especially the tempting assortment of imported French cheeses. The first difference that dawned on me was that all the goods were under glass enclosures or on the shelf behind the women at the counters. Customers could look but not touch (and presumably not steal). Even though this was lunch hour in the middle of Moscow, few customers were in the store. Those that were seemed to be taking their time, or at least they were there for a long time. Bustling customers were not running in and out as they do at a 7-Eleven.

The reason of course is that there is no such thing as running in and out of a gastronom. For each item purchased, the customer has to visit the counter twice: first to identify the item he wants and pick up a slip identifying that item, and second to pick up the item itself after he has gone to the cash register to pay for it. In Soviet days, I gather there were often lines at the counters. Some convenience. Now, the lines are gone because people shop elsewhere. In Soviet times, 90 percent of all food retailing sales was in gastronoms. It should come as no surprise that by 1997, that percentage had dropped to 40. A wide variety of new types of stores have appeared, including kiosks and pavilions, retail and wholesale markets, and agricultural markets. They took market share away from the gastronoms because the retail and wholesale markets had lower prices, the agricultural markets had better produce, and the kiosks and pavilions stayed open much longer. It should be easy to be more productive than the gastronoms. Surprisingly, however, in 1997 labor productivity in food retailing in Russia was only 23 percent of the U.S. level and almost exactly the same as for gastronoms themselves. The reason is that there are almost no supermarkets in Russia.

Supermarkets Can't Make Money

The big jump in retailing productivity comes when large chains of huge supermarkets replace the traditional mom-and-pop stores and open-air markets. In the United States, 70 percent of food retailing sales is in supermarkets. Supermarkets are two to three times as productive as traditional food retailing. They give customers lower prices and a wide variety of high-quality products. They allow one-stop shopping for a household's food needs for a week. That's real service. Only it does not work this way in Russia.

In Russia, supermarket prices are higher, not lower, than the prices in retail and wholesale markets (Exhibit 7.4). They are higher by about 15 percent. As a result, the market share of retail and wholesale markets has gone from 0 in 1990 to 16 percent in 1997. It's supposed to work the other way. In Poland it did. Poland had the same Soviet-style food retailing structure in 1990. In 1997, supermarkets had 18 percent of food retailing sales. Retail and wholesale markets had only 3 percent. What's gone wrong in Russia?

The low prices of supermarkets come primarily from much lower procurement costs of food items. What about the cost structure of the retail and wholesale markets? Off went one of our team members to interview the operators of the freestanding containers and booths in these markets around Moscow. It turned out these operators paid 10 percent less for the goods they sold than supermarkets. They paid less because they bought foreign goods smuggled into Russia without paying import

Exhibit 7.4: Informal Markets and Supermarkets in Russia

Index price in gastronoms = 100

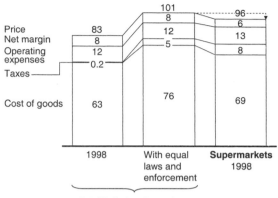

tariffs and they bought counterfeit imitations of branded goods. Over 30 percent of vodka on the consumer market in Russia is counterfeit. In addition, these operators pay virtually no taxes. They pay no taxes because new tax laws give them huge preferences and they often don't pay even that. Thus they save 6 percent of the final sales price by illegally paying less for goods, and they save 8 percent by not paying taxes. If they did not sell smuggled or counterfeit goods and if they paid normal corporate taxes, their prices would be 4 percent higher than for supermarkets.

Recent surveys showed that over 80 percent of Russian consumers would prefer to shop in supermarkets even if prices were equal. They don't like walking through the mud either. However, their income is low enough that they will do so to get lower prices.

The other reason supermarkets normally pay less for food products is that they set up sophisticated logistics systems based on sourcing at least 70 percent of their food products locally. In Russia, that is not possible. It's not possible because the Soviet-era food processing manufacturers have been protected against investments by global best practice food processors. Incumbent food processors can remain profitable by not paying their taxes. Moreover, foreign investments in incumbents are deterred by local governments' preventing improvement of productivity through restructuring operations and laying off excess workers. Finally, the advertising needed to establish brands is not allowed as an expense deduction for tax purposes in many regions, and counterfeit products diminish the value of brands.

As a result, the Russian food processing industry is not restructuring and growing. Thus it is not able to meet the needs of best practice supermarket chains. Part of the sophisticated logistics system that best practice supermarkets set up is a rationalized wholesaling sector, as I described in chapter 4 on the United States. Thus, market distortions in food retailing and food processing are not only preventing performance improvement in these sectors, they are also preventing improvement in the wholesaling sector.

Global Supermarkets Go Everywhere Else

Poland and Brazil have roughly the same per capita income as Russia. Supermarkets account for 36 percent of food retailing sales in Brazil and 18 percent in Poland. They account for only 0.2 percent in Russia. Clearly, Russia is performing way below its potential. In 1990 food retailing in Russia and Poland looked very much the same. Supermarkets came to Poland through foreign direct investment by such global best practice retailers as Carrefour and Tesco. They came because the playing field was level. The stalls in bazaars and other markets in Poland are all registered with the government and must use cash registers. The result is they have to pay their taxes. They can't compete with the supermarkets. In addition, global best practice food processors have invested in Poland. They provide the food products supermarkets need. Poland imports only 14 percent of food consumption. Russia imports 40 percent. Foreign direct investment into Poland has been the key. It accounted for half of all business investment in consumer goods manufacturing and trade in Poland in 1998. The corresponding figure for Russia was negligible. In Poland, foreign investors setting up "transplant" food processing factories and supermarkets calculated they could make a profit.

Carrefour, perhaps the most successful global food retailer, has not entered Russia. Carrefour feels it could overcome the bureaucratic hassle to obtain land and build stores. It also feels it could manage the bribery and even threats to physical security. *However, it cannot overcome the prospect of not making money.*

Food retailing is perhaps the best example of how Russia is distorting the playing field for competition enough that the most productive operators in the world could not be profitable. In those circumstances, clearly, privatization, price decontrol, and even access to the global capital market are not enough to cause productivity improvement. The playing field also has to be reasonably level.

This is a serious problem for Russia. We often underestimate the importance of food retailing. Food retailing is the critical link connecting customers with the production of food and its processing. Best practice food retailers around the world have taken the lead in improving the efficiency of the growing and processing of food to make sure that consumers get enough of what they want to eat at the lowest price possible. Food retailing is also a big sector in its own right. In Russia it employs 2.6 million people, or slightly more than the combined total employment of steel, dairy, confectionary, cement, hotels, and software. Thus, food retailing matters more in determining Russia's average labor productivity than all these industries combined.

I said earlier in this chapter that substantial Western investment in the Russian oil industry would be a leading indicator that Russia was on the path to rapid performance improvement. A second leading indicator would be Carrefour's decision to invest substantially in Russia.

Economic Potential: Russia Could Grow Very Fast

Russia's economy is dysfunctional. This should not be a surprise. For about seventy years, a totalitarian Soviet government decided where people would work and what they would produce. It was the most extreme form of the producer mentality. Then overnight in the early 1990s, most of the productive assets were put into private hands and prices were set free. Consumers now had major influence through bidding up the prices to get what they wanted and simply not buying what they did not want. The Soviets had put massive emphasis on heavy manufacturing and agriculture. The Russian consumers wanted light manufacturing (consumer) goods and better quality food than the Soviet system provided. The economic forces at work called for a wrenching change in where people work and what they produced. Such a change was bound to be painful.

The tragedy of Russia in the 1990s was that it got the pain but not much of the change. The pain came from a dramatic drop in real output. Output per capita dropped by 40 percent between 1991 and 1997. The private firms stopped investing so much in heavy manufacturing and the consumers went for imports. The Russian government exacerbated the switch in demand to imports of consumer goods by trying to maintain a grossly overvalued exchange rate. Employment didn't change nearly as much as output changed. Natural attrition in manufacturing and construction caused employment to drop by about one-third there. However, output dropped by over 50 percent. The result was that productivity in the old part of the economy carried over from Soviet days dropped by 40 percent to about 17 percent of U.S. productivity. Private owners were reducing their investment plans and consumers were changing their spending patterns much faster than new jobs were being created to provide the goods and services consumers wanted. Russia was a poor country to start with and now it is much poorer.

Poland's experience was very different. Poland had much of the same Soviet-style economic structure and was even poorer than Russia in 1989. However, by the end of the 1990s, Poland was significantly richer than it was in 1989 and significantly richer than Russia. The differences in performance came primarily from the differences in performance of new businesses created after 1990. In Poland, new businesses, primarily in services and consumer goods manufacturing, were built near global best practice standards. They were built near these standards because much of the new business came from global best practice companies investing in Poland. In general merchandise retailing, new hypermarkets and specialty retailing chains captured 20 percent of the market by 1999 and operated at 75 percent of the productivity of corresponding U.S. retailers. These retailers included Carrefour, Allkauf, Tesco, IKEA, Levi-Strauss, and Adidas. Forty percent of all business investment in Poland in the 1990s was foreign investment. Foreign investment was less than 1 percent of business investment in Russia.

Virtually Nothing Close to Global Best Practice

The real tragedy of Russia in the 1990s is that the new businesses built after the dissolution of the Soviet Union are no better than the old Soviet businesses in 1991. Both groups had average productivity of 30 percent of that of the United States. Only a handful of operations are close to U.S. productivity. There are a few first-class Western hotels and token investments in confectionery and dairy products by global best practice firms, including Mars and Danone. However, employment in these operations is only 1 to 3 percent of total sector employment. In other words, at the end of the 1990s there were virtually no businesses in Russia operating at close to global best practice, unlike in Poland (and Brazil).

I have already discussed in the food retailing section why global best practice companies have not invested in Russia. They can't make any money there. The same thing is true in confectionery. Mars, one of the most successful consumer goods companies worldwide, built a new plant in Russia and found that its return on sales was negative. As I explained in the food retailing case, the reason more productive firms in Russia are less profitable than less productive firms is that the playing field is not level. Sometimes distortion comes from unequal tax laws; sometimes, from unequal tax collection. Other times it's unequal payment of electricity and gas bills or unequal willingness to accept overvalued barter goods. Sometimes it's unequal government allocation of land for housing construction and retail developments. Sometimes it's unequal harassment by government officials administering licensing and regulatory matters. As I illustrated in the food retailing case, Poland took care of these problems, and global best practice companies invested substantially.

Only one tiny corner of the Russian economy seemed to be free of these distortions. It was customized software services, which software companies provide to other companies to help them conduct their operations more efficiently. This was a new business after 1990 and so there were no incumbents to protect. Everybody paid their taxes; they did not use much energy; they didn't need much land; and the government officials had not found them yet. Unfortunately, they have not been found because they are so small. The software industry in Russia employees only 8,000 people, compared with 640,000 in the United States. However, the productivity of the 6,000 people providing customized software services was 70 percent of that of the United States.

Russia Is Growing at Half Its Potential and That's Not Sustainable

Our team made an estimate of how fast Russia could grow if it removed the market distortions discussed above and investors had confidence it would maintain macroeconomic stability. Poland is a good benchmark for Russia because the starting points in 1990 were so similar. Poland's economic policies were not perfect. It still has not rationalized its land and housing markets, and thus two big industries at the heart of its economy, housing construction and retailing, are underperforming. Nevertheless, Poland has done many things right. In the middle of the 1990s, Poland achieved a growth rate of 6 percent with a business investment rate of 13 percent. Russia has the potential of doing somewhat better because of its oil opportunities. Thus, we estimate Russia's potential to be GDP growth of 8 percent per year, with a business investment rate of 19 percent.

Poland's growth rate has diminished recently. I believe it's because of lack of further reform in the core of the domestic market and some uncertainty on the part of outsiders about just how committed Poland's government is to further reform. In part because of this diminished growth in Poland, we cross-checked Russia's potential by using the method we used for Brazil. We estimated the rate at which productivity could grow and then estimated the investment rate that would keep employment from falling. In particular, we assessed the potential for productivity improvement in companies using the old Soviet assets. About 25 percent of these assets should just be bulldozed. On the other hand, in the remaining 75 percent of old Soviet assets, labor productivity could be increased from 20 to 65 percent of that of the United States through restructuring. The restructuring would include making all the investments economically viable today at Russia's labor and capital costs.

The experiences of Poland and Brazil as benchmarks for how output and demand will evolve as Russia gets richer indicate, not surprisingly, that the fastest growth would be in light manufacturing, trade, and business and personal services. Combining these output growths with the estimates of productivity growth from our industry studies suggests that employment in heavy manufacturing in Russia would continue to decline, light manufacturing would hold steady, and trade would increase. Although we did not examine business and personal services, we assumed that employment would increase there because it had done so in Poland. Using this method yields about the same economic growth potential for Russia as using straightforwardly the Poland benchmark for everything. Of course, the precise numbers don't matter all that much. It is clear that Russia should be growing much faster and could benefit greatly from more foreign investment.

Russia's growth rate for the past couple of years has been better, about 4 percent per year, or half its potential. The conventional wisdom that it is caused by the major currency devaluation in the financial crisis of 1998 and by higher oil prices seems plausible. The devaluation would certainly curtail imports of consumer goods and increase demand from Russian consumer goods companies, which have lots of spare capacity. Moreover, higher oil prices would certainly help stabilize public finances and generate some confidence in macroeconomic stability. However, our study of Russia ended before these effects appeared and so I don't know. What is clear is that the market distortions in Russia have not been removed. Russia is locked in a trap of being unable to generate new, high-productivity jobs and therefore feels it cannot let the jobs in the old, unproductive incumbents be destroyed. The creative destruction process is not working. My two leading indicators that Russia is on a path of rapid reform have not shown up yet. They are major Western oil investment (well beyond the level of the 2002 BP commitment) and Carrefour hypermarkets. In the next section, I will discuss why Russia has such horrible market distortions and what it will take to get rid of them.

Missing Individual Rights Cause Market Economy Failure

Russia is not growing in a sustainable way. It is true that its productivity is increasing and productivity is the engine of growth. However, Russia's productivity growth today is primarily "cyclical." By cyclical, I mean the growth is caused by factors that have a transitory rather than sustaining effect. Capacity utilization in factories is increasing. The substantial devaluation of Russia's currency in 1998 made imported goods much less attractive, and Russia's consumer goods factories have lots of spare capacity. Russia is not improving the efficiency (structural productivity) with which it produces goods and services. It is just producing more of them. Once Russia's factories reach full capacity, this growth process will stop. That would only bring Russia back to where it started in 1990. To grow beyond that point, Russia needs to improve the way workers use their time in factories and offices to produce goods and services. (Russia's government finances are also temporarily healthier because of the recent high oil prices. This situation has diminished the risk of inflation and increased business confidence.)

Russia is not improving its structural productivity because workers are not leaving old industries, such as steel and oil, and going to work in new industries, such as housing construction and food retailing. This evolution is the way all countries have grown. It is not working in Russia. The reason it is not working is that the old industries are not laying off people. These industries in today's advanced economies have been laying off workers for a few decades. These industries in Russia are not laying off people because the workers, the plant managers, and the government officials where the plants are located don't want this to happen.

The careers and income of the plant managers and, without doubt, many local government officials depend on the plant's operating. The workers perceive correctly that they have no place else to get a job. Therefore, the workers, the managers, and the local government officials do everything they can to keep obsolete plants from closing and potentially viable plants from major layoffs. What they have found they can do in Russia is not pay the plant's electricity and gas bills and its tax bills to the government. Sometimes they pay without really paying by sending the government grossly overvalued barter goods rather than cash. Workers also often don't get paid very much. Many spend much of their time growing potatoes. Understandably, they would rather do something else. They could wake up from this nightmare if they simply left for better jobs elsewhere. They don't because such jobs don't exist.

Better jobs in growing industries don't exist because new, more productive businesses in those industries can't make profits. They can't make profits because they are not competitive with less productive incumbents or even new businesses starting up with productivity no better than the incumbents. Sometimes more productive businesses are not competitive because they have to pay their taxes and sell legitimate goods whereas their competitors don't pay their taxes and sell counterfeit goods (as happens in food retailing). Other times more productive businesses are just not allowed to compete because, for instance, they can't get enough land for large-scale single-family housing developments. The net result is that Russia gets a lot of new businesses but productivity does not improve. The engine of growth is not there. Therefore new jobs are not being created in what should be the growing part of the economy, consumer goods manufacturing and services. The workers in the old part of the economy are right to fight to stay put.

The Way Forward

How can Russia perform nearer to its economic potential? Well, there are lots of ideas floating around. From the World Bank you hear a lot about better corporate governance, stopping corruption and establishing the rule of law, and even decentralization of governmental authority. In our ten industry studies in Russia, differences in corporate governance were not among the most important factors causing Russia to have low productivity compared with the United States. Stopping corruption and establishing the rule of law sounds pretty good as far as it goes. The problem is it doesn't go very far. First, I worry about holding up early twenty-first-century advanced economy practices as a standard for poor countries at the stage of economic development at which these advanced economies were one hundred years ago. Second, you don't hear much about how to accomplish stopping corruption and establishing rule of law. And decentralization of governmental authority, which I will come back to later, would be moving in the wrong direction.

In Russia itself, social concerns are sometimes given as the reason for not closing down obsolete plants. These concerns have some validity when workers have no place else to go. Perhaps, it would be better if the plants were closed and the workers given a direct unemployment subsidy. However, neither scenario is great, and the prospect of thousands of idle Russian factory workers milling around doing nothing is not appealing. The social concerns would go away, of course, if the newer parts of the economy were moving in a productive way. Therefore, Russia needs to fix that and then the social concerns should go away.

Mancur Olson

So how does Russia get rid of all the barriers to productivity improvement in consumer goods, housing construction, and services? I have just stepped over the line from exclusively economic analysis to a mixture of economics, sociology, and politics. The most penetrating answer to this type of question has been given by Mancur Olson. His recent book, *Power and Prosperity,* published shortly after his death, summarizes the results of thinking about these questions over his whole career. He concludes that two conditions are necessary for advanced economic performance: "secure and well-defined individual rights" and "absence of predation."

By individual rights, Olson primarily means property rights. Property rights are clearly important. However, here and further in chapter 11, I will argue that other aspects of individual rights are more important for poor country development. These other aspects are more closely related to "liberty" and the freedom to choose. In the economic sphere, the most important individual right is the freedom to be a consumer and to buy what you want. An important part of these "consumer rights" is the right to buy from anybody in an economy in which any potential producer of what consumers want is free to produce those items on an equal basis with any other producer. Russia abuses these individual rights by distorting the playing field for producers, which will lead us to Olson's second condition, the absence of predation.

As for property rights in Russia, contracts are often not fulfilled and not enforced by the courts. Minority shareholders are exploited sometimes by majority shareholders and all shareholders are exploited sometimes by managers. This, however, is not the main factor holding Russia back. Strong global businesses can manage this risk. Smaller Russian and foreign businesses probably cannot. The establishment of secure property rights in the advanced economies occurred over much of the nineteenth and early twentieth centuries. It's unrealistic to expect this to happen overnight in Russia, or anyplace else, for that matter. For this reason, economic development was led in the advanced economies by larger, stronger businesses. Small and medium-sized businesses followed in their wake. We should not expect something different in today's poor countries.

The Predators Are a Majority

However, in today's Russia, even the larger, stronger, and more productive companies do not flourish. The reason is that Olson's second condition is missing. Absence of predation is a joke in Russia. Government and its bureaucrats give favorable treatment to incumbents and less productive new entrants through legislation and regulation and their application. Lobbying for such treatment undoubtedly includes substantial bribery. Olson's analysis unfortunately lets us down at this point, however. He assumes that the special interests served by preferential treatment "are always tiny minorities." He solves the problem by concluding that such tiny minorities "cannot get away with this if even the intellectual elite understands what is going on." By intellectual elite, I guess Olson means academics and probably academic economists.

Olson has more confidence in intellectual elites than I do, even in the circumstances he assumes. However, the circumstances in Russia are different. There, the special interests are almost everybody. Everybody perceives they stand to lose if the economy is allowed to evolve. They are right if their special-interest favoritism is the only favoritism that is fixed. The result in Russia today is that nobody is giving up their favoritism. In these circumstances, everybody loses, because the only way for Russia to have structural productivity growth and create good new jobs is for everybody to give up their favoritism.

We found this same gridlock in Japan. There, the special interests are currently a majority, but by no means everybody. Toyota is not Toyota because of favorable treatment by the Japanese government. However, the special-interest majority keeps the LDP in power. In return, the LDP keeps the provisions favoring the special interests in place. The result is that over 50 percent of Japan's economy is not advanced.

Putin Needs More Power, Not Less

So what should Russia do? Russia should do pretty much what it looks like it is doing now. Forget about decentralizing governmental power. That's naive. Even in the advanced countries, local governments are more corrupt and more susceptible to protecting special interests than central governments. Olson points out it is better to have one big thief than lots of little ones. The big thief is interested in economic development because he will then have more to steal. The many little thieves don't see it that way because each can influence only a small part of the economy. Besides, in Russia, the "big thief" is democratically elected. To continue in office depends on making economic progress. In Russia, the central government needs to consolidate strong power to make the needed changes. That's how the United States got many of the fundamentals of its economic policy right in the first half of the twentieth century.

It's also naive to think that even a strong central government in Russia can establish corruption-free institutions and enforce the rule of law overnight. Building corruption-free departments of justice, commerce, energy, and social welfare is impossible. Just bringing them to good standards takes decades. Certainly Russia should move in this direction. However, the only step that will cause substantial progress quickly is to reduce drastically the ability of government to treat special interests favorably. That means reducing the number of permits required for housing construction and getting rid of the bureaucrats administering these permits. It means structuring the energy distribution systems so that the local distribution companies are under central government control and users are metered separately so that delinquent payers can be cut off. It means simplifying and reducing taxes so that collection is easier and noncompliance less damaging. It means real land reform that places land clearly in private hands and reduces local government authority to zoning within an overall land development plan. And much more. It also means a much smaller, although stronger, central government.

Can this be done? President Putin seemed to start out on this track. His timing looked good. Strong measures by central governments are tolerated in a democracy if people feel things have gotten so bad that they're willing to give somebody with plausible new ideas a chance. Russia seems this way today. It's too bad Russia didn't move this way in 1990. Then people also felt things were so bad that they had to change. However, strong local forces thwarted central authority. Moreover, it looks like the central government didn't know what to do in important respects. The Harvard advisers missed the critical importance of a level playing field.

Poland was different. There the central government had enormous credibility because its leadership had led the overthrow of the Soviet-imposed regime. Equally importantly, Poland had Leszek Balcerowicz, the first finance minister after the Soviet-supported regime fell. He knew what to do. We will never know whether the failed reform in Russia in the early 1990s was because of compromises necessary to prevent a reversion to Communism or because of lack of understanding of what is really needed. I believe it's both.

Should we worry about a strong central government in Russia? We should watch it closely. However, the initial signs are good. President Putin seems genuinely interested in bringing Russia into the "club" of advanced democratic countries. A necessary condition for his success at this endeavor will be that Russia remains a democracy. It's also important for Russia's economic development itself. The Russian people need to give their president the benefit of the doubt for some time. However, he must always feel responsible to them, and they must always feel they can change presidents if this one doesn't succeed.

Knowing How to Change Economic Policy Is Not Enough; Rights Have to be Established

Does President Putin know what to do? Olson wrote, towards the end of his last book, "Research and education have some effect, I think, which is one of the reasons why I have written this book." His final sentence is, "If those of us who are professionally concerned with ideas about how society should be governed—and all of us who are intensely interested in the policies that largely determine how our economies and societies perform—work hard enough and well enough, there may be further understanding."

President Putin's initial economic program was based substantially on the findings of our examination of the Russian economy. However, the forces against reform remain powerful and accomplishments are modest. Just as in Japan, the special interests are not small. They include all the old Soviet companies, workers who don't see any new jobs for themselves, and government bureaucrats and local politicians who depend on the system for their jobs and some extra income. Reform in Russia will take longer than anyone would have believed.

I began this chapter with the fact that Russia's market economy has a worse economic performance than under the central planning of the Soviets. Does this fact undermine the case I am making in this book? Well it would if we didn't get to the reasons for this outcome. To do that, understanding individual markets, including how individual firms compete in these markets, is essential. At that level in Russia, competition is sufficiently distorted that the best firm does not win. It's possible to win by being no better than the old Soviet firms. Since Russian consumers are now free to buy what they want from whomever they want, they buy from better firms outside Russia whenever they can. It's no more complicated than that to see why Russia's economic performance has fallen. The establishment of democracy in Russia failed to recognize one individual right in particular. That is the right of consumers to buy from producers who have a fair chance of getting the consumer's business. That right is critical to consumers because it's through intense, fair competition that consumers get innovative products and services and the lowest prices. Achieving that right requires a level playing field with equal competition. Russia needs to give its people this right.

CHAPTER EIGHT

India: Bad Economic Management from a Democratic Government

India is probably the single most important country to understand in to-day's global economic landscape. One billion people live there. Within this decade it will pass China as the world's most populous country. It is heartbreakingly poor. Its per capita income is 7 percent of the United States' per capita income and only 59 percent of China's. The majority of people in India live in desperately poor conditions not seen anywhere in advanced economies and rarely in Brazil and Russia.

India defies generalizations. Something of everything is there. The Oberoi hotel chain is the best in the world, and Infosys is one of the top global software firms. The Taj Mahal is the only man-made structure that has ever exceeded my expectations. In 1974 on a World Bank mission to India, I got up before any sign of dawn and took a bicycle rickshaw to see the Taj. I passed the smoky fires of homeless people sleeping beside the road. And then there it was, emerging pure white out of nothing. The bejeweled white marble slowly turned rose pink as the cold dawn light warmed. To understand India, you have to understand the mixture.

The Mix That Is India

In India, 60 percent of the people work in agriculture, compared with 25 percent in Brazil and 14 percent in Russia. Thus, understanding how India will evolve out of agriculture is perhaps the most important issue in development economics. Indian dairy and wheat farmers have a productivity of about 1 percent of U.S. farmers'. Rural wages in India are so low that sharing a tractor is likely as far as mechanization will go now. Seventy percent of all land devoted to wheat farming is already tilled using tractors. Combine harvesters are not economic. Wheat farmers might double their productivity by increasing their yields through better farming practices. However, Indian farming will be stuck at current productivity levels until rural wages increase enough to justify more mechanization. Thus something has to happen outside agriculture.

Of the remaining 40 percent of employment, only about one-half is in "modern" business enterprises, like steel mills and commercial banks. By modern, I mean organizations large enough to have substantial division of labor, to capture economies of scale, and to use a fair amount of capital equipment. These enterprises are industrialized. In India, these enterprises have an average productivity of 15 percent of the productivity of corresponding enterprises in the United States, or two and one-half times the average for all India.

The remaining 20 percent or so of employment is in the transition sector. This sector shows up in all poor countries and consists of the entry-level jobs for people drawn out of agriculture. In total, the productivity of the transition sector is about 7 percent of corresponding U.S. productivity. These businesses are usually one- to two-person operations with very little equipment. Typically they are street vendors, rural counter stores, and tailors. Because they are not amenable to industrialization, they have virtually no productivity growth potential.

The Modern Sector Holds the Key

From this picture, it's clear that there is only one source of meaningful change in India's economic situation. That's the modern sector. Its productivity ought to be much closer to 100 percent of U.S. productivity than it is. Productivity improvement in the modern sector will cause incomes of those working there to increase. The experience of other countries indicates that as incomes increase, individual demand swings from the absolute necessities of life, food and basic shelter, to the new goods and services these modern sectors produce. The experience of other countries also shows that demand for these new products and services increases faster than productivity in the modern sectors. Hence, to meet demand, total employment in the modern sector has to increase.

In fact, the experience of other countries and India's potential to build new capacity in the modern sector both indicate that as productivity grows, the modern sector will be unable to fulfill demand for goods and services outside agriculture. The residual of demand will be met then by the transition sector. Because its productivity is so low, it will take a lot of jobs to fulfill this new demand. If India were performing at its potential, the transition sector would create even more jobs than the modern sector over the next decade or so. Even though the productivity is low in transition jobs, it's probably five to ten times higher than in agriculture. Thus, the creation of these jobs is a good thing and is a crucial intermediate step in India's evolution out of agriculture. It's important to keep in mind, however, that the process needs to start with productivity improvement in the modern sector.

So what's keeping the modern sector in India from realizing its potential? There are lots of things. Brazil doesn't need to learn from the economic experiences of other countries. Brazil over the past thirty years has tried almost everything. India really doesn't need the experience of other countries either. India is trying everything right now. India's government seems to be trying to control the economy. It is not trying to control through central planning by telling everybody what to do. It is trying to control through regulation by telling everybody what they cannot do. *This regulation has the result of distorting and diminishing competition.*

Foreign direct investment in retailing in India is prohibited. Import duties protect the Indian steel industry from global competition. Licensing protects incumbent milk processing plants from new entrants. About 830 products are reserved for manufacture by firms below a certain size. Unequal taxes and tax enforcement favor low-productivity, small-scale enterprises from steel to retailing.

In addition to telling businesses what they cannot do, the government continues to own a huge section of India's economy. *Enterprises owned by the federal and state governments account for about 40 percent of the total business capital stock in India.* India continues this practice despite evidence from India itself that productivity in government-owned enterprises is always less than half the productivity in private enterprises in the same business, and often no more than 10 percent of private sector productivity.

Finally, India has a special problem. It is not clear who owns land in India. Over 90 percent of land titles are unclear. A clear title to land is the first thing an investor insists on before breaking ground to build an expensive plant. If it turned out someone else owned that land, that someone else would have the power to stop plant operations. Unclear land titles most affect industries which use a lot of land. These industries are housing construction and retailing. The result is that there is huge demand for the very little land with clear titles. Not surprisingly, the ratio of land costs to per capita income in New Delhi and Bombay is ten times that ratio in the other major cities of Asia, such as Tokyo, Singapore, Bangkok, and Seoul. Also not surprisingly, India has very few supermarkets and large-scale single-family housing developments.

So if you thought market distortion in Russia was bad, India is considerably worse. You really have to see it sector by sector to believe it. That's what the next sections of this chapter are about.

Dairy and Wheat: Rational Farmers

India produces more milk than any other country in the world, and more wheat than any other country except China. Dairy is the single largest industry contributor to India's GDP and employment. It accounts for 5 percent of GDP and 13 percent of employment. Hours worked producing milk in India are equivalent to 45 million full-time employees. *That means dairy in India has more employment than any other sector in any economy in the world.*

Dairy and wheat (and rice) farming in India have saved it from starvation. Since 1950 milk production in India has increased about fivefold, and wheat production, about sevenfold. This increased production has come from more cows and acres of wheat and from increases in yields, wheat per acre and milk per cow. Remarkably, yield in wheat in India has reached the U.S. level.

The Green Revolution Worked

A "Green Revolution" really occurred in India. The improved strands of wheat (and rice) and the improved farming practices were developed by the worldwide international agricultural research system initially funded by the Rockefeller and Ford Foundations in the 1960s. It's a great example of the application of global best practice plant breeding techniques and farming methods to improve economic performance. In this case, the performance improvement was not discretionary. It undoubtedly meant the difference between life and death for many millions of people.

It is amazing to find wheat farmers in India achieving U.S. yields. It's the first hint that farmers know what they're doing. Indian wheat farmers could further increase their yields by about 30 percent. However, it's clear their performance on yield is the best economic performance we found anywhere in India (with the possible exception of a couple of private retail banks). Yield was not as good in dairy. It is only 10 percent of the U.S. level. Thus the "White Revolution," as it is called in India, was not as successful as the Green Revolution. Yields in dairy could increase fivefold through improved breeds of milk animals and improved farming practices.

The story of the Green Revolution is understood fairly widely. What is not understood is why Indian farmers use seventy-five times as many hours as the United States to farm each acre of wheat and, for dairy, fifteen times as many hours per cow. The result is that labor productivity in wheat and dairy farming are both about 1 percent of U.S. productivity. We are all aware of the huge improvements in agricultural productivity from mechanization. Photographs of the United States always include a huge combine harvester in the middle of an endless wheat field in Kansas.

Our team member conducting the wheat farming study was a young graduate of the Indian Institute of Technology. IIT, as it is called in India, provides an elite engineering education for India's best. Competition for entrance is brutal. Graduates go on to leadership roles in India, and the rest of the world for that matter. These graduates come from and move in a world far different from the world of India's farmers. It is understandable that our team member assumed that India's poor, uneducated, and often illiterate farmers must be doing something wrong.

Farmers Know What They Are Doing

As the wheat farming study developed over several months, a tone of amazement crept into our team member's presentation of his results, and a tone of respect for India's farmers appeared. Careful calculations showed that India's farmers were mechanizing wheat farming to almost exactly the right degree. Seventy percent of them were using tractors. Probably about 90 percent should be. Only a few large farmers in Punjab should be using combine harvesters and they were. The reason manual harvesting was preferable to combine harvesting was in part because rural labor to help in harvesting was so cheap and the huge combine harvesters cost the same around the world. The other reason was that manual harvesting preserves twice as much of the wheat stalks (fodder) as combine harvesting. The fodder is valuable for feeding the dairy cattle which the wheat farmer also keeps. He can tend dairy cattle because wheat farming takes by no means all the time he and the other members of his family can work. Virtually all wheat farming is combined with dairy farming for this reason.

We found a similar story in dairy farming. Big changes to full-time dairy farming with mechanization did not make economic sense. Moving to full-time dairy farming with a bigger herd would cost more per unit of milk produced. The farmer would then have to buy fodder instead of getting it free of middleman and transportation costs from his wheat farming. He would also have to pay for some external labor. Economies of scale don't offset these extra costs. Use of milk machines is simply out of the question at today's rural labor rates. It's much cheaper to milk by hand.

Of course, India should go on with the increases in yield for wheat and dairy. Yield increases in dairy are significant and will increase India's dairy productivity to about 3 percent of the level in the United States. To improve yields Indian dairy farmers need the transfer of knowledge from agricultural extension services. These government workers have played crucial roles in the transfer and application of research results by the farmer. They were necessary for the Green Revolution to be successful. They were also necessary for the remarkable productivity improvements over the last century in U.S. agriculture. Modern private food processors sometimes can also play this role. With the atrophy of the Indian agriculture extension services following the Green Revolution, private dairy processors in India could pick up this role. After all, they want to increase the milk available within reasonable transportation distances. However, private dairy processors are restricted because the Milk and Milk Products Order (MMPO) allows government to control new entrants through licensing. The government uses this power to protect the incumbent cooperative dairy processors. Without competition, these cooperatives have little incentive to improve performance through helping farmers increase their yields.

So let's say Indian dairy and wheat farmers do improve their yields up to the current potential. That will bring their productivity to 2 to 3 percent of the U.S. level. Then they're stuck. It doesn't make sense for them to go any further. This sounds like a Catch-22. If they do what farmers in all economies further down the development path do, they're worse off. How do Indian farmers get out of this trap? Well, the one thing we can conclude so far is that it's out of their hands.

It's out of their hands because the way out of this trap is for many Indian wheat farmers, their children, and other rural laborers to have something better to do with their time than wheat farming. If they could get better jobs in the modern sector, or even in the transition sector, they would leave what they're doing and move to cities and towns for these jobs. Many small combined dairy and wheat farms could not survive without a large supply of family labor. There would be little free time for the wheat farmer to tend the dairy cattle. At the same time, the reduction in rural laborers would eventually cause the price of this labor to rise to the point that combine wheat harvesters and milking machines would be economic. At this point, wheat and dairy farming would split apart, with dairy farmers tending much larger herds and wheat farmers cultivating more acres. Productivity would begin increasing rapidly in agriculture. This is exactly what happened in Thailand. However, it did not start to happen until Thailand was four times richer than India is today.

The Indian wheat farmer knows that tractors are in but combines are out. How does he know this? My guess is that he doesn't move to combines because he has not seen it demonstrated successfully. The agricultural extension services connected with the Green Revolution demonstrated to Indians that use of tractors as part of good wheat farming practices was economic. They didn't demonstrate the successful use of combines because they could not do so. To me, this explanation is more plausible than the wheat farmers' doing discounted cash flow analysis.

This does not take anything away from the savvy of Indian wheat farmers. There are numerous cases of business managers in other industries in Brazil and India not making investments that competitors in the same industry in the same country have shown to be economically successful. Often, business managers did not make economic investments because governments either subsidized them or protected them in some other way from their more productive competitors. Of course, this situation is a vicious spiral because the continued existence of the less productive businesses means that the more productive businesses are less successful. Thus the power of the demonstration of the success of the more productive way of conducting business is diminished. Indian farmers always had to pay attention to more successful methods because they were so poor.

The dairy and wheat farming cases also give some insight into how the different parts of an economy interact in fits and starts to move GDP per capita up. We know from Adam Smith that the initial move out of agriculture came from productivity improvements in agriculture freeing up labor that could produce goods and services that landowners wanted. However, as India demonstrates, the increases in agricultural productivity come in step functions. Sometimes agriculture gets caught on one step, and it's not economic to move to the next step up until something changes in the rest of the economy. That's where India is today. Agriculture will not move very far without the rest of the economy creating enough good jobs to soak up a significant amount of today's rural labor. Those new jobs will come from growth in the rest of the economy. And that growth will be triggered by productivity increases there. That's what the rest of this chapter on India is about.

Automotive Assembly: Model for the Rest of India

After studying the automotive assembly industry, it is very difficult not to be inpatient with India for its lack of reform. The automotive assembly industry in India shows by itself almost all the good and bad effects of different economic policies. India need go no further to see what to do.

Before 1983, the Indian government controlled and protected two auto companies. Today those companies have a productivity that is 6 percent of productivity in the U.S. auto industry. Their market share has dropped from 40 percent in 1990 to 4 percent in 1999. In 1983 the government granted a license for a new entrant, Maruti, to set up as a fifty-fifty joint venture with Suzuki. Suzuki is one of Japan's six auto companies, all of which are high productivity. By 1990, Maruti had 60 percent of the Indian car market, and it now holds about the same percentage after reaching a high of 80 percent in 1998. Maruti's productivity is about 55 percent of the U.S. level. The reason Maruti's share has fallen recently is that passenger car production was delicensed in 1993. As a result, many of the world's best auto companies have invested in India, including Honda, Daimler-Chrysler, Ford, General Motors, and Hyundai. These new firms have already captured 25 percent of the market.

Over the period since delicensing, productivity in this industry in India has grown 20 percent per year. Output has increased even faster, causing employment to increase a little (1 percent per year). What better evidence could the Indian government ask for to show the benefits of competition and foreign direct investment?

The pre-1983 plants are a mess. Parts and materials are lying around all over the place, and substantial numbers of workers simply mill around. It's about what you'd expect to be the result in an industry that had only two companies and where production volumes were determined by the government and imports were prohibited. Nehru was an admirer of the Soviet Union, and this was big, state-controlled industrialization.

An Anomalous Event

Then in 1983, something strange happened. The government granted one license for a joint venture with a global automotive company close to best practice. Given that nothing else like this was going on in India at the time, it's hard to believe this action came from a change of heart about economic policy. In India, the story is that Indira Gandhi's son, Rajiv, wanted to get into the auto industry and needed help. He turned to Suzuki and got the government to grant one license. I don't know whether this story is right or not, but it's more plausible that Maruti is in India because of favoritism than because of good economic policy. Fortunately for India, the Japanese auto companies were not skilled in managing an oligopoly. They were used to competing fiercely. That meant they focused on improving operations. That's what Suzuki did with Maruti in India.

Finally, in 1993, the industry was opened entirely for foreign direct investment. Many of the major auto companies in the world came. They already are achieving a productivity 25 percent of the U.S. level and are still ramping up production. Capacity utilization for most of them is still 30 percent or less. If India were to grow at its potential of about 10 percent per year, these car companies would have no difficulty achieving high capacity utilization. Moreover, with India's low wage rates, it should have a comparative advantage in automotive exports.

India's productivity potential at current wage rates is about 85 percent of the United States'. The remaining 15 percent would come from investment in automation that is not yet economic. The foreign producers in India are not all that close to the 85 percent. Most of the lean production techniques of the Japanese have been adopted at least to some degree. In particular, lean inventory (*kanban*) techniques have been applied. These new plants are clean as a whistle compared with the pre-1983 plants. The relative low skills and lack of education of the workforce, however, has caused it to take longer to train Indian workers in lean production. Nonetheless, productivity is improving rapidly and will continue to do so as long as competition remains intense.

On this note, there is one black cloud on the horizon. India has retained a high import tariff of 44 percent on cars. This tariff precludes imports. In chapter 6 on Brazil, I explained how import protection had resulted in appallingly low automotive productivity, despite Brazil's automotive industry being entirely foreign direct investment from major European and U.S. car companies. In Brazil, these companies arranged matters such that there were only one or two competitors in each car segment. And these companies know from home country experience how to run an oligopoly if they get a chance. India faces the same risk. I'm not as worried about India as I would have been about Brazil because the Japanese and Korean auto companies have a history of intense competition. Nevertheless, high import tariffs are an unnecessary risk for India and should be removed.

Labor Laws Can't Be All That Bad

The Indian automotive case illustrates one more point. In every industry in India with large-scale companies, the conventional wisdom is that the principal reason firms could not improve was difficulties with the workforce because of labor laws. Reading the Indian newspapers, as I did every morning over a hearty "English breakfast" in the Bombay Oberoi, you would think the most important issue in the economic policy debate was labor market reform. In fact, managers' complaints about difficulty in managing the workforce because of labor laws and regulations are common around the world. Managers never complain because there's not enough competition to stimulate them to better performance. However, they sure can complain about labor.

Labor laws in India require that state governments approve any layoffs in companies with more than 100 employees. These labor laws are hindering managers from adopting lean production techniques as fast as they want to. Lean production is a constant process of reducing labor hours worked in some functions as work is reorganized and conducted more efficiently. Moreover, the pre-1983 plants have large numbers of excess workers doing nothing.

This sounds like a huge problem. What government is going to approve layoffs that large bodies of workers oppose? In fact, in some industries in India, managers have successfully found an alternative way for gaining acceptance of layoffs. The method is voluntary retirement schemes (VRS). The most progressive companies in the United States use these schemes all the time to reduce the workforce. These schemes cost some money. However, the worker should have some compensation for the difficulty caused for him by his unexpected layoff without cause, other than a company productivity improvement.

However, the pre-1983 plants can't use VRS. They have so many excess workers and have become so weak financially that they could not afford to solve their excess worker problem with VRS. However, the fundamental reason these plants have a problem now is not the labor laws. The real reason is that competition didn't force them to solve the excess labor problem with VRS long ago when they were financially able to do so.

Despite the problems the labor laws may have caused the Indian automotive industry, the facts argue that these labor laws cannot have been all that important. After all, with these laws in place, the industry has grown 21 percent a year for the past seven years, productivity has increased at 20 percent per year, and employment has grown a little.

Why is India's overall performance so bad and India's performance in automotive so good? How do other industries differ from automotive? Well, just let me count the ways. That's what the next sections are about. Of course, underlying this question is the one that asks why India doesn't make all the other industries look like automotive.

Apparel: Small Is Not Beautiful

The basics of life are food, clothing, and shelter. India is doing fine in food production. That's not true for clothing and shelter.

Apparel shows why India is not evolving rapidly out of agriculture through transition jobs to modern businesses. India is trapped in a situation where tailors can provide shirts cheaper than manufacturers. In addition, China's manufacturers can provide shirts for the world market cheaper that India's manufacturers. Thus, the Indian apparel industry is going nowhere.

Seventy percent of all apparel workers are tailors. These are little three- to four-person operations that design, measure customers, stitch, and sell clothing all in the same spot. For shirt making, their productivity is about 10 percent of U.S. shirt makers'. Small manufacturers for the domestic market have about 20 percent of total employment. Their productivity is about twice that of tailors. Finally, larger manufacturers for exports have about 10 percent of total employment and a productivity that's 35 percent of that of the United States. The overall industry average productivity is about 16 percent of the U.S. average.

There's nothing wrong with India's having so many tailors. If India were moving rapidly towards its potential, the number of tailors would have to grow to help satisfy an explosive demand for shirts. However, the principal cause of this evolution has to be rapid productivity growth in the modern sector. This is not happening in apparel.

Big Is Out

In India, the price of ready-made shirts from domestic manufacturers is about 35 percent higher than the price of a tailor-made shirt. The manufacturing cost of the shirts is about the same as the tailor-made price. However, the manufactured shirt has to get to the customer. In India that's a huge problem because of the undeveloped retail sector. The Indian retailing sector adds about 40 percent to the cost of getting a man-ufactured shirt to the customer. This margin is 20 percent in modern discount stores. Thus, domestic manufacturing of shirts is not growing as it should.

Two things have to happen to get domestic manufacturing of shirts moving. First, the productivity of the retailing industry has to improve significantly. The second thing is that shirt manufacturing productivity also has to improve significantly. The way shirt manufacturing produc-tivity will improve is through foreign direct investment bringing best practice operations and capital to build large-scale plants. At least, that's the way China did it and it worked there.

This doesn't happen in India. Neither Indians nor foreigners can build large-scale plants oriented towards serving the huge Indian mar-ket. The reason is the "Small-scale Reservation" law. For most seg-ments in apparel, this law restricts investments in fixed assets to about $200,000 for firms producing more than 50 percent of their output for the domestic market. A minimum efficient scale shirt manufacturing plant requires five hundred sewing machines and costs about $700,000. China (and Sri Lanka) have many plants like this. In contrast, manufac-turers serving the domestic market in India have on average twenty sewing machines. A plant this small can get no efficiencies from large production runs of the same item. It would take too long to fill an order this way. That means smaller orders and higher costs from more fre-quent switching of products. No wonder tailors are more competitive than manufacturers. A tailor probably has three to four sewing ma-chines and no distribution and selling costs.

Why would India penalize itself this way with the Small-scale Reser-vation law? It has to be ideological. Perhaps its origin is Mahatma Gandhi's reverence for the traditional, self-sustaining Indian village. In-dira Gandhi put the Small-scale Reservation law in place. By that time, the small-scale ideology had undoubtedly become a broader rejection of influences from the world outside. Western societies have incidences of "small is beautiful" movements. Beyond the true believers, many of us hold sentimental feelings for a romantic image of a more beautiful and simpler life in previous ages. History suggests life then was closer to Hobbes's "nasty, brutish, and short."

Foreign Direct Investment Not Interested

A possible way around the small-is-beautiful constraint would be for-eign direct investment in large-scale plants in India exporting over

50 percent of their production. That might work except for the fact that there is a competitive market for foreign direct investment. For apparel, China clearly beats India in this market. It's understandable that Hong Kong and Taiwan would invest in China. However, Japan and Korea also do so. The United States invests in Sri Lanka. Nobody invests in India.

India is not attractive for foreign direct investment for a whole variety of reasons:

- High-quality fabric is not available in India and has to be imported.
- Labor laws make investors uncertain about their ability to close down plants in India if market conditions change.
- The huge domestic market in India is not readily available because of the undeveloped retail industry and the 50 percent limit on the amount of production that can be sold domestically.
- Red tape in customs procedures and port operations delays the import and export of products, thus raising doubts about whether fast-changing international fashion trends can be met from India.

The net result is that apparel exporters in India have around fifty machines in their plants, compared with five hundred in China. China's exporters are 55 percent as productive as U.S. producers, compared with 35 percent in India. China has 20 percent of the world's apparel export market. India has 2 percent (Exhibit 8.1).

Exhibit 8.1: Apparel Exports

$ Billions

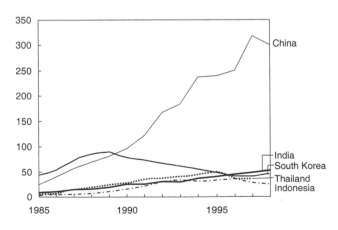

Ironically, India gets its 2 percent because many importing countries give it a guaranteed market under the Agreement on Textiles and Clothing (the follow-on agreement to the old Multifiber Arrangement). India's share of apparel exports is only half as big in countries not giving guaranteed markets as it is in countries giving guaranteed markets. In China, the situation is reversed. Its share is three times higher in countries without market guarantees than in countries with such guarantees. These guarantees will expire in 2005. Then, all markets will become more like the non-guaranteed markets of today. That means China's global market share of exports will go up even higher and India's will fall even lower.

What a mess India has made of its apparel sector.

Housing Construction: No Wheelbarrows

Shelter is the third basic need after food and clothing. India does even worse in housing construction than it does in apparel. Housing construction labor productivity is 8 percent of the U.S. level, compared with 16 percent in apparel. The amount of housing per person is a little square, eight feet by eight feet. If four people six feet tall laid down perpendicular to each other, with the head of each at the feet of another, the area inside the square they formed would be a little smaller than the average amount of shelter per person in India. China has four times as much shelter per person, Brazil, seven times, and the United States, ten times.

Moreover, about half the housing in India is traditional huts made out of mud, cardboard, straw, tin sheets, and stones. These huts have no plumbing and no flooring. The materials have low durability and the huts need constant repair. None of the benefits of industrialization, standardization, and scale can apply to the building of these huts. The productivity of such construction is 2 percent of U.S. housing construction productivity. It cannot get much better.

Most of the rest of housing in India is single-family houses built out of brick. Less than 10 percent of housing is multifamily apartment houses. India's productivity in both these types of housing is 15 percent of the United States'. The potential at today's prices of labor and equipment is 90 percent.

It is easy to understand why India's productivity is so low. Indian construction workers don't use wheelbarrows. Wheelbarrows are used everywhere around the world and certainly in Brazil and Russia. In India, workers move materials on the tops of their heads. They do this despite being smaller and weaker than workers in Brazil. You would think wheelbarrows would be the first thing construction workers out in the hot Indian sun would use. Not so. When asked why not, construction foremen said they couldn't get up steps with wheelbarrows. At the suggestion of boards being used to form an inclined plane for wheelbarrows to run up and down on, the response was that this is a good idea. No one seems to have an incentive to think about how to improve productivity. Why not?

In the housing construction industry in Europe, Japan, Korea, Brazil, Russia, and Poland, many factors, sometimes repeating themselves, cause lower productivity. Materials were not standardized in Japan, causing every house to be different. Suburban infrastructure was not provided by local governments in Europe, thereby preventing development. Zoning laws in Korea prevented large-scale single-family housing developments. Mortgages were not available in Brazil, causing houses to be built one paycheck at a time. Russia and Poland were different because the government had recently owned all land and had not really privatized land in urban areas. There, the government was still managing the use of land, bad as that might be.

No One Knows Who Owns the Land

India has all the problems for housing construction found outside Russia and Poland. In addition, India has an even worse problem in the allocation of land than the government's doing it. In India, everybody was sure that the land was privately owned and did not belong to the government. Therefore, the market should successfully allocate land pretty well. Unfortunately not. In India, nobody knows for sure who the actual owners are. Over 90 percent of land titles in India are subject to dispute. Needless to say, there's no point in talking to a bank about lending you the money to build a house if you can't prove to the bank that you're going to build the house on land that you own. Most importantly, if you didn't repay the bank, the bank would probably be unable to sell the house to somebody else without clear title. Moreover, this situation makes it virtually impossible to put together large parcels of land for big multifamily and single-family housing developments. Every potential development site has some land without clear title.

Competition Is Over Land, Not Productivity

India has all the penalties in housing construction productivity from lack of mortgage financing and lack of large-scale developments. These would be bad enough. However, India has a unique penalty that is worse than the other two. So little land is available with clear title that competition in housing construction is focused almost entirely on gaining control of what little land there is. There's no time for worrying about improving the productivity of construction methods and using such things as wheelbarrows. They don't matter. If you're not one of the few developers with some clear titles, you're not in the housing construction business.

You can just imagine what a corrupt business housing development in India has become. The skills for success include running an intelligence gathering network to be the first to know about land with clear title becoming available. Skills are also necessary for your title cases to be adjudicated at the head of the backlog line stretching for a hundred years. The land shortage is so great that developers will pay practically anything for it. The ratio of urban land cost to GDP per capita in India is ten times almost anywhere else in Asia (Exhibit 8.2). The housing shortage is so great that potential homeowners will also pay anything, including giving developers and contractors profit margins twice those in Brazil and six times those in the United States. In these circumstances, who cares about productivity? There is no cost-based competition. If there were, contractors would probably just use substandard materials more than they already do. They can get away with this because of lack of materials standardization.

Why does India have such a problem with land titles? The most straightforward cause is bureaucracy and red tape. It's too much of a hassle for owners to see land registration through to the end, and too complex for government bureaucrats to keep straight. More pernicious are tenant rights, the Urban Land Ceiling Act, and a high land registration tax. Indian law gives renters occupancy rights that dilute the owners' rights to sell without mountainous paperwork. Sales without this paperwork proceed anyway. Moreover, in most urban areas, the Urban Land Ceiling Act restricts land ownership to less than 500 square meters. That's a square 70 feet on a side. You can barely get two to three townhouses on such a plot. Certainly not a high-rise apartment building or a large-scale single-family housing development. To get around this law, owners register sub-parcels in different variations of their own name or under the names of other family members. Over time, this obfuscation causes real problems as the descendants of family members think they really own the land. After all, it's in their parents' names. Finally, a high tax on land registration causes many transactions to go unrecorded. The potential for chaos is clear.

Exhibit 8.2: Land Costs Relative to Income

Index New Delhi = 100; ratio of land costs per sq.m. to GDP per capita in 1999

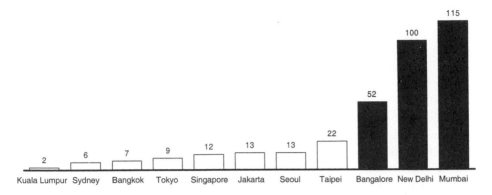

Of all the industries examined in India, the market in housing construction was the most distorted. Even more disturbing was that the problem with land titles caught Indian policymakers by surprise and was not even on the World Bank priority list for reform in India.

Food Retailing: Reinventing the Wheel

In early September 2001, we presented our findings on India's economy to Prime Minister Vajpayee and his cabinet. The response was polite but noncommittal. Among many recommendations, perhaps our strongest was to allow unrestricted foreign direct investment in retailing. At the time, foreign direct investment in retailing was restricted to franchise operations. Within a week of our meeting with the prime minister, India announced a total ban on all foreign direct investment in retailing. We never have had a recommendation rejected so quickly. On the other hand, most of our recommendations have found their way into the latest five-year plan prepared in the middle of 2002. The Indians still go through the motions of preparing such plans although they don't pay much attention to them anymore. We'll see what happens this time.

In previous chapters, I have recounted the huge role the retailing industry has played in the evolution of economies to advanced stages. I have also noted along the way how this role has been grossly underappreciated virtually everywhere. First of all, retailers are the only businesses in the consumer goods chain physically and continuously in contact with consumers. They can know exactly what consumers buy on a daily basis. That means retailers are in by far the best position to know what consumers want. Of course, if you think consumers are also dumb and don't know what they should want, then this doesn't matter to you. I happen to belong to the school of thought that the purpose of economies is to provide what we, as consumers, want. Of course, this objective needs to be met within the appropriate safeguards for such things as product safety, environmental quality, truth in advertising, etc.

As retailers have competed among themselves to make profits and thereby improve productivity, they have taken actions that have improved productivity along the whole consumer goods chain. They realized that once they reached a sufficient scale, they could bypass monopolistic, unproductive wholesalers. They could build their own logistics systems and purchase directly from consumer goods manufacturers. They also found that their large volume purchases gave them leverage to insist that small, fragmented consumer goods manufacturers consolidate to lower costs, thereby increasing productivity. In the food chain, large-scale food processors then often assisted farmers to apply higher productivity practices. In theory, this rationalization of the consumer goods chain could have been led by any party along the chain. In reality, we know retailers were the leaders. The reasons are that consolidation could proceed in smaller increments in retailing and retailers were more confident about the benefits of major changes because they knew better how consumers were likely to react to them.

Today, India gets none of these benefits. In food retailing, modern supermarkets in India have only a 2 percent market share. Sixty percent of all food is sold in mom-and-pop counter stores, and the rest through street markets and street vendors. The productivity of counter stores and street markets/vendors is less than 10 percent of U.S. food retailing productivity. That's not surprising. What is surprising is that the productivity of the supermarkets that are in India is only 20 percent of U.S. supermarket productivity. In Brazil, the productivity of hypermarkets and supermarkets is 50 percent of the U.S. level. These two types of food retailers have 35 percent of the food retailing market in Brazil. In Poland, the productivity of hypermarkets and supermarkets combined is 75 percent of U.S. supermarket productivity, and in the past ten years their market share has gone from 0 to 18 percent.

The reason the productivity of supermarkets in India is so low is that their managers don't know what to do. Neither did the managers of the first supermarkets in the United States fifty years ago. They had to learn how to use employees efficiently through multitasking and part-time employment. They also had to learn how to understand systematically the purchasing patterns of customers and to apply that understanding to their purchasing, logistics, merchandising, and marketing activities. They also had to learn how to bypass wholesalers and help rationalize food processing. I'm sure that Indian supermarket managers will learn this too. However, it may take fifty years. There's no need to wait that long. Supermarket/hypermarket managers from France, the United Kingdom, and the United States now go around the world applying immediately what took them fifty years to learn. In Brazil, it took modern hypermarkets and supermarkets only 15 years to capture a 35 percent market share; in Thailand, ten years for a 40 percent share; and in China, ten years for a 10 percent share. It seems this is happening everywhere, except for India (and Russia, as explained in the previous chapter). Why not in India?

India Not Attractive to Global Food Retailers

Well, even if global best practice hypermarkets and supermarkets were allowed to invest in India, they still probably wouldn't come. First of all, they would have great difficulty getting the land for a large number of stores. I have already discussed the problem of unclear land titles in the housing construction case. The same difficulty would apply to assembling enough parcels of land for a large store, with accompanying parking lot and storeroom. Zoning laws also restrict the amount of land available for commercial use. Closely associated with the land difficulty is the lack of urban and suburban infrastructure. Many of the local governments are simply bankrupt. Property taxes are so low that local governments find it impossible to discharge their responsibilities for providing roads, water, sewer, and electricity (if power is publicly owned).

Second, supermarkets/hypermarkets would have great difficulty sourcing food products locally. Global best practice food retailers require 70 percent local sourcing to enter a market. It's too expensive to have to import because of perishability, reliability, and quality control problems. In China, Carrefour, which established twenty-two hypermarkets within four years, sources 90 percent of its food products locally. In India, 75 percent of processed food is still produced by small-scale industries protected by the Small-scale Reservation law or by non-industrial operations. In these circumstances, global retailers cannot lead a consolidation in the food processing industry from which they could efficiently source.

Finally, they probably couldn't make any money. The playing field is not level. Large global retailers would pay their taxes, set at 38.5 percent in India. Counter stores pay a lower rate of 22 percent, and they often evade that. Moreover, counter stores have the advantage of residential rather than commercial rates for electricity and controlled rent prices set long ago. Today, prices for branded goods are 2 to 3 percent higher in supermarkets than in counter stores. Normally, they're 10 percent lower. Global best practice supermarkets might beat the counter stores today. However, as their actions demonstrate, they would probably believe there are many more attractive places to invest around the world. And of course, even if they wanted to invest in India, they couldn't.

1991 Medical Exam Ignored the Heart

The conventional wisdom today is that the 1991 reforms removed virtually all the important constraints on how business is conducted in India. Licenses to do business were abolished for most industries. Yes, things could be worse than they are now in India, and they were worse before 1991. However, abolishing licenses just removed the outer peel of the onion. Underneath lay a morass of barriers to India's economic progress. Food retailing shows how pernicious these barriers are at the heart of India's domestic economy. And retailing is the real heart of all economies. India is differentiated from every other major developing country, with the exception of Russia, by not having any global best practice food retailing. High-productivity food retailing has been part of the development story in Brazil, Thailand, Poland, and China. In the introduction to this chapter, I gave a conceptual argument about why productivity growth in the modern part of developing economies is necessary for the country to move forward. Reality seems consistent with this theory.

And just when you think you have seen the extent of India's problems, along comes electric power.

Electric Power

Although many industries in our 118 industry studies in thirteen different countries are performing below their potential, electric power in India is the worst.

Electric power depends much more heavily on capital than most sectors. The technology for generating electricity and distributing it is built into the capital. The same capital is available everywhere in the world. Moreover, the engineering understanding for building and maintaining an electric power system is also readily available everywhere. Thus, India's productivity potential should be very close to that of the United States. It is for the generation of electricity, with a potential productivity of about 90 percent of the U.S. level. However, India achieves only 34 percent of the productivity of the United States in the generation of electricity. For distribution of electricity, India suffers a penalty because individual customers use much less electricity even though it takes just as much capital to build the distribution system right up to their factory or house. Thus, India's potential productivity for electricity distribution is about 40 percent of U.S. productivity. Incredible as it may seem, India achieves only 4 percent. That's getting down close to the same relative performance that India's farmers have.

The Business of Government Is Not Running Businesses

The reason India's performance is so bad is that the electric power industry is 95 percent government owned. States own about 60 percent of generation and virtually all of distribution. The federal government owns the rest of generation except for a few private power generators. They achieve 80 percent of U.S. productivity. Best practice private electricity distribution companies achieve 33 percent of U.S. productivity, or 80 percent of India's potential. Since 1991, private firms have been allowed in electricity generation. Very few have shown up. The reason is that they have grave doubts they will be paid for the electricity they generate. That's where India's problems start.

Electricity distribution is a natural monopoly. It makes no sense to build two or more competing distribution networks. In most states in India, the state government's Electricity Board owns the distribution system. Virtually all these Electricity Boards are bankrupt. They are bankrupt because, believe it or not, they lose 35 percent of the electricity they take from power plants. Technical losses experienced by all systems are about 10 percent in both India and the United States. The remaining losses of 25 percent are not really a mystery. Sometimes the Electricity Boards simply have not placed meters on customers' lines. Other times, the electricity is stolen through illegal (and dangerous) taps into the electricity wires. These nontechnical losses amount to about $3 billion per year. That's equivalent to 1 percent of India's GDP.

The nontechnical loss rate for the best of the privatized state Electricity Boards is 2 to 3 percent. The privatized distribution systems know that the state governments will not bail them out if they run out of cash. The government-owned distribution systems know they will be bailed out, because that's what the state governments have done over and over again. Whether the state governments would bail out the government-owned distribution companies to pay for electricity bought from private electricity generators remains to be seen. That's what worries private investors and keeps them away from electricity generation.

The result is that most electricity generation is also government owned. This generation has all the problems you can imagine of businesses with no competition and an unlimited line of credit. Shortcomings include having ten times as many administrative support personnel per megawatt of electricity generated as the United States and four times as much plant shutdown time as the United States.

India tries to control the cost and improve the operating performance of generating plants through regulation. Needless to say, it is difficult for one government body to regulate another. After all, both bodies are meant to be serving the public's interest. Then on top of this weakness, India uses old-fashioned regulation. It allows the government-owned electric power system to set prices so that it gets a guaranteed rate of return. That is, if they didn't lose so much electricity. It would just be too much if they were allowed to take losses into account in their calculations. It's bad enough as it is. Under this system, there is no incentive to reduce costs. In contrast, U.S. public regulators use "price caps" to force down electricity prices and put pressure on electric power systems to reduce costs and operate more efficiently. The public regulators have no conflict putting this pressure on private electric power systems, whose primary mission is to create shareholder value.

The amounts of money at stake here are huge in anybody's world. If India were to grow at its potential over the next ten years, $350 billion in investment would be required to expand its electric power system. The effects of privatization and good regulation would reduce that bill by about $35 billion. That's not small change.

India Has to Get Serious about Privatization

How does India get out of this morass? Well, it has to start with the privatization of the electricity distribution system. Private generators will not appear until they have confidence they will be paid for their electricity. That means the distribution systems have to be financially viable. The overwhelming change needed for financial viability of the distribution systems is stopping the losses of electricity. Even in India, the small amount of privatization of distribution systems has shown that private companies can do this. Overwhelming evidence comes from other countries. At the time Argentina privatized its electricity distribution system in 1992, it had losses of about 25 percent. Within three years of privatization, these losses had reduced to 15 percent.

Of course, you could say maybe these electricity losses don't matter so much anyway. After all, somebody's probably using electricity. They just aren't paying for it. Well it's not that simple. First of all, thefts are putting the distribution systems into bankruptcy. And that's stopping the privatization of electricity generation. And that's stopping productivity improvements in generating plants. However, much more important is the grossly nonlevel playing field caused by tolerance of this theft. Modern, large-scale industrial enterprises are not the ones stealing electricity. In fact, their tariffs are set at about 150 percent of the cost of generation. They are set at this high level to cross-subsidize farmers, who pay about 10 percent of the cost of generation.

Among the parties stealing electricity, or just not being metered, are many small, low-productivity businesses. Free electricity helps them sell at lower prices than larger, more productive competitors. Counter stores have lower prices than supermarkets. That stops retailing from evolving to higher productivity operations. And the evolution to higher productivity operations in the modern sector is the only way India will ever pull workers out of subsistence jobs in agriculture and move them through transition jobs to good jobs in modern enterprises. That's why privatizing electric power in India is important.

How the Rich Countries Should View India

In any discussion of the Indian economy with an Indian, software comes up sooner or later. It's raised to make the point that India is progressive. That things are changing rapidly. That India is in the forefront of the information technology revolution that will be the dominant characteristic of economic evolution from this point on.

Indians are justifiably proud of their software industry. Infosys is one of the very top big software companies in the world. India's relative productivity in software is about 50 percent of that of the United States and twice as high as the relative productivity of any other industry we studied in India. India's productivity in software would be even higher if its domestic market demanded more complex products. Moreover, foreign customers outsource to India most heavily for low-value services related to the maintenance of large, old mainframe systems and other legacy systems.

I intentionally have not included a summary of India's software industry in this chapter. The reason is that the software sector makes relatively little contribution to India's overall economic performance. This is true for virtually every industry in any economy. An economy is too big and too complex to be saved or ruined by any one industry. Beyond that, software is a very small sector. Currently, software employs 0.1 percent of Indian workers, or about 350 thousand people. Even in the United States, software employs only about 1 percent of the workforce. I once made a rough calculation of how many people in India would be employed in software if India performed all the software work for the entire world. That number came to about 7 million. That's only 2 percent of the Indian workforce. In contrast, there are about 25 million Indians working in retailing and 50 million in dairy farming. In determining the standard of living in India, the productivity of these workers swamps the productivity contribution of software workers. The productivities relative to the United States are 6 percent for retailing and 0.6 percent for dairy farming. India's software industry is certainly worth having. Performance there, however, needs to be matched by the other 99.5 percent of India's GDP for India to get out of being a poor country.

More Barriers to Productivity Improvement Than Anywhere Else

The problems in the other 99.5 percent of India's economy are massive. In our industry studies of India, we found every single barrier to productivity improvement that we found in other countries. In many cases, the barriers in India were stronger. On top of that, a few barriers are unique to India. India provided the clinching evidence of the impression that began to form as we studied progressively poorer countries. The more numerous and the more intense the barriers to productivity improvement, the poorer the country. I will come back to this point more systematically in the next chapter. Also, in India, barriers that distorted the markets in which goods and services are sold (product market) were the most important type of barrier. This also was a finding common with the results from other countries.

Of these product market barriers, India has by far the tightest restrictions on new competitors entering markets. The most important of these restrictions is on foreign direct investment. The most severe restriction on foreign direct investment is the outright prohibition of foreign direct investment in retailing. As I have explained earlier in this chapter, retailing is crucial. It may very well be the most important industry in any economy. India is forcing itself to "reinvent the wheel" in retailing rather than reaping the advantage of applying everything the rest of the world has learned about retailing in the past fifty years. In addition to unusually high tariffs on imports, and licenses prohibiting new entries in some sectors, such as dairy processing, India has a unique restriction on new entrants. The Small-scale Reservation law limits production of some eight hundred products to small-scale firms. This law, for instance, makes it impossible for India with its small-scale apparel plants to compete with large-scale Chinese manufacturers.

In addition, India severely distorts the playing field for competition among existing firms. For instance, small, unproductive steel minimills get away without paying their energy and tax bills. Sounds like Russia. In retail, small, unproductive counter stores can sell at prices below the (admittedly unproductive) Indian supermarkets. This should not be true no matter how unproductive Indian supermarkets are. It is true because tax and labor laws give counter stores an advantage. Again, sounds like Russia.

The economics literature does not pay much attention to these product market barriers. That literature discusses primarily labor markets and capital markets. This is because there is a huge amount of publicly available data on both labor markets and capital markets. There is this old joke of the drunken man looking for his keys under the lamppost when he obviously lost them somewhere else. When asked why he was looking under the lamppost, he replied that's where the light is. The point is product market distortions cannot be easily extracted from publicly available data. They usually apply specifically to one industry and sometimes to only a class of firms within that industry. It's just not possible for economists, who typically work at the small scale of an individual, to find all these product market distortions. The only possibility then is widespread surveys of opinions about the importance of these distortions. Those surveys have some value, but they are not always convincing. Their most serious shortcoming, however, is that they give no insight into the specific laws, regulations, and practices that need to change to remove the distortions.

Beyond product market distortions, there are also land market distortions. At least the potential effects of product market distortions are mentioned in the economics literature. You see virtually nothing there on land market distortions. Land market distortions were not even part of the economic debate in India. And given the huge newsprint space devoted to this debate in India, you would think nothing could be left out. In India, there are our old friends, zoning laws and low property taxes. As in even France and Germany, zoning laws limit competition among housing developers and retailers. And as is also the case in Germany and many other countries, low property taxes preclude local government authorities from financing infrastructure needed for large-scale housing and commercial developments. Finally, as you might suspect, there is also a unique distortion in the land market in India. About 90 percent of land titles are unclear as to who really owns the land. As I explained regarding the housing construction industry, this distortion causes competition among real estate developers to be over finding and acquiring land with clear titles rather than over construction productivity.

Finally, India has more government ownership of businesses than any other country we studied. Businesses owned by the federal and state governments have 40 percent of all employment in the modern sector in India. Productivity growth in the modern sector in India will be the most important cause of further economic evolution in India. Thus, all this government ownership is a big problem. In India, government-owned businesses invariably have lower productivity than private businesses (Exhibit 8.3). India has no equivalent of Korea's General Park, who made POSCO, the state-owned steel company, one of the best in the world. Government-owned businesses simply do not have as strong a profit motive as private businesses. Their shareholders, the government, are not as unhappy as private shareholders if businesses don't make money. More importantly, the government-owned entities face no risk of going out of business. Governments cannot let businesses fail in large part because the workers won't let them. The governments always cave. They cave by sending good money after bad to subsidize the businesses. This leads to another problem, big government.

On Top of Bad Policymaking, the Size of India's Government Distorts Micromarkets

India's governments spent 32 percent of India's GDP. That's a little lower than Brazil's 39 percent. These numbers need to be compared with the 8 percent or so of GDP the governments of France and the United States spent when these countries were close to Brazil's GDP per capita in 1913. Of course, Brazil's GDP per capita is 21 percent of the United States'. India's is 7 percent. When the United States was at India's level of today, the United States had virtually no government. I have discussed the problem of poor countries having big governments in the chapter on Brazil. In India's case, the size of the government reflects the degree of government intervention in the market economy. It reflects both extreme government ownership of business and extreme government regulation of business. The costs of these activities are a substantial drain on national savings. That money could be put to much better use invested in

Exhibit 8.3: Public vs. Private Productivity: India

Index U.S. = 100 in 1998

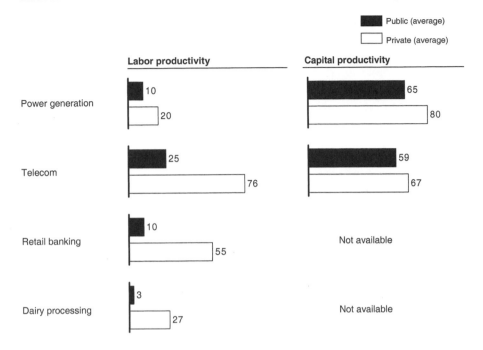

increasing India's productive capacity. Moreover, the high levels of government revenue necessary to finance the high expenditures require that taxes on modern enterprises be high. There is nobody else to tax. As I explained in the retail case, that distorts competition between much more productive supermarkets and low-productivity, traditional stores. This translates directly into a lower productivity growth rate because it slows the rate at which supermarkets spread over India. Also important is that big government creates the potential for market distortions through illegal bribery and other forms of favoritism serving special interests.

There is a lot of frustration and even the appearance of a lack of urgency about India's economic problems. I believe the frustration and the lack of urgency come from more than just so little progress. There is simply more ideological difference among political forces in India than in any other country we studied, with the possible exception of Russia. There is an element of the business community in India that would be at home in any country in the world and could compete successfully anywhere. Their notions of good economic policy are virtually identical to those of progressive businesspeople everywhere. It is true that many potential members of this group in India leave the country for better opportunities elsewhere. Throughout my career, some of my professional colleagues for whom I have had the most respect have come from India.

There is another group of politicians, academics, and journalists in India who remind me of the economic thinking I met in Oxford in the early 1960s when Harold Wilson, a former Oxford don, was the Labor Party prime minister. In those days, the United Kingdom was nationalizing industries and caving to labor unions. There was disdain around Oxford for "making profits" in industrial enterprises, although apparently it was acceptable for those reading "Greats" (classics) to make a pile of money in the City (in London) keeping their hands clean in finance. The feeling was that smart people knew better. They should protect the innocent worker and the finer things in life from greedy, uncouth industrialists. They should go to government and run the country. I suspect that some of India's political elite were there at Oxford (probably at Nuffield College, the center of this thinking) at about that time. Unfortunately for India, they were gone by the time of Thatcher's revolution.

Finally, there is another element in India's thinking that is more foreign, certainly to Westerners, but I also believe to many other people, including some Asians. This is the feeling that material things just don't matter that much in this life. Of course, there is nothing "wrong" about this view. However, if you hold it, you certainly don't have the same sense of urgency about getting economic policies right for rapid GDP growth.

Dilemma for Rich Countries

India presents the rich countries with the most important dilemma over development assistance. In the United States, many influential political groups are dissatisfied with the progress achieved by poor countries in the past fifty years despite substantial financial and technical assistance from the rich countries and the international development banks they have established. India has more poor people than any other country on earth and has received more of this assistance than any other country. Right now, the United States is leading an effort to grant development assistance only to countries with economic policies causing rapid GDP growth. The objective is to use the resources where they will have the most benefit and to provide countries incentives to improve their policies. On this score, India would get much less development assistance. In fact, many countries would fall into the same category. Because India has been such an outsized example of economic development failure, if penalizing bad economic policy is not applied to India, then the new criteria for giving assistance will have little credibility.

I doubt that the rich world can walk away from India like this. The plight of the desperately poor is too heart-rending. I still remember vividly from 1974 the exquisite human face of a young boy lying asleep on a railroad bridge near the main train station in Delhi. I hoped he was asleep from exhaustion but knew it was probably from near starvation. Somehow we have to find a way to get clean water and some books to these people regardless of whether they ever improve their economic policy. On the other hand, economic policies in India are the principal reason India has not made more progress economically. It's not going to be possible to ask taxpayers in the United States to transfer part of their wealth to make up for wealth India could be creating if it had better economic policies.

PART THREE

CAUSES AND IMPLICATIONS

CHAPTER NINE

Patterns: Clear and Strong

In the past seven chapters, I have described the economic performance of the rich parts of the world, Japan, Europe, and the United States, the performance of one middle-income country, Korea, and the performance of three poor countries, Brazil, Russia, and India. In this chapter, I will gather together the explanation of why countries have the economic performance they do.

Jared Diamond, in his book *Guns, Germs, and Steel,* argues conclusively that in AD 1500 the wealth and power of Chinese and European civilizations did not come from racial superiority but from geographic happenstance. Domesticable wild grains and wild animals naturally occurred in only two places on earth, China and the Middle East. These occurrences caused the evolution from hunting and gathering to agriculture to occur first in these places. The transition to agriculture triggered a great increase in the productivity of acquiring food. This increase in productivity then caused more rapid development of these two civilizations. The increased food productivity of the Middle Eastern civilizations diffused easily into Europe because Europe was roughly at the same latitude and climatic conditions were similar (unlike Africa).

Today, however, Europe and China have very different economic performances. China's GDP per capita is about 10 percent of the United States', the leading "European" civilization economy. Most of the people in the world live in countries with economic performance much closer to China's than to the United States'. However, a few countries, for example Korea, are in the middle. Moreover, most of the countries with origins in the European civilization have economic performance much closer to the United States' than to China's. Latin America is the exception. (Some speculative work suggests this is because Spain and Portugal colonized Latin America to exploit resources and not to settle.

Britain, on the other hand, colonized North America and Australia, at least in part, to settle people there.)

This situation is almost the opposite of what we would expect at first thought. In the past five hundred years, and especially in the last 150 years, interaction among all parts of the world has increased dramatically. We would expect that new products and services and better ways of producing them would transfer rapidly around the globe. We would thus expect the initial advantage of China and Europe in 1500 to have largely dissipated. In fact, we see the opposite, with the economic gap between poor countries and European civilization countries widening manyfold. Moreover, China has become a poor country relative to European civilization countries.

It's Competition Policy

Our most important finding is that poor countries' policies have kept them poor. And these policies can and must be fixed, as I will get to in the next two chapters. Of course, many of the policy failures of these countries are widely known. Good conventional wisdom about proper economic policies is embodied in the "Washington Consensus" of the early 1990s. However, that policy prescription failed to recognize sufficiently the critical importance of intense and fair competition in economic development. Policies creating macroeconomic stability and fair, intense competition are by far the most important conditions for rapid economic growth. The importance of macroeconomic stability has become obvious to virtually everybody. Low inflation, government solvency, and slowly adjusting exchange rates are necessary for economic growth to match growth potential. *What is by no means obvious is the importance of competition.*

Economists often don't give competition sufficient emphasis because they assume that businesses always maximize their profits. I was staggered at a working dinner in the White House with Clinton's economic team when a member of the Council of Economic Advisers challenged my contention that the productivity in the U.S. automotive and steel industries had been hurt by the government's allowing an oligopoly to exist in those industries in the 1950s and '60s. He contended that a monopolist had just as much incentive to cut costs as everybody else since everybody was profit maximizing. That statement reflected such a naive understanding of how the real business world worked that I could barely maintain my patience to explain how things were. After all, my tax dollars were going to pay his salary while he gave the president economic advice based on such a grave misunderstanding.

The reality is that productivity improvement is hard work. Cost-cutting makes some people very unhappy, especially if they are the costs cut. Changing the way people do their work is also hard. People get set in their ways. Moreover, producing new things or doing things a new way involves risk. It might not work out. Many managers do just enough of these things to keep their jobs. The thing they really want to avoid is going out of business.

A monopolist can go on this way for a very long time. However, intense competition causes more productive firms to rapidly take market share away from less productive firms. The less productive firms either change their ways and began to improve about as fast as the more productive firms or they go out of business. As I explained in chapter 4 on the United States, Wal-Mart's higher productivity in the 1990s forced the other general merchandise retail stores to either rapidly increase their productivity or go bankrupt. The resulting productivity increase in the retailing sector contributed significantly to the acceleration in labor productivity in the entire U.S. economy in the second half of the 1990s.

The competition not only needs to be intense, it also needs to be fair. Straightforwardly, if less productive firms have an unfair advantage through, for instance, a government subsidy or a tax preference, then no matter how intensely more productive firms compete with them, the more productive firms will do less well. In the extreme, the more productive firms don't even bother to enter the market. That's the case today in food retailing in Russia.

I hope the importance of fair and intense competition has come through in the last seven chapters. A systematic array of the important causal factors in all the industries in all the countries shows clearly the importance of competition. It is even possible to make rough quantitative estimates of how much differences in competition contribute to productivity differences. These calculations show the same conclusion. I will not present them here because they are beyond the scope of this book. Moreover, they are not necessary to know the conclusion. The conclusion about competition comes right out of reading the country stories themselves.

The other thing that should emerge from the past seven chapters is that the less intense the competition is and the more distorted it is, the worse the productivity. In the next sections of this chapter, I will use the retailing and housing construction industries across all the countries I have described to show how this is true. What causes India to have the lowest productivity in housing construction? It's that competition is more distorted in India than anywhere else. It's so bad that competition is not even over prices and costs and productivity. It's over inside access to the small amount of land with clear titles.

As the industry studies in the past seven chapters showed time and time again, differences in competitive intensity and distortions in competition come directly from differences in policies. Government-owned firms immediately create unfair competition. They are almost invariably less productive than privately owned firms. Governments invariably subsidize them rather than letting them fail. As a result, for example, the productivity of the retail banking sector in Brazil is far below potential. Other policies that diminish or distort competition are unequal tax laws and unequal tax enforcement. Trade tariffs and foreign direct investment restrictions also diminish and distort competition. Land use restrictions such as zoning laws limiting the size of developments, and lack of provision of road, water, sewerage, and electricity infrastructure also retard development and thus diminish competition.

Competition occurs in the market in which goods and services are sold. This is the product market. Most economic analysis ends up attributing most of the differences in economic performance to differences in labor and capital markets. This conclusion is incorrect around the world. Differences in competition in product markets are by far more important. That means that policies governing competition in the product markets are the most important policies, along with, of course, macroeconomic policies. In later sections of this chapter I will review why labor and capital markets are less important than product markets. I will also address why education and infrastructure, both high on the World Bank's priority list, are much less important than getting competition right.

Patterns by Industry across Countries

From the beginning of the drafting of the manuscript for this book, I had planned to write sections about retailing and housing construction in each of the country chapters. I did this for several reasons:

- Although no one industry is big enough to influence heavily whole economies, retailing and housing construction are large industries. Retailing accounts for 11 percent of employment in the United States and 12 percent in Japan. Housing construction accounts for about 2 percent of employment in the United States and about 4 percent in Japan. In contrast, the combined share of U.S. employment accounted for by the high-tech industries of metalworking, computers, instruments, drugs, chemicals and plastics, consumer electronics, and electrical machinery and equipment is only 0.75 percent.

· Retailing has heavy influence outside its boundaries. Retailing is the industry in immediate contact with individual consumers and thus in the best position to know what they want. That marketing knowledge has allowed retailers in the advanced countries to consolidate massively. The resulting bargaining power has allowed retailers to bypass wholesalers and force the consolidation of consumer goods and food processing industries. It has even led to food processors helping farmers become more productive.

· Housing construction is among the most local of all businesses. It has no global firms and no national firms in large countries. Yet it is one of the most sensitive industries to macroeconomic conditions because of its dependence on mortgages. Because of the use of monetary policy, the housing construction industry is carrying the United States through the economic disruption caused by the bursting of the information technology bubble in 2000. At the same time, housing construction is extremely sensitive to local land use policies (as is retailing).

· Neither retailing nor housing construction get the attention they deserve. Despite their being part of our everyday lives, as industries they are much less visible than the heavily traded sectors, such as automobiles and steel, and the high-tech sectors, such as computers and pharmaceuticals.

· Because these industries are hidden at the core of our domestic economies, it is much more difficult to establish the conditions under which they will have high productivity.

· Finally, I wanted to be in the position at this point in the book to provide a synthesis across countries for a couple of industries.

This synthesis gives tangible evidence of how productivity performance varies with competitive dynamics and laws and regulations. No such comparisons on a global scale are now available. As I have said earlier, the major finding of this synthesis is that product market regulations, including land market factors, are the most important causal factor for economic performance, along with, of course, macroeconomic policies. These product market and land market effects show up only at the industry level. Therefore, to include them in a worldwide synthesis requires synthesis at the industry level. Here I will synthesize retailing and housing construction across countries.

Retailing

Labor productivity in retailing varies as widely around the world as does GDP per capita. European countries have about the same productivity in retailing as the United States. Productivity in retailing falls off rapidly outside Europe. The labor productivities in retailing for the other countries covered in this book, as a percentage of labor productivity in the United States, are as follows: Japan, 50 percent; Korea, 32 percent; Poland, 24 percent; Russia, 24 percent; Brazil, 14 percent; and India, 6 percent (Exhibit 9.1). The two countries whose labor productivity in retailing is way out of line with their GDPs per capita are Japan and Korea. Their relative labor productivity in retailing is way below their relative GDPs per capita. As I explained in the chapters on those countries, both Japan and Korea have paid little attention to retailing because they have not considered it very important.

Supermarkets versus Mom-and-Pops

The general pattern as we look across countries from the highest productivity to the lowest is that as productivity decreases, more causal factors limiting productivity appear and the causal factors themselves intensify. Some of these factors we can quantify. We know that the general pattern of evolution in retailing has been from small, low-productivity mom-and-pop stores to high-productivity department stores, hypermarkets, supermarkets, convenience stores, etc. In the United States, modern supermarkets are four to five times more productive than mom-and-pop stores. Thus, the mix between modern stores and mom-and-pop stores accounts for a large part of all the productivity gaps. This mix effect starts to show up strongly with Japan and Korea. The Japan and Korea chapters describe the large number of mom-and-pop stores left in these countries.

Then, when we get to Brazil and India, another effect kicks in. The mom-and-pop stores drop out of the official economy and become the transition activities, as people desperate for a better life try to move from subsistence living in rural areas to better jobs in cities and towns. The productivity in these mom-and-pop stores is far below the productivity of mom-and-pop stores even in Japan and Korea. Finally, in In-

Exhibit 9.1: Retail Labor Productivity

Index U.S. = 100

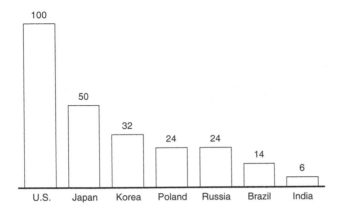

dia, the last causal factor directly related to stores shows up. In India, even the modern stores have very low productivity. Supermarkets in India are only about 20 percent as productive as supermarkets in the United States.

You Can't Build without Land

Why is it taking so long for modern retail stores to displace mom-and-pop stores outside the United States and Europe? In every country, these modern stores have the potential to provide food and general merchandise to customers at significantly lower prices than the traditional stores. Well, to compete with the traditional stores, modern stores have to be built. That's where the problem starts. To build a store you have to have land to build it on. In all the countries we studied, with the exception of Brazil, that's a problem.

Zoning laws in France, Germany, the United Kingdom, Japan, Korea, Poland, and India restrict the development of large modern stores. In Russia, land allocation by city governments serves the same purpose. In India, on top of zoning restrictions is the problem that for the land that is available for development, most of the land titles designating ownership are unclear. In addition, in Japan and Korea, laws give mom-and-pop stores substantial influence over decisions whether governmental bodies will allow large stores to be built. If large stores can't be built, then competitive intensity is diminished and productivity is lower. Japan has a special wrinkle. Even if the large stores are built, the government provides subsidized loans to the mom-and-pop stores to keep them in business.

High Taxes Create Nonlevel Playing Field

When we get to Russia, Brazil, and India, another problem appears. Even if the modern stores were built, they would make little or no money. This is because the traditional stores don't pay any taxes and the modern stores do. Moreover, in Russia the informal retail operations have been selling counterfeit goods and smuggled goods. The dramatic fall in the value of the ruble has solved some of the problem with smuggled goods, and Russian consumer goods companies are now helping to crack down on counterfeit goods. Nevertheless, the tax burden is unequal.

This matters a lot because the tax burden is high. The tax burden is high because the governments of these countries spend a lot of the GDP. They have to raise this money through taxes. In retailing, the only businesses they can tax are the modern retailers. The employment taxes and value-added and sales taxes they pay go right into their cost structure because these taxes have to be covered by the sales price. This sales price is in competition with the sales price of informal retailers not paying these taxes. Because of volume discounts, modern retail chains can procure food and consumer goods at much lowers prices than informal stores. The modern stores also have significantly higher productivity. Despite all this, the modern stores can just barely underprice the informal stores in Brazil and India, and they are more expensive in Russia. The result is that modern stores are expanding very slowly in Brazil and India and not even attempting to compete in Russia. Thus, retailing is stuck at its current low productivity in Russia, Brazil, and India. This is why they're having such a difficult time rising above the low GDP per capita plain in the global economic landscape. I will come back to this point more generally in the next chapter.

Finally, in India we have the problem that even the modern retailing stores have low productivity. That's because India prohibits experienced modern retailers from investing in India. Indian retailers are reinventing the wheel for modern retailing. They will do it, but it will take a long time. Here's a desperately poor country shooting itself in the foot, or more accurately, in the stomach.

To sum up then, hopefully without oversimplifying too much, this is the situation in retailing around the globe. Land use policies reflected in zoning laws affect most countries' productivity in retailing. The exceptions are the United States and Brazil. Once we get to poor countries, unequal taxes create a huge nonlevel playing field that allows the informal, low-productivity activities to continue and prevents the modern high-productivity retailers from expanding. And then India, the poorest of the countries we studied, outright prohibits foreign direct investment in retailing. India thus denies itself global best practice know-how in retailing. On top of this, India has the special land problem of unclear land titles. All these factors diminish competitive intensity in retailing. India has the most factors, with the most intense distortions, and the lowest productivity. The overall pattern of increasing restrictions on competitive intensity and increasing distortions in competition leading to lower levels of productivity seems clear.

Barriers Also Matter Because the Frontier Is Alive

The productivity performance of retailing at the frontier in the United States has been important recently. As I described in chapter 4 on the United States, the productivity growth rate accelerated in the United States in the second half of the 1990s. Retailing and wholesaling combined contributed an amazing 50 percent of the total acceleration. This part of the acceleration was caused primarily by the competitive dynamics within the retailing industry.

By 1995, Wal-Mart had built up such a strong productivity lead over its competitors that competitors faced the choice of either improving productivity rapidly or going out of business. They reacted strongly. Even though Wal-Mart accelerated its rate of productivity improvement, its competitors improved so fast that Wal-Mart's market share just barely improved from 1995 to 2000. The net result for the United States was a productivity acceleration.

As part of the competitive dynamics among retailers in the 1970s and '80s, the big chains of supermarkets and general merchandise stores began to bypass the inefficient wholesaling industry and perform the wholesaling function for themselves. Wholesaling was inefficient because it is almost a natural monopoly for many items in many regions of the country. The volume of business would support one but not two wholesalers, at least doing business in the small-scale, labor-intensive, paper-based way wholesaling was done at the time in the United States.

The big retailers noticed and began to perform wholesaling in an industrialized and automated way. The wholesalers finally began to see the light in the late 1980s. They consolidated, invested in assembly line op-

erational equipment, and applied simple information technology to reduce labor and improve reliability. This modernization of the wholesaling industry reached full speed in the middle 1990s and made a major
contribution to the improved performance of the U.S. economy. This
contribution was caused to a significant degree by retailers under considerable competitive pressure looking for a way to gain an advantage
on their competitors.

Thus part of the pattern of retailing is the spillover effects from good
performance in retailing to the improvement of the wholesaling, consumer goods, and food processing industries. The spillover effects can
even extend to improving agriculture. Furthermore, the experience in
the United States shows that innovations in retailing have been so strong
over the past twenty-five years that if barriers are not in the way of their
application, they can accelerate the national rate of productivity growth
all by themselves.

Housing Construction

Housing construction is a very difficult sector for countries to get right.
No country may have it right. They may not have it right in the sense
that housing construction gains virtually no benefits from globalization.
Virtually no transfer of best practice around the world occurs. No big
companies are competing intensely through innovation and cost reduction in several countries. Housing construction is predominantly a local
business, conducted by small, local companies, producing their products a few at a time in many different locations.

The complexity in housing construction arises from the process of
bringing all the components together at one location in the right sequence and at the right time to create the most expensive product by far
purchased by consumers. Most of the components going into the construction of a house are procured locally. Land, labor, and materials.
Each of these components has its own local complexity, especially land,
as I will get to in a moment. Moreover, because housing is by far the
most important product purchased by consumers, consumers pay a lot
of attention to the style and content of housing. Local styles vary considerably. Sometimes, unproductive styles can become entrenched if
they don't have to compete with other styles of much higher productivity. Thus housing is by far the most local of the significant economic sectors. A few attempts at cross-border housing construction have been
tried. None have succeeded to any appreciable degree.

Given the local nature of housing construction, we shouldn't be sur-

Exhibit 9.2: Housing Construction Productivity

Index U.S. = 100

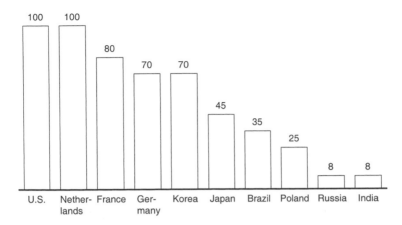

prised that labor productivity varies enormously. No best practice companies are forcing labor productivity convergence through foreign direct investment. In our studies of individual countries, the Netherlands had about the same labor productivity as the United States; France was at 80 percent of the U.S. level; Germany, 70 percent; Korea, 70 percent; Japan, 45 percent; Brazil, 35 percent; Poland, 25 percent; Russia, 8 percent; and India, 8 percent (Exhibit 9.2).

Land Again and Mortgages

As the previous chapters have described, the reasons for these differences in productivity are manyfold. However, the pattern of the way construction is performed reveals two big differences. The first is that in all countries with the exception of the United States and the Netherlands, construction companies have great difficulty getting enough land to build large-scale single-family housing developments. As people get richer, they show around the world they prefer single-family housing to multifamily housing. If many of these houses can be built at the same place at the same time, then some of the inefficiencies of housing construction described above can be overcome. The coordination problems of land, labor, and materials have to be solved only one time for several houses as opposed to being solved one at a time for single houses.

The second big difference is that, starting with Brazil and continuing through Poland, Russia, and India, the coordination problem of building even a single house is enormous. It is enormous because houses have to be built at the rate the owner can save enough money to pay for the next stage. This rate is often unknowable, even to the owner. The reason houses have to be built on a "build as you save" basis is that no mortgage financing is available. And no mortgage financing is available in Brazil, Russia, and India because of lack of confidence of local and foreign investors in the maintenance of macroeconomic stability. In particular, investors worry that inflation will not be controlled and that high or hyper inflation could wipe out the value of their loans. Poland has had a good macroeconomic track record since coming out from under the Soviet sphere. Mortgages are beginning to become available there.

The mortgage problem is one of the clearest examples in all our industry studies where previous macroeconomic instability continues to cause low productivity. Given the volatility of macroeconomic performance in poor countries, this limit on productivity growth is likely to persist for a long time. In fact, one of the few leading indicators of whether a country is going to increase productivity rapidly and rise off the low GDP per capita plain is the appearance of housing mortgages. Another important leading indicator is whether global best practice retailers such as Carrefour, Tesco, and Wal-Mart invest substantially in the country. Whether they invest is determined by whether they can get land on which to build and whether they can make any money if they do build. Whether they can get the land depends on many of the same factors that determine whether large-scale single-family housing developments can occur.

So we come back to the land issue. Getting land for single-family housing developments gets tougher and tougher as we move towards the poorer countries. The first problem that shows up is in France and Germany. There, limited land is available on the outskirts of cities and towns for housing development. Little land is available because local governments do not provide the basic infrastructure needed for additional housing. This infrastructure includes roads, water, sewage, and schools. The local governments don't provide this infrastructure because they don't have the authority to tax the developments to finance infrastructure.

Netherlands Cross-Check

Thank goodness for the Netherlands. The Netherlands allows us to cross-check our causal story about construction. There is a problem with always using the United States as the standard. It implies that the United States is perfect and everybody else isn't. Well, that's certainly not true. The difficulty is that the United States has the highest productivity in virtually every industry. The exceptions are a few manufacturing industries in Japan (and retail banking in the Netherlands). The result is that it is simply difficult to learn how the United States can achieve higher economic performance from the experience of other countries. That does not mean, however, that the United States cannot improve its economic performance. It can and is doing so, but more in a trial-and-error mode than from learning from the experience of others. For these reasons, whenever another country has the same or higher productivity in an industry, it is important to see if the causal factors are the same as those coming out of my story, which is so heavily influenced by the United States.

The Netherlands has about the same productivity in housing construction as the United States. The Netherlands handles the infrastructure development issue in a way equivalent to the United States. (It, of course, also has the macroeconomic stability causing mortgages to be available.) The Netherlands and the United States match responsibility for providing development infrastructure with the authority to tax to finance it. However, they achieve this match at different levels. In the United States, local governments have the authority to tax developments and the responsibility to provide infrastructure. In the Netherlands, the central government has the responsibility for the infrastructure and the taxing authority. The result is the same either way. Both countries get large-scale single-family housing developments at high productivity. Despite claims that Germans feel large-scale single-family housing developments are low quality, Germans like the Netherlands' prices and find the quality OK. They buy such housing near the border and commute to work in Germany.

Korea and Japan face more than just infrastructure development issues. In Korea, zoning laws up until recently have simply precluded the acquisition of land for large-scale single-family housing developments near cities. As I discussed in the Korea chapter, it remains to be seen whether the removal of these laws will be followed by denial of such developments through indirect means. In Japan, it's the tax laws themselves that give individuals strong incentives not to sell land while they're alive. Capital gains taxes are high and inheritance taxes are low. Poland and Russia (especially) are having difficulty creating a workable land market given the recent history of government-owned land and subsidized housing.

Finally, in India, the land market is chaos because of unclear land titles. Competition there is all about finding land with clear titles and not about improving housing construction productivity. Of course, India also suffers a high housing construction productivity penalty because many people are so poor that they can afford only makeshift (subsistence) housing. Such housing has virtually no productivity improvement potential. However, we can't argue that India is poor because it is poor. As I discussed in the India chapter, India will emerge from building subsistence housing only by building nonsubsistence housing at higher productivity.

One important anomaly appears as we look across all these countries. Whereas Japan is considerably richer than Korea, its housing construction productivity is only 70 percent of Korea's. The reason is Japan has not standardized basic construction materials and basic construction methods. This standardization occurred in the United States in the 1920s. It occurred in Korea because the government allocated financing to big construction companies to build cookie-cutter apartment houses all around the big cities. It hasn't happened for single-family housing in the poorer countries, but standardization is not their biggest problem now. However, for Japan it is a big problem today. Without standardization, rich Japanese cannot assess the quality of existing housing. Banks cannot either. The only housing that consumers trust and that banks will finance then is new housing. Therefore, there is virtually no secondary market in Japan. And new single-family housing is built one house at a time using nonstandard methods. Since that's all the Japanese can get, they pay the high prices for their small houses.

Thus, in housing construction, as in retailing, we can see how the buildup of constraints on the range and intensity of competition causes lower productivity, which leads to lower GDP per capita. If you cannot get land for large-scale single-family housing developments, then companies cannot build such housing in competition with one-at-a-time housing or multifamily housing. Moreover, if no secondary housing market exists, then builders face little competition since the competition only concerns new housing. Of course, as the housing construction cases in each of the country chapters show, there is more to the distortion of competition in many of these countries than I have explained here. Here, I have limited the discussion to only the big patterns that affect most countries and that explain most of the productivity differences. Housing construction is especially valuable because it shows not only the effects of increasingly distorted competition but also the effects of macroeconomic instability.

Labor and Education: Why Didn't These Dogs Bark?

Many people feel deeply that education is the key to the development of societies. They also feel it is key for economic development, which is, of course, an integral part of societal development. I believe these views are correct.

These views are correct because education is necessary for the social, political, and philosophical development of societies. As I explain in chapter 11, education is the means through which societies acquire political philosophies based on individual rights. These rights are necessary for political and social developments that overcome the privileges of "special interests" and satisfy individual or consumer desires better. The economic experiments around the world over the past hundred years show that so far, such conditions are the only ones that have led to high economic performance.

Where I disagree with many about education is over whether education is a current constraint on the ability of the current workforces around the world to be trained now on the job to work in operations with much higher productivity levels. The trainability of the current labor force is not a constraint to significant economic development in any country around the world. This finding is at the core of my contention that it's economic policy that causes the global economic landscape to look the way it does.

The public debate on education is confused. All people around the world seem broadly to have the same capabilities. Education is viewed as the way to realize this potential. There is much truth to this argument. However, it is carried too far. It is carried to the point of contending that increasing education is one of the very highest priorities for promoting rapid economic development in poor countries today. That priority is wrong. Again, it's fortunate it's wrong. It would take two or three generations to build significantly different educational systems in poor countries and to put enough people through these systems to potentially make a difference in economic performance. We do not have to wait that long. Thank goodness.

Trainability Is Not the Same as Education

The reason we do not have to wait for significantly different educational systems is that today's workers around the world can be trained on the job to achieve much higher labor productivity, even to a level close to global best practice in many cases. Twelve years ago, the biggest economic question was the performance of the U.S. economy relative to Japan and Germany. The conventional wisdom at the time was that the U.S. economy was going down the drain. The poor skills of the U.S. workforce were often cited as one of the primary reasons. U.S. managers complained regularly about the inability to hire workers who could read, write, and do arithmetic. U.S. high school students scored poorly on standardized international tests in science and mathematics. Public officials in Europe and Japan labeled the U.S. workforce lazy and incompetent.

It came as a great surprise to everybody, both in the United States and abroad, when our early work showed in industry after industry that the U.S. workforce achieved higher labor productivity than anyplace else on earth. The only exceptions were a handful of manufacturing sectors where Japan had the global lead. How could this be? Well, of course other factors such as more capital, or more technology, or bigger scale, or better organization of operations could be offsetting a labor disadvantage in the United States. In general, the United States did not apply more capital, did not have access to different technology, and did not build operations on a larger scale. The primary U.S. advantage was better organization of operations. These better organizations are usually more demanding of workers. The U.S. workforce was able to work in ways that were more productive.

The most important evidence came from the performance of Japanese automotive transplant factories in the United States. Japan was, and remains, the global leader in automotive assembly productivity. The factories of Toyota, Honda, and Nissan in the United States achieve about 95 percent of the productivity they achieve in Japan. They achieve this productivity by training U.S. workers on the job. They do the same thing with Japanese workers in Japan. They estimate the additional training required by the U.S. workforce causes them about a 5 percent productivity penalty.

Of course, these factories are virtually all in the U.S. Midwest and not in big industrial cities. Maybe the Japanese got the best of the workers in predominantly rural areas. However, these workers were the product of the U.S. educational system. Any lack in their education did not penalize their trainability to any significant extent. The Japanese probably would not have had as good an experience with workers educated in the school systems in the urban core of some large cities. However, when the transplant evidence is combined with the finding that U.S. workers across the board almost always work at the highest labor productivity in the world, we have the basis for a strong conclusion.

Whatever shortcomings the U.S. education system may have, it is not an important constraint on U.S. relative economic performance.

The trainability of workforces is not a constraint today on economic development in poor countries. Brazil, Russia, and India could all clearly double their GDPs per capita with today's workforce. The disappointing returns on investment in education in poor countries are documented by statistical evidence in chapter 4 of William Easterly's recent book *The Elusive Quest for Growth*. The evidence on which I rely comes from studying why labor productivity in most sectors in poor countries is so low. A whole variety of factors explains this, without ever having to get to the trainability of the workforce. Of course, these other factors could just be masking a constraint from labor force trainability. If countries fixed all the other factors, then they still might not make significant economic progress because of labor force trainability.

Uneducated Workers Can Achieve Best Practice and Educated Ones Often Do Not

Fortunately, there are tests of whether this is true. In every economic sector in developing countries, there is a reasonably wide range of productivity across firms. Most important evidence is from firms that achieve productivity much higher than industry average. Sometimes this productivity is even close to global best practice. These examples indicate that the local labor forces are capable of achieving much higher labor productivity than they do now. However, the other factors have to be fixed for them to do so.

Perhaps the most important evidence of this conclusion came from the United States and Brazil. In the U.S. construction industry, there are workers equivalent to many Brazilian construction workers. In Houston, Texas, illiterate agricultural workers from Mexico not speaking any English are achieving best practice labor productivity in housing construction. In Brazil itself, the two leading private retail banks are owned locally and achieve near global best practice productivity. Similarly, a Honda transplant factory there is near Japanese performance levels. Carrefour, the French hypermarket, achieves in Brazil about 90 percent of its productivity at home.

In Russia, the evidence is somewhat different. Education ministries and the World Bank would love for poor countries to have an educational system as good as Russia's. However, in industry after industry the productivity of whole sectors and individual firms is uniformly low. The productivity is so low that Russia's overall GDP per capita is significantly below that of Brazil. Brazil clearly has an educational system inferior to that of Russia. Russia shows for sure that economic policies are more important than education for economic performance.

Even in India, there are a couple of examples that help to prove the point. India's labor productivity overall is about 8 percent of the United States'. However, India got the policies roughly right for one sector, automotive assembly. In this sector, India allowed foreign direct investment by one of the smaller Japanese automotive companies, Suzuki. The resulting joint venture company, Maruti, has 60 percent of the car market in India and achieves about 55 percent of U.S. automotive assembly labor productivity. India stopped the licensing restriction on automotive companies in 1993. Since then, many of the world's best automotive companies have invested in India, including Honda, Daimler-Chrysler, Ford, General Motors, and Hyundai. Since 1993, labor productivity in automotive assembly has grown 20 percent per year. This performance is being achieved with the Indian workforce and the educational system as it now exists. Even the illiterate wheat and dairy farmers are doing the right thing economically. They are investing in tractors and combining both wheat and dairy farming in the same household. Given rural wage rates, it is not economic for them to invest in harvesting combines or to do wheat or dairy farming alone.

Finally, I should mention Korea. Korea is neither rich nor poor. Korea is one of the few countries in the middle. Since 1960, Korea has made a massive investment in education. In 1960, 80 percent of the Korean workforce had no education beyond primary school. In 1995, 80 percent of the Korean workforce had education beyond primary school. The corresponding figure for the United States was 90 percent. Thus, it doesn't look like education would be a constraint for Korean labor productivity. However, the Korean workforce achieves only about 35 percent of U.S. labor productivity. Korea achieves 50 percent of U.S. GDP per capita primarily by working 40 percent more hours. That's not the effect education advocates have in mind.

What Is the Role of Education?

This book is not about education. However, I'll add here a few speculative thoughts. After reading Diane Ravitch's book *Left Back, A Century of Failed School Reforms,* about the U.S. education system, I was left wondering if anybody knew what education was really about. I have begun to suspect that economic development causes education to develop even if governments don't force it as Korea has done. After all, that's how education got started. When we were all hunters and gatherers 10,000 years ago, we did not have time for education. We did not even have time to wonder much about anything besides finding enough food. Only when our productivity for food production increased did we have time for other things.

Jared Diamond gives us a good explanation of this transition. We wanted to do things that would make us richer and more powerful. We also wanted to know things about which we were simply curious. Who are we? What are we? Where are we? Why are we? Education arose naturally as successive generations wanted to learn what those going before them had learned and thought. We began to make the trade-off between simply working more now and learning more to work in more valuable ways later. We also wanted to learn more to satisfy our curiosity. The more productive we became, the more we had time for education. We demanded that education.

No doubt, as education increased, our productivity potential increased. If our policies pushed us to achieve that potential, then we could afford more education. As I will come back to in chapter 11, this increasingly high level of education probably is necessary, but not sufficient, for the complex political systems necessary for advanced economic performance. It's possible that poor countries today will not get out of their poverty traps without political changes. Those political changes may only be possible with broader education. The point is, however, that education is not a constraint on the ability of today's workforces to achieve substantial productivity improvement around the world. It's the other way around. Constraints on productivity improvement are the reason education is not developing faster around the world.

Capital: Many Hear the Wrong Bark

Capital is, of course, a crucial element in economic performance. Buildings, machinery, equipment, vehicles, etc. are all obviously an integral part of the production of goods and services. However, the way capital affects economic performance is not well understood.

First of all, capital is not an issue for the rich countries. Capital intensity is the amount of capital a worker has at his disposal to make his work more productive. Differences in capital intensity among the rich countries explain virtually none of the differences in labor productivity. Moreover, the technologies embedded in the machinery and equipment are available for application everywhere in the rich countries. Differences in labor productivity arise because of the different ways firms have chosen to organize their labor and capital. As I have discussed in previous chapters, those choices are heavily influenced by the nature of competition, which is determined primarily by government rules and regulations.

In the rich countries, there are large differences in the efficiency with which capital is used. These differences are caused by many of the same factors that cause the labor productivity differences. The net result is that more capital is used per worker in Germany and Japan than in the United States. However, because the capital is used less efficiently, it does not give them higher labor productivity. The grumblings in the United States about crumbling infrastructure and overall insufficient investment for growth have subsided in the 1990s. The economic performance of the U.S. economy showed that whatever the shape of its infrastructure, infrastructure was not keeping the United States from having the highest GDP per capita among the rich regions of the world. Moreover, the inconvenience from construction on streets, bridges, highways, and airports suggested that the infrastructure was being fixed before it fell down. In addition, the United States has much higher capital productivity than the other rich countries. Therefore, the United States needed less capital for high economic performance. In summary then, capital is not much of an issue for the rich countries.

Not so for the poor countries. Capital is a big issue for the poor countries. Much of the public debate about economic development in the poor countries is over how to get more capital to them. We see all over the rich countries skyscrapers, huge manufacturing plants, gigantic retail stores, laptop computers, superhighways, and endless comfortable housing. We see very little of these things in poor countries. We assume that if poor countries had all these things, then they would be as rich as the rich countries. Since it takes capital to build or buy these things, we assume the solution is for the rich countries to send lots of capital to the poor countries. I am, of course, oversimplifying to make a point. However, I'm not oversimplifying by a whole lot, especially in the way the World Bank has been thinking. Again, Easterly in *The Elusive Quest for Growth* explains why this thinking is conceptually wrong. He also provides the statistical evidence about how substantial flows of capital to poor countries have led to disappointing growth.

What Capital Does Not Do: Automatically Increase Labor Productivity

I am not going to go through the conceptual arguments nor am I going to repeat the aggregated statistical evidence. What I am going to do is describe the role capital does and does not play in improving economic performance in poor countries. This point of view comes out of the industry studies, primarily in Brazil and India. It is consistent with Easterly's analysis but told in terms of industries and firms rather than the "production functions" of economists.

In Brazil, the average labor productivity in the eight industry studies was about 25 percent of the U.S. average for these eight industries. Lack of capital accounted for only about one-third of this 75 percentage point gap. This means that Brazil could close two-thirds of its labor productivity gap with the United States without any additional capital. Brazil could do this by organizing the labor and capital it does have in a much more efficient way. I have explained how in chapter 6 on Brazil. These results mean that Brazil's current potential labor productivity is about 75 percent of the United States' without any additional capital. Brazil is simply grossly underperforming its potential. It gets even worse. Of the remaining 25 percentage points attributable to capital, all but 5 to 10 points could be closed by making investments that are economically viable today even at Brazil's low wage rate (and assuming interest rates consistent with macroeconomic stability). Thus, Brazil's true labor productivity potential is 90 to 95 percent of the United States' today.

Of course, the industry studies in Brazil excluded agriculture. So, Brazil's potential could be somewhat lower. However, agriculture accounts for only 25 percent of Brazil's employment. Moreover, the average productivity of all the industry studies of 27 percent is only slightly higher than Brazil's overall productivity of 22 percent from aggregate analysis. Thus, Brazil's labor productivity potential cannot be much below 90 percent of the United States'.

The same general result is true for India. Of course, India has about 65 percent of its employment working in agriculture, where productivity improvement potential is very low at today's rural wage rates. In addition, India has 15 percent of its employment in what we called "transition" sectors. These sectors included such activities as domestic help, tailors, and builders of mud houses. These sectors also had virtually no potential for labor productivity improvement given the nature of the activity. However, about 20 percent of India's employment was in what could be called "modern" sectors. These sectors included activities found in the rich countries. Of the modern sectors, we did industry studies in retailing, apparel manufacturing, dairy processing, wheat milling, automotive, retail banking, housing construction, electric power, steel, telecom, and software. The (weighted) average labor productivity of these industries taken together was 15 percent of the productivity of the same industries in the United States. Without any additional capital, India could increase the labor productivity in these industries to about 40 percent of that of the United States. Again, India could do this by better organizing the way capital and labor are applied, as I explained in chapter 8 on India. Most of the remaining productivity gap with the United States could be closed only with the application of capital not economically viable at today's low wage rates. Still, 40 percent without any additional capital is a lot higher than 15. India also is grossly underperforming potential in its modern sectors.

So, does this mean that firms and industries in Brazil and in the modern sectors in India could dramatically increase their performance without any significant increase in capital? Yes! Does this mean that Brazil and India can become rich countries without any additional capital? Unfortunately no.

What Capital Really Does: Increase Capacity for Growth

To grow into a rich country is another matter. Here we see the true role of capital in economic development. The easiest way to think about growth is this: Under intense, fair competition, firms will strive to maintain or increase profits by increasing productivity. One of the ways they increase productivity is to reorganize to produce the same goods and services with fewer people. Once this happens, the economy has spare labor capability. Entrepreneurs can put those spare workers to work, but they need to build the offices and manufacturing plants where they can work. They need to add to the capacity of the country to produce goods and services. That takes capital. That is the primary role of capital in changing poor countries into rich countries. In Brazil, 60 percent of the capital needed to double its GDP per capita is to increase capacity. About 15 percent is to improve labor productivity, and 25 percent, to maintain existing capital. In India, 70 percent of the capital needed to double its GDP per capita is to increase capacity.

Of course, the total capital required to increase capacity depends on the efficiency with which the capital is employed. In the modern sectors, India's capital productivity is about 30 percent of the United States'. Improving the way capital is organized, eliminating spare capacity, and improving a variety of other factors, including building plants to the right scale and producing and marketing a higher value mix of products, would increase capital productivity in these sectors to its potential at current prices of about 90 percent of the United States'. These changes would reduce the amount of capital India would need to double its GDP by a factor of three. This makes a huge difference. If poor countries were performing at their potential for both capital and labor productivity, much less capital would be required to grow and labor would become available much faster, enabling faster growth. We found that many of the same causal factors constrained both labor and capital productivity. Thus improving the rules and regulations governing competition would improve not only labor productivity but also capital productivity.

It's easier to reach capital productivity potential than labor productivity potential. Much of the capital needed to grow goes to particularly capital-intensive modern sectors such as electric power and telecommunications. The equipment that's economic to use all around the world has the same capital productivity potential because it's based on the same technology. However, the way labor is organized to operate the equipment in these and all other industries can be vastly different. If labor productivity is not at potential, then performance is constrained because labor is not as available as it would otherwise be to operate new capacity.

Thus we need both labor and capital productivity at potential. It's amazing and sad how far both are below potential in poor countries. It's sad because that's what makes them poor. Poor country growth is not confined to a slow, agonizing process of potential slowly inching up as per capita income increases, thus making more capital investment economic. If it were, then massive amounts of capital would surely be needed and it would take a long time. Poor countries have the potential to grow much faster than almost anybody thinks. The reason is that labor productivity can increase dramatically without additional capital, and much less capital is needed for new capacity. And the actual amounts of capital needed are sufficiently small that they are within the reach of poor countries. All this applies, of course, only if the poor countries get their economic policies right.

Growth

Of course what really matters is economic growth. The only way rich countries will get richer and poor countries will get rich is by economic growth. Given the shape of the global economic landscape, by far the most important growth question is for poor countries. I can imagine a world fifty years from now in which the differences in economic performance among the rich countries are about the same as they are now. I cannot imagine another fifty years going by with as many people remaining poor. Either the poor countries must get considerably richer or the rich countries will have to organize the world in an apartheid-like way. Nobody wants a global apartheid. Therefore, the most important global problem facing us today is economic growth for the poor countries.

The great news is that the poor countries have the potential to grow very fast. We calculated point estimates of potential growth rates for the next ten years in India to be 10 percent per year, and in Brazil, 8.5 percent per year. These growth rates would roughly double GDP per capita in these countries over ten years. If people in poor countries realized such growth, their economic well-being would certainly improve during their lifetime. Moreover, the economic well-being of their children would be dramatically better than theirs. That would be enough to give some meaning to the lives of many people in poor countries. The problem is growth rates in virtually all poor countries are nowhere close to potential. India is struggling to grow at half its potential. Brazil's growth is meager, and often Brazil doesn't grow much at all.

Our approach to explaining why poor countries are poor did not start with growth rates, as most conventional economic analysis does. Conventional growth analysis just did not seem to have the potential to provide the desperately needed better understanding. So we started with trying to understand the reasons for the differences in economic performance as they exist today. The single best measure of economic performance is GDP per capita. GDP per capita is simply the product of labor productivity and the fraction of people who work. Since most people work, the great differences in economic performance come from differences in labor productivity (Exhibit 9.3). Therefore we sought to understand the reasons for the current differences in labor productivity. I have discussed these results in each of the country chapters. This approach seemed worthwhile. Changing the conditions causing low labor productivity should cause labor productivity improvement. That would be a good thing.

First Figure Out Where We Are, Then How Fast We Can Move

At the start of the planning for the Brazil project, a former member of the president's Council of Economic Advisers advised me to change our approach to focus on growth. All conventional economic development analysis is done that way. The debate about economic development is conducted only in those terms. Work not conducted in those terms

Exhibit 9.3: Productivity and GDP per Capita

Index U.S. = 100 in 1996

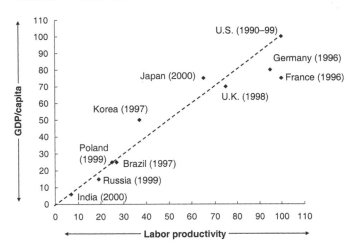

would have no connection and no influence. I did not take this advice. Analyzing the fundamental causes of differential growth rates seemed to me to be too complex to do in one step. Intuitively, understanding the differences between two moving objects is simply much more difficult than for two objects standing still. So our approach was the same as for the rich countries. At least, this approach would tell us something new and different about the changes needed in poor countries to increase labor productivity. My hope was that then it would be possible to make some estimates about how fast labor productivity could potentially increase and derive some potential growth estimates. That approach worked.

To understand growth potential, you have to understand two things. You have to understand how fast labor productivity can grow and whether adequate capital is available for additional capacity. Labor productivity always tells you the amount of goods and services produced by the people who are working. If we just increased labor productivity and added no capacity, then the amount of goods and services produced would stay the same and lots of people would be unemployed. We have to build new factories and office buildings to provide places for these people to work. That requires additional capital. Since capital also can be applied with different efficiencies, we have to understand capital productivity and how fast it can increase. The more efficiently we use capital, the less capital we need to create additional capacity and new jobs for growth.

Korea Tells Us How Fast We Can Move

As I have discussed earlier, we estimated how fast labor productivity could increase in poor countries by looking at how fast it had increased elsewhere. Korea turned out to be a valuable benchmark. In the past fifty years in many industries, Korea has improved labor productivity dramatically. Korea is a great example for us because fifty years ago Korea was a poor country. As I explained in chapter 5 on Korea, these labor productivity improvements were accompanied by massive applications of capital. In the capital-intensive industries, Korea's capital productivity was very low. There are no recent examples in any country of dramatic increases in labor productivity and capital applied at high capital productivity at the same time. That is not a serious shortcoming. Korea's capital could have been applied at best practice capital productivity without affecting its labor productivity performance. Korea has an example of just that. General Park built POSCO Steel at global best practice in both labor productivity and capital productivity.

Get the Policies Right and the Capital Is Easy

A more difficult issue for us was whether adequate capital would be available. The conventional wisdom in Brazil and India was that they would have to invest at Korea's rate of about 33 percent of GDP to achieve an economic growth rate like Korea's. Brazil could achieve its potential growth rate with an investment rate of 26 percent, and India, with a rate of 30 percent. Still, these rates are 7 points higher than the current investment rate for Brazil, and 6 points higher for India. The majority of these investment gaps could be closed with improved fiscal policy in these countries. Both countries run substantial government deficits. These deficits are a plague on their economies. They threaten macroeconomic stability in both countries. Neither country will achieve its growth potential as long as this cloud hangs over them. Interest rates will remain too high and foreign direct investment will be scarce. Both countries have channeled a substantial part of domestic savings to finance these deficits. In effect, the savings have been used for current consumption rather than business investment. Both countries could get close to the investment rates needed to achieve their growth potentials by eliminating these government deficits.

Foreign direct investment is the other source of capital to close investment gaps. Poland attracted about half of all its business investment in the 1990s from abroad. However, foreign direct investment will come on a sustained basis only if countries have a track record of stable macroeconomic conditions and only if the more productive businesses created with foreign investment can make money. There is an aversion in many poor countries to foreign investors making money from business operations in their countries. If these countries want to grow at their economic potential, they have to get over this. The facts are that most of the value created in these foreign-owned operations goes to local workers and local consumers. Labor is roughly two-thirds of the cost of these operations. Moreover, as the best practices brought by foreign investment are copied, and even improved upon, by locally owned operations, resulting competition causes most of the value created by these businesses to benefit the local consumers through lower prices.

Foreign investors are hungry to invest in poor countries. They are hungry because the financial returns are potentially so much higher than they can achieve on average in their home markets. The evidence of this is that every time a poor country looks like it's achieving macroeconomic stability and conducting substantial microeconomic reform, foreign investment leaps in. Poland is a great example, but China, Brazil, Argentina, Chile, Korea, Russia, and even India are good examples. Japan was a good example in the 1960s and '70s. Many times these investors have been burned. They seem to be ever hopeful. Their memories are short. They will keep trying. However, their investments will not be sustained without substantially improved macro- and microeconomic policies in most poor countries.

One more issue about our growth potential estimates remains. If all reforms needed to achieve macroeconomic stability and intense, fair microeconomic competition are made, will the very high growth really happen? After all, thousands of businesspeople have to act to make it happen.

First of all, businesspeople can act this fast on a national scale. Japan and Korea are examples showing this within the past fifty years. The governments in these countries influenced the way businesspeople acted. That influence has led to economic difficulties in both countries recently, as I discuss in the chapters on Japan and Korea. Would businesspeople act as fast without the heavy hand of government? I think so, because they acted even faster at Toyota, Honda, and Sony, which did it on their own.

Will Rapid Development Really Happen?

Entrepreneurial spirits abound in Brazil, Russia, and India. It looks like in all these countries that people want the same things in the economic sphere of life. That means some people will work very hard to get rich themselves. The fabulous thing about a market economy with intense, fair competition is that most of the benefits of the efforts of these people go to consumers and not to themselves. Sure, the most successful entrepreneurs become fabulously rich. However, their personal wealth is a tiny fraction of the total value created by the enterprises they build. Moreover, we have the tragic evidence that the most aggressive and entrepreneurial members of these poor countries are doing everything they can to move to the rich countries. They perceive they can achieve more of their potential there. They want the conditions they see in the rich countries. It seems reasonable that if the poor countries provide these conditions, these entrepreneurs will stay home.

Of course, it's possible that the poor countries really don't want rapid economic growth. Or said another way, maybe they perceive that the trade-off between rapid economic growth and other things important to them is unfavorable. They also might be wrong about the nature of the trade-off. In the next chapter, I will leave this world of "hard," "fact-based" economic analysis and move into the fuzzy world of political economy. Why have countries chosen to govern their economies as they have, and why are reforms needed to achieve economic growth potential so hard to make?

Why Bad Economic Policy around the World?

Does GDP per Capita Matter?

Fifty years ago, we thought we would have solved the problems addressed in this book by this time. The Western democracies were having remarkable geopolitical and economic successes. They had just won a war against the totalitarianisms of Fascism and Japanese imperialism. The totalitarianism of Communism was slowly becoming visible. However, the Western democracies defeated that one too.

The economic successes were also phenomenal. The bad policies leading to the economic depression of the 1930s were analyzed, understood, and remedied. The steady economic progress caused the economies of the Western democracies to rise far above other economies around the world. Japan adopted democracy and a market economy and also developed rapidly.

The empirical evidence about what worked and what didn't seemed clear-cut. Everybody would just do what the Western democracies had done. Everything would work out fine. Or so we thought.

That the world still has so many poor people in so many countries is especially frustrating. It is frustrating because we can see how the world could be otherwise. The innovations of the past fifty years in the Western democracies and Japan are transferable today to virtually every corner of the earth. These innovations improve productivity and cause today's high material standard of living in the rich countries. They can be applied in the poor countries. Companies have done this many times. Most times innovations are applied by outside companies. The previous chapters have given several examples. They include Carrefour in Brazil and Poland, Suzuki in India, and IBM in Japan. Sometimes locally owned companies apply the innovations. Examples are POSCO Steel in Korea and selected private retail banks in Brazil and India. Perhaps the most encouraging finding reported in this book is that the workforces around the world can now apply most of these innovations. Of course, substantial capital is needed to expand capacity. However, there is plenty of capital in the world. It has proved that it will flow anywhere with the prospect of making a good profit.

Why hasn't this adoption of innovations occurred on a vast scale? It would take forever for the wheel to be reinvented everywhere. Maybe that's what we're in for. I continue to be struck by India's not using the wheelbarrow in housing construction. Maybe it just won't be reinvented or adopted in some places. Is that OK? Before getting into some of the political reasons behind bad economic policies, I will say little bit about why GDP per capita matters.

Consumers Want More Than the Basics

Mancur Olson, in *Power and Prosperity,* points out that much of the gain from a market economy is realized even if competition is grossly distorted. The reason for this, of course, is the economic concept of the consumer surplus. This concept is that the value to consumers of most of the goods they purchase is above the price they actually pay. The first quart of water we consume each day is very valuable to us because it keeps us alive. The cost to produce that quart is well below its value. So water producers can make more profits by producing more water. This process ends up where the cost of producing water equals the value to us of using that water, for instance, to water our lawns and wash our cars. Governments could fix water prices so high that we only bought the quart of water necessary to keep us alive. We still would get much of the value from water consumption. So maybe it doesn't matter so much that governments distort competition and that GDP per capita is so low for most people.

This thinking is held in several quarters. It considers much of the material well-being of the rich countries to be unnecessary. Often this thinking is combined with environmental concerns that the production levels for high GDP per capita will ruin the global environment. The UN has produced an index of country performance that combines GDP per capita and the quality of life measures of life expectancy and education. This index gives countries diminishing credit for higher GDPs per capita. The UN adjusts GDP per capita because "achieving a respectable level of human development does not require unlimited income." The UN adjustment is technical, without any basis in what people want. (Instead of comparing countries using the ratios of their GDPs per capita, the UN compares the ratio of the logarithms of their GDPs per capita.) So whereas Mexico's GDP per capita is 24 percent of the United States', the UN economic index shows Mexico's economic performance to be 77 percent of the United States'.

It's hard to believe that Mexicans are risking their lives to cross the U.S. border illegally to get only another 23 percentage points of economic well-being. Another 76 percentage points is more plausible. A few interviews with the illegal immigrants might raise some questions about the UN index. The index also indicates that the Soviet Union was very successful because it had higher GDP per capita and higher educational levels than Mexico. A centrally planned economy can perform as well or even better than a severely distorted market economy. The Soviet Union collapsed primarily because its well-educated people saw their counterparts in the rich countries living with more material goods. The Soviet leadership had promised such prosperity and not delivered.

Economic Growth: The Cause of Global Warming or the Solution?

The environmental objection to higher GDP per capita requires a little more attention. The concern is that higher GDP per capita is leading to the production of more "greenhouse gases" in the earth's atmosphere. These gases trap more of the sun's rays and result in a warming of the earth. The main economic impact comes from additional melting of the polar icecaps and the resulting flooding of coastal areas. This effect would cost the world a few percentage points of GDP to fix a hundred or so years from now in the most severe cases.

Advocates for limiting the production of greenhouse gases have always faced a difficult political task. The difficulty is that fixing the problem a century from now costs relatively little in world GDP terms. However, even at today's low economic growth rates, the world will be a few times richer in a hundred years than it is today. Thus, even after paying the costs to remedy the effects of global warming a hundred years from now, the people living then will still be much richer than the people living today. In this situation, it is understandably hard to persuade today's people to take a cut in economic pay to mitigate economic effects that will show up only one hundred years from now, when the world's people will be considerably richer.

The concerns about global warming have gotten considerably murkier just recently. It turns out that the estimates of the production of greenhouse gases over the next hundred years have been based on assuming that the poor countries of the world grow much faster than they have ever grown in the past. Even the low end of the temperature increase projections has been based on such high economic growth rates. It's as if the climate change analysts have assumed that all the barriers to high economic growth rates identified in this book will be overcome.

I hope they are right. I would much rather have my children, grandchildren, and great-grandchildren have to deal with the problem of global warming than with the problem of a huge economic difference between rich and poor countries. The consequences of global economic disparities are much more troubling than the consequences of global warming. However, given all the difficulties for poor countries to achieve high economic growth, I'm afraid it's much more likely that the next generations will be dealing with the global economic disparity problem than with a global warming problem. Let's hope I'm wrong. If so, then the world a hundred years from now will be rich enough to take care of any global warming problem.

Why Be Rich?

After making the point that even distorted markets yield much of the potential economic value to consumers, Olson turns to the rich countries. He says that "to achieve rapid economic growth or high levels of income, however, a society needs to obtain gains from the mutually advantageous trades, such as those that involve borrowing and lending and goods purchased for future delivery, that are not self-enforcing" (by which Olson means trades that are not consummated at the same time and place and thereby fully controllable by each party). Olson goes on to say that "incomes are low in most of the countries of the world, in short, because the people in those countries do not have secure individual rights," which Olson says are necessary for trades that are not self-enforcing. I will address later the degree to which Olson is right about causality. The point I want to make here is that Olson says nothing about the importance of achieving rapid economic growth or high levels of income. After arguing that much of the potential economic value to consumers is achieved at relatively low levels of GDP per capita, the question hangs about the importance of further economic growth and high levels of income. If these don't matter, then why bother?

First of all, a large number of the world's people don't even get (a clean) quart of water a day. They may get the quart, but it contains all sorts of things detrimental to their health. Perhaps 500 million people in

India live this way. Unquestionably, rapid economic growth would be important for them. The question becomes more serious after economies provide a secure subsistence living at a minimum. The simple empirical fact is that people clearly want more than a subsistence living. Their desire for more is reflected in everyday behavior around the world all the time. Perhaps the most dramatic evidence is the huge immigration pressure from poorer countries to richer countries. Whether this desire is good or bad is another question. It just is. Since this is what people want, the burden of proof rests with those wanting to deny them their desires. The case for denial has not been made in a convincing way.

We can go deeper and refer back to Marvin Harris's anthropological theory, with which I started the Prologue of this book. Harris's theory is that more productive societies inevitably replace less productive societies. Maybe that also is too bad. However, that's the way the world has worked. There could be an interesting debate about whether the world has to work this way. I believe that as long as there is some competition among societies, the world does have to work this way. Today, this competition is often ideological or simply commercial. Even ideological competition is heavily about which structure of society can provide more of what people want. The ideological competition between the United States and the Soviet Union was settled by which society could provide more of the goods and services the people of both societies wanted. It was decided by which society was economically the most productive.

As Jared Diamond points out, China in AD 1500 illustrates what happens when there is no competition for a regime and that regime decrees that economic innovation stop in crucial areas like shipbuilding. The society stops improving productivity. Since China later came into competition with Western societies, it was headed for trouble. However, if the whole world had been under the emperor of China, then Harris's theory might not have held up. Since it seems highly unlikely that the whole world would come under a regime like the one in China in AD 1500, Harris's theory seems safe.

Historically, this process of more productive societies replacing less productive ones has often proceeded through wars and even annihilation of whole peoples. Today, the sanctity of the nation-state provides some protection for less productive societies. However, the recent invasion of less productive Iraq by the more productive United States is an example of historically common behavior. I believe this war will finally be judged by whether the overthrow of a dictator in Iraq results in a more productive Iraq, which will give the Iraqi people more of what they want. That's what the aims of the United States seem to be boiling down to.

However, to get more of the goods and services people want, most of them would not volunteer to be invaded by the United States, or anybody else for that matter. When the conditions are right, as in Japan and Korea recently, the people get what they want by themselves. This process will probably progress as Harris would predict on an anthropological timescale. What is different now is that for the first time, the world has the potential for rapidly giving people more of what they want. This book is about what they would need to do to get it.

But are the very high income levels of the rich countries really necessary? Their desires for more goods and services seem never-ending. Is this OK? Well, with that high per capita income has come the technological capability and surplus of resources to provide militarily for national security. The Soviet Union, a command economy, was also able to provide militarily for its national security, at a much lower per capita GDP than the United States. However, it was not able to provide both "guns" and the "butter" its people wanted. The United States could. Thus the Soviet Union failed in its competition with the United States.

Democracies Have to Produce Economic Results

I believe the advanced democracies are successful in the world today because they are able to provide both guns and butter. If their economies began to weaken to the point of not being able to provide both, then the guns part would suffer first. The large European countries have already significantly reduced their military expenditures. Part of this reduction is because they perceive reduced threats to their societies now that the Soviet Union has fallen. They also know they can depend on the United States to defend the democratic way of life. But part of the reduction is because they are having increasing difficulty providing the butter their people have come to expect. The advanced democracies need to produce the butter in order for their citizens to be willing to pay for the guns.

All the rich countries in the world are democracies and all want to remain that way. Threats to the democratic way of life exist around the world. The U.S. invasions of Afghanistan and Iraq have been justified on these grounds. The GDP per capita of the rich countries has given them the means to protect themselves against these threats. As long as these threats exist, the rich countries want higher GDPs per capita than the sources of these threats. Higher GDPs per capita are important to the democracies for this reason. Later, I will get to the point that real democracies are the best way for the poor countries to get richer. The bet the rich countries are making is that if the poor countries become more democratic, richer, and thus militarily more capable, the threats to the rich countries' democratic way of life will diminish. That bet seems necessary to take.

The alternative is an apartheid world. Interactions between rich and poor countries would be tightly controlled by the rich. Rich countries would be constantly intervening militarily within the poor countries to remove threats to the rich. Immigration from poor to rich countries would be controlled by physical barriers and shoot-on-sight policies like the Soviet Union used. No one wants that kind of world.

Happier reasons for high income exist. High income allows greater realization of human potential. As countries have gotten richer, they have become willing to trade some current consumption for other things in life. Rich countries invest substantial resources in response to our inquisitive and creative natures. Research and the arts flourish with increasing wealth. We are able to identify the cause of AIDS and develop drugs to slow its progression. We devote resources to the preservation of the Grand Canyon so that all future generations can enjoy it. We clean up our air and water to improve quality of life. We send the majority of our young people to tertiary educational institutions to increase the realization of their human potential. National Public Radio brings the world to the most remote corners of our country. We can argue about how to make the trade-off between consumption and investment in human potential. Poor countries don't have that luxury. What is really holding them back?

Social Objectives

Bad economic policies often result from attempts to achieve social objectives. Most people consider the social objectives to be "good." The problem is that to achieve these objectives, governments often distort markets severely. These distortions often limit productivity growth, slow overall economic growth, and cause unemployment. Many times, the adverse, unintended consequences of such distortions undermine the achievement of the social objectives. The good news is that in some cases alternative means are available for achieving the social objectives without distorting the market nearly as much. In other cases, there is a legitimate trade-off between social and economic objectives. In these cases, there is no "right answer."

Preserving Existing Jobs

The most pervasive problem is the social objective of maintaining employment. Employment is a special social concern. High levels of unemployment have historically been associated with political instability. Moreover, high levels of employment mean that most members of society are working to contribute their share in creating a better life. Such high levels help prevent strife between those who work and those who don't. The problem arises because the objective of high employment levels is often translated into the objective of maintaining existing jobs. The protection of the European automobile industry against the Japanese for so long is a good example of an attempt to preserve existing jobs.

Literally, if all existing jobs were simply preserved, there would be little productivity growth, and therefore little economic growth. Productivity increases primarily through the application of new ways of producing goods and services and through the introduction of new goods and services requiring the creation of new production processes. In this evolutionary process, old jobs are constantly destroyed and new jobs are constantly created. Some firms manage this process better than others and consequently increase in size. Other firms shrink or disappear. Two hundred and fifty years ago virtually everyone worked in agriculture. In the rich countries, we have destroyed virtually all those agricultural jobs. Now, only 3 percent of the workforce in the United States works in agriculture. The remaining 97 percent of us are not sitting around unemployed eating what the 3 percent produce. Most of us have jobs producing manufactured goods and services, which have been the source of virtually all U.S. economic growth in the past 250 years. This process continues today. Without it, there would be no economic growth.

Attempts to preserve existing jobs take many forms. Sometimes they are direct limits on competition, which would increase pressure for lower prices, lower production costs, and higher productivity. The steel tariffs imposed by the United States in early 2002 are a great example of a costly policy to preserve existing steelworking jobs. Sometimes the policy is a direct subsidy for unproductive enterprises. The subsidized loans for the mom-and-pop retailers in Japan is an example. Sometimes, the policy is a requirement for government approval of any layoffs. India requires government approval of any layoffs in any company with more than 100 employees. Such approval is often withheld.

People usually don't like to lose their job and to have to find another one. It's anxiety producing. We also want a never-ending increase in our material well-being. We can't have it both ways. Especially in the United States, the overall interest of the consumer has won out. We may not like it, but we change jobs. We do seem to like the results of the productivity increases that occur. Moreover, those unlucky ones having to change jobs can be compensated. The government can subsidize retraining and pay some level of unemployment insurance. The problem is that unemployment insurance diminishes the incentive to find another job. There is no right answer here. However, the level and duration of unemployment benefits in Europe seems to have contributed to a worrisomely high level of unemployment, with much of it more than six months in duration.

In the United States the lack of restraint on the nature of competition has resulted in rapid innovation in new goods and services and new job creation. As a result, employment levels have remained high. Labor markets are less flexible in virtually every other economy. By the time we get to India, the conventional wisdom among business leaders is that the preservation of existing jobs is a major constraint on economic growth.

These attempts to preserve jobs often fail. They fail in two ways. The first is that business managers find ways around the labor laws and regulations. Voluntary retirement systems ("early retirement") are used from the United States to India to reduce workforce size. Even the large state-owned steel company in India, SAIL, has used this method successfully. The use of voluntary retirement systems seems like a good way around the labor restrictions. Workers are compensated somewhat for their firing, which had nothing to do with their performance.

The second way attempts to preserve jobs fail is through business failures. If businesses are unable to reduce their labor force and increase productivity as fast as their international competitors, then these businesses eventually face the prospect of running out of cash. At that point, some businesses fail and jobs simply disappear. The failed attempt to protect the big U.S. steel companies over the past two decades is a good example. In other cases, the prospect of business failure causes labor to relent and accept reductions. The massive reduction in the workforce of the German automotive industry in the early 1990s, in which Daimler-Benz laid off almost 100,000 workers, is a good example. In such cases, the eventual employment level in the industry is lower than it would have been if the industry had kept pace with its competitors. The market share lost during the period of productivity lag is usually gone for good.

Since attempts to protect existing jobs usually fail eventually, they are not as important as constraints in the product and land markets that prevent the applications of new business innovations with higher productivity. However, there is no doubt that attempts to preserve existing jobs slow down productivity improvement and economic growth.

Adverse Unintended Consequences

Unfortunately, governments often go further than simply attempting to preserve existing jobs. Sometimes, they try to control the type of job that exists. France and Germany are examples. France's government sets a minimum wage for the entire economy that is about twice the level of the minimum wage in the United States. Many of Germany's unions negotiate a similar minimum wage. The objective of these efforts is to achieve a more equal income distribution by raising the income of workers at the bottom.

This policy, however, has backfired. The higher wage costs have forced up the prices of the products that minimum wage workers produce so high that consumers in France and Germany will not pay them. The result is that goods are not produced and services not delivered. That means the jobs don't exist either. Especially hard hit are low-skill jobs in service industries. Half the workers in the U.S. retailing industry have wages below the minimum wage in France. There are no bag packers in French hypermarkets. Toys "R" Us employs 30 percent fewer workers in its stores in France than in the United States.

Much of this unintended unemployment consequence could be avoided. The United States has used for some time the Earned Income Tax Credit to increase the after-tax income of low-wage workers. After all, it is after-tax income that should really matter. Employers face the market wage or a very low minimum wage. Thus, they adjust their workforces according to the productivity of workers and consumer demand. The government then adjusts the after-tax income of low-wage earners to be whatever can be agreed upon in the political process. Thus, the market is almost undistorted and society's income objectives for low-wage earners are met. Employment objectives are also met better because the Earned Income Tax Credit is tied to work and thus provides an incentive to work. (Because this tax credit phases out with increasing income, the incentive to earn higher compensation is diminished. However, enhancing the income of low-wage earners and getting them into the workforce is more important.) The Labor government in the United

Kingdom adopted this tax credit when it signed the EU Social Charter, rather than adopt the high minimum wage of the Continent.

The problem of adverse unintended economic consequences of social policies gets worse in poor countries. Maybe it's because there are so many social problems to fix. In Russia, the Soviet planners placed many small and medium-sized industries in one-company towns in remote areas. The steel industry is a good example. Small steel mills employing two to three thousand people account for one-third of all employment in the Russian steel industry. Thirteen of these small steel plants are in towns where the steel plant employment accounts for 20 percent or more of total town employment. If these plants shut down, these workers would have very little chance for reemployment in their towns. On the other hand, twenty of these small steel plants are in towns where steel employment accounts for less than 10 percent of town employment. If these plants shut down, many of the workers could find other jobs locally.

None of the small steel plants are economically viable. They all should be shut down. However, they are all kept open. They are kept open with the objective of preserving the towns in which they operate. They don't run out of cash because they don't pay their electricity and gas bills and they don't pay their taxes. The local authorities prevent the national energy companies from shutting off their energy. The local authorities also simply do not collect taxes from them. Of course, the special interests of the local managers (and workers) are at stake here. Some financial interests of the local authorities are probably also at stake. The result is that the much more productive big steel plants cannot expand as fast as they could if these small plants were not kept alive. A far better solution would be to level the playing field for energy costs and taxes, let the small steel plants die, and give unemployment and relocation benefits to displaced workers in towns not viable without the steel plants.

An even more dramatic example of a social policy backfiring is the Small-scale Reservation policy in India. Eight hundred thirty-six manufactured products can only be made in small factories. One of these products is apparel. As I described in chapter 8 on India, many apparel importing countries now guarantee market shares for exporting countries. China's market share in the importing countries not guaranteeing market shares to exporters is much higher than in the countries guaranteeing market shares to exporters. That means where there is free competition, China does much better than where there is no competition.

For India, the situation is reversed. India does much worse where there is free competition than where there is no competition. The market share guarantees to exporters are going away in 2005. That means that free competition will be everywhere. At that time, China's export share will certainly increase, and India's, decline. All this because as a matter of social policy, India has limited apparel production to factories not big enough to be competitive in a global market with free competition.

High Taxes and Informal Workers Don't Mix

The last example I will give of the interaction between social and economic policies is the "informal sector." The informal sector includes all employment that is not registered with the government. Fifty percent of all workers in Brazil are informal. The figure in India is probably about 75 percent. These workers are street vendors, mud and cardboard house builders, tailors, housecleaners, etc., and most agricultural workers. Often they live near subsistence. They pay no taxes. Tax laws that might apply to them often favor them over their more productive, formal competitors. These people are so poor that the public agrees with favoring them in this way. Thus in retailing, housing construction, and even many manufacturing industries, the competitive playing field is distorted because of concern for the poor.

Of course, even if this social concern did not exist, it would be infeasible to collect taxes from most of these people and their enterprises. Although the tax amount for each individual would be tiny, there are so many of these informal workers that the tax revenues forgone are significant. Of course, the missing revenues have to be made up from those who can be taxed and for whom there is not the same social concern. These enterprises are the relatively few formal companies. These companies are usually industrialized and much more productive. Taxes on the sales, value added, employment, and profits of these companies make up for the missing revenue from the informal sector.

As I discussed in chapter 6 on Brazil, the taxing of these enterprises forces their prices to be so high that they have a hard time competing with informal businesses. At best they are able to take market share away from the less productive firms very slowly. Sometimes, their prices would have to be so high that no one would buy from them. Then they can't make any money and choose not even to try. The size of the governments in Brazil, Russia, India, and most poor countries is so big today that the taxes collected from these productive enterprises have to be large. The solution to this conflict between social and economic objectives is not to tax the poor workers and their enterprises. The solution is to reduce the size of government. This will reduce the tax burden on productive enterprises and make competition more equal. The productive enterprises will grow faster and economic growth will be higher.

In summary, we see that policies to achieve social objectives often distort markets in ways that undermine the social objective itself or compromise the really important economic objective of growth. It's hard to imagine circumstances where the social objective is so important that economic growth should be compromised. After all, the bigger the economic pie, the more resources there are to be devoted to solving social problems. Where the motivation for social improvement is genuine, an understanding of the unintended adverse economic consequences of distorting markets should result in better policy. Where the motivation is really protection of special interests, then the only solution is preventing the special interests from prevailing. I will come back to how we can achieve better understanding of unintended adverse consequences and how we can deal with the special interests in the next chapter.

Informality and Big Government

As I described in chapter 6, Brazil has substantial informality. I initially thought of informality as a data collection problem. I wasn't surprised that roughly half of the employment in Brazil was unconnected with the government. Brazil is a poor country. Many people would be working at near subsistence levels. People have been working in such ways for a few thousand years. They weren't connected with the government over most of this time. We wouldn't expect them to be so now.

Informality Distorts Competition When Taxes Are High

Brazil shows that the effects of informality on economic development in today's world are profound. The effects go far beyond informal workers simply being unproductive. In Brazil the competition between informal workers and the far more productive formal workers is impeding economic growth. The reason is that informal workers don't pay their taxes and sometimes make or sell cheap, illegal goods. The firms of formal workers pay their taxes and most times sell legal goods.

In retailing in Brazil, supermarkets can just barely undersell counter stores despite the supermarkets' much higher productivity and lower cost of (legitimate) goods to be sold. Informality is also inhibiting the emergence of specialized firms (special trades) in the Brazilian housing construction industry. If firms trained workers in specialized construction skills, they would have to pay the workers commensurate with their productivity. Otherwise, the firms would lose these workers to other firms trying to do the same thing. The trained workers would then demand that the firms pay employment taxes on them so that they would be eligible for the benefits of government programs. If firms refused, the workers would go to formal general-purpose construction companies. So special trades firms have to be formal and pay their taxes. They compete for jobs with informal firms using cheap, unskilled labor. The productivity advantage of the special trades companies is not enough to overcome their extra costs. So, they have not developed.

Even though the effect of informality shows up in Brazil, it is difficult to fully appreciate it. Sometimes it takes the extreme example of a situation for its significance to be recognized. The extreme example is Russia. There, productive, formal firms often could not compete with informality. The costs of formal firms were higher. They could not make any money at all. So they did not even try. And the firms deciding not to try were the most productive in the world. Carrefour felt it could overcome all the bureaucratic and corruption problems of Russia. However, Carrefour could not overcome the problem of not making money.

Informality took a different form in Russia than in Brazil. In Russia, the informal firms were not small retailers in cardboard shacks in slums. The Soviet government planned the entire economy. It did not plan for slums; so there weren't any. Virtually all business enterprises were established in permanent places and thus known to the government. In Russia, the government itself has created informality. It has done so by not requiring some firms to pay their taxes and by preventing electricity and gas companies from shutting down firms that do not pay their energy bills. Some of these "informal" firms in Russia are steel companies employing two to three thousand people. The government knows about them all right. It just doesn't make them obey the law. This is happening many places in the Russian economy. We found it in steel, cement, dairy, confectionery, food retailing, and general merchandise retailing. In Russia, we came to appreciate fully that competition can be distorted enough to keep more productive firms from replacing less productive firms.

In India, informality is a serious problem for economic growth. Sixty-five percent of India's employment is in agriculture, which is mostly informal. Of the 35 percent remaining, about 20 percent is in firms organized similarly to firms in advanced economies. The remaining 15 percent of workers are in the "transition" sector, which is virtually all informal. These are the tailors, the builders of mud and cardboard houses, the cubbyhole retailers, the porters, etc. The transition sector shows up as societies evolve out of agriculture to the production of modern goods and services. It has productivity about five times the productivity of agriculture in India, but very little potential to improve that productivity. The only sector with substantial potential to improve its productivity is the modern sector. Virtually all India's economic growth from this point will be caused by productivity growth in the modern sector.

In many cases, the best of the modern sector firms cannot grow at their potential because of competition with informality. Sometimes the competition is with informal firms like those in Brazil. Supermarkets competing with cardboard shack retailers is an example. Other times the competition is with small steel mills that don't pay their taxes and energy bills as in Russia.

The effect of nonpayment of taxes and energy bills in India is not as prominent as in Brazil and Russia. The reason is that India has many more direct and intentional distortions of competition that favor unproductive firms. These distortions come from such matters as government ownership of large parts of the banking, steel, telecom, electric power, and dairy industries. The distortions also include the Small-scale Reservation discussed earlier in this chapter. However, if all these distortions were removed, India would still have this problem we found originally in Brazil. Productive firms would have a very difficult time competing with unproductive firms not paying their taxes.

What's New Today—Big Government

As I begin to think about the important messages for this book, this difficulty of competing with informal activities stood out. However, I realized that this problem has been around forever. Despite that, the Western democracies and Japan have grown and reached very high per capita income levels. How could they do this? Is something different today? Yes, and the difference is big government.

Today the governments of poor countries spend large fractions of GDP. For Brazil, it's 39 percent, for Russia, 37 percent, and for India, 32 percent. The U.S. governments today spend about 37 percent of the GDP. However, that's not the right comparison. In 1913, the United States and France had GDPs per capita near those of Brazil and Russia of today, but well above that of India today. Both countries' governments spent less than 10 percent of the GDP. For the United States, the

Exhibit 10.1: Government Spending

Government spending
Percent of GDP

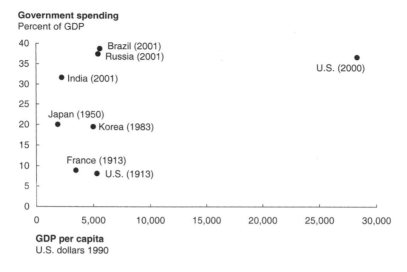

GDP per capita
U.S. dollars 1990

percentage was 8, and for France, 9. In 1950, Japan's GDP per capita was slightly below the current figure in India. Then, Japan's government spent about 20 percent of the GDP. In 1983, when Korea's GDP per capita was about the same as Brazil's today, Korea's government expenditures were also 20 percent of GDP (Exhibit 10.1). These government expenditures have to be financed. They are financed primarily through taxes. When government expenditure levels are high, the taxes have to be high. In poor countries the only entities that can be taxed are the formal corporations and some individuals.

It gets even worse. In Brazil, taxes paid (or collected by) formal corporations account for 70 percent of all revenues when sales, value-added, employment, and profit taxes are all taken into account and capital items are excluded. (In India the percentage is 67 excluding capital items.) Of the 38 percent of GDP collected as government revenue in Brazil, 12.4 percentage points come from sales and value-added taxes, 7.2 percentage points from employer contributions to the government-run pension system, 4.0 percentage points from corporate profit taxes, and 1.3 percentage points from other corporate taxes (Exhibit 10.2). Only 2.0 percentage points come from individual income taxes. Capital items account for 2.9 percentage points of GDP in revenue. (Of the 20.7 percent of GDP collected as revenue in India, excluding capital items, 8.9 percentage points come from sales and excise taxes, 2.5 percentage points from import duties, 1.9 percentage points from corporate profit

Exhibit 10.2: Government Revenues

Percent of GDP

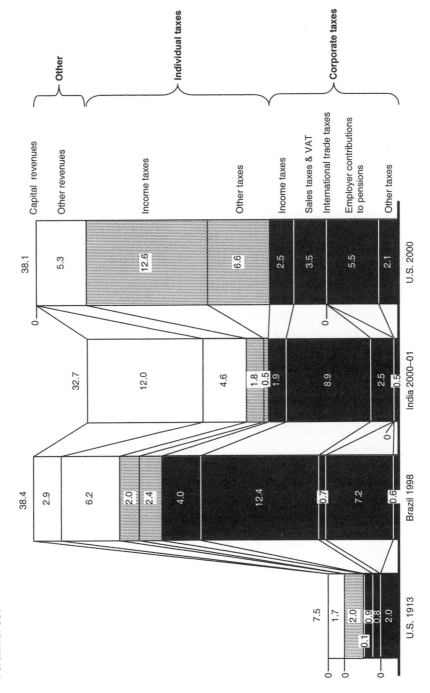

taxes, and 0.5 percentage points from other corporate taxes. Individual income taxes provide only 1.8 percentage points. Capital items account for 12.0 percentage points of GDP in revenue.)

Today, taxes paid by or through U.S. corporations are only about 36 percent of all government revenue. The corporate tax burden in Brazil is thus almost twice as high as in the United States as a percent of GDP (25 percent versus 14). Again, today is not the right comparison. We should be comparing with the United States in 1913. Then, corporations paid roughly the same percentage of all taxes in the United States as they pay today. That means that the corporate tax burden in Brazil today is seven times higher than the corporate tax burden in the United States in 1913. This time the comparisons are rough approximations of absolute amounts per capita since the GDPs per capita are about the same. That's a huge absolute difference. Another way of putting this difference is that Brazilian corporations are paying in taxes 21 more percentage points of GDP than U.S. corporations did in 1913.

We don't know what was done with this 21 percentage points of GDP in the United States in 1913. But we do know that it was in private hands, some combination of private corporations and private individuals. The corporations would have invested most of their part. Private individuals would have saved some of their part. Maybe about 10 percentage points ended up in business investment. That would make a huge difference in growth. As I discussed in the last chapter, there is no way of getting around economic growth's requiring additional capital for investment in additional business capacity.

Angus Maddison, an economic historian, has estimated that the U.S. GDP grew at 4 percent a year between 1900 and 1913. That means that GDP per capita was growing at 2.3 percent. At this time the United States was overtaking the United Kingdom as the economic frontier in the world. The United States was having to develop most of the innovations leading to productivity improvements. Brazil's annual GDP per capita growth, on the other hand, has been only about 1.3 percent since 1990. And it didn't have to develop any new business innovations. All it had to do was adopt innovations developed elsewhere. Our calculations were that Brazil needed to increase business investment only by 7 percent of GDP to grow at 8.5 percent per year. Of course that's the amount needed if Brazil increases its capital productivity to current potential. If it doesn't, then even more capital would be needed.

In Brazil, the difference (21 percentage points of GDP) in corporate tax burden from the United States of 1913 is in the hands of the government. Undoubtedly, a substantial part of it goes for consumption.

That's what happens to most transfers, which include pensions. Sure, some of it goes to physical infrastructure and investments in human capital. Physical infrastructure in 1913 did not hold back U.S. economic development. As I reported in the chapter on Brazil, about 11 percent of GDP in Brazil goes for health and education. That's not out of line with today's 13 percent in Germany and 9 percent in Japan, although higher than the 6 percent in Korea. It's considerably more than the United States and France invested in these areas in 1913. In that year, U.S. governments invested 1.8 percent of GDP in health and education. Considerably more medicine is available today to improve people's lives than in 1913. However, that increase in spending on health care should be traded off mostly against current consumption and not business investment.

Brazil, like all other countries at Brazil's stage of development, will not get rid of informality. The only way to level the playing field between informal activities and formal companies is to reduce the tax burden on formal companies. That means the government has to spend much less. Brazil's government is simply too big. That, and Brazil's history of macroeconomic instability, are the main impediments to economic growth today.

Where Are the Tax Monies Going?

So the question remains, what is Brazil doing with the 28 percent of GDP its government spends on things other than health and education? Astoundingly, Brazil's governments spend 11.3 percent of GDP on welfare and the government-run pension system for private and public sector employees (Exhibit 10.3). Most of this is for pensions (10.6 percent). In 1913, the U.S. government spent 0.6 percent of GDP on welfare and pensions. In 1970, when Japan's GDP per capita was about twice what Brazil's is today, Japan's government spent only 3.1 percent of GDP on welfare and pensions. Even today, the U.S. government spends only 5.4 percent of GDP on pensions. The contribution to Brazil's public employee pensions alone is 4.7 percent of Brazil's GDP.

Of course one of the reasons the United States and Japan had such low pension and welfare expenses was that people worked longer and died earlier. Now people everywhere live longer and retire earlier. Maybe the rich countries can afford this, although Germany and France are finding that their current retirement schemes are unsustainable. However, it's clear that Brazil cannot afford it because of its consequences of slowing economic growth.

Exhibit 10.3: Government Programs

Total government expenditures as percentage of GDP

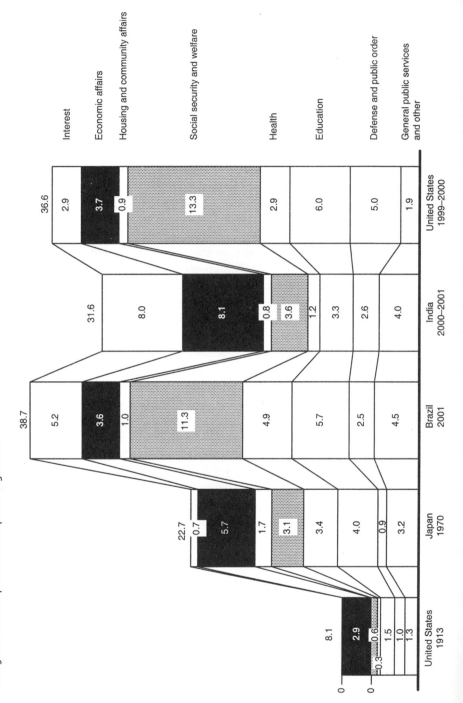

India's story is different. India's governments spend only 3.6 percent of GDP on welfare and pensions. However, 8.1 percent of GDP goes for economic management and subsidies for agriculture, electricity, rail, and a few other industries. Even Japan's government, which was admired for state management of development, spent only 5.7 percent of GDP on economic management in 1970. India's big government comes in large part from direct government intervention in markets to achieve social and economic objectives, whereas Brazil's big government comes more from direct social welfare payments to individuals.

Where Did These Big Governments Come From?

Well, the stories of India and Brazil are different. India's big government comes from the ideology and politics of its political leadership at the time of independence in 1948. Jawaharlal Nehru led this group. Brazil's big government is much more recent. It comes from the compromises reached in the establishment of its Constitution of 1988, when democracy replaced military rule. President Fernando Enrique Cardoso implemented this Constitution and oversaw the creation of Brazil's big government.

The only thing India's and Brazil's stories have in common is that they both were based on political philosophies developed in Europe in the twentieth century. Nehru tried to adopt many of the economic management techniques practiced by the Communists in the Soviet Union. Nehru is quoted as saying, "Our problems in India today are the same as those that faced Russia some years ago and they can be solved in the same manner in which Russians solved theirs. We should draw a lesson from the USSR in the way of industrialization." Of course, it's not a surprise that Nehru's policies were an economic failure. Brazil's 1988 Constitution is based on the social welfare political philosophy adopted by most European states following World War II. All such states have big governments. Such governments are not severely distortionary in Europe because they can be financed by relatively equal taxation on all individuals and businesses. As I have explained above, that is not true for a poor country, such as Brazil, where 50 percent of all employment is outside the reach of government tax authorities.

India's story is well documented. Even as early as 1931, Nehru's political party, the Congress party, adopted a platform that the chief industries in India's economy should be owned and controlled by the state. Nehru had a great distrust for the British and for capitalism in general. He wanted to remove the inequalities in wealth in Indian society. He felt that a few favored business leaders could be trusted to act in the interests of the poor in India. These leaders adopted a highly self-serving plan in 1944. This plan called for India to be "self-reliant," with the government strictly controlling the importation of foreign technology and capital. They didn't want any competition.

Nehru certainly realized that India's government had no capability to manage every single business in the country the way the Soviet Union tried to do. So he resorted to planning and government subsidies as the way to make the economy come out the way he wanted. He got plenty of help from prominent economists and other intellectuals from India and around the world in this attempt. This program was carried on by Nehru, his daughter Indira Gandhi, and her son Rajiv Gandhi, right up through Rajiv Gandhi's election defeat in 1989. During this period, central government expenditures in India went from 10.2 percent of GDP in 1970 to 20.6 percent in 1987. They have declined only a couple of points since then.

Brazil's story is less well documented, in part because it is relatively recent. We do know that Brazil's 1988 Constitution guaranteed a set of economic rights for all Brazilians. A minimum percentage of government revenues must be allocated to education. Health assistance must be available to all Brazilians. Regional governments must dedicate at least 12 percent of revenue to health care. Local governments must dedicate a minimum of 15 percent of revenue to health care. Minimum levels of welfare and pensions were specified for everybody under a government-run program. Amendments to the Constitution have allowed for abuses of the pension system. Such abuses include joining the civil service for a year or so near the end of one's career, retiring on full pension benefits, and taking another job.

The specificity of Brazil's Constitution seems strange, at least to an American. The U.S. Constitution, which has served Americans well for over two hundred years, contains values and principles, not economic programs. This is not the place to debate the merits of different constitutions. I will only say that it's difficult to anticipate conditions a few years down the road, let alone a couple of centuries. Thus, the inflexibility of Brazil's Constitution seems risky. In fact, this inflexibility is already coming back to haunt Brazil. Both Presidents Fernando Enrique Cardoso and Lula have tried to reform the bloated pension system. However, change requires a constitutional amendment. Such amendments have to pass with 60 percent of the votes of the total membership of each of the two houses of Congress. That's tough, as all who have witnessed the difficulty of breaking a filibuster in the U.S. Senate have seen.

On top of this, all the civil servants designing the new system, all the members of Congress who vote on the constitutional change, and all judges, who will interpret whether the change is constitutional, benefit from the current system. We can't tell yet whether pension reform will succeed in Brazil. However, what we do know is that under the 1988 Constitution, government expenditures on welfare and pensions went from 6.3 percent of GDP in 1986 to 11.3 percent in 2001.

How did Brazil get into this predicament? It started with the technocrats in the civil service designing a reform program to be implemented through the 1988 Constitution. Then in the actual hammering out of the Constitution, the politicians weighed in because they saw a chance to get benefits for both their constituents and themselves. Pretty soon the security blanket was extended to everybody. However, the civil servants and the politicians seemed to come out especially well for themselves. The business community initially rejected the reforms because they were too costly. However, in the end they cynically agreed to the financing of the social welfare system through taxes they thought they could pass through to the customer. These taxes are sales taxes, value-added taxes, and employment taxes, rather than corporate (or individual) income taxes. They agreed in return for avoiding land redistribution. They didn't realize that their informal competitors would not be passing the taxes through to customers in the price of goods and services and that they would thereby be at a competitive disadvantage.

Special Interests, Elites, and Corruption

No businessperson ever asked for more competition. Businesspeople spend considerable efforts trying to find market segments with little or no competition. That way they can charge higher prices. That's the way a market economy is supposed to work. Being able to charge higher prices means the business has found a market segment where customers really want their product. Of course, the unusually high profits attract competitors. Prices fall to the cost of production plus the profit margin that keeps businesses operating. Volume goes up. The consumer ends up with most of the economic value created.

It's up to government to make sure markets are open to competition. If governments have credibility on this matter, then the more productive businesses are advocates for fair competition. They know they will do well under such circumstances. As Jeffrey Sterling, chairman of P&O Steamship and Navigation Company, put it at a Global Institute CEO Conference in 1992, "We would all like to have monopolies. However, we know we are not going to get them in our countries. Therefore, we must work for fair competition."

The problem is that unproductive businesses want protection from productive businesses. We should not blame them. That's human nature. We should just prevent them from having their way. Their way is against the common good. Their way causes economic stagnation. Unproductive businesses go to great lengths to get protection. They lobby, bribe, gather votes for, and promise jobs to government officials. They also hide their special interests underneath noble-sounding social objectives whenever they can. In this case, we have to sort out the legitimate social and economic trade-offs from the preservation of special interests. Olson says this "predation" of special interests is one of the two main causes of failure of market economies to work well. The other is lack of property rights. As I said in the Russia chapter, I don't agree with Olson about the extreme importance of property rights when countries are poor. However, I do agree with him about predation.

Predation in Poor Countries

Competition is generally fair in the rich countries. It is not in the poor countries. After decades of problems on this score, Brazil is in much better shape today. Russia and India are not. Perhaps the most blatant example of unfair competition we found was the Moscow government's allocation of housing construction contracts to the unproductive old Soviet construction companies. Such problems are in virtually every sector we studied in Russia. The same thing is true in India. The Small-scale Reservation policy, which applies to 836 products including apparel, is one example. Government-owned businesses are another. In India, governments own 40 percent of business capital stock. Government-owned businesses are virtually always unfair competitors. They are unfair because governments will subsidize them before letting them fail. Government-owned electricity generators and distributors in India are the worst example of this we found in any country.

The special-interest problem is a much more serious issue today in poor countries than it has been historically. Sure, special interests have always been everywhere. However, before globalization the special interests in poor countries just kept the better local companies from expanding as fast as they could. These better local companies were usually far behind the rich countries. Thus special interests held back productivity improvement only modestly and economic growth potential was limited.

On a global scale, virtually all businesses in poor countries are unproductive. In the advanced countries, businesses operate at much higher productivities in virtually every economic sector. With globalization these businesses have shown they have the ability to re-create their more productive operations virtually anywhere in the world. Thus, through allowing these more productive companies to set up operations locally, poor countries have the potential to improve productivity more rapidly than in the past. However, local producers are threatened by this possibility. Thus, most businesses in poor countries today are special interests against opening up their home markets to foreign competition. These local businesses are the secret enemies of globalization. By influencing the local political process to keep foreign competition out, they constrain economic development more than local special interests have in the past.

For agriculture and a small part of manufacturing, this means trying to limit trade. However, services are the largest part of almost all economies. Businesses transfer more productive ways of providing services almost entirely through foreign direct investment. Local businesses in poor countries are also against local entrepreneurs applying global best practices in their home markets. However, they are not as much a threat as foreign companies. That's too bad. It's easier for special interests to keep foreigners out than to prevent local businesspeople from starting more productive new businesses. This is a big problem. It is simply inconsistent for poor countries to ask rich countries for money when they keep out investments by highly productive rich country companies. The investments by the more productive companies would raise poor countries' productivity and growth rates far more effectively than sending money.

Labor often is another special interest. Labor has historically organized in groups to bargain with management about pay and working conditions. The balance in these negotiations has been usually satisfactory. If businesses are competing intensely and fairly, then labor special interests are kept in check. If not, then labor bargains with management for a share of the extra profits and usually gets it. The resulting higher labor costs or productivity-constraining work rules then put businesses at a competitive disadvantage when competition finally comes. Then, labor is usually reasonable and adjusts its conditions before businesses run out of cash or capital flows elsewhere.

The one circumstance in which labor special interests are not held in check is with government-owned businesses. There, the risk of businesses running out of cash or capital flowing elsewhere does not exist.

That's because if labor objects strongly enough, governments will not let publicly owned businesses fail. This works in part because public workers often have a lot of votes. It's also because public workers have successfully engaged in civil disobedience to prevent publicly owned businesses from being closed. They also engage in civil disobedience to prevent privatization. They do this because they know that their jobs are not secure in privately owned businesses. Such civil disobedience happens even in the advanced economies. A few years ago, Air France workers laid down on the runways at Charles de Gaulle to prevent Air France's privatization. These tactics are much more prevalent in poor countries.

It's understandable that public workers in poor countries resist privatization. Job insecurity is a serious concern in poor countries. The risk of losing a job there is not just having to take another job at a somewhat lower wage. The risk in poor countries is falling back down to near subsistence living. That's why all workers in poor countries lobby for regulations protecting existing jobs. Private businesses in virtually every case have been able to find ways around job protection rules and regulations. However, this has not been true for the lobbying of public workers against privatization. This is a big problem in India, where governments own so much of the assets of business.

Elites Want to Control Others and Reward Themselves

One special interest in poor countries deserves far more attention than it gets. This special interest is the elites. Elites dominate public life in many poor countries. They certainly do in Brazil and India. In Brazil it's the technocratic and political elites. In India, it's the political, business, and intellectual elites. These elites are responsible for big government. Government is the means through which they can not only get their way about how the economy should run but also provide for themselves.

I've already discussed in this chapter how big government in poor countries distorts market competition. It distorts competition because formal companies have to pay extraordinarily high taxes to finance big government. Big government also makes extensive corruption possible, as I will explain in a minute. Corruption is perhaps the principal way special interests get their protection. Thus the causal chain leads step-by-step from the elites to corruption.

Peter Bauer, no friend of elites, quotes Sir Arthur Lewis as saying that "the advantage of economic growth is not that wealth increases happiness, but that it increases the range of human choice." Through economic growth, ordinary people get to choose what they want. Bauer goes on to say, "It is well-to-do and established politicians, academics, media men, clerics, writers and artists who are apt to dismiss economic choice as unimportant."

Sometimes big government comes from a belief by the elites in government planning, as in India. Planning gives the elites their chance for power. Once they have it, they are not going to let it go. Primacy of planning is a short step away from government control. The elites believe they are smart enough to figure out who should do what. Since those are the right things to be done, government should ensure that they are done. It's easy to see how this mindset leads to public ownership of business, licensing of business activity, control of international financial and material goods flows, prescribed prices and wages, and even restrictions on the movement of labor.

The result is big government. The Soviet Union carried these ideas to the extreme. However, despite the fall of the Soviet Union and substantial market reform around the world, many poor countries are left with big governments and elites still inclined towards many of these ideas. Ambivalence about the value of market economies strongly pervades the civil services of Brazil, Russia, and India. It's in large part because market economies take power away from civil servants and give it to ordinary people. Elites everywhere hold ordinary people in disdain. This is especially true when the ordinary people are very poor and uneducated.

Sometimes the big government comes from a belief by the elites in social objectives, as in Brazil. These social objectives are usually commendable. They are usually based on redistribution of wealth to alleviate poverty. What they don't realize is that through a complicated mechanism at the micro level, the redistribution chokes off economic growth, which is the only way to eliminate poverty.

These elites also strive to preserve and reward themselves. Their beliefs naturally generate substantial feelings of self-importance. This importance should be rewarded materially. After all, their educated peers in advanced economies are living very well. They should too. Hence the high salaries and unrealistic pension benefits of government workers in Brazil.

More importantly, however, extensive government interventions create the possibility for special interests to be protected. Taxing modern, productive steel mills in Russia but not the small, obsolete mills keeps the small mills in business. Licensing regulations in India for dairy prevent private dairies from competing with the government-favored cooperatives in many markets. Tariffs on imported cars in Brazil protect complacent multinationals producing in Brazil. Prohibitions on foreign direct investment in retailing in India prevent Carrefour, Tesco, and Wal-Mart from competing with Indian retailers in India.

Public officials, of course, get something in return for these favors. Government officials and businesspeople are only human. If the potential for corruption exists, it will occur. Punitive laws against it and vigorous prosecution of it help some. However, the most effective remedy is to diminish the potential for it. That means getting rid of big government. And that will require ordinary people throwing the elites out of power. Democracies provide a way for doing this.

CHAPTER ELEVEN

New Approaches

Which Development Path?

During the past one hundred years, political leaders and economists have advocated many different theories of economic development. The theories have included Lenin's Communism, Nehru's self-reliance, and Rostow's take-off strategies. Many different things have been tried across many different countries. We now have an enormous body of evidence. We are just beginning to learn what we can from this evidence.

As I described in chapter 1, our sample of country studies suggests that there have been three primary development paths over the past century (Exhibit 11.1). The Western democracies have achieved very high GDPs per capita by following a high-productivity path. Japan has also achieved high GDP per capita. Korea has reached a middle income level rapidly. Korea will likely reach the high-income group soon. Both Japan and Korea have followed a high labor and capital input path. Their productivity has also increased. It has increased in part because of the technology embedded in the equipment they have used. Finally, most of the world's people live in countries where productivity is low and capital inputs are also low. As in India, sometimes workers in rural areas in these countries have substantial idle time. (China is among these low-productivity, low-capital countries. It is too early to tell what path it is on. Its large, inefficient state-owned sector would suggest its path is certainly not as steep as Japan's. However, its still small private sector along the coast benefits from lots of foreign direct investment and may be on a high-productivity path.)

Thus, we seem to have found two development paths that have worked. They are the path of the Western democracies and the path of Japan and Korea. As I discussed in the chapters on Japan and Korea, their development paths have turned out not to be sustainable. Productivity really is the engine of growth. Japan's productivity growth has slowed appreciably and so has its growth rate. Korea got into trouble

Exhibit 11.1: Economic Development Paths

Percent U.S. 1995 level

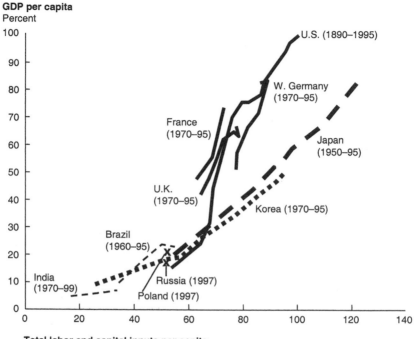

GDP per capita
Percent

- U.S. (1890–1995)
- W. Germany (1970–95)
- France (1970–95)
- Japan (1950–95)
- U.K. (1970–95)
- Korea (1970–95)
- Brazil (1960–95)
- India (1970–99)
- Russia (1997)
- Poland (1997)

Total labor and capital inputs per capita

earlier because of its low productivity. Both Japan and Korea borrowed substantial amounts from abroad when they were about half as rich as Korea is today. Japan used much of this money well by financing its global best practice manufacturing firms. For reasons I discussed in the chapter on Korea, Korea has not developed such global best practice firms. POSCO Steel is the one exception. As a result, Korea had a financial crisis; its productivity was so low that it did not earn enough on its borrowed capital to repay its foreign debt. Korea will remain vulnerable to financial crises as long as its productivity remains low and it owes money abroad.

Why Not Copy Japan and Korea?

Japan and Korea are in great shape compared with most of the world's economies. It is very tempting to say just copy them. You can see how

they could be copied. Governments have heavily guided these economies. Japan's and Korea's governments have orchestrated a high savings
rate by ignoring or suppressing the development of consumer goods and
their distribution. Their governments have used the banking system to
channel the savings to capital-intensive industries. This approach is
guaranteed to lift countries out of poverty if executed well. The global
markets ensure that equipment is available with embedded technology
yielding substantial productivity improvement. What difference does it
make if such a path runs into difficulty later? Countries can get out of
poverty this way.

Some countries may be able to follow the Japan path. But not many.
The reasons are that most people will not save and invest as much as the
Japanese and most governments will not use the savings as well as the
Japanese. Maddison has estimated that during the period from 1950 to
1973, business capital stock per capita grew in Japan at the annual rate
of 6.8 percent, while the corresponding growth rate for the major developing countries of Asia and Latin America was 3.4 percent. Some countries have tried the high-investment path. Perhaps the Soviet Union is the
most extreme example. For this same period, business capital stock per
capita grew at 7.1 percent in the Soviet Union. Brazil also tried this in
the 1970s. India tried, starting with Nehru. These countries all failed.
Korea (and Taiwan) in the 1970s and '80s are the only exceptions.

The countries that tried and failed at the Japan path failed because
their governments never came close to the competence of the Japanese
government, principally its Ministry of Finance. Many of the best and
the brightest young people in Japan went to work in the Ministry of Finance. They executed their policies well. They were largely devoid of
corruption. They were lucky to be matched with a group of world-class
entrepreneurs achieving global best practice productivity in automotive,
machine tools, consumer electronics, and steel. These entrepreneurs did
their thing without much government help. Their exports earned the
foreign exchange to pay back Japan's foreign borrowings from the time
when Japan was poor. No other country has had this combination of
high competence in its Ministry of Finance and world-class entrepreneurs in a few heavily traded manufacturing sectors. Korea doesn't really have either one. The entrepreneurs are probably there. As with most
countries, they just haven't shown themselves. The United States could
not follow the Japan path. The world-class entrepreneurs have shown
themselves. However, the best and the brightest in the United States do
not go to work at the U.S. Treasury. Most countries will not have the
equivalent of Japan's Ministry of Finance.

Most countries also will not have Japan's savings rate. For the entire period from 1983 to 2000, Japan's gross national savings has hovered around 30 percent of GDP, compared with 15 to 18 percent in the United States. Savings rates are a result of deep societal behavior patterns. We do not understand why different societies have such different levels of savings. One factor that had to matter to the Japanese people was that they trusted their government during Japan's high-growth period. They were willing to put their savings into government-controlled or -guided banks. The government used some of this money to repay foreign debt. Much of the remainder went to Japanese corporations. The Japanese people had faith that they were in good hands. For a long time it seemed as if they were. Now, of course, more than a decade of economic stagnation has ruined the credibility of the Japanese government, and particularly the Ministry of Finance. How much longer will the Japanese savers prop up the economy of Japan? If they decide to invest abroad for higher returns, Japan will have a financial crisis.

People in most poor countries do not trust their governments. They don't trust them for good reason. Their governments have squandered much of the people's savings on misguided programs of one kind or another. Their governments have stolen the rest and put it in foreign bank accounts. People in poor countries still save a lot. They don't have much else to do with their money. However, some put their money in their mattresses and others send it abroad. The upshot is that they will not put as much money in domestic financial institutions as the Japanese. Thus, the Japan path is out of reach for most poor countries.

High-Productivity Path

That leaves the high-productivity path of the Western democracies. That path is not easy either. However, about 750 million people in a couple of dozen countries have been following it. That suggests it might not be so rare as the Japan path. The high-productivity path even sounds a little easier. The essential ingredient is intense, fair competition. That includes allowing foreign firms to compete equally with domestic firms. The foreign firms solve much of the capital and technology availability problem. That sounds easier than betting on re-creating the Japanese Ministry of Finance and hoping that a Toyota and a Honda appear. Moreover, countries on the high-productivity path have not run into the problem of economic stagnation at high income levels. Thus, the high-productivity path seems a better bet than the Japan path. However, as I discussed in the previous chapter, many factors work against it.

Competition is not intense and not equal in most economies for three reasons: special interests, big government, and weak economic understanding. I will discuss how countries might overcome these problems in the remainder of this chapter.

Special Interests Thrive off Government

Special interests have been around forever. When they gain favoritism, competition is not equal and productivity suffers. One hundred years ago, the governments of the Western democracies were not the way special interests were held in check. Then, special interests often held each other in check.

In those days, the Western democracies had such small governments that they didn't do much of anything at all. Protecting the country militarily was government's primary function. Governments did so little to regulate economies that special interests had little opportunity to gain favoritism. In an economy with few rules, special interests naturally play off against each other. Companies are free to enter and leave markets. Competition is intense and often ruthless. Predatory pricing and attempts to gain monopolies are common. However, since special interests cannot gain legal privileges, competition is often fairly equal. Attempts to curtail the worst abuses of predatory and monopolistic behavior were made early. The U.S. antitrust laws date from 1890 (Sherman Act). However, the major thrust towards curtailing market abuses in the United States occurred in the 1930s. This thrust was in response to the excesses of 1920s and the Depression of the 1930s. In the first part of the twentieth century, the special interests kept each other somewhat in check.

Poor countries don't do this now. The difference is they have big governments. These governments attempt to regulate their economies. Sometimes they attempt to correct the market abuses of special interests. However, they also provide a means through which special interests can gain legal or illegal favoritism. Moreover, their sheer size distorts competition because more productive firms end up having to finance big government. In some cases it even means that productive firms don't enter markets because they can't make any money. Thus, big government is a new problem for poor countries to have to overcome.

Weak economic understanding is not a new problem for poor countries. One hundred years ago economic understanding everywhere was weak. Economics was just getting started as a serious discipline. No question, without the strong macroeconomic understanding developed by the economics discipline in the past fifty years, the advanced economies of today would not be possible. These monetized economies are too complex to operate without sophisticated government monetary policies and institutions. However, the understanding to develop such policies and such institutions did not exist when the Western democracies were poor one hundred years ago. Yet these economies began to grow out of their poverty.

Thus we're left with the one primary thing that's different between the poor countries of today and today's rich countries when they were poor. It's the size of their governments and what those governments do to control their economies.

Reduce Big Government and End Bad Policies

Poor countries today cannot follow the historical development path of the Western democracies. They cannot for two reasons. They already have big governments that exercise substantial control over their economies, often with bad policies. Second, innovations by businesses in the rich countries make them many times more productive than the businesses in poor countries. Businesses can apply these innovations in the poor countries. By this means, poor countries have the potential to increase productivity much faster than the rich countries could when they were poor. It takes much longer to create an innovation than to transfer it. These innovations are slowly diffusing from rich countries to poor countries. They are diffusing despite many barriers to this process.

So we can't say that the poor countries should just do what the Western democracies were doing when they were poor. We would not want to even if we could. Poor countries today have an opportunity that rich countries did not when they were poor. Poor countries today can grow much faster. They can grow much faster by applying diffused innovations from the rich countries. However, the other difference between poor countries today and rich countries when they were poor significantly reduces the speed at which this application of best practice can occur. Big government and its economic policies are preventing poor countries from rapidly realizing their potential.

So what should everybody do about this? Well, we have to start from where we are today. That means we have to start with big governments in poor countries. We also have to start with the many bad policies in place. The most obvious step needed is to reduce the size of government in poor countries. It's unrealistic, however, to reduce them to the size of the governments in France and the United States in 1913. The world has moved on. Modern health care practices can be applied in poor countries. These practices are rapidly improving life expectancy, primarily through reducing infant mortality. This is a good thing. It costs money. Poor countries should be spending substantial amounts for health care, and many are. Second, education should get more money than it did in France and the United States in 1913. But not because it's needed to increase the current workforce's ability to apply more productive work processes right now; it's not. Rather, education should get more money because it's needed if people are going to change the size of their government and what it does through a democratic process, as I explain later in this chapter.

However, beyond health care and education (and public infrastructure) there is a serious question of what poor country governments should be doing. As I mentioned in chapter 6, Brazil's government spends about 11 percent of GDP on health care and education. However, total government spending amounts to 39 percent of GDP. This book is not about fiscal policy in poor countries. However, this subject needs serious attention. Where have the World Bank and the IMF been? Sure, these institutions have argued for fiscal discipline and stability. That has meant balancing budgets, not making them much smaller. Without doubt, Brazil should curtail its exorbitant government-run pension system. Also, India, a desperately poor country, should not be spending money on a pretentious nuclear weapons program. At least not when it's asking the rich countries for money to make up for the money it's spending on that program. And that's just the tip of the iceberg.

How to Reduce Government Size

So reducing the size of poor countries' governments is one thing to do. How do poor countries do this? The previous examples of government reductions are not encouraging. Over the past twenty years, four countries have made reductions in the size of their governments that might be relevant for poor countries today. These countries are Ireland, Canada, New Zealand, and Chile. Ireland and New Zealand are upper-middle-income countries and Canada is a rich country. Chile is the only example near the top end of the poor countries. Ireland, Canada, and New Zealand all had government expenditures around 50 percent of GDP. Chile's government expenditures were 34 percent of GDP before reductions. Thus, Chile's government size before reductions is the only example close to Brazil and India today.

The government reduction programs in all four of these countries were caused by bad economic performance. Ireland's unemployment was 17 percent in 1987, and its government debt exceeded 100 percent of GDP. New Zealand had fallen from the seventh-highest GDP per capita in the OECD in 1960 to eighteenth place in 1984. Inflation had been more than 10 percent every year for a decade and foreign debt had increased from 11 percent of GDP in 1974 to 95 percent in 1983. Canada's federal government deficit was 8 percent of GDP in 1984, and, by the early 1990s, its risk premium on the international bond market was well above that of most other rich countries. The socialist government in Chile in the 1970s had almost destroyed its economy.

As part of economic reform programs, each of these countries reduced government expenditures as a fraction of GDP by a significant percentage (Exhibit 11.2). These percentages were 36 percent for Chile (1984–90), 27 percent for New Zealand (1990–97), 24 percent for Ireland (1987–90), and 18 percent for Canada (1993–98). At the end of the government reduction programs, Ireland's government expenditures were 41 percent of GDP; Canada's, 44 percent; New Zealand's, 35 percent; and Chile's, 22 percent. Chile thus ended up with a government about the size of Japan's in 1970. The end point for the other three countries was a bigger government than Brazil's and India's today.

All four countries had some reduction in the real level of government expenditures. However, for Chile, New Zealand, and Canada, most of the reduction came from holding the growth of government expenditure while GDP grew. This is a significant accomplishment. In Ireland, most of the reduction came from real cuts in government expenses. That's impressive. In both Canada and Chile, 84 percent of the reduction came from GDP growth and 16 percent from real cuts. In New Zealand 64 percent came from GDP growth and 36 percent from real cuts. In Ireland, 31 percent came from GDP growth and 69 percent from real cuts.

Thus far, Chile looks like the best example for poor countries. It's on the borderline between poor and middle-income countries. Its government expenditures as a fraction of GDP before reductions were similar to Brazil's and India's today. It made the highest percentage reduction. Its reductions brought it down to Japan's level of 1970. However, Chile is not a good example in one crucial respect. It made its reductions under a military government, whereas Ireland, New Zealand, and Canada made their reductions as democracies. Thus, we need to look at Ireland, New Zealand, and Canada to see how they made their reductions.

The pattern in Ireland, New Zealand, and Canada is strong (Exhibit 11.3). All three made their reductions across the board. All major

Exhibit 11.2: Government Reductions

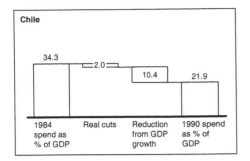

Chile

| 1984 spend as % of GDP | Real cuts | Reduction from GDP growth | 1990 spend as % of GDP |

34.3 — 2.0 — 10.4 — 21.9

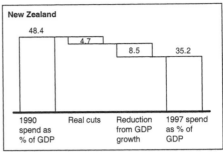

New Zealand

| 1990 spend as % of GDP | Real cuts | Reduction from GDP growth | 1997 spend as % of GDP |

48.4 — 4.7 — 8.5 — 35.2

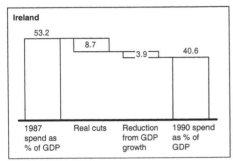

Ireland

| 1987 spend as % of GDP | Real cuts | Reduction from GDP growth | 1990 spend as % of GDP |

53.2 — 8.7 — 3.9 — 40.6

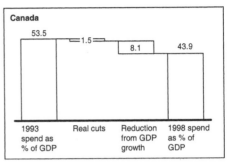

Canada

| 1993 spend as % of GDP | Real cuts | Reduction from GDP growth | 1998 spend as % of GDP |

53.5 — 1.5 — 8.1 — 43.9

areas of their government expenditures were reduced. Moreover, the political party in power when the reductions were made did not campaign that it was going to make reductions if elected. This brings to mind Lula's campaigning in Brazil's presidential election of 2002 on a populist political platform but proposing serious government reduction once elected. The political fate of the parties reducing government is mixed. In Canada, the Liberals were reelected handily in 1997 and remain in power. In Ireland, Fianna Fail lost seats in the next election and had to form a coalition government. It was defeated in the subsequent election. In New Zealand, the National Party was reelected once but then lost in 1996.

Chile's government cuts were selective and are probably a good example for Brazil (Exhibit 11.4). Before reductions, Chile's government spent 13.6 percent of GDP on pensions and welfare. Brazil's percentage for these items today is 11.3. Chile reduced these items to 7.2 percent of GDP.

So what's the bottom line here? The bottom line is that it takes strong political leadership to reduce the size of government in a democracy. This is not necessarily a suicide mission. The Liberal Party in Canada has shown that if strong actions are explained to a sophisticated

Exhibit 11.3: Patterns of Government Cuts

Change in percentage points of GDP

Chile, 1984–90

New Zealand, 1991–97 (1990 not available)

Ireland, 1987–90

Canada, 1993–98

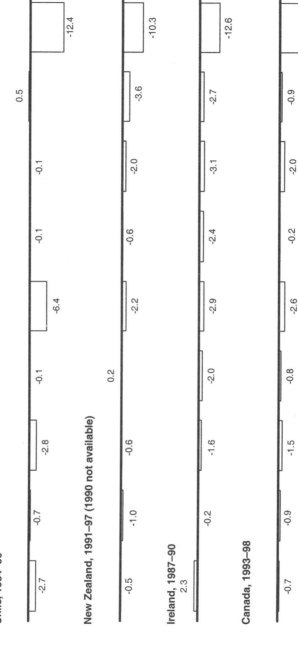

	Chile, 1984–90	New Zealand, 1991–97	Ireland, 1987–90	Canada, 1993–98
General public services, other, and nondistributable residual	-2.7	-0.5	2.3	-0.7
Defense and public order	-0.7	-1.0	-0.2	-0.9
Education	-2.8	-0.6	-1.6	-1.5
Health	-0.1	0.2	-2.0	-0.8
Social security and welfare	-6.4	-2.2	-2.9	-2.6
Housing and community affairs	-0.1	-0.6	-2.4	-0.2
Economic affairs	-0.1	-2.0	-3.1	-2.0
Interest expense	0.5	-3.6	-2.7	-0.9
Total	-12.4	-10.3	-12.6	-9.6

Exhibit 11.4: Chile Model

Total government expenditures as percentage of GDP

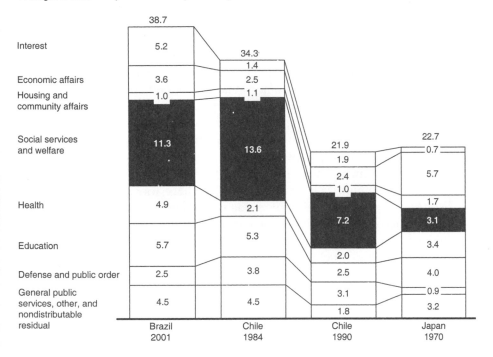

	Brazil 2001	Chile 1984	Chile 1990	Japan 1970
	38.7	34.3	21.9	22.7
Interest	5.2	1.4	1.9	0.7
Economic affairs	3.6	2.5	2.4	5.7
Housing and community affairs	1.0	1.1	1.0	1.7
Social services and welfare	11.3	13.6	7.2	3.1
Health	4.9	2.1		3.4
Education	5.7	5.3	2.0	4.0
Defense and public order	2.5	3.8	2.5	0.9
General public services, other, and nondistributable residual	4.5	4.5	3.1	3.2
			1.8	

electorate, politicians are not necessarily punished. However, none of Canada, Ireland, and New Zealand had as tough a set of reductions to make as Brazil and India do today. Chile is the only country to have dealt with problems like that.

Does this mean that the only way out of the poverty trap caused by big government in poor countries is through military governments? I hope not. However, the way out of this trap is not clear. The multi-national development and financial institutions, the World Bank and the IMF, have not dealt with it. And yet they seem the only possibility, apart from the Chile solution. Clearly, for these institutions to have impact, a much stronger interventionist approach would be necessary. That of course would bring all sorts of local objections to outside interference. And yet we cannot go on as in the past. That path leads to an apartheid world, except maybe where military governments fix things as in Chile. This problem should preoccupy the rich countries for the next generation.

How to Find and Fix Bad Policy

The second thing poor countries need to do is to fix the bad economic policies. We cannot go back to the world of France and the United States in 1913. Then, those countries had very little economic policy in place. Their growth out of poverty came from a free-for-all in the competitive marketplace. However, we wouldn't go back there even if we could. The rich countries have learned some valuable economic lessons the hard way. We now know how to achieve macroeconomic stability. We need an independent central bank, staffed by well-trained and competent professionals, with a mandate to control inflation and keep the economy running near to full capacity. We need a flexible exchange rate. We need to keep government deficits in check.

The rich countries have also learned the hard way about monopolistic and oligopolistic behavior, predatory pricing, price fixing, insider trading, accounting conflicts of interest, perverse incentives from stock options, import tariffs, producer subsidies, government ownership of business, property rights, land use policies, and many other matters affecting the intensity and fairness of competition. These are the ways special interests gain favoritism. The so-called Washington Consensus about good economic policy in developing countries is hopelessly superficial about the importance and complexity of achieving intense and fair competition. To become rich, poor countries have to deal with these issues. Even if poor countries could wipe the slate clean, it would not make sense to do so. Poor countries have the opportunity to benefit from the hard lessons learned by the rich countries. Poor countries can replace bad policy with good policy. However, this is much easier said than done.

The reason it is so difficult is that market distortions occur at the market level. And in an economy, there are a few hundred different markets. Maybe fifty to a hundred markets really matter. However, that's still a pretty big number. It's a big number because the effort required to analyze any single market for distortions to competition is substantial. It requires analyzing the comparative performance of firms in that market and potentially in that market. It requires understanding why firms' performances differ. And it requires understanding whether the competitive dynamic of more productive firms replacing less productive firms is working. If it's not working as well as it potentially could, then it requires understanding why not. Why are the incentives shaped by policy not leading to productive firms replacing unproductive firms as fast as potentially possible?

This work requires complex microeconomic analysis. It requires extensive data. Sometimes this data needs to be created from scratch. Governments in poor countries usually do not have it. It requires analysts who understand how microeconomic markets work. In particular, it requires analysts who understand how businesspeople react to incentives. It also requires experience in understanding the incentives that economic policies generate. Finally, it requires substantial resources to accomplish this work. It needs to be done in many markets at the same time. The reason is that the benefits of removing distortions in any one market are amplified by removing the distortions in other markets. Richer workers in other markets then demand more products and services produced at higher productivity in the first market. The economy then has more output produced at higher productivity in the first market than it would if productivity increased only in the first market.

Who can do this work? Certainly poor countries cannot today. It's difficult enough for the rich countries. And the rich countries have a much better policy base from which to work on improvements. The obvious candidate for this work is the World Bank. The World Bank has sufficient resources to do this work for the largest poor countries. It has bright, well-educated people who have the potential to do this work. However, it does not have sufficient people experienced in the rough-and-tumble competitive world of business. All banks have this problem to some extent. Their relationships with their borrowers are based heavily on bottom-line financial performance, or simply on whether debt service is up-to-date. Bankers have great difficulty understanding the complex microeconomics of their borrowers. It's difficult enough for the borrowers themselves. So we would be asking a lot of the World Bank to take this on. However, there is no real alternative. The World Bank has to get this work started.

Perhaps, once the World Bank learns how to do this work, it can build institutions in developing countries that can carry it on. The World Bank has created over the years a series of development banks in its client countries. Perhaps these banks could pick up this work over the longer term. However, they have a banking and development planning perspective today. That's not a promising starting point. Perhaps we simply need a new class of institutions in poor countries. Perhaps these institutions should be positioned as central banks should be. Central banks are responsible for macroeconomic policy today. It should have independence. It should be established by law and report on its actions to a legislative body. These new institutions perhaps should have the same role and positioning for microeconomic policy. Unfortunately, microeconomic policy is much more complex. However, we have to try something.

It will not be easy to get the World Bank to take the lead in this new approach. World Bank employees will have to be trained to get their hands dirty in the data and analysis of the business world. They will also have to change their mindset from that of planning and monitoring to one of achieving intense and fair competition. That won't be easy.

Even if the World Bank did this work and found the microeconomic policies needing change, what would cause the poor countries to make these changes? By now, the special interests are deeply entrenched. Moreover, in many cases, the special interests are not tiny fractions of the societies, as Mancur Olson thought. Often, the special interests are practically everybody. Except, of course, the desperately poor.

Serve Consumers' Interests

So even if we find the bad policies, how do we get them fixed? This is a serious question. The reason it is serious is that usually so many special interests are against fixing bad policies. These bad policies favor the special interests. The special interests are behaving exactly as we should expect. We're not going to be able to change how they behave. What we have to change is the mindset with which economic policy decisions are approached. We have to change the mindset from serving producers and workers to serving consumers. Unless economic policy is guided by serving consumer interests, it is headed for trouble.

Olson wrote that usually special interests were a tiny minority and that the intellectual elite can overcome that minority. In Russia, India, and even Japan, special interests made up an effective majority. Moreover, in Brazil and India, the intellectual elite was a special interest itself. In Russia, we found unequal competition in every sector we studied. Small steel and cement producers do not have to pay their taxes or their energy bills. Former Soviet construction companies get housing contracts from the Moscow government. Wholesale markets get favorable tax treatment and often don't pay even that. Hotels are still mostly government owned and run no risk of having to shut down. In India, we found much the same. Large manufacturers are not allowed to compete with small apparel producers. Foreign retailers are not allowed to compete with domestic firms. Government-owned banks and telecom providers are protected from failing. Licensing protects many existing dairy processors.

In Japan, the LDP remains in power because its political base of special interests gives it a majority. Those special interests are construction workers, mom-and-pop shopkeepers, health care workers, farmers, and other unproductive workers that rely on the government for protection. The LDP protects these groups with government subsidies and regulations. These low-productivity groups make up 80 percent of the Japanese economy.

So how do societies overcome special interests when they are not a tiny minority? Even worse, what can they do when special interests are a majority? Well, India can't rely on the intellectual elite. That elite in conjunction with the political and business elites put in place all the protections that have created today's special interests. Societies have to do something radical. They have to change their mindsets about the purpose of economies. They have to change their mindsets from serving the interests of producers and workers to serving the interests of consumers.

The purpose of economies is consumption. We realize the benefits of an economy when we use goods and receive services. We want to use goods to do things we could not do without them. We want services to have other people do things for us that we cannot do or would rather not do. These benefits are the value created by an economy. We can choose to consume everything right now or save to consume later. However, consumption is what we want from an economy. Of course, production and work are necessary for consumption. We cannot consume what we have not produced. *Thus, production and work are a means to consumption.* They are not a final objective themselves.

Many societies get this wrong. They see production as the creation of value. And they are right as far as that goes. *However, they fail to make the link between production and consumption.* The goods produced have value only because consumers want them. If consumers want something different from the goods that are produced, then the economy is performing below potential.

Stopping at the mindset that production is what creates value leads to all sorts of difficulty. First of all, it sometimes leads to producing enterprises being created unnecessarily and often as fast as possible. Governments make this happen. They do this by deciding what kind of factories should be built and channeling capital to them. Japan and Korea are good examples. We have seen how this approach leads to productivity well below potential. *Second, governments view producing enterprises as being so valuable that they protect them regardless of their performance.* This locks in low-productivity operations. Producers play on this misplacement of value on production. When less productive producers are threatened by more productive producers, the less productive producers run to the government for protection. They argue that they will go out of business if not protected. Governments don't want to lose this production because it's valuable. They protect it.

Existing producing enterprises always have political influence. All the people associated with a firm vote. Firms also have money they can spend to influence politicians and other voters. A few producers gain a lot from any tariff protection, whereas the loss is spread over many, many consumers in trivial amounts. No wonder the producer interests are heard.

When the political influence of firms meets a political mindset valuing production, favoritism and protection of existing firms are usually the result. We see this today especially in India, Russia, Korea, and Japan. However, no country is without it entirely. Bizarrely, the George W. Bush administration in the United States has recently reversed a long-term trend in the United States towards less protection of domestic producers. It has placed tariffs on imported steel and significantly increased agricultural production subsidies. These actions were taken for blatantly political reasons. It's business as usual in many parts of the world. However, the high economic performance of the United States has come from less protection and favoritism of special interests, not more. This strategy will likely backfire on the president because U.S. consumers are no fools.

Consumer Power

Only one force can stand up to the influence of producer and worker special interests. That force is consumer interests. After all, everybody, producers and workers alike, is a consumer. Consumers are not naturally organized as are producers and workers. However, in the United States they have formed effective political lobbying groups. These groups have been helpful in achieving good economic policy, but they are not the primary reason consumer interests have been served. The primary reason is the mindset of political leadership in the United States.

That leadership has adopted to a significant degree the mindset that economic policy should serve consumers first. That mindset has by and large been successful politically in the United States. The reason it has been successful is that consumers are also voters. They are vaguely aware that fair and intense competition among producers serves their interest. For sure they want to buy imported goods from all over the world at the cheapest price possible. They feel they have rights. Political leadership can make arguments against protection and favoritism of producer and worker special interests by appealing to consumer rights. These arguments resonate with U.S. consumers. They probably don't understand deeply the substance of the argument. However, they certainly understand that political leadership seems to be taking their side. Moreover, special interests cannot effectively argue against the consumer mindset of political leadership. They cannot do so because that mindset is valid. Thus, political leadership in the United States can be successful with a platform of protection of consumer rights.

This championing of consumer rights in national politics in the United States goes right back to the height of the Industrial Revolution in the late nineteenth and early twentieth centuries. Unlike in Europe at that time, a populist movement favoring labor against business never was successful in the United States. The principal reason is that voters in the United States recognized that what is good for labor is not necessarily good for the consumer. For instance, labor might prefer a high minimum wage over a low minimum wage coupled with an Earned Income Tax Credit. The consumer would prefer a low minimum wage and the Earned Income Tax Credit. The consumer's preference creates a bigger economic pie with less unemployment. However, labor is happy with its high minimum wage and union-guaranteed job. Fortunately, in the United States the consumer has won out over both labor and business.

As early as 1906, a successful senator from Wisconsin, Robert La Follette, said in his first speech on the Senate floor, "The welfare of all the people as consumers should be the supreme consideration of the Government." Although Theodore Roosevelt talked extensively about the dangers of concentration of economic power in business, he did not appear to appeal to the concept of the consumer. He did say that his Progressive movement's purpose "is to establish in this world the rights of man, the right not only to religious and political but to economic freedom." Walter Lippmann wrote in 1914, "We hear a great deal about the class-consciousness of labor. My own observation is that in America today consumers' consciousness is growing very much faster."

Later on, Franklin Roosevelt said in his presidential campaign of 1932, "I believe that we are at the threshold of a fundamental change in our popular economic thought; in the future, we're going to think less about the producer and more about the consumer." He went on to say that "consumers have the right to have their interests represented in the formation of government policy." Then, when campaigning for president in 1960, John F. Kennedy said, "The consumer is the only man in our economy without a high-powered lobbyist. I intend to be that lobbyist."

This consumer mindset resulted in legislation aimed at protecting consumer rights and serving consumer interests through fair competition. The most important conditions for fair competition are no monopolies or oligopolies, no predatory pricing aimed at either business competitors or certain customers, and a fair tax code administered fairly. The milestones for establishing the conditions for fair competition were put in place early. The Sherman Act of 1890 declared illegal "every contract, . . . trust, . . . or conspiracy in restraint of trade or commerce." It also made monopolies illegal. Its explicit intent was to preclude activities that "prevent full and free competition" and those that "advance the cost to the consumer." The Supreme Court ruled in 1911 that both Standard Oil and American Tobacco had violated the Sherman Act by lowering prices with the intent of driving competitors out of the market and achieving monopolies. The Court found that American Tobacco had priced below its production cost and was guilty of what the Court came in 1963 to call "predatory pricing." The Court also ruled in 1911 that the Sherman Act forbade manufacturers from fixing the prices at which retailers had to sell the manufacturers' products (resale price maintenance). Such practice prevented retailers from competing on price. The Clayton Act of 1914 forbade price fixing and price discrimination (predatory pricing) where it lessened competition. The Federal Trade Commission Act of 1914 declared illegal "unfair methods of competition."

Of course it took a long time for government agencies and the courts to interpret these acts. Initially the courts interpreted the acts narrowly, but by the 1930s action was in full swing. The Federal Trade Commission brought only 43 price discrimination cases from 1914 to 1936, and only 8 of these were upheld by the courts. Because of the slow progress, Congress passed the Robinson-Patman Act in 1936 to amend the Clayton Act to strengthen the prevention of price discrimination and, in particular, predatory pricing. Price discrimination cases multiplied rapidly. From 1936 to 1957, the Federal Trade Commission concluded 429 price discrimination cases, 311 of them with cease-and-desist orders.

The federal tax system was made professional in 1952. All tax officers became civil servants except for the head of the Internal Revenue Service. Finally, in 1982, the Department of Justice formally adopted the use of sophisticated microeconomic tools (Herfindahl indices) to check whether proposed mergers and acquisitions would result in oligopolies.

The United States has this mindset of an economy serving consumers (and law protecting consumers) to a greater degree than any other comprehensive economy. Why is this so? As I discussed in chapter 4, this mindset has long historical roots. Back in the days of Adam Smith, the hereditary aristocracy of Europe viewed consumption as their privilege only. Consumption was a luxury. Ordinary people were meant to produce. They were meant to be fed and housed and that was all. The United States was originally settled by many of those ordinary people wanting to leave that system behind. They successfully fought a revolution to make sure such a system was not imposed in the United States. As Gordon Wood explains in *The Radicalism of the American Revolution*, at the time of the American Revolution, a few million farmers in the United States saw no reason why they should not have rights to consumption also. Thus, the consumption mindset and the notion of consumer rights were built into U.S. society from the beginning. Perhaps on this dimension the U.S. society is most exceptional in the world today.

The consumer mindset has begun to spread more around the world over the past few decades. Margaret Thatcher broke the coal miners special interest in the United Kingdom by appealing to consumers' interests. Examples elsewhere are hard to find. On the European continent, the elites have resisted change to this mindset. Only a decade ago, Continental Europe seemed to believe that "national champion" producing companies were the way to better economic performance and successful economic competition with the United States. That mindset has changed. Europe is taking actions in competition policy much more consistent with consumers' interests. However, Europe is coming to this position in a roundabout way. National champion companies did not achieve world-class productivity. Most of them were not able to compete successfully with U.S. and Japanese producers in global markets. Our productivity studies may have helped them realize this. In any case, failure of the national champion strategy in Europe has caused the European Commission to turn to competition in an attempt to achieve global best practice.

This strategy will work unless it is thwarted by the protectionist sentiments at the national level. We will know the European Commission has succeeded when Fiat has to compete intensely with Toyota in Italy. This strategy, however, may be fragile. It is based more on competing with the United States than on serving consumers' interests. It's much easier to walk away from a strategy of competing with the United States. All it takes is the argument that European society has different objectives. "We don't want the American economic way of life with its crime, poverty, long working hours, short vacations, pollution, etc. We like it the way it is in Europe." That argument is already coming from several quarters in Europe. However, once a mindset is changed to serving consumption and the notion of consumer rights is accepted, it's virtually impossible to change strategy. That's because consumers are everybody, and in democracies, everybody can vote.

Most of the rest of the world is a long way from the consumption mindset and consumer rights. They don't even aspire to achieving global best practice through fair competition. As a result, most of these countries are poor. They will remain poor until they change their ideas about consumption and competition. And the only way they will change their ideas is through better economic understanding, education, and a working democracy.

Improve Economic Understanding

In 1991, I called on Ed Denison at the Brookings Institution. I wanted to see whether Ed would be interested in joining the Academic Advisory Committee I was forming for the first Global Institute project. That project was on productivity in the service industries.

Ed Denison was one of the pioneers of growth accounting studies. These studies attempted to explain economic growth in terms of changes in variables that could be measured for economies as a whole. The technique was based on the growth model developed by Bob Solow, for which he was awarded the Nobel Prize in economics in 1987. The model attempts to determine how much of economic growth could be explained by increases in hours worked and additional investment in plants, equipment, and housing—assuming that the additional hours and the additional capital are applied with current levels of productivity. Sometimes the hours worked are adjusted for increases in education levels, on the assumption that a more educated labor force can work with higher productivity. Any residual economic growth beyond what could be explained by these changes must be caused by technological improvement or business innovation in the way work is organized.

I found Ed in a small office with metal furniture and a few bookshelves. Here was a man who had spent most of his career producing important reports with detailed statistical tables showing what economics knew about what causes economic growth around the world. I explained that the concept for our project was a series of industry case studies, measuring productivity across countries and explaining the reasons for the differences in terms of the strategic, organizational, and operational choices managers had made and why they had made the choices they did.

Ed got very interested in the project. He said all his work and the work of others on growth accounting had ended up explaining a disappointingly small part of economic growth. Sometimes, their work explained as much as half of economic growth rates. Other times, it explained virtually none of the growth. Ed said he had concluded that the only source of adequate explanation of economic growth resided in the area I was proposing to study. This was the nitty-gritty world of business operational practices, business innovation, business technological choices, business competition, and incentives for business. In other words, how and why productivity improvements occurred. The challenge was to do this work on a large enough scale and with enough solid evidence to draw conclusions. This book is about the results of the twelve-year program of the Global Institute to conduct studies around the world along these lines. Ed Denison was the first to anticipate where these studies might lead. Unfortunately, in 1991 Ed's health was failing. It would have been too much of a burden for him to advise us.

As a theoretical physicist by training, I have always been frustrated that more issues are not settled in economics. Of course, the one huge difference is that in physics we can run experiments in the laboratory to sort out which theories are right. In economics, it is not possible to run such controlled experiments. However, all is not lost. Every day in every economic sector in every economy a natural experiment is running. We have attempted to understand the results of those natural experiments. Bob Solow calls this a new style of work. He says that "it is not a rival or alternative to standard economic analysis, but a way of implementing it, especially in situations where complete statistical data are either unavailable or unlikely to tell you what you want to know."

It takes substantial resources to collect valid data and do the analysis in even one industry in one economy. And the need for such resources grows quickly when it is a matter of doing studies of enough different industries in enough different economies to puzzle out why economic performance differs. You have to understand operational differences, the incentives for managers making operational decisions, and the source of those incentives in the laws, regulations, and ownership rights that govern business conduct.

It's hard to say new things in economics. Economists have said many things over the years. A good example is when we brought out the results of our first country study in Sweden. We said that the competition authorities needed to be tougher on anticompetitive behavior. An economist from the Swedish National Academy said that Swedish economists had already said that. However, other Swedish economists had said otherwise. Only with our micro studies did the competition authorities become convinced that they should become more aggressive in stopping anticompetitive behavior.

The problem is that many of the points of view in economics are in conflict. They have not been put forward with enough evidence and logic to be convincing. Thus, the primary challenge in economics is to sort out which views are right. Our approach was to go after the evidence that Ed Denison and his colleagues could not get. This evidence was at the microeconomic level. At that level, it is possible to construct satisfying explanations of what causes what. Often we lit on things because the other likely causes didn't seem to pan out. We found our work convincing in a way that much of the work in economics has not been.

This work needs to be continued. If we want to improve economic performance, we have to understand what is causing economic performance to be what it is now. From looking at other natural experiments, we can find out how changing economic policies would change economic performance. As I said earlier in this chapter, the World Bank should take the lead in continuing this work for poor countries. Rich countries need it too. It's not easy to see where it should be done in rich countries. At a Brookings Microeconomic Conference where we reported some of our results, Zvi Griliches asked how academics could possibly compete with this work. They usually don't have the access to the workings of business and they don't have the resources. National governments do not have the time horizon or the staff for this work. Probably, it should be done in a think tank under the National Academy of Sciences. The U.S. National Academy of Sciences has a good track record of bringing together academics and businesspeople to address high-priority national issues.

A broader issue is that economists need to dramatically improve their communication of the findings of economics to the public. As a boy, knowing nothing about physics, I was turned on to that subject by the books of George Gamow. He explained the atom and the universe in ways understandable to the public and fully consistent with good physics. Richard Feynman's books have done the same thing more recently. We don't have the equivalent of these books in economics. We need them. The debate about economic matters is pretty bad in most countries. We found it better in Sweden, the United Kingdom, Australia, and the United States. The *Economist* is usually reliable on economic matters. The *Wall Street Journal* and the *New York Times*, only sometimes. The occasional good article will appear in the *New Republic* and the *New York Review of Books*.

I asked Francis Bator why he and his peers did not write more in widely read publications. He said the bad drives out the good. The good just gets lost. Everybody thinks they can comment on economic issues. That's not true for physics. We need more good stuff written by economists, understandable by the public, and characterized by the reputable economics writers in leading publications as "the most authoritative work to date." Those were the words Sylvia Nasar used in her 1992 *New York Times* story about our comparative evaluation of the economic performance of Japan, Germany, and the United States. Adam Meyerson of the *Wall Street Journal* told me on the Washington Metro one morning that our work had changed the economic debate in the United States. Sylvia's story was perhaps the most important communication of our results.

Education and Democracy

How does a society come to have a consumption orientation, respect for consumer rights, a smallish government not captured by special interests, and even a good economic debate? It's obviously not easy. Not many societies today are this way.

This is where education really comes in. Education is the organized system for helping the members of a society to understand themselves and the world in which they live. It's not the only way. Simply living accomplishes much of this. However, education, at least theoretically, is much more efficient. Through education, we learn the lessons of the past. Through living we learn only the lessons that current experience can teach us. Our species has been around for some time now. Just as in economics, we should learn the results of the natural experiments of the past.

From our studies of the past, we know that we have begun to think about ourselves as individuals only recently, perhaps for the past two to three thousand years. The latest thinking about the evolution of our species based on mitochondrial DNA analysis indicates all humans today are descended from the people who lived in the Rift Valley of Africa 100 to 200 thousand years ago. That means our thinking about ourselves as individuals has been around for only 2 to 3 percent of the time the modern form of our species has existed. Who knows where these ideas got started. The ideas probably occurred many places. What we do know is that these ideas took hold in the pre-Grecian civilizations of the Middle East only a few thousand years ago. Only the intellectual elite held them. Even then, education of that elite was how the ideas were passed on. The ideas waned for perhaps a thousand years afterwards. Then only a little more than five hundred years ago, they exploded in the European Renaissance. They diffused to the common man, the ordinary man, the middle class to an unprecedented degree in the United States at the time of the American Revolution. A consumer orientation and recognition of consumer rights by a large part of society was a direct consequence.

Education has been the primary means through which this point of view has been transmitted to all reaches of U.S. society, to immigrants, and from generation to generation. For some time now, this point of view has been simply taken for granted. The realm into which individual choice has been extended continues to grow. In the economic realm, individual choice has been strong for over three hundred years and dominant for most of the past century. The notion of individual rights has also gained substantial ground in European societies over the same three hundred years. However, these ideas have faced greater resistance there because of the special interests in place when the ideas appeared. The battle is not quite over yet there. Frustration in overcoming historic special interests in Europe has led to the extreme points of view of Communism, Fascism, and Socialism. These extremes have set back the cause of the individual.

In the rest of the world, the notion of primacy of individual choice has not spread very far. After seeing the exhibition entitled "The World in 1492" at the National Gallery in Washington, Lawrence Stone, the eminent British historian of Wadham College, Oxford, and Princeton, remarked, "You can see that the Renaissance really happened." The art of that time from around the world showed enormous differences in how we viewed ourselves. European art at that time revealed an intense study and understanding of us as individuals. Art from the rest of the world showed stylizations.

The Role of Education

Will these ideas about us as individuals spread to the rest of the world? Theoretically, education would provide everybody exposure to these ideas. Exposure was enough for these ideas to catch on in Europe. We don't know for sure whether exposure would be enough elsewhere. We do know that many educated people around the world want to come to live in Europe and, especially, in the United States. In any case, education would give people the choice of adopting these ideas or not. For this reason, education must be a high social priority around the world. This is not because greater education is needed immediately to allow the current workforce to work at higher productivity. It is needed because it is the best hope for these people to get out of their current poverty trap. Only through adopting a consumption orientation and a respect for consumer rights do these societies have a good chance of overcoming the power of special interests, including the elites behind big government.

Of course, the content of education matters. In the Western democracies, education takes for granted the value of individual rights. These values are passed on to most people in an uncritical way. They are accepted by most in an uncritical way. This will not be the case in other parts of the world. At best, it will take a long time for these ideas to spread widely. In the Western democracies, these ideas had to overcome resistance from the hereditary aristocracy. In the rest of the world, these ideas have to overcome resistance from the elites themselves, and particularly religious leaders. That may be even harder. It may be harder because the elites and organized religion have a dominant influence on the content of education. Nevertheless, it is impossible to seal off societies from these ideas and the way people who hold these ideas live. These ideas took hold in the common man in the Western democracies in large part because the common man could see how he suffered under the ancient regime. The hope now is that the common man around the world can see the beneficial results of respect for individual rights.

This is no longer simply a theoretical matter. We have natural experiments showing what happens in societies where individual rights are respected. These societies are not perfect by any means. Providing equal opportunity for everybody is an aspiration that will never be reached. However, we must keep trying to do better. Mitigating the effects of the unequal distribution of the misfortunes of life is also a goal we will never reach completely, but we must keep trying. Redistributing material rewards to take into account unequal opportunity and chance, while at the same time grappling with the human traits of greed and envy, will always leave everybody somewhat dissatisfied. However, immigration patterns suggest that many people consider societies that respect individual rights much better than what they leave behind. Part of the attraction undoubtedly is that these individual rights greatly increase the opportunities for improving the immigrants' material standard of living.

Even if these ideas catch on around the world, there is still the question of how they lead to a consumer rather than a producer mentality. This is the easy part. These ideas lead straightforwardly to democracies. In democracies, consumers can get their way. Leadership will learn sooner or later that it can achieve political power by putting consumers first. In a democracy, such a platform can win. However, it doesn't always win. It doesn't win when democracies are not based on a deep desire of the people for individual rights.

The spread of democracies around the world has been faster than the spread of beliefs in individual rights. The two large democracies outside Europe and North America are Japan and India. The United States imposed democracy on Japan at the end of the Second World War. The British brought democracy to India. Japan and India show that democracies can be captured by special interests, including, in India, the intellectual elite. Thus, just having a democracy is not enough to get out of poverty or to achieve the highest economic performance. It depends on what the democracy is based on. The great struggle that began in the Middle East three thousand years ago is still going on and will go on for a long time. It's the struggle between individual rights and special interests.

The future of the global economic landscape depends on how this struggle progresses. Without substantial progress on individual rights, most of the world's people will remain in poor countries. That's why there are so few middle-income countries today. If individual rights are recognized and respected, societies have the potential of achieving very high economic performances. They rapidly move through middle income to high income levels. Without individual rights, countries remain poor. Korea is an exception. It has taken a special path not available to most economies. It has achieved middle-income levels. However, without a conversion from a production orientation to a consumption orientation, Korea will not achieve high income levels. Japan is showing the limits of the production orientation. It has reached the bottom of the high-income group, but it is now stagnating.

Because of the lack of economic success in many of the world's societies, frustration, envy, and wounded pride are building around the world. Thus, as I discussed in the previous chapter, we are facing the prospect of an apartheid world, as the rich countries attempt to protect themselves from the effects of these changes. The U.S. invasions of Afghanistan and Iraq mark a turning point in the behavior of the rich countries. We can expect to see more of this behavior. That is, unless we make rapid progress on spreading respect for individual rights around the world. Maybe forcible "regime change" is the only way to "free" societies and to allow them to follow their natural instincts to respect individual rights. I doubt if this approach really works because I don't think respect for individual rights is a natural instinct.

How societies gain a respect for individual rights is another subject not for this book. It's probably deeply evolutionary in nature. It will or will not happen because of the examples set by the Western democracies and how the people around the world learn about and react to those examples. It really does seem that the evolution of our species, in the broadest sense, has converted from genetic changes to changing ideas. The Western democracies seem to have demonstrated that there is a chance that our species can live with and benefit from the ideas of individual rights. However, this situation has been around for only a few hundred years. That's not very long on an evolutionary timescale. However, we have no choice but to bet heavily on promoting this way of living. The alternative of an apartheid world is not attractive to anyone. It's hard to see how an apartheid world could be stable for very long, especially since regime change is not likely to succeed in automatically leading to democracies respecting individual rights.

Of course, we don't know where a world based on individual rights would lead. The United States is now the oldest surviving government in the world. Yet nobody's in charge. Elites are deeply uncomfortable with the lack of control such a world carries with it. That might be the biggest test for our species right now. Can we live with the uncertainty and lack of control of a world in which individual rights win out? That's going to be determined by who we are as a species. That's our biggest natural experiment.

CHAPTER TWELVE

So What?

I raise the question of "so what?" in two respects. The first is that readers accustomed to standard economic reports may be missing all the usual data tables, quantitative analysis, and regression coefficients. They may be thinking at this point that this book simply amounts to a set of assertions and some anecdotal stories. So what? It may or may not be true.

My intention from the beginning has been not to write an economic report. I have had in mind explaining what I learned over the past twelve years to the readers of the *New York Times,* the *Wall Street Journal,* and other leading periodicals. I have wanted to write this book that way because the problems for the world raised here will be with us for a long, long time. They will require sustained effort by the American society as a whole, along with our friends in the other rich countries, to avoid our being overwhelmed by them. Such an effort has to be based on a broad understanding of the challenge and general agreement about the objective. What we are up against in this effort is the second "so what," which I will address below.

For those worried about the first "so what," I will simply point to the nineteen economic reports issued by the McKinsey Global Institute since 1992 on the topics addressed in the first eight chapters of this book. These reports are listed after this chapter. They total about 3,000 pages of text and contain about 5,000 exhibits displaying data and the results of quantitative analysis. Along with aggregate analyses and synthesis of results, these reports include 118 individual microeconomic industry studies spanning 29 different microeconomic industries including agriculture. All these reports are available to be downloaded, without charge, after a simple registration process, under the McKinsey Global Institute section of McKinsey & Company's Web site (www.mckinsey .com).

The Real "So What"

The real "so what" of this book is how hard economic development is. If it were not so hard, there would be far more middle-income and rich countries. I had no idea this would be the main "so what" when I started this book. The problem of the world's poor did not receive the attention it needed in the second half of the twentieth century. The reason is understandable. The world had an even bigger problem. That problem was avoiding thermonuclear war between the United States and the Soviet Union. Only now that the risk of thermonuclear war is close to zero can the world get a clear look at the problem of the world's poor countries.

Perhaps the achievement of avoiding thermonuclear war holds some insight for dealing with the problem of global economic development. One thing stands out. Thermonuclear war was avoided through the leadership of the United States, in cooperation with most of the Western democracies and Japan. It was not solved by the UN or its multilateral agencies. The United States took the lead for many reasons. Among them was that the United States perceived it had the most to lose if thermonuclear war broke out. Another was that the United States was the one country that had the power to determine the outcome. It was clearly the highest national priority over a forty-year period.

There was a clear strategy, "containment," with the objective of preventing something from happening. The strategy included educating the leadership of the Soviet Union on the consequences of thermonuclear war—that there would be no winner, only losers. Herman Kahn's book *On Thermonuclear War* laid out the whole story in 1960. The United States kept most of the rich countries by its side through tolerant and patient diplomacy. The United States needed its Western European allies, and they knew it. That's the price of being the leader.

Of course, during the Cold War, it was never clear that the outcome would be as good or as quick as it turned out to be. You do the best you can on a sustained basis and hope for the best. Nevertheless, avoiding thermonuclear war in the second half of twentieth century is a great achievement of the Western democracies under U.S. leadership. Why can't we just do the same for the problem of the world's poor countries and solve this problem over the next forty to fifty years?

"New Paradigm?"

Right after the Berlin Wall fell and the Soviet Union dissolved, there was a brief flurry of discussion about a new paradigm to replace the paradigm of the Cold War. Most of the comments were about shifting from military to economic matters and usually concerned global economic competition. These discussions fizzled quickly because they were unfocused and contained little that was new. Global economic competition was nothing new. The most fundamental basis of the competition with the Soviet Union had been economic and not military. There was some attention to the world's poor associated with the fiftieth anniversary of the establishment of the World Bank and the IMF. A review of the record of these institutions and their mission was meant to be part of the marking of the anniversary. Again, nothing much came out of these reviews.

In retrospect, it should not be surprising that a new paradigm did not come out of talking and thinking around a table. Sometimes it takes an extreme event to expose the true threat to people's way of life. That came to the rich countries and, in particular, to the United States with the terrorist attack on New York's World Trade Center on September 11, 2001. Of less attention, but potentially of greater seriousness, was North Korea's development of the capability to produce nuclear weapons.

These two events involved two of the world's poorest countries, Afghanistan and North Korea. Moreover, the evidence of potential mischief, at the least, from Iraq and Iran accumulated. These events and potential threats so far rank nowhere near the seriousness of thermonuclear war. However, they might be the beginning of a trend that could unravel the Western democracies. After all, the threat of thermonuclear war was abstract to most people and not part of their everyday state of mind. Terrorist attacks, on the other hand, actually happen and thus are not abstract. Their psychological impact on people's sense of well-being is dramatic. The only long-term, high-confidence strategy for the world not to be overwhelmed by terrorism is for economic development to go so well that terrorists have no place to incubate or hide. That should be the new paradigm. What does the world do under this new paradigm?

The current U.S. strategy seems to be "preemption," rather than the "containment" and "deterrence" of the Cold War. Deterrence does not work when the aggressor is irrational or has very little to lose. Terrorists fit both of these characteristics. Thus preemptive attacks on specific terrorist organizations make sense.

The U.S. strategy involves more than preemptive attacks on terrorists, however. It includes economic development. Here, preemption becomes "intervention." The U.S. attempt to build a modern democracy and a well-performing economy in Iraq following the invasion is exactly this kind of intervention. This intervention in Iraq is naive. Intervention for economic development and preemptive attacks on terrorists have virtually nothing in common. The United States knows how to make a military attack on terrorists. The United States does not understand what a long, difficult process economic development is.

This book is about the things developing countries need to do to become rich. I have been surprised by the length of the list and the complexity of the process to get them done. I have also been impressed by how long it takes. Most of the things to do have to be done by the poor countries themselves.

This book shows the pernicious effect on productivity growth of distortions in markets coming from predation. Big government contributes, often unwittingly, to this predation. Predation cannot be remedied from the outside. Countries have to do this for themselves. Capital won't do it, educating the workforce for the job market won't do it, infrastructure won't do it, and lectures from outsiders won't do it. Countries themselves have to want to do it to serve consumers better.

"Consumerism" has a bad name in many quarters, including some in the United States. *However, serving consumers is the purpose of economies.* If you are not interested in getting consumers what they want, then forget about economic development. Societies with political philosophies based on individual rights are the only societies that have served consumers so far. Such philosophies cannot be imposed from the outside. They have to grow up from within. Broad leadership to move in this direction is required for a start, and liberal education is necessary to sustain development. The record for the world over the past fifty years indicates these things are hard to do.

That countries have to do most things for themselves is understood by only a few in both rich and poor countries. One of those is Leszek Balcerowicz, president of the National Bank of Poland and formally deputy prime minister and finance minister. In October 1999, he wrote, "There isn't one voice of the emerging countries. They all have very differing experiences. But broadly speaking, there are two categories. One is those countries which had been affected by crises—often of their own making—and they tend to blame external forces. And they call for help. Then there is a second group—the smaller one, to which Poland belongs—which thinks that it is the quality of internal policy that decides how much a country is affected by external forces." Another apparently is the new president of Brazil, Luiz Inácio "Lula" da Silva. He was quoted in the *New York Times* of May 31, 2003, as saying, "I'm fed up with meeting presidents of Latin American countries who blame imperialism for the misfortunes of the Third World. That's nonsense. We are victims only of our own incompetence." That last quote was surprising because Lula was elected president on a populist campaign platform. Both observations, Balcerowicz's and Lula's, are fully consistent with the findings in this book.

So the government-managed approach used so successfully by the United States in the Cold War will not work for economic development. There's already evidence that this is true. That has been the world's approach for the past fifty years. We have bet that the World Bank, the IMF, and other UN agencies would solve this problem. They haven't. They haven't because the solution has to come from the bottom up.

What to Do?

How can the United States and the other rich countries help the poor countries improve economic policy? The United States does not have much leverage. In the Cold War, the United States had enormous leverage over the Soviet Union. If the Soviet Union started a nuclear war, then it would also suffer enormous destruction. There is no such leverage available to get good economic policy. Sending money has been tried and has not succeeded.

U.S. leadership in economic affairs is less natural than in military affairs. The United States is the one rich country that has produced both guns and butter. Most other rich countries have produced mostly butter. That means the U.S. military capability makes it the natural leader in military matters. Other countries have little choice but to follow the U.S. lead because the United States can go a long way in military matters alone. That is not true for economic matters. Any U.S. economic development strategy towards the poor countries could be undermined by Europe and Japan, which together have an economy greater than the United States. That does not mean that the United States should forgo leadership. The U.S. economy is widely viewed around the world as the single most powerful economy by far. Thus the United States is the natural leader on global economic affairs. However, that leadership role is more complex to perform than for military affairs. Moreover, the big question still is what to do as leader.

Intervention as a strategy has limited use. People simply don't want to be told or forced to do things. Moreover, an overlay of actions without the deep societal changes which would lead to these actions naturally will not succeed. Thus the U.S. strategy should be to take actions that lead poor countries to want to make the changes themselves.

Perhaps the easy step is for the United States to give recognition to poor countries that make the needed changes by themselves. Thus part of the U.S. strategy for global economic development should be "inclusion," rather than the "preemption" and "intervention" of the fight against terrorism. However, this "inclusion" should be selective. The United States should favor poor countries that have good enough economic policy to cause rapid economic growth near potential. The United States should favor those countries with money and economic agreements.

The hard part is leading the poor countries to wanting to make the changes in the first place. There, the only way is to persistently provide the evidence that these economic policies work. They lead to high economic performance. Most people around the world and even in the United States have no idea why the U.S. economy has such high performance. The United States needs to understand its economy better and to explain it better to the rest of the world.

U.S. Story

This book is not about the United States. It is really about the rest of the world. However, I end up giving the United States a lot of attention because it is the benchmark. It has the highest overall GDP per capita and the highest productivity in most microeconomic industries. Over the past twelve years, I tried many times to use non-U.S. benchmarks for other countries. I did this to avoid the usual "we don't want to be like the United States" reaction. However, in every country the local people preferred using the United States as the benchmark. People all over the world really want to know more about the United States and how they compare. The United States is the standard in the minds of most people. So it's important to get the U.S. story straight.

The U.S. story starts with the political philosophy on which the United States was founded a little more than two hundred years ago. This philosophy held that individual rights were foremost. The U.S. Constitution was the first constitution in the world to write down the values and principles of individual rights. *There are no economic rights in the U.S. Constitution.* And yet the United States has the strongest economy in the world. The political philosophy of individual rights led immediately to an economic policy orientated towards serving the interests of consumers. Consumerism in the United States is over two hundred years old.

These ideas were held broadly in American society at the time. As the eminent Harvard historian of colonial and revolutionary America, Bernard Bailyn, says in his book *The Ideological Origins of the American Revolution,* "The spokesmen of the Revolution—the pamphleteers, essayists, and miscellaneous commentators—were not philosophers and they did not form a detached intelligentsia. They were active politicians, merchants, lawyers, plantation owners, and preachers, and they were not attempting to align their thought with that of major figures in the history of political philosophy whom modern scholars would declare to have been seminal."

Given this orientation two hundred years ago, it is not surprising that the United States moved quickly to establish laws to serve the interests of consumers when the Industrial Revolution took off a hundred years later. I was amazed to learn about the rules for fair competition laid down in the Sherman Act of 1890. The act's original language said its purpose was to preclude activities that "prevent full and free competition" and those that "advance the cost to the consumer." Most countries in the world still do not have this necessary foundation for high economic performance.

In understanding and explaining itself, the United States has to get much more thorough. It has to address many of the misunderstandings about the United States that are rampant around the world. I have already discussed the misunderstanding that U.S. economic policies cause more poverty than the policies of the other rich countries. The U.S. economy actually causes less poverty than in virtually all the Western European countries. As an entirely separate matter, the Western Europeans decide through their political process to redistribute more income than the United States and thus have less poverty on an after-redistribution basis. That is a political or even a moral issue. It is not an economic issue. Also, many people around the world attribute the high crime rates in the United States to the U.S. economic system. However, the upper Midwest of the United States, including the metropolitan area of Minneapolis/St. Paul with its population of about 3 million people, has crime rates, including violent crimes, about as low as France. Yet this part of the United States has the same economic system as all the rest. This suggests that the higher U.S. crime rate comes from something besides the economic system.

It is discouraging to think about how long the U.S. political and economic system has been in development and how far poor countries have to go. In retrospect, the Cold War seems much easier to deal with. Maybe that's because it's over and it ended successfully. However, I don't think so. Societal change is much more difficult than military conflict. The United States is learning that in Iraq. All this suggests to me that the next fifty years are going to be a difficult, frustrating time for Americans, and for many around the world. However, it's still early days. The problem is not yet anywhere close to being as serious as the thermonuclear confrontation with the Soviet Union. However, the problem of poor countries and terrorism may become that serious. Who knows how the United States will react then. Leaders equivalent to those of the Cold War era (Truman, Marshall, Kennan, John Kennedy, McNamara, Rickover, etc.) have not emerged. If the problem gets bad enough, hopefully they will. The world needs them from time to time. There seems to be no end to history.

MCKINSEY GLOBAL
INSTITUTE REPORTS

U.S. Productivity Growth, 1995–2000: Understanding the Importance of Information Technology Relative to Other Factors. Washington, 2001.

India: The Growth Imperative. Mumbai, 2001.

Why the Japanese Economy Is Not Growing: Micro Barriers to Productivity Growth. Washington, 2000.

Poland's Economic Performance. Washington, 2000.

Unlocking Economic Growth in Russia. Moscow, 1999.

Driving Productivity and Growth in the UK Economy. London, 1998.

Productivity-led Growth for Korea. Seoul, Washington, 1998.

Productivity—The Key to an Accelerated Development Path for Brazil. São Paulo, Washington, 1998.

Boosting Dutch Economic Performance. Amsterdam, 1997.

Removing Barriers to Growth and Employment in France and Germany. Frankfurt, Paris, Washington, 1997.

Health Care Productivity. Los Angeles, 1996.

Capital Productivity. Washington, 1996.

Australia's Economic Performance. Sydney, 1995.

Sweden's Economic Performance. Stockholm, 1995.

Employment Performance. Washington, 1994.

The Global Capital Market: Supply, Demand, Pricing and Allocation. Washington, 1994.

Latin American Productivity. Washington, 1994.

Manufacturing Productivity. Washington, 1993.

Service Sector Productivity. Washington, 1992.

All reports are available without charge at http://www.mckinsey.com.

RECOMMENDED READINGS

Bailyn, Bernard. *The Ideological Origins of the American Revolution.* Cambridge: Harvard University Press, 1967, 1992.

Das, Gurcharan. *India Unbound.* New Delhi: Penguin Books, 2000.

Diamond, Jared. *Guns, Germs, and Steel: The Fates of Human Societies.* New York: Norton, 1997.

Dower, John W. *Embracing Defeat: Japan in the Wake of World War II.* New York: Norton, 1999.

Easterly, William. *The Elusive Quest for Growth.* Cambridge: MIT Press, 2001.

Landes, David S. *The Wealth and Poverty of Nations.* New York: Norton, 1998.

Lewis, Bernard. *What Went Wrong: The Clash Between Islam and Modernity in the Middle East.* New York: Oxford University Press, 2002.

Olson, Mancur. *Power and Prosperity.* New York: Basic Books, 2000.

Porter, Michael E. *The Competitive Advantage of Nations.* New York: Free Press, 1990.

van Wolferen, Karel. *The Enigma of Japanese Power.* New York: Knopf, 1989.

Wood, Gordon S. *The Radicalism of the American Revolution.* New York: Knopf, 1992.

INDEX

Note: Italicized page numbers indicate exhibits.